Received this day from Georgia Lloyd
via Greenwood Press.

Strengthening
the
United Nations

STRENGTHENING THE UNITED NATIONS

A Bibliography on U.N. Reform and World Federalism

Compiled by
JOSEPH PRESTON BARATTA

Bibliographies and Indexes in World History,
Number 7

GREENWOOD PRESS
NEW YORK • WESTPORT, CONNECTICUT • LONDON

Library of Congress Cataloging-in-Publication Data

Baratta, Joseph Preston.
  Strengthening the United Nations.

  (Bibliographies and indexes in world history,
ISSN 0742-6852 ; no. 7)
  Includes indexes.
  1. International organization—Bibliography.
2. United Nations—Bibliography. I. Title. II. Series.
Z6464.I6B37 1987 [JX1954]   016.3412   87-134
ISBN 0-313-25840-6 (lib. bdg. : alk. paper)

Library of Congress Catalog Card Number: 87-134
ISBN: 0-313-25840-6
ISSN: 0742-6852

First published in 1987

Greenwood Press, Inc.
88 Post Road West, Westport, Connecticut 06881

Printed in the United States of America

The paper used in this book complies with the
Permanent Paper Standard issued by the National
Information Standards Organization (Z39.48-1984).

10 9 8 7 6 5 4 3 2 1

Copyright Acknowledgments

The author and publisher are grateful for permission to reprint from the following
works.

From THE PEOPLE, YES by Carl Sandburg, copyright 1936 by Harcourt Brace
Jovanovich, Inc.; renewed 1964 by Carl Sandburg. Reprinted by permission of publisher.

Joseph Preston Baratta, "World Federalism." Reprinted with permission from Ervin
Laszlo and Jong Youl Yoo (editors) *World Encyclopedia of Peace*, copyright 1986
Pergamon Books Ltd and the Institute of International Peace Studies.

Ramon Gordon cartoon, in I. A. Richards, *Nations and Peace*. Copyright © 1947, 1974
by Simon & Schuster, Inc. Reprinted by permission of SIMON & SCHUSTER, Inc.

Every reasonable effort has been made to trace the owners of copyright materials in
this book, but in some instances this has proven impossible. The publishers will be glad
to receive information leading to more complete acknowledgments in subsequent printings of the book, and in the meantime extend their apologies for any omissions.

In memory of my mother,
Beatrice Wood Preston Baratta

and my father,
Joseph John Baratta, Lt. Col., U.S. Army (Ret.)

Contents

Preface

This bibliography is based on the compiler's research over seven years into the history and issues of world federal government. Most of the publications can be found in large urban and university libraries. Those visited for this bibliography include:

Boston Public Library;
Mugar Library, Boston University;
Olivart Collection, Harvard Law School;
Lilly Library, Indiana University;
Regenstein Library, University of Chicago;
Library of Congress;
New York Public Library;
Dag Hammarskjold Library, United Nations.

Many publications, though rare, can still be found in used book stores. The more important journals, such as *Common Cause*, should soon appear in a microfilm reprint edition under the compiler's direction by the Clearwater Company.   More recent books can often be ordered from the organizations listed in the last section.

Special appreciation is extended to Warren Kuehl, Alan Henrikson, Winston Langley, Finn Laursen, John Logue, Hanna Newcombe, Guy Marchand, Roy Pryce, John Roberts, Patrick Armstrong, Henry Usborne, Humphrey Tonkin, Harold Taylor, Stillman Williams, Richard Falk, and Richard Dean Burns for advice and suggestions.   Acknowledgement is gratefully made to Harcourt, Brace, Jovanovich for permission to quote a few lines from Carl Sandburg's *The People, Yes*.   Appreciation is also extended to Pergamon Books, Ltd., and the Institute of International Peace Studies for permission to quote from my article on "World Federalism" in Ervin Laszlo and Jong Youl Yoo (eds.), *World Encyclopedia of Peace*, copyright 1986.   In the case of the Eleanor Roosevelt cartoon by Derso and Kelen, it proved impossible to trace the copyright.   The publishers will be glad to receive information leading to more complete acknowledgments in subsequent printings of the book, and in the meantime extend their apologies for any omissions.

This bibliography was completed during the United Nations International Year of Peace.

Strengthening
the
United Nations

Introduction

The aim of this bibliography is to provide a reasonably exhaustive listing, organized on historical lines, of works from all countries and in all major languages dealing with the strengthening of the United Nations and its system of international organizations. The governing assumption here has been that true peace can only be permanently maintained by effective international institutions, on the model of strong, yet constitutionally limited, national and federal states. Particular attention is given to the concept, politics, and establishment of a world federation.

World federation is a form of international organization in which the nations would share power for certain specified general purposes, beginning with the maintenance of peace, in a common or world government ruling by law. Courts and tribunals of a world federal government would replace war as an institution for reaching decisions in international disputes. A world legislature, acting under majority rule and limited by due processes for the protection of minorities, would be the supreme organization.

The modern doctrine of world federalism has its roots in recent history. The idea of creating a political union of states and peoples in order to abolish war may be traced back for centuries -- back to Woodrow Wilson, Immanuel Kant, Abbé de Saint-Pierre, William Penn, Henry IV, the duc de Sully, and even Dante -- but until the collapse of the League of Nations in the 1930s most such proposals of international union were not strictly federalist. Kant, for instance, spoke only of a *confederation* of free and independent states. The League of Nations (and its successor the United Nations) was the great realization of the dreams of a confederal system of nation states; for all its limitations, it was a triumph in the slow and painful progress of international law.

But the failure of the League to stem the course of international conflict before the Second World War, and then the untold sorrow of the war itself, caused many observers to search for the inadequacies in what had been achieved so far in international organization. Many argued, as did Clarence Streit in *Union Now* (1939), that the League failed not only because it never achieved universality in membership and because the *nations* had failed it, but also because the League had preserved the principle of the absolute national sovereignty of states, as reflected in the rule of unanimity for decisive action. If international organization were to work effectively for the prevention of war, particularly at times of grave crisis when the defense of the majority was at stake, that principle had to be

made less absolute by the division of sovereignty in accordance with the
proven principle of federal government. That is, the nations would have to
delegate certain sovereign powers (those relating to their general or common interests, such as peace) to the international organization, while re-
taining all others. They would have to create a constitutionally limited,
federal world government, empowered to rule by law enacted under majority
rule.

It will be helpful to clearly distinguish the terms confederation and
federation.

A confederation is a voluntary association, or a league, of sovereign
states. States are said to be sovereign -- though in fact by joining a
league, as in entering into treaties and alliances, they accept limitations
on their freedom of action -- because, in accordance with international
law, they retain the right to reject the league's recommendations, and because they enforce its decisions only by national law. There is no higher
power, not even the union, that can compel a state to implement the decisions of the majority. Hence, a league is a very weak form of union.

Its weakness is vividly made manifest in the principle of collective
security, the mode of enforcement contemplated under the League and now the
United Nations. Collective security was an advance on unbridled national
adventurism and balance of power politics, but it is still the imposition
of sanctions and ultimately war on the offending state itself. Such a measure is so indiscriminate that states, to protect themselves when joining a
league, have insisted on a rule of unanimity or veto in the council that
makes the enforcement decision. The veto vitiates the whole system. It
prevents enforcement in the cases that really matter, when some nation is
apparently launched on a course of aggression, and it establishes a psychological climate of inaction and powerlessness. Historically, collective
security has been exercised only twice: very inadequately by the League
when applying economic sanctions against Italy after its invasion of Ethiopia in 1935, and more severely by the United Nations when it deployed military forces against North Korea in 1950. The latter action was only possible because the Soviet Union (which possesses a veto) happened not to be
sitting in the Security Council while boycotting the U.N. for its refusal
to seat the People's Republic of China. And, as is well known, it was the
United States that led the action politically, commanded the forces, and
supplied most of the troops and matériel, in keeping with its policy of
resisting communist expansion. In the years since then, U.N. "peacekeeping" forces (lightly armed for patrol and observation purposes only) have
conducted thirteen valuable operations designed to stabilize cease-fire
lines and to encourage negotiations, but but they have hardly had much
impact on the 150 wars that have occurred since 1945.

A federation, on the other hand, is a government of peoples. Since
the system of states members and action on states has proved ineffective,
federalists argue that a supranational, or world federal government, vested
with powers to enact law binding on individuals must be created. Individuals would be made citizens of the world as well as national citizens. They
would participate in the election of world representatives, and they would
be subject to world laws just as to national laws. Three levels of government, then, are required in order to complete the rule of law: local, national, and world.

A world federation must be constituted, like democratic republics generally, with representative institutions -- primarily a world legislature,

plus a world executive and world judiciary -- so that the people have a
sense of participation in the making of the laws, and hence will obey them
willingly as rules of action truly in the common interest.   Constitutional
safeguards, as well as continual public vigilance, will be required to prevent abuses of power.   Special protections would have to be provided for
human rights and the rights of minorities. World law, enacted by the majority, must yet prove to be a greater protector of human equality than the
present struggle for human rights in an anarchy of national states. If this
difficult, constantly readjusted political condition can be established, it
would be possible to maintain world peace by court action on individuals
accused of violating the world laws, instead of collective security action
against states.   Hence, the level of violence, threatened and actual, in
modern life -- and, incidentally the magnitude of government, even the
world government, designed to protect people from violence -- would be dramatically reduced.   The idea is to bring mankind as a whole into a social
contract: world federation would be established by a revolutionary exercise of the sovereignty of the people.

     Thus, the rule of law would replace collective security as the means
by which the human race would establish true peace.   Peace, federalists
say, is not merely the interim between wars, but is the presence of order,
produced by law, in turn produced by government.   Peace is itself only a
condition for the fulfilment of human potential, for the good life.   When
peace is established, then will come the great achievements of science and
religion, modern industry and development, social planning and free enterprise, liberal education and the arts.   But the essential point is that
these things are based on *law*.   "Law," Mark Van Doren once explained, "is
merely the thing that lets us live in peace with our neighbors without having to love them." It may not be so good a thing as religious consciousness
or even maturity of character, and someday perhaps we may have no more need
for government, but in politics, with men as they are, law is an indispen-
sible minimum.

     The world today seems very much in want of good laws above the nation-
al level. What people everywhere need to see is that the rule of world law,
commonly enacted, would not be a loss of freedom, or a sacrifice of sovereignty, but would be an immense gain in order, in non-violent processes for
the resolution of disputes and in more equitable planning for development.
The rule of law on the national level is the actual basis of our freedoms;
the rule of world law could produce the mutual confidence that would be the
basis of an almost unimaginable material and spiritual world prosperity.

     The great advantage of a government is that it permits orderly change,
whereas a league tends to be a guardian of the status quo.   The reason is
that a government can enact law while a league cannot. Law has both a large
rational element and a coercive element.   It is enacted by a deliberative
process, with respect to the complexity of human circumstance, and it is by
nature a general rule of action or standard of conduct binding on individuals, who are the persons that ultimately need government.   The recommendations of a league, on the other hand, reach only to states, which retain
the ultimate power to govern individuals and hence are not bound. The great
difficulty for the rule of law on the world level is to vest a coercive
power reaching to individuals in the world federal government, but to do so
in such a way that the rational power of the law generally obviates need
for recourse to punishment.   World law would require world police forces
and even elite world military forces as part of its enforcement apparatus,
but their function would be merely to overawe wrongdoers.   No effective
world law could rely to any appreciable degree on its power to punish vio-

lators, who would include national leaders; it must so manifestly represent the will of the world community, and be so deliberately formulated in accordance with the planetary constitution, and in short be so *just* within the complex historical circumstances of our times, that the law would command universal respect and adherence *without* fear of punishment.

In brief, what humanity must do in order to establish a better ordered world, in the language of Hamilton and Madison in *The Federalist* (No. 20), is to abandon *violence* for *law*, to give up the "destructive *coercion* of the *sword*" for the "mild and salutary *coercion* of the *magistracy*."

If powers were granted to the federal world government to protect human rights and to regulate economic life, as probably would be necessary even to achieve peace and international security, the mild and salutary coercion of world law would be felt at all levels of every society, and most vividly at top levels of national government and economy. The rule of world law plainly implies interference in the domestic affairs of states, just as treaties do. The difference is that, under the latter, the highest legal recourse is to national courts, whereas, under the former, it is to new world courts.

The whole question of world federalism then becomes: Is humanity ready to accept the rule of world law?

World federalists argue that the global expansion of Western industrialization, finance, and economic techniques, the spread of European forms of liberal and socialist democracy, the counter-flow of non-Western cultural ideas from the post-colonial world, the shrinking of distances by modern transportation and communications, and in short the interdependence of civilized life today on the planet make the acceptance of world law *possible*. The world is already one, they say; only law and politics lag behind.

Moreover, the global problems of nuclear war, traffic in armaments, erosion of human rights, the international debt crisis, worsening poverty in the underdeveloped world, international terrorism, overpopulation, environmental pollution, and the militarization of space -- problems that cannot be solved on a short-sighted nationalistic basis -- make the acceptance of world law *necessary*. The traditional idea of national sovereignty, which seems to block all progress toward effectively solving our common problems, is a false freedom, if it compels people and their governments to live in constant fear of their neighbors in an anarchical society. Real freedom and prosperity will come when human beings join together under a common rule of law.

World federalists say that they, who wish to extend the rule of law, are the realists, while those who put their faith in a league of sovereign states or, worse, who suppose that peace can long be maintained by deterrence or competition in arms are the utopians.

The example of national federal systems, of which about seventeen of various degrees of centralization have been formed since the founding of the United States, has always been prominent in the minds of world federalists. An extensive republic like the U.S., with its numerous and disparate peoples, cultures, languages, and religions, or like the U.S.S.R., which is also a federal republic, is an image in miniature of what a world federation would be like.

Federal world government would not mean the abolition of nations.

Rather, the nations (sometimes themselves federal systems) would be preserved as subordinate authorities. Provincial, state, and urban authorities would, of course, also be preserved. Indeed, it is argued, world
federalism is the most acceptable way, in an atomic age and in an interdependent world, by which nations and more local authorities can be preserved. They also must be preserved, under a world federation, as sources
of law better adapted to national and local circumstances. World federation is the only acceptable form of international organization that is
strong enough to abolish war, yet not so strong as to endanger the political and cultural diversity of mankind. "Unity and diversity" has been the
watchword.

     Two typical proposals of world federation are the *Preliminary Draft of
a World Constitution* (1948), by the University of Chicago's Committee to
Frame a World Constitution, and *World Peace through World Law* (1958), by
Grenville Clark and Louis B. Sohn. These span the range between "maximal"
and "minimal" proposals, respectively, that is, proposals that would vest
the world government with powers to achieve peace and justice, and those
that would limit it to powers to maintain international security. The whole
spectrum of international organization, then, in the order of decreasing
centralization of power, would look as follows:

          World empire;
          World communist or capitalist state;
          Maximal world federation (Chicago Committee);
          Minimal world federation (Clark and Sohn);
          League of sovereign states (United Nations);
          Balance of power (Western Alliance, Warsaw Pact);
          Anarchy of independent states, untempered even by
               international law;
          Social and political chaos, following bid for empire.

     World empire, many people think, will be the way that the world is
finally united. But judging by past attempts to unite the world by force
(Philip II, Napoleon, Hitler), a new attempt by one nation to conquer the
world would under modern conditions surely lead to nuclear war and hence to
a breakdown of civilization, as represented by the last item of the list.
World federalists are absolutely opposed to a bid for world empire. They
resist the trend toward a Pax Americana or a World Soviet Dictatorship. Use
of force will destroy the respect for law and the viable national and local
authorities on which a realistic world union depends. The only wise course,
consistent with the best spirit of our times, is to follow the relatively
nonviolent precedent for the establishment of most national federal systems.

     There has been great variety in world federalist proposals. In addi-
tion to the Chicago Committee's draft of a world constitution and the
Clark-Sohn plan, there have been well over fifty other model world constitutions. One of the most recent is the *Constitution for the Federation of
Earth* (1977) by the group centered about Philip Isely. There have also
been countless proposals of U.N. reform, though none quite on the scale of
the Clark-Sohn plan. The more recent include the revised Charter of Harold
Stassen, the Binding Triad proposal of Richard Hudson, a fourteen-point
plan by the Campaign for U.N. Reform, and a fifteen-point plan by the World
Association of World Federalists. These at least show that a lawful federation of the modern world is conceivable, and they could easily serve as
draft negotiating documents for a realistic program of political action.

Many proposals have not been model world constitutions but political
appeals to the public or to governments to assemble in a U.N. review conference or world constitutional convention, where official representatives
would undertake to draft a new charter of union. The proposals of the U.S.
mainstream organization, United World Federalists, were largely such appeals. Its successor organization, the World Federalist Association, and
the international organization, the World Association of World Federalists,
have also, since about the time of the Korean War, emphasized strengthening
the U.N. through Charter amendment and functional development of international law under the present Charter.   A very large literature of commentary, criticism, and international education, reflected in this bibliography, has been produced in virtually every country of North America, Latin
America, Europe, and the Soviet bloc, and in major countries of Africa, and
Asia.

A brief history of the world federalist movement will cast some light
on its contribution to peace.

The political opportunity to undertake national policies leading to
world federation was greatest, though still small, from about 1944 to 1950,
that is, from the last year of the Second World War to the point when the
Cold War was generally accepted as the dominant "reality" of international
relations.   The Soviet Union and the United States were allied in the war,
of course, and this fact gave encouragement to those concerned with the
structure of the peace.   Many private persons and some with connections to
the U.S. government, like Grenville Clark, made formal proposals for limited, federal world government by 1944.   But the United States was uninter-
ested in anything stronger than a league of sovereign states, largely because of fear of Senate rejection as in 1920.   The Soviet Union was reluc-
tant to submit even to a league after its disastrous experience with the
League of Nations during the Munich crisis of 1938.   Nevertheless, the
times did not permit a turning away from international organization.   The
great powers, as they guided the formation of the United Nations Organization at the Dumbarton Oaks conference (1944) and San Francisco conference
(1945), permitted some relaxation of the principle of national sovereignty,
since unanimity was required only of the five permanent members of the Security Council, but they made the General Assembly only an advisory body of
state representatives (one-nation-one-vote), and they granted the International Court of Justice no compulsory jurisdiction.

It was after the U.N. Charter was signed in June, 1945, that atomic
bombs were first used in war.   On August 6, 1945, the United States dropped
an atomic bomb on the Japanese city of Hiroshima, followed by another in a
few days on Nagasaki.

Mankind entered the atomic age.   To many internationalists who had
suffered through the war, the United Nations belonged to an *antiquus ordo
seculorum*.   It had not been vested with powers to govern states that had
nuclear weapons at their disposal.   Atomic fear emerged, particularly in
the U.S., as the main motivation for immediately calling another international conference to establish a world federation.   "One world or none!"
was the rallying cry of atomic scientists and world federalists alike.
They talked of world government in five years; if not achieved by 1950,
when Russia probably would have developed atomic bombs, a general nuclear
war would become inevitable.   Continuation of the national pattern of recurrent warfare would lead to nuclear destruction of all civilization.
Grenville Clark hosted the first Dublin conference of prominent internationalists in October, 1945; they issued a ringing call for immediately

replacing the U.N. with limited, federal world government.   But the Truman administration and the Senate deflected the call as mere obstructionism to the new United Nations.

Outside the United States, atomic fear was less of a motivation.   In Europe and Russia, there was much more public concern about reconstruction after the war and about satisfying basic needs for food and shelter. A Polish peasant, when told about the dangers of atomic war, looked about him and asked, "Is it worse than this?" In the colonized territories of Africa and Asia, after British power had been humbled by Japan, humanity was on the move with demands for independence, economic assistance, and an end to racial discrimination.   American appeals for world government to control atomic energy sounded suspiciously like attempts to fix the status quo under American domination. G.A. Borgese, an Italian emigré professor and secretary of the Chicago Committee to Frame a World Constitution, sensed this difference in values when he declared that *justice*, not mere abolition of war, was the universal object of world federation.   "Peace and justice stand or fall together," the Committee declared in their draft world constitution. Borgese was not optimistic. Limited world government, he warned, was too strong for the United States, too weak for the rest of the world, including Russia.

Nevertheless, the movement for world federation made some notable progress.   In the United States, twenty-one states passed resolutions recommending U.S. participation in a world federal government. Resolutions were introduced in Congress, and there were hearings on world federation in the House in 1948 and 1949 and in the Senate in 1950. In Europe, the constitutions of France, Italy, West Germany, and the Netherlands were modified to permit limitations of sovereignty in order to participate in a European or world union. (Twenty national constitutions now have such provisions.) By 1951, the World Movement for World Federal Government had member organizations in twenty countries, with a total membership of 150,000 people.

But the movement was too small and too slow to form to influence policy or to bring about a new convention to draft a world constitution or to amend the U.N. Charter.

The United Nations soon proved inadequate to exert an effective mediating influence on the two great powers that emerged from the war.   The United States did make an historic effort to establish the international control of atomic energy (the Baruch plan), which had implications for world federation, but the plan was not well thought out and negotiations were pressed in an atmosphere of atomic threat.   By the end of 1946, when the Baruch plan was effectively defeated, both the United States and the Soviet Union were accusing each other of Hitlerite ambitions.   The U.S. abandoned its foreign policy of cooperation with Russia and settled on the containment policy, which was announced in March, 1947. Soviet policy apparently was more ambiguous, but the Truman Doctrine and the Marshall Plan provoked a strong reaction with the formation of the Cominform and the beginning of the ideological campaign against "cosmopolitanism" (world government and friendliness with the West) later that year.   Both countries, despite protestations of support for the U.N., ceased to base their national security on the international security organization, and they returned openly to national programs of preparedness and military defense. The posture was one of war.   It was called Cold War only when hostile operations like those of World War II failed to develop.

Since the Cold War has endured to the present, despite periods of

peaceful coexistence and detente, are we to say that world federation is
impossible? Is the world permanently two?

     G.A. Borgese viewed the Cold War as a struggle about the principle of
justice on which the necessary world federation would be based.   In an age
of nations, no nation could feel secure as long as any other possessed a
threat to its existence.   Hence, expansion has been a strategic necessity
for both sides. Ultimately, the security interest of states will lead to a
world political union, achieved by force or consent. The course of national history, from a broad perspective, was clearly toward union, as is shown
by attempts in recent centuries to unite the feuding nations by force. But
the nations of Europe gradually wore themselves out with their wars, and,
by the end of the last general war (the ninth by some reckonings), only two
great, sovereign powers remained, Russia and America. They found themselves
the bearers of the two great traditions of Western democracy -- liberalism
and socialism. America was the champion of liberty; Russia, of equality of
condition. If the world had to be united, one would make it over by creating a world government of minimal powers in order to preserve popular freedoms, including freedom of business enterprise.   The other would create a
world government of maximal powers in order to bring the protection of the
state to the people against concentrations of private industrial and financial power.   It was a small difference in valuations, perhaps, for America
recognized the principle of equality before the law; and Russia, freedom
from class exploitation. It was a difference rather like that in past ages
about whether salvation came by faith or by works.   In the mid-twentieth
century, it was very nearly enough to plunge the world in fire.

     World federalists have attempted to solve this modern political diffi-
culty.   The purpose of their model world constitutions is to demonstrate
that the two main strands of justice are sufficiently shared to make possible a union by consent between East and West, North and South.   A mixed
capitalist-socialist system is usually proposed.   It could be democratic
yet contain a strong central authority.   Protections could be provided for
political and economic freedoms, for liberal as well as civil and social
human rights, for private as well as socialist enterprises.   Procedures in
the world legislature could permit maximum representation of diverse peoples and interests, but, when all processes for the protection of minorities were satisfied,   enactments would have the force of law.   The world
legislature is usually made unicameral precisely to avoid the paralysis
that democratic assemblies are liable to. Federalists argue that the political struggle between capitalism and communism, and now between the developed and underdeveloped worlds, can at least conceivably be brought under
one world legal order, much as has been done under national governments for
the struggle between capital and labor. Moreover, apart from national ideologies -- made rigid by the military necessity that they serve to prepare
the people for war -- all nations now in fact have mixed systems, part public, part private. What is needed are peaceful processes for the settlement
of disputes, which would obviate the need for claiming a right to recourse
to arms.   With such processes, ideological differences would not prove to
be insuperable obstacles to union.

     Grenville Clark and Louis B. Sohn, for instance, carefully provided
that the U.N. Economic and Social Council be reconstituted to give representation to the twelve nations with the highest gross national products;
then they proposed that a World Development Authority, under the Council,
be established with powers to make grants in aid or interest-free loans to
governments or organizations for economic and social projects considered
necessary for the "creation of conditions of stability and well-being."

The Chicago Committee, more radically, provided for an extensive bill of rights and duties, a broad grant of powers, a world planning agency, and a clause permitting public purchase of business that had acquired the "extension and character of a transnational monopoly."

There are four major problems for world federalists: membership, representation, powers, and approaches.

On membership, virtually all world federalists are agreed that universality is the ultimate goal; most hold that it is the immediate goal. Universality is the great achievement of the United Nations.   Every weakness in the U.N. has been tolerated rather than tamper with the principle of universal membership, and every attempt to evict one country (the Soviet Union in the early days, and in recent years South Africa or Israel) has been rejected as a threat to the peace. Nevertheless, a minority of federalists argue in favor of a partial union first -- notably Clarence Streit and his followers, who have proposed an Atlantic union of liberal democracies. One would also have to include among the partialists Winston Churchill, Robert Schuman, Jean Monnet, and all those, mostly under Monnet's inspiration, who have toiled for European union.

In a universal world federation, representation is the most vexed problem. Should representation be proportional to population, which is the strictly democratic principle, but which would give predominance to poorer, more populous, and less "politically experienced" countries like India? Or could representation be "weighted" somehow to make active participation more attractive to the great powers?   Grenville Clark and Louis B. Sohn proposed that the U.N. General Assembly be reorganized according to a system (subject to periodic amendment) of weighted representation cleverly scaled with respect to population, wealth, education, and traditional great power ranking: the U.S., U.S.S.R., China, and India would each be allocated 30 votes;   mid-sized powers like Britain and France, West Germany and Japan, 16; smaller nations, 8; and so on through seven steps to the smallest state, which would be granted one. This scheme produced a total of 625 world representatives. Clark and Sohn urged that the representatives be elected by the people wherever possible, so that representatives develop a sense of responsibility to the people instead of to national governments; elsewhere, appointment by parliaments, national monarchs, or communist parties would have to be tolerated.

The Chicago Committee earlier proposed an ingenious alternative scheme of regional popular elections and nine electoral colleges, which eliminated the invidious weighting scheme. But it had the same effect, since the nine regions (nicely coincident with the world civilizations that Arnold Toynbee distinguished) had different populations. These representatives were to be finally elected by all the electoral colleges in plenary session, so each representative would in principle represent the whole world. There were to be 99 of them.   Little has come of such schemes because of opposition by national officials, who stand to lose power, and by poorer, populous countries, who resent the implied slight to their people.

The powers to be delegated to a world federation could range all the way from the minimum necessary to preserve the peace to the maximum desirable to promote justice throughout the world.   Grenville Clark argued that only minimal powers were acceptable for delegation by the nations at present; amendment could provide for gradual expansion of powers as the world federation proved trustworthy. This was the doctrine of "minimalism." G.A.

Borgese and the Chicago Committee,   at the other extreme ("maximalism"),
contended that   a mere security government   would be a world police state;
the federation had to start with powers to achieve justice, for injustice
was at the root of the crisis of modern civilization.   Hence, in addition
to powers to preserve the peace, the world federation would have to have
powers to regulate world commerce, supervise world communications and transportation, lay world taxes, issue world money and control world finance,
prepare plans for equitable economic development, regulate emigration and
immigration, and supervise the rectification of borders and the creation of
new states.

     Most of the federalist movement has followed Clark. But in the course
of time, each side has seen the validity of the other's views. The minimal-
ists have seen the need for greater social and economic powers and certainly for constitutional provision for development of such powers; the maxi-
malists have softened their ideal demands for the sake of more immediate
practicality.   A more balanced view,   which some have called "medialism,"
has prevailed.

     The greatest problem of world federalism is the political transition.
Most federalists have argued that the only practical course is to conduct a
campaign of public education to persuade people that it is in their own
self-interest, particularly in peace, to reach an international agreement
for the non-violent establishment of world federal government.   Federalists
have always resisted talk and hints of preventive war, use of force, and a
national bid for empire.   The preferred method is to convene a general review conference for the reform of the United Nations, as provided for in
Article 109 of the Charter, or to convene a new world constitutional convention, like that in San Francisco in 1945. This is commonly known as the
approach of U.N. reform. The approach is official, legal, and "realistic."
Appeal is made not to moral sentiments or to the sense of human brotherhood, but to national interests. The politics of U.N. reform has consisted
largely of lobbying with legislators and high executive officials to produce a resolution or other national initiative for a new conference. United
World Federalists saw its purpose almost entirely as lobbying in Congress
for a world federalist resolution.   The World Federalist Association con-
ducts a broader educational program but still attempts to influence Congress.

     A variant on this official approach is the "parliamentary" approach,
in which national parliamentarians, including members of the U.S. Congress,
would introduce the federalist resolution themselves.   The British Parliamentary Group for World Government began this approach.   It is carried on,
with more political "realism," by Parliamentarians for World Order (now
Parliamentarians Global Action).

     A minority of federalists have argued that national governments are
natural enemies of a project that would reduce national sovereignty, so an
appeal must be made directly to the people in order to produce a wholly new
social contract.   They propose to hold popular elections of delegates to a
world constitutional convention, using state electoral machinery wherever
possible; these delegates, legitimated by their election, would then assemble in convention to draft the world constitution.   This is the peoples'
convention approach. It is unofficial, revolutionary, and "utopian." Most
proponents see it as an educational device to bring greater grassroots popular pressure to bear on officials, in order to move them to undertake U.N.
reform.   Henry Usborne, a British Member of Parliament, led a difficult
campaign to hold such a peoples' convention in Geneva by 1950.

Still another approach would be to form a transnational political party aimed at winning national offices for the purpose of carrying out a program of establishing world federation. A more modest variant would be to form an advisory committee of leaders of national political parties and trade unions on the model of Jean Monnet's Action Committee for a United States of Europe.

Actually, all federalist approaches are revolutionary, in the sense that they all aim to create favorable political conditions for the transfer of sovereign powers from nations to a higher governing authority. What is proposed is no less than the dissolution of the external sovereignty of nations. But federalists argue that -- since sovereignty is really the right of the people to institute new government, laying its foundations on such principles and organizing its powers in such form as to them shall seem most likely to effect their safety and happiness -- there can never be a "sacrifice" or dissolution of sovereignty. Rather, sovereignty is *strengthened* by uniting governments. Far from being a loss, establishing federal world government would be a gain of immense powers of social coop- eration, analogous to what has been achieved under the U.S. federal Consti- tution, which was bitterly opposed at first. Even the provision in Article 109 that each of the Big Five must ratify any amendments to the Charter need not be a barrier, if there were overwhelming popular demand for a stronger United Nations. Delegates to a U.N. Charter review conference could provide that the new Charter should go into effect when ratified by some large majority of states plus, say, three or four of the five "perma- nent members," just as the delegates to the Philadelphia convention of 1787 provided that the new U.S. government should go into operation when the Constitution was ratified by nine of the thirteen states, and not unani- mously, as required by the Articles of Confederation.

World federalists say that the times themselves are revolutionary. We are witnessing the rise of the working classes to power in the West, and the awakening of the impoverished masses in Latin America, Africa, and Asia. These events reduce even the Cold War between Russia and America to a mere ripple on the wave of history. Revolutionary times call for a revo- lutionary response.

Critics of world federalism have tended to bridle at the arguments of world law and to examine its root assumptions, particularly those of world community and world democracy. There has been much searching for alterna- tives short of a challenge to national sovereignty in the present period when nationalism remains stronger than ever.

Reinhold Niebuhr, who withdrew early from the Chicago Committee, im- mediately sensed that a precondition for the popular acceptance of world law was a shared sense of values, of world community. Law cannot work merely by virtue of the penalty attached; there must be respect for the law and voluntary obedience. In the world today, Niebuhr observed, there was hardly enough sense of belonging to a common community of humanity to pro- vide that ready obedience to the rule of world law. Dean Acheson once ob- served that government simply does not work where five percent of the popu- lation refuse to obey the law, as Truman was finding out with the coal strikers of 1946 or the British with the situations in India or Palestine. World community must precede world government.

G.A. Borgese and the rest of the Committee replied that government helps to *create* community, as the history of the U.S. federal government

shows.   A world government would begin to create the habits of submitting
to a higher law by which the power of national traditions can be broken.
He and others argued, mostly from world literature and ordinary people's
demand for peace,   that world community existed sufficiently for a beginning. There is no gradual way to peace. The problem of war must be rooted
out by a decisive act, as at Philadelphia in 1787. It is a problem of *will*.
Hence, world community and world government will develop together.

There has been extensive debate on this point, and much of the argument amounts basically to an assertion that there does not exist the will
to begin to establish world law, or that there does.   The balance of opinion, however, in the early days went decidedly toward Niebuhr.   Today, it
is shifting to the view that world community is steadily forming.   Federalists continue to maintain that law and community are interlinked parts of
one process and evolve together.

The Soviet Union has been unable to distinguish proposals of world
federation, which have been made mainly by American private citizens, from
the foreign policy of the United States. World federalism, Russian writers
say, is a mere front for Wall Street imperialism. This identification is a
mistake, but that it is even made indicates how difficult it will be, after
many years of Cold War, to bring the political struggle between capitalism
and communism into a representative world legislature, courts, or conciliation tribunals, where it would be allowed, by either the Soviet Union or
the United States, to reach decisive conclusions.   Both countries believe
in "democracy," but there is a deep division in our times between the concepts of liberal and people's democracies. Until the slow reconciliation of
these concepts is accomplished, there can be no establishment of a working,
world democracy.

Federalists reply that the real difficulty is not the concept of democracy, but the posture of war, which destroys the trust essential to the
working of any government. Communist governments, which are democratically
as nearly alike as possible, have several times been at war against one
another or on the verge of it, most notably the Soviet Union and the People's Republic of China.   What is essential for world federalism is that
all nations renounce the right to wage war.   Before the Soviet Union will
do that, it must be convinced that its defense and its progress toward
communism will not be put at the mercy of hostile Western majorities.   The
United States must be willing to demonstrate the value of its democratic
way of life and capitalist enterprise by example and leadership of world
public opinion, without the adjunct of military power.   If these difficult
political conditions can be met, there is no reason why Americans and Russians, with other peoples, cannot participate in a limited, federal world
government, just as they have begun to do in the United Nations, and as
communists and other democrats have learned to do in such European countries as Italy and France.

Many critics have shown that the proper analogy for world federation
is not the Thirteen States of 1787, but the British Commonwealth or historic Europe. The Commonwealth has developed gradually and is still not bound
together by law; in Europe, national fears and differences are much more
typical for the world at large.   The attempt to unite Europe, then, has
much more significance for the world than Philadelphia. The "Communities,"
as Walter Hallstein and Jean Monnet describe them, are a new form of international organization -- neither confederations nor federations.   The Spinelli plan for European Union, passed by the European Parliament in 1984,
is certainly the most significant recent draft constitution for the practi-

cal federation of modern states.   The council-commission-summit structure
of the Communities has been cited by Maurice Bertrand as a new model for
the reform of the United Nations.

Functionalism, a theory of closer international relations first pro-
pounded by David Mitrany in 1943, has proved to be the most successful of
all alternatives to world federation.   Mitrany rejected schemes to change
constitutions or to merge sovereignties.   Instead, he urged support for
international organizations like the International Labour Organisation and
other programmes and specialized agencies that have since been incorporated
into the United Nations system.   These organizations, some of which have
been created by simple executive agreements without formal enactment in
law, perform services ("functions") for citizens of national states.   Over
time, as they perform necessary functions beyond the ability of nation
states in an interdependent world, the people of those nations will gradually develop loyalty to the new supranational institutions. Mitrany called
the process "federalism by installments." Its success can be seen most
clearly in the Third World, whose Group of 77 (now actually 124) continues
to look to the United Nations for development assistance and political redress.

Over the years, there has been much quiet progress in the United Nations, despite an atmosphere, as the Secretary-General warns, of a retreat
from multilateralism.   A typical achievement was the signing of the Law of
the Sea in 1982 by 119 nations.   (Only eighteen, however, have ratified it
to date.)   By 1985, there were no less than 188 multilateral treaties on
deposit with the Secretary-General, dealing with every subject of interest
to the international community: human rights, economic development, disarmament, protection of the environment, and the like. The current conventional wisdom at the U.N. is that substantive Charter amendment is imprac-
ticable, given the deep divisions between East, West, and Third Worlds. But
much could be accomplished through interpretation of the Charter, as in the
case of peacekeeping, which is entirely based on a loose construction of
Article 99, or as in the relationship of the specialized agencies to the
Secretariat, which is technically an administrative matter.

Quite a bit of work has been done in the last twenty years on the alternative of "world order" to traditional power politics by the group at
the World Policy Institute centered around Saul Mendlovitz and Richard A.
Falk.   Six volumes of the World Order Models Project have now been completed.   These virtually describe a world ordered by law but avoid the clear
concepts of law.

The theorists of world order, European union, functionalism, and the
United Nations have developed a new vocabulary that avoids the historically
loaded connotations of federalist terms. These may help to overcome ground-
less fears during the transition. Some equivalents are:

Subsidiarity	= Federalism
Competence	= Sovereignty
Consensus	= Majority rule
Norms	= Laws
Cooperation	= Friendly relations
Common action	= Binding law
Union	= Government
Implementation	
of decisions	= Coercion of governments
Multilateralism	= Internationalism

Peace making	= Collective security
Peace keeping	= International police operations
Mandate	= Grant of powers
Central governance	= World government

By the 1980s, there was some renewed interest in world federal government by writers groping for a solution to the problem of nuclear war. Jonathan Schell and Freeman Dyson have raised the idea only to reject it. The
U.S. Catholic bishops, in their recent Pastoral Letter, come close to advo-
cating world government as a long-term political solution to the problem.
Many of the arguments have the ring of atomic fear, similar to arguments of
Americans in the 1940s. Less is heard of arguments about the positive promise of world federation, as G.A. Borgese used to make.

Thinkers as widely separated in recent times as Arnold Toynbee, Andrei
Sakharov, and Saul Mendlovitz have predicted world government by the year
2000, but world federalists have been unable to found an influential institute of world federal law or a world university to guide the historical
processes tending in such a direction.

The peace movement, at least in the West, was divided, poorly funded,
and seemingly without an adequate concept of the goal. Randall Forsberg,
one of the moving spirits of the movement for a nuclear weapons freeze, has
written an important article on the "Seven Steps to Peace," of which the
first is a halt in production of nuclear weapons, and the seventh is establishment of limited, federal world government, but few people have noted
it. The world federalists, as the reader can see from the section on organizations, remained divided, too. The World Association of World Federalists
did not embrace them all, and in principle it remained a league of sovereign organizations. Even those who aim to unite the world cannot unite
themselves. Nevertheless, there is evident by the 1980s a great, diffuse,
world-wide popular movement in opposition to nuclear arms and to the politics of neglect of humanity's global problems. Some have called it a movement of "respiritualization." It may be symbolized by the teachings of the
Bahá'í religion, which holds (and has held since the 19th century) that
world peace can practically be achieved only by a political union or federal world government, which will produce what Bahá'ís call the Lesser Peace;
such a lawful world order will then provide the social and spiritual conditions for the perfection of religion, or what they call the Most Great
Peace.

What is the relevance of world federalism to the search for peace?

Its primary contribution is an adequate conception of the goal. Peace
is not the interim between wars; it is a positive thing, an active social
condition, chosen deliberately and consciously maintained. Peace is the
presence of justice, that is, of order, of law, and of government. World
peace will require *institutional* change in order to provide for the regular, orderly resolution of international disputes and for international cooperation in the common interest. Federalists argue that structural change
-- U.N. reform -- may precede "trust," and indeed will help to create it.
If peoples and governments already trusted one another, cooperating and
competing without violence, there would be no need for world government, or
for the United Nations for that matter. The U.N. is weak today because it
has not been structured to reach decisions that seem fair or can be en-
forced, even in matters about which there are not great East-West differences, like the Iran-Iraq War. World federalists express the need for
stronger international institutions in the familiar language of federal

government, but no doubt new and unprecedented institutions will have to be created, for the whole human race is far more diverse than any community yet united under a federal system. Europe is probably the best model.

The achievement of the rule of world law will largely depend on new, enlightened national leadership. Jean Monnet used to say that, for the hard work of uniting sovereignties, men act only when faced by a crisis. The world now is faced by a massive crisis, symbolized by the threat of nuclear war. At the moment, it is only a crisis of the mind. To bring about an agreement to establish a stronger form of international organization, we need now not more arguments based on atomic fear, for they move people not toward world federation but toward more ready expedients like deterrence. We need a new positive vision of peace.

What federalists are really calling for is a new kind of world political wisdom. The works listed in this bibliography, collected over a long time period and over the broad face of the globe, all have a bearing on the summoning of such wisdom.

Edith Wynner and Georgia Lloyd, *Searchlight on Peace Plans: Choose Your Road to World Government* (Dutton, 1944; 1949). Used by permission of Edith Wynner and Georgia Lloyd.

Organization of Bibliography

This bibliography is organized generally according to the end sought by the authors: union of democracies, United Nations, international control of atomic energy, universal federation (several sections divided by time and nationality of author), European federation, and world order. Several other sections are provided for context or completion, such as diplomacy, the peace movement, and bibliographies.

All works listed here have some connection to world federalism, pro or con. Critical works especially have been sought. Works strictly on international law, with no conception of a compromise of national sovereignty, have not been included. No attempt has been made to list all articles in world federalist journals, such as *Common Cause*, though a few more important and representative ones have been included. The reader is referred to the journals themselves. Much historical material remains in the archives. The bibliographies have been combed for works of general significance. For small-scale or partisan writings, the reader is referred to the bibliographies. Generally, all books, pamphlets, and articles on world federalism that were widely read and had any political significance are here.

The divisions involve some chronological overlap, particularly in the cases of "Universal Federation--U.S. to 1955," "United Nations," and "League or Federation--U.S. Wartime Views." Individuals generally were known as supporters of the United Nations or as advocates of world federation (though federalists did support the U.N. in the sense that they wished to keep it until they could reform or replace it). During the war, however, until the Moscow Declaration of 1943, there was much fluidity of view. Prominent individuals, such as Nicholas Murray Butler, then talked of federation, but, with the official U.S. commitment to a league structure in the U.N., they later switched to the U.N. A few, like Stringfellow Barr or Henry Wallace, switched to world federation. Others, like Grenville Clark, were consistent advocates of world federation from early years. Many commented on others' positions. The sections preserve the distinctions individuals themselves would have made.

In this bibliography, individuals are categorized by the areas of their advocacy or criticism; in cases where they might be so placed in two sections, they are listed twice. There is some repetition. A division is made in American works about the year 1955. This marks the end of the more euphoric period in the movement, when world government seemed five years away; thereafter, federalism was struggling with the realities of the Cold

War.   A similar time division is not made for works published outside the
United States because their numbers are not unmanageable.   Works by single
individuals are arranged chronologically, not alphabetically.   The author,
nation, and subject indices are extensive and accurate.   These arrangements
should help the researcher to find works in similar areas of interest and
to follow an author's progression of thought.   Readers may want to look for
the same author in subsequent sections.   Quincy Wright is a good example.

The works listed here provide a rich field for original research and
inspired teaching.   Much needs to be done to bring greater coherence to our
thought on the central problem of the age.   Many federalist writings,   especially in recent years, seem conceived in isolation from main currents in
foreign policy as well as from kindred spirits in other countries.   Diplomatic history has become a specialized field. U.N. publications are written
in a language of their own. The peace movement seems to shrink from a clear
conception of its goal.   It is hoped that this bibliography will serve to
bring students, scholars,   citizens,   and policymakers into closer dialogue
in forming a creative response to the challenge of war in the twentieth
century.   It should be useful for the study of international organization,
foreign policy, diplomacy, history, federalism, and peace.   A certain light
-- confident in human powers to achieve peace as the positive condition for
a good life for all people -- shines from the works listed here and offers
us hope.

"You fellows mind if we start the ball rolling?"
   —copyright 1949 by Herblock in The Washington Post on July 27, 1949
Used by permission of HERBLOCK CARTOONS.

1

Essential Works

Robert M. Hutchins once remarked that it was possible to silence a world federalist simply by asking him what was meant by world federal government. The following works, particularly those by Grenville Clark and Louis B. Sohn and by the Committee to Frame a World Constitution, make that meaning clear. It must be a government, representative of all the world's nations, peoples, classes, and minorities, vested with powers ranging from the minimum to the maximum, that can, by constitutional processes, enact law reaching to individuals.

Albert Einstein brings to bear the broad scientific view on the problem of atomic energy, which he helped to release. Clarence Streit's *Union Now* develops the implications of federalism from the precedent of the American Revolution. *The Federalist* explores such root assumptions of world federalists as the necessity for world law reaching to individuals. Emery Reves' *The Anatomy of Peace* lays bare the notion of national sovereignty. Arnold Toynbee's "The International Outlook" takes the long historical view.

Henry Stimson, in his article published after the containment policy became the fundamental foreign policy of the United States, marking the onset of the Cold War, warned that "lasting peace and freedom cannot be achieved until the world finds a way to the necessary government of the whole." He left this as a "challenge to Americans."

[1] Adler, Mortimer J. *How to Think about War and Peace*. New York: Simon & Schuster, 1944. 307 pp.
"The *only* cause of war is anarchy. . . . It is the only cause we can control." A book that lives up to its title. But world government, Adler thought, was 500 years distant. After the atomic bomb was used, he changed his estimate to five years.

[2] Clark, Grenville. *A Plan for Peace*. New York: Harper & Bros., 1950. 83 pp.
First of the genre of warnings on nuclear war, with the difference that Clark proposed a realistic solution of steps toward world federation.

[3] Clark, Grenville, and Sohn, Louis B. *World Peace through World Law*. Cambridge: Harvard University Press, 1958; 2nd ed., 1960; 3rd, 1966. 540 pp.
Model for United Nations reform.   Minimalist.   There is no clearer statement anywhere of what exactly must be done to establish the rule of law. Clark and Sohn's World Equity Tribunal and World Conciliation Board are of particular interest for the settlement of *political* disputes. Translated into ten languages, including Russian.

[4] Committee to Frame a World Constitution. Robert M. Hutchins, president; G.A. Borgese, secretary. "Preliminary Draft of a World Constitution." *Common Cause*, 1 (March, 1948), pp. 1-40.   Reprinted as *A Constitution for the World* by the Center for the Study of Democratic Institutions, Santa Barbara, Calif., 1965. 112 pp.
Model world constitution. Maximalist.   The problem of representation is ingeniously solved through a system of regional electoral districts that conform to the civilizations. Its preamble, list of powers, tribune of the people to protect minorities, and constitutional checks and balances are of particular interest.

[5] Hamilton, Alexander; Madison, James; and Jay, John. *The Federalist Papers*. New York: Modern Library, n.d. [1787-1788]. 622 pp.
Nos. 9, 10, 15, 16, 17, 21, 23, 39, and 46 are especially relevant today, on analogy with the international situation under the U.N. Charter.

[6] Hutchins, Robert M. "The Constitutional Foundations of World Order." *Common Cause*, 1 (December, 1947), pp. 201-08.
Bold statement marking failure of national leadership to take the initiative for necessary world federation.

[7] Nathan, Otto, and Norden, Heinz, eds. *Einstein on Peace*.   New York: Schocken, 1960. 704 pp.
Chapters 9-14 clearly reveal Einstein's thinking on world government in the atomic age.

[8] Reves, Emery. *The Anatomy of Peace*. New York: Harper & Bros., 1945. 275 pp.
Powerful argument against national sovereignty.   There is no freedom without law, no real national independence without world law. Book appeared just before atomic bomb, then sold 70,000 copies in eight printings in 1945 alone. It was widely excerpted, translated into many languages (including Czech and Arabic), and often was the only book people had read about world government, in addition to Streit's *Union Now*. Reves, however, was very sketchy about his solution. He

doubted that the world's peoples could cooperate in time to establish
a world federation by peaceful means.   He closed the book with an
appeal for world government as a war aim in an expected bid for world
empire by either the United States or the Soviet Union.

[9] Stimson, Henry L. "The Challenge to Americans." *Foreign Affairs*, 26 (October, 1947), pp. 5-14.
"Lasting peace and freedom cannot be achieved until the world finds a
way to the necessary government of the whole." Corrective to Kennan's
"X" article.

[10] Streit, Clarence K.   *Union Now*:   *A Proposal for a Federal Union of the
Leading Democracies of the North Atlantic*. New York: Harper & Bros.,
1939. 315 pp.
The book which started the world government movement.   Chapters 2-3
particularly relevant.   Originally, Streit proposed an anti-fascist
Atlantic Union, and he was remarkably tolerant toward the Soviet Union.   Later in the Cold War period, he edited his book so that Russia
took the place of Nazi Germany as the enemy to be overwhelmed by the
Union's "preponderance of power." Book has sold over 250,000 copies
in eight editions.

[11] Taylor, Edmond. *Richer by Asia*. Boston: Houghton Mifflin, 1947.   431
pp.
Book which raised the consciousness of the American world government
movement to the importance of the undeveloped world.   Gandhi's relevance.

[12] Toynbee, Arnold.   "The International Outlook." *Civilization on Trial*.
New York: Oxford University Press, 1948, pp. 126-49.
Political issue is not whether, but which way the world will be unit-
ed.

[13] Wells, H.G. "The Next Stage in History" (Book 9) in *The Outline of His-
tory*. New York: Macmillan, 1920. 2 vols.
See especially Chap. 41: "Man's Coming of Age. The Probable Struggle
for the Unification of the World into One Community of Knowledge and
Will. . . .   How a Federal World Government May Come About. . . ."
Suppressed in 1949 Postgate edition.

[14] White, E. B. *The Wild Flag*. Boston: Houghton Mifflin, 1946. 188 pp.
"The most appalling thing in the world that I know of is world government, except the lack of it." A slim book written with good humor and
intelligence. The place to begin.

[15] Wofford, Harris. "Road to the World Republic." *Common Cause*, 2 (August,
1948), pp. 23-28.
Classic argument for forming a world federalist political party.

2

Union of Democracies

Clarence Streit was a *New York Times* correspondent at Geneva covering the League of Nations during its last years. The experience convinced him that a league of sovereign states was too weak to keep the peace in the modern world and had to be replaced by a world federation.

It was natural for him to think first of a union of similar liberal democracies, which in 1939 meant the United States, Britain, the British Commonwealth, France, the non-fascist West European states, and their empires, including most of Africa, India, Indonesia, and Australia. Streit conceived this union as opposed to the fascist Axis. He had extraordinary influence in Great Britain, where his ideas formed part of the backdrop for Winston Churchill's proposal of a Franco-British union in June, 1940. Later after the war, the Soviet Union took the place in his mind of the enemy to be overwhelmed by the union's preponderance of power.

Streit has been criticised from many quarters for proposing a partial union that would probably precipitate the very war that world union is designed to prevent. World Federalists formed as a splinter group from his public organization over the issue of universality.

Nevertheless, Streit received powerful support from people in high places. Supreme Court Justice Owen Roberts joined the cause. After the North Atlantic Treaty was signed in 1949, Roberts, former Secretary of War Robert H. Patterson, and former Under Secretary of State Will L. Clayton formed the Atlantic Union Committee. Their aim was to transform the NATO alliance into a political union opposed to the Communist bloc. United World Federalists expended most of their energies opposing the Atlantic Union program in the Congressional hearings of 1949 and 1950.

In the years since, there has been much interest in the developing Atlantic community and in its potential for union. But Atlantic union has not made as much progress as European union. The reason seems to be that the United States would be added to the former. Atlantic union is conceived as an anti-communist superstate, while European union is designed to maintain a delicate balance between the existing superstates.

[25] Acheson, Dean. *The Problem of International Organization among Countries of Europe and the North Atlantic Area.* Washington: U.S. Department of State Publication 3861, 1950. 8 pp.

[26] Allen, Harry C.   *The Anglo-American Predicament*: *The British Commonwealth, the United States, and European Unity.* New York: St. Martin's, 1960. 241 pp.

[27] Angell, Norman. *The Political Conditions of Allied Success*: *A Plea for the Protective Union of the Democracies.* New York: Putnam, 1918. 350 pp.

[28] --------, and Roberts, Owen J. "U.N. or World State?" *Rotarian*, June, 1946, pp. 12-15.
By champions of Atlantic Union. After Dublin Conference.

[29] --------. *The Steep Places.* New York: Harper & Bros., 1948. 247 pp.
By 1948 the author of *The Great Illusion* was firmly in the Atlantic Union school.

[30] "Atlantic Union's Streit: Nationalism Is the Poison." *Time*, March 27, 1950, pp. 22-25.
Cover story.

[31] Ball, Mary M. *NATO and the European Union Movement.*   London: Stevens, 1959. 486 pp.

[32] Beveridge, Sir William.   *Peace by Federation?*   London: Federal Union, Federal Tracts No. 1, 1940. 35 pp.

[33] Bieri, Ernst, et al. *Basic Values of the Atlantic Community.*   Foreword by Paul Van Zeeland. Leyden: Sijthoff, 1961. 135 pp.
Papers at Bruges conference of 1957 on the future of the Atlantic alliance.

[34] Boothby, Robert. *Citizenship of the Free World*:   *A Plea for Organic Union.* Sackville, New Brunswick: Mt. Allison University, 1956.   70 pp.

[35] Brailsford, Henry Noel. *The Federal Idea.* London: Federal Union, 1940. 15 pp.

[36] Catlin, George E. G. *One Anglo-American Union . . . A British Response to Streit.* Introduction by J. C. Wedgwood; preface by Ernest Barker. London: A. Dakers, 1941. 155 pp.

[37] --------. *The Atlantic Community.* London: Coram, 1959. 146 pp.

[38] Cerny, Karl H., and Briefs, Henry W., eds.   *NATO in Quest of Cohesion*: *A Confrontation of Viewpoints.* Foreword by Gen. Lauris Norstad.   New York: Hoover Institution on War, Revolution, and Peace, 1965.   476 pp.

[39] Chaning-Pearce, M., ed. *Federal Union*: *A Symposium.* London: Cape, 1940. 336 pp.

[40] Clark, Grenville.   *A Memorandum with Regard to a New Effort to Organize Peace and Containing a Proposal for a Federation of Free Peoples in*

the Form of a Draft, with Explanatory Notes on a Constitution for the Proposed Federation. New York: By the author, 1940. 38 pp.

[41] Clayton, Will L. "We Must Trade Sovereignty for Freedom." *New York Times Magazine*, October 22, 1950, p. 13.

[42] Cleveland, Harold Van B. *The Atlantic Idea and Its European Rivals.* New York: Council on Foreign Relations, 1966. 186 pp.

[43] Conant, Mary H. "How Federal Union Would Fit with United Nations." *Christian Science Monitor Magazine*, September 8, 1945, p. 9.
United States of World should begin with nucleus of nations that are based on solid democratic foundations. Others to be admitted as they adopt a democratic form of government.

[43]a Cooper, Richard N. *The Economics of Interdependence: Economic Policy in the Atlantic Community.* New York: Council on Foreign Relations, Atlantic Policy Studies, McGraw Hill, 1968.

[44] Curry, W. B. *The Case for Federal Union.* Hammondsworth, Middlesex: Penguin, November, 1939. 213 pp.
Equivalent in England to Streit's *Union Now.*

[45] Curtis, Lionel. *World Revolution in the Cause of Peace.* New York: Macmillan, 1949. 135 pp.

[46] Deutsch, Karl Wolfgang, et al. *Political Community and the North Atlantic Area: International Organization in the Light of Historical Experience.* Princeton: Princeton University Press, 1957. 228 pp.

[47] Eagleton, Clyde. "The League of Nations and Federal Union." *New Commonwealth Quarterly*, 5 (1939), pp. 119-30.

[48] Fawcett, Charles B. *The Bases of a World Commonwealth.* London: Watts, 1941. 167 pp.

[49] Ford, John Howard, and Streit, Clarence. "We Need Hamilton's Plan Now." *Freedom and Union*, January, 1948, p. 5.
Argument for Atlantic Union on basis of Marshall Plan.

[50] Goodman, Elliot Raymond. *The Fate of the Atlantic Community.* New York: Praeger, Atlantic Council of the United States, 1975. 583 pp.

[51] Greaves, H.R.G. *Federal Union in Practice.* London: Allen & Unwin, 1940. 135 pp.

[52] Griessemer, Tom. "Hitler? Stalin? Streit? World Domination or World Federation: The Choice Free Peoples Face." New York: Committee of Inter-Democracy Federal Unionists, 1940. 15 pp.

[53] Hartley, Livingston. *Atlantic Challenge.* Forword by Elmo Roper. Dobbs Ferry, N.Y.: Oceana, 1965. 111 pp.

[54] Henrikson, Alan. "The Creation of the North Atlantic Alliance." In John Reichart and Steven Strum, eds., *American Defense Policy* (Baltimore: Johns Hopkins University Press, 1982), pp. 296-320.
Historically rich essay on the origins of NATO -- the end of the "no entangling alliances" tradition and the beginning of actual permanent

U.S. commitments to the Atlantic community of nations. Suggestive about widening the alliance in membership (Egypt, ASEAN, even the Soviet Union) and in functions (revived European Defense Community, greater social and economic integration in accordance with Art. 2, cooperation with the United Nations). "There is 'a new world' -- a world in which the Soviet Union has achieved nuclear parity, of economic weakness in the United States, and, perhaps most important, of nearly a hundred emerging countries on the continents of Latin America, Africa, and Asia. [As President Carter said at Notre Dame in May, 1977,] 'We can no longer have a policy solely for the industrial nations as the foundation of global stability, but we must respond to the new reality of a politically awakening world.'"

[55] Herter, Christian A. *Toward an Atlantic Community*. New York: Council on Foreign Relations, Harper & Row, 1963. 107 pp.

[56] "History Is Catching Up with 'Union Now': Has the Time Come to Call a Constitutional Convention?" *Fortune*, April, 1949, pp. 77-78.
In post-North Atlantic Treaty, Atlantic Union Committee period.

[57] Hoffman, Rose. "Europe and the Atlantic Community." *Thought*, 20 (1945), pp. 21-36.

[58] Huntley, James. *Uniting the Democracies*: *Institutions of the Emerging Atlantic System*. New York: New York University Press, 1980. 392 pp.

[59] Jensen, Merrill. *The New Nation*: *A History of the United States during the Confederation, 1781-1789*. New York: Knopf, 1950. 433 pp.
Prompted by Streit's *Union Now*, Jensen admitted only that the "weakness" of the U.S. Congress under the Articles was due to its constitutional reliance on "persuasion" rather than "coercion" (pp. 348, 428). This is the very difference between a confederation and a federation, between a league and a union.

[60] Joad, C. E. M. *The Philosophy of Federal Union*. London: Macmillan, Federal Tracts No. 5, 1941. 40 pp.

[61] Johnsen, Julia E., comp. *International Federation of Democracies (Proposed)*. New York: H. W. Wilson, The Reference Shelf, Vol. 14, No. 8, 1941. 263 pp.
Early opinion inspired by Streit.

[62] Keeton, George W. "Federalism and World Order." *New Commonwealth Quarterly*, 5 (1940), pp. 6-10.

[63] Kefauver, Estes. "The Case for Federal Union." *The Progressive*, July, 1950.
Atlantic Union Committee statement; next in series was one for United World Federalists by Cord Meyer.

[64] Lambert, R.S. "Federal Union -- Panacea or Delusion?" *Food for Thought*, 11 (1941), pp. 3-12.

[65] Mahabharati, Alokananda. *Ending the Communist Menace*: *Atlantic Union or World Union*. Calcutta: Arunachal Mission, World Peace Office, 1962. 60 pp.

[66] Meeman, E.J. "Freedom through Union: Make the Potential Strength of the Free World Actual." *Vital Speeches*, 16 (November 15, 1949), pp. 89-93. Address before Tennessee State Exchange Clubs, Knoxville, June 24, 1949.

[67] Moore, Ben T. *NATO and the Future of Europe*. Foreword by William C. Foster. New York: Council on Foreign Relations, Harper, 1958. 263 pp.

[68] Middleton, Drew. *The Atlantic Community*: *A Study in Unity and Diversity*. New York: McKay, 1965. 303 pp.

[69] Morrison, Philip, and Wilson, Robert R. "Half a World . . . and None: Partial World Government Criticized." *Bulletin of the Atomic Scientists*, 3 (July, 1947), pp. 13-14.
Answer to Urey in previous issue. Preponderance of power in the "democratic" Atlantic Union would not "persuade" the Communist countries to join, but would provoke them to form an opposing union and perhaps even precipitate the very war union is supposed to prevent.

[70] Munk, Frank. *Atlantic Dilemma*: *Partnership or Community?* Foreword by Henry Cabot Lodge. Dobbs Ferry, N.Y.: Oceana, 1964. 177 pp.
Includes "Common Defense" and "Towards a Political Community."

[71] Nesslein, Floyd F. *United We Stand*. Washington: Freedom & Union, 1969. 136 pp.
Brief account of Streit's movement from his League of Nations days to NATO and after.

[72] Roberts, Owen J. "Real World Parliament to Keep Peace: The Lessons of Past Failures." *Vital Speeches*, 12 (May 1, 1946), pp. 426-28.
Speech by former Supreme Court Justice in favor of world government.

[73] --------; Schmidt, John F.; and Streit, Clarence K. (Publius II). *The New Federalist*. New York: Harper & Bros., 1950. 109 pp.
Federalist principles applied primarily to Atlantic union.

[74] Rockefeller, Nelson A. *The Future of Federalism*. New York: Atheneum, 1964. 83 pp.
"This Communist new order . . . is based on a *false* federalism whose pattern may be found in the Soviet Union itself."

[75] Roper, Elmo. *The Goal Is Government of All the World*. New York: Atlantic Union Committee, 1949. 21 pp.

[76] Ross, Carl A. *Union Now and Peace Now*: *For a New Northwest Ordinance*. Albion, Mich.: By the author, 1939. 14 pp.

[77] Schwarzenberger, Georg. *Atlantic Union*: *A Practical Utopia?* London: Federal Educational and Research Trust, 1957.
"Is it not glaringly obvious that such a scheme would perpetuate Anglo Saxon supremacy in the Western world? . . . Anglo-Saxon supremacy in the Western world is a fact. It needs no Atlantic Union to establish it."

[78] Schwimmer, Rosika. *Union Now for Peace and War? The Danger in the Plan of Clarence Streit*. New York: By the author, 1939. 19 pp.

[79] Steed, Wickham; Harsfall, W.; et al. "Union Now? (A Debate)." *New Commonwealth Quarterly*, 5 (1939), pp. 157-69.

[80] Strausz-Hupe, Robert; Dougherty, James E.; and Kintner, William R. *Building the Atlantic World*. New York: Harper & Row, 1963. 400 pp. Streitian. Defeat of Communism a higher value than toleration of differing eco-political systems.

[81] Streit, Clarence K. *Union Now: A Proposal for a Federal Union of the Leading Democracies of the North Atlantic*. New York: Harper & Bros., 1939. 315 pp.
The book which started the world government movement.

[82] --------. "Union Now." *Reader's Digest*, June, 1939, pp. 99-102.

[83] --------. *World Government or Anarchy? Our Urgent Need for World Order*. Chicago: World Citizens Association, 1939. 57 pp.
Chapters 2-3 from *Union Now*, reprinted by Anita McCormick Blaine's group.

[84] --------. *Union Now with Britain*. New York: Harper & Bros., 1941. 240 pp.
Book which provoked the splintering of World Federalists from Streit's Federal Union organization.

[85] --------. *Freedom against Itself*. New York: Harper & Bros., 1954. 316 pp.
Cold War anti-communism.

[86] --------. *Freedom's Frontier -- Atlantic Union Now*. Washington, D. C.: Freedom & Union Press, 1961. 308 pp.

[87] Szent-Miklosy, Istvan. *The Atlantic Union Movement: Its Significance in World Politics*. New York: Fountainhead, 1965. 264 pp.

[88] Terry, J. William. "Federation or League." *Changing World*, 13 (April, 1941), pp. 11-12.
Criticism of a partial federal union. "If enduring peace can be attained only through an organized world community, and if the creation of such a community must await the democratization of peoples who are without democratic traditions, enduring peace is apt to be a long way off."

[89] Wilcox, Francis O. *The Atlantic Community: Progress and Prospects*. Boston: World Peace Foundation, International Organization 17, 1963. 308 pp.

[90] Wofford, Harris, and Findley, Paul. "Universal Union vs. Union of the Free." *Freedom and Union*, November, 1947, pp. 6-9.

3

League or Federation—
U.S. Wartime Views

America was strongly isolationist in the 1920s and '30s. The Senate rejected U.S. participation in the League of Nations in 1920, the "lost generation" decried its part in the "war to end war," and by 1935 a host of writers had convinced the public that the munitions makers and merchants of death were the cause of wars. The Neutrality Acts were intended to keep the country out of war by preventing the President from again supplying war matériel to belligerents as Wilson had done.

When World War II broke out, in part because Roosevelt had so little power under the Neutrality Acts to prevent it, a group of far-sighted internationalists set themselves the task of building American public opinion in favor of U.S. participation in another international security organization after the war. One of them was James T. Shotwell, a historian associated with the Carnegie Endowment for International Peace. He organized the Commission to Study the Organization of Peace a few months after Hitler invaded Poland. Shotwell and Clark Eichelberger, the Commission's director, drew over 100 able internationalists and publicists to their cause. They had a brief federal period, as one can see in the works of Butler, Corbett, Kelsen, and even Shotwell, but after the U.S. commitment to a league in 1943, the Commission worked for a new league of sovereign states. Forty-seven Commission members attended the San Francisco conference of 1945 as delegates or consultants in order to assist at the establishment of the United Nations.

Breaking the political appeal of isolationism was a major accomplishment of these internationalists. World federalists had no similar influence.

Several other figures who later would be significant for world federalism, though they themselves remained cautious, were Henry Wallace and Wendell Willkie. Wallace's speech, "The Century of the Common Man," was practically a proclamation of a world New Deal as a war aim, and Willkie's book, *One World*, gave a name to the aspirations of a generation of internationalists.

[100] Adler, Mortimer J. *How to Think about War and Peace*. New York: Simon
      & Schuster, 1944. 307 pp.
      "The *only* cause of war is anarchy. . . . It is the only cause we can
      control."

[101] Agar, Herbert; Borgese, G. A.; et al.   *The City of Man*: *A Declaration
      on World Democracy*. New York: Viking, 1940. 113 pp.
      Eloquent on the issue of World War II.

[102] Alguy, Jeremiah. *Permanent World Peace*. New York: Standard, 1943.   304
      pp.

[103] American Historical Association, Historical Service Board, *Can We Pre-
      vent Future Wars?*   War Dept.   Educational Manual EM-12, GI Round-
      table. Madison, Wisc.: U.S. Armed Forces Institute, 1944.   28 pp.

[104] Aufricht, Hans.   "Post-War Planning and Limitation of Sovereignty."
      American Journal of International Law, 38 (1944), pp. 119-24.
      Commission to Study the Organization of Peace legal opinion.

[105] Barney,   Nora Stanton.   *World Peace through a People's Parliament*:   A
      Second House   in World Government.   Committee to Win World Peace
      through a People's Parliament, n.d., c. 1944.
      Barney was an architect and civil engineer. Plan was known to Gren-
      ville Clark.

[106] Barr, Stringfellow. "The Education of Free Men." *New Republic*, August
      31, 1942.
      Barr's early federalist (Streitian) thinking.

[107] Bartlett, Ruhl J. *The League to Enforce Peace*. Chapel Hill, N.C.: Uni-
      versity of North Carolina Press, 1944.   252 pp.
      History of 1915-1920 predessor to world government movement.

[108] Bassett, Noble P. *Constitution of the United Nations of the World*. Bos-
      ton: Christopher, 1944. 64 pp.

[109] Becker, Carl L.   *How* New *Will the Better World Be?*   New York: Knopf,
      1944. 246 pp.
      Nationalism, sovereign independence, national interests, and balance
      of power will remain political realities after the war.

[110] Birdsall, George A.   *A Proposed World Government*. Arlington, Va.: Shaw,
      1944. 110 pp.
      Similar to Bishop.

[111] Bishop, Rufus Walter.   "A Proposal for Permanent World Security with
      Suggested Methods for Its Application." Dittoed, n.d., c. 1944; in
      Clark Papers.
      Bishop was in Sgt. Alvin York's platoon during the famous Argonne
      battle in which their company was reduced from 200 men to 80.   His
      plan, which would give the world assembly more power than Clark's at
      this time, was typical of popular interest in federalism.

[112] Bonnet, Henri.   *The United Nations*: *What They Are, What They May Be-
      come*. Chicago: World Citizens Association, 1942. 100 pp.

[113] --------. *Outlines of the Future*: *World Organization Emerging from the*

War. Chicago: World Citizens Association, 1943. 128 pp.

[114] Bordwell, Percy. "A Constitution for the United Nations." *Iowa Law Review*, 28 (1943), pp. 387-421.

[114]a Borgese, Giuseppe Antonio. *Common Cause*. New York: Duell, Sloan & Pearce, 1943. 448 pp.
"The Common Man, in plainest words, has not yet found the Common Cause." Broad political and philosophical tract on the issues of World War II, written during period of Western defeats. Source for Borgese's and the Chicago Committee's later effort to establish a world republic.

[115] Boucher, Anthony [William A. P. White]. *Q. U. R.* 1943.
Science fiction novelette of a black man as president of a world federation of nations. Most science fiction, which became a literary genre at this time, preferred the distopia.

[116] Boulding, Kenneth. *New Nations for Old*. Wallingford, Pa.: Pendle Hill Pamphlet, 1942. 40 pp.
Humanity needs to move beyond national patriotism. The nation state is a temporary convenience, or, in fact, an obsolescent institution. A work of the Quaker Graduate Center for Social Study while Boulding was chairman of the economics department at the University of Michigan.

[117] Brecht, Arnold. "Limited-Purpose Federations." *Social Research*, 10 (May, 1943), pp. 135-51.
Based on paper read at Institute on World Organization, Washington, D.C., September 12, 1942.

[118] Briggs, Asa G. "As to a Super-State." *World Affairs*, 107 (September, 1944), pp. 166-71.
No sovereign international organization can successfully govern the world. Comment on first report of Commission to Study the Organization of Peace.

[119] Butler, Nicholas Murray. *The Family of Nations: Its Needs and Its Problems*. New York: Scribners, 1938. 400 pp.
The Columbia University president's pre-war speeches in favor of world federation.

[120] --------. *Toward a Federal World*. New York: Carnegie Endowment for International Peace, 1939. 17 pp.

[121] --------. "Leadership of the United States in World Organization for Prosperity and Peace." *International Conciliation*, 371 (June, 1941), pp. 567-86.

[122] Commission to Study the Organization of Peace. *Preliminary Report and Monographs*. New York: Commission to Study the Organization of Peace, 1940. 39 pp.
James T. Shotwell: "National sovereignty must yield more and more to the community of nations. The world must evolve from League to federation."

[123] --------. *Building Peace: Reports of the Commission to Study the Organization of Peace, 1939-1972*. Metuchen, N.J.: Scarecrow, 1973.

2 vols.
1. Preliminary,   November, 1940;
2. Transitional,   February, 1942;
3. U.N. and Organization of Peace,   February, 1943;
4. Fundamentals of the International Organization, November, 1943.

[124] Corbett, Percy Ellwood. *Post-War Worlds*. New York: Farrar & Rinehart, 1942. 233 pp.
Institute of Pacific Relations series.   Analysis of many plans for
federation, including those of Lionel Curtis and Clarence Streit.

[125] Corliss, John B., Jr. *Constitution of the World State*. Detroit: By
the author, 1943. 20 pp.
Minimal world government with weighted representation (China, India,
U.S., and U.S.S.R. each to have 20 representatives).

[126] Corwin, Edward S. *The Greatest Project of All Time*, *a Federation of
the Nations That Will Insure a Lasting Peace between Them*: *The Constitution and World Organization*. Freeport, N.Y.: Books for Libraries, 1944; reprinted, 1970. 64 pp.
By the great scholar of American government.

[127] Davis, Forrest. "Roosevelt's World Blueprint." *Saturday Evening Post*,
April 10, 1943, pp. 20-21, 109-10.
Roosevelt stressed his faith in only two instrumentalities of the
League of Nations: the plebiscite and the mandate. One of few pub-
lic sources on FDR's concept of a post-war security organization.

[128] --------. "What Really Happened at Teheran." *Saturday Evening Post*,
May 13, 1944, pp. 12 ff., and May 20, 1944, pp. 22 ff.
A superstate with its own capital, centralized bureaucracy, and
armed forces FDR called "nonsense."

[129] Dexter, Lewis A. "Implications of Supranational Federation." *American
Sociological Review*, 7 (June, 1942), p. 400.
Analysis of federalism in terms of values: prestige, power, excite-
ment, moral habits, income.

[130] Dulles, John Foster. *Toward World Order*. Delaware: Ohio Wesleyan Uni-
versity Press, 1942. 27 pp.
Merrick-McDowell lecture delivered at Ohio Wesleyan University,
March 5, 1942, on the occasion of a conference called by the Federal
Council of Churches to study the bases for a just and durable peace.

[131] Eagleton, Clyde. "Organization of the Community of Nations." *American
Journal of International Law*, 36 (1942), pp. 229-41.

[132] Eaton, Howard O., ed. *Federation*: *The Coming Structure of World Government*. Norman, Okla.: University of Oklahoma Press, 1944.   234
pp.
Wartime statements.

[133] Fike, Linus R. "No Nation Alone: A Plan for Organized Peace." New York:
Philosophical Library, 1943. 96 pp.

[134] Fisher, Irving. *Winning the Peace*. Address before luncheon meeting of
the second annual national convention of Federal Union, St. Louis,
June 26, 1942; in Clark Papers. 10 pp.

Classic argument for federation by Yale professor emeritus of economics.

[135] Freeman, Harrop A. *Coercion of States in International Organizations*.
Philadelphia: Pacifist Research Bureau, 1944. 57 pp.

[136] Gibson, Harold Elmer. *Federal World Union*.   Jacksonville, Ill.: Midwest Debate Bureau, 1942. 45 pp.
Debate topic. 1942-1943: "Resolved: That the United Nations should establish a permanent federal union with power to tax and regulate international commerce, to maintain a police force, to settle international disputes, and to enforce such settlements. . . ."

[137] Gill, Charles A. *World Republic*. Philadelphia: Dorrance, 1943.   119
pp.
"What the average man or woman, not only in America, but all over the world wants [is] . . . a plan of World Democratic Government."

[138] Guillet, Cephas. "A Plan for a Peaceful World." New York: By the author, 1944. 23 pp.

[139] Hall, Arnold H. *The Science of World Government and a Charter*. Boston: By the author, 1944. 16 pp.

[140] Hamilton, Kingsley W. "Aspects of the Coming Postwar Settlement." *International Conciliation*, 393 (October, 1943), pp. 543-63.

[141] Hard, William.   "Are We on the Wrong Road toward Peace?" *Reader's Digest*, September, 1944, pp. 1-8.
Typical article in favor of "world union" before end of war.

[142] Harrison, Richard Edes. *Look at the World*: *The Fortune Atlas for World Strategy*. New York: Knopf, 1944.
Atlas which conveyed the new airman's view of the world.   Contains "One World, One War." Harrison emphasized the Arctic for the future, drawing attention to the Japanese attack on Pearl Harbor from the north.   Several perspective maps over the pole, as a Russian bomber pilot might approach America, chillingly illustrated the danger. Cf. article by Alan Henrikson.

[143] Hemleben, Sylvester J. *Plans for World Peace through Six Centuries*.
Chicago: University of Chicago Press, 1943. 227 pp.

[144] Hirsch, Rudolph, comp. *Plans for the Organization of International Peace, 1306-1789*. New York: New York Public Library, 1943. 14 pp.

[145] Hoffman, Ross J.S.   *The Great Republic*:   *A Historical View of the International Community and the Organization of Peace*. New York: Sheed & Ward, 1942. 167 pp.

[146] Holmes, Henry Wyman. *New Hope for Human Unity*.   New York: Macmillan, 1944. 111 pp.
Kappa Delta Pi lecture series.

[147] Hoover, Herbert, and Gibson, Hugh. *The Problems of Lasting Peace*. New York: Doubleday, Doran, 1942. 209 pp.
"Moral suasion" to keep peace in future.

[148] Hovgaard, William. *The United World.*   Forward by Karl T. Compton.
Brooklyn: 1944. 31 pp.

[149] Hudson, Manley O.   "The International Law of the Future: Postulates,
Principles, and Proposals." *American Bar Association Journal*, 30
(1944), pp. 560-63, 590-91.
Harvard Law study on future U.N. Charter. By judge of League's Permanent Court of International Justice who influenced Grenville Clark.

[150] --------. "A Design for a Charter of the General International Organization." *American Journal of International Law*, 38 (1944), pp. 711-
14.

[151] Hunt, Ben Bridges. *Vice-President Wallace and the World Congress.* Austin, Texas: Van Boeckmann-Jones, 1943. 22 pp.

[152] Johnsen, Julia E., comp. *International Federation of Democracies (Proposed).* New York: H. W. Wilson, The Reference Shelf, Vol. 14, No.
8, 1941. 263 pp.
Early opinion inspired by Streit.

[153] --------. *World Peace Plans.* New York: H.W. Wilson, The Reference
Shelf, Vol. 16, No. 5, 1943. 281 pp.
Increasing weight of opinion for "world-wide collaboration" after
the war.

[154] --------. *Reconstituting the League of Nations.* New York: H.W.   Wilson, The Reference Shelf, Vol. 16, No. 7, 1943. 304 pp.
Includes Commission to Study the Organization of Peace, Ely Culbertson, and Amos Peaslee on world federation.

[155] Josephson, Harold. *James T. Shotwell and the Rise of Internationalism
in America.* London: Associated University Presses, 1975. 330 pp.
Shotwell, director of the Carnegie Endowment for International
Peace, was the leading protagonist of internationalism and collective security in the U.S.   Historian turned activist.   Idealist --
believed that man, through exercise of reason, could remake his
world.   "Shotwell never achieved more than secondary importance as
molder of public opinion or as a State Department advisor."

[156] Joyce, James Avery, ed. *World Organization*: *Federal or Functional? A
Round Table Discussion.* London: C.A. Watts, 1945. 54 pp.
Comment on Mitrany's, *A Working Peace System*, by Patrick Ransome,
George Catlin, Edvard Hambro, C.B. Purdom, J.A. Joyce, H.G. Wells,
and David Mitrany, February 5, 1944.

[157] Kelsen, Hans. *Law and Peace in International Relations.* Cambridge:
Harvard University Press, 1942. 181 pp.
Idea of a universal world federal state may, after a long and slow
development, be realized.   Meanwhile, an international court with
compulsory jurisdiction would be a next step.   By prominent professor of international law.

[158] --------. *Peace through Law.* Chapel Hill, N.C.: University of North
Carolina Press, 1944. 155 pp.
Argument that a strong world court, rather than a world legislature,
could be the next step in strengthening the United Nations, since a
court would avoid questions of sovereignty and majority rule.

[159] Laserson, Max M.   "On Universal and Regional Federalism." *Journal of Legal and Political Sociology*, 2 (October, 1943), pp. 82-93.
Comments on Ely Culbertson's plan.

[160] Laski, Harold J. *Reflections on the Revolution of Our Time*. New York: Viking, 1943. 419 pp.
Replies to Gilbert Murray on abrogating national sovereignty.

[161] Lippmann, Walter. *U.S. Foreign Policy*: *Shield of the Republic*. Boston: Little, Brown, 1943. 177 pp.
Against isolationism.

[162] --------. *U.S. War Aims*. Boston: Little, Brown, 1944. 235 pp.
Part V: "On the Formation of a Universal Society."

[163] Lin Mou-sheng.   "Toward World Organization." *Contemporary China*, 3 (May 31, 1943), pp.
Text of address at Institute for Post-War Planning, Temple University. Plan for a federal U.N. pact after the war.

[164] Li Yu-ying.   "Federalism and World Confederation." *Free World*, 4 (December, 1942), p. 231.

[165] Lloyd, Lola Maverick, and Schwimmer, Rosika.   *Chaos, War, or a New World Order: What We Must Do to Establish the All-Inclusive, Non-Military, Democratic Federation of Nations*. Chicago: By the authors, 1924; enlarged ed., 1942. 7 pp.
Draft world constitution , to be written in a peoples' convention if national governments fail to act. Pacifist (no police forces).

[166] MacIver, R.M. *Towards an Abiding Peace*. New York: Macmillan, 1943. 195 pp.
"MacIver's is one of those rare books which fill the reader with the joy of discovering a man who knows the truth, has the courage to speak it, and speaks it most beautifully" (*World Government News*).

[167] Maddox, William P. *European Plans for World Order*. Philadelphia: American Academy of Political and Social Science, 1940. 44 pp.

[168] --------.   "The Political Basis of Federation." *American Political Science Review*, 35 (December, 1941), pp. 1120-27.
Warns against oversimplifications and points out objective and realistic problems for federalism.

[168a] Mahon, Charlotte B., comp. *Our Second Chance*. New York: Woodrow Wilson Foundation, 1944. 54 pp.
Cf. Divine.

[169] Marriott, John A.R. *Commonwealth or Anarchy?   A Survey of Projects of Peace from the Sixteenth to the Twentieth Century*. New York: Columbia University Press, 1939. 227 pp.

[170] Millspaugh, Arthur C.   *Peace Plans and American Choices*: *The Pros and Cons of World Order*. Washington: Brookings Institution, 1942. 107 pp.

[171] Moore, Alvin Edward. *The World Republic*. Pinemore, Va.: By the author, 1942. 144 pp.
Another private draft world constitution. Maximal powers, proportional representation.

[172] Nash, Philip C. *An Adventure in World Order*. Boston: Beacon, 1944. 139 pp.
Proposed U.N. constitution.

[173] National Opinion Research Center. *The Public Looks at World Organization*. Chicago: NORC, Report No. 19, April, 1944.

[174] National Peace Conference. *To Prevent a Third World War -- World Government. Why? How? What kind? What Must We Do to Get It?* New York: Commission on the World Community, 1941. 13 pp.

[175] Nearing, Scott. *United World: The Road to International Peace*. Mays Landing, N.J.: Open Road Press, 1944. 265 pp.
A mix of pacifism and world government.

[176] Neilson, William A., et al. "The Coming World Order." *Free World*, 3 (1942), pp. 338-57.
A Round Table discussion.

[177] Newfang, Oscar. *The Road to World Peace: A Federation of Nations*. New York: G. P. Putnam's Sons, 1924. 372 pp.

[178] --------. *World Federation*. New York: Barnes & Nobel, 1939. 117 pp.

[179] --------. *World Government*. New York: Barnes & Nobel, 1942. 227 pp.
A lone voice.

[180] Orfield, H. M. *A Monroe Doctrine for the World: The American Peace Plan*. Minneapolis: 1945. 48 pp.

[181] Parker, John J. "World Organization." *Proceedings* of the American Society of International Law, 38 (1944), pp. 20-39.

[182] Parkes, Henry Bamford. *The World after the War*. New York: Crowell, 1942. 240 pp.
By the prominent American historian.

[183] Paullin, Theodore. *Comparative Peace Plans*. Philadelphia: Pacifist Research Bureau, World Organization Series IV, No. 1, 1943. 87 pp.

[184] Peaslee, Amos Jenkins. *A Permanent United Nations*. New York: Putnam, 1942. 146 pp.

[185] --------. *Some Financial Problems of World Government*. Address before the Institute of Foreign Affairs, Earlham College, May 15, 1942. Richmond, Ind.: 1942. 14 pp.

[186] Pound, Roscoe; McIlwain, Charles; and Nichols, Roy F. *Federalism as a Democratic Process*. New Brunswick: Rutgers University Press, 1942. 90 pp.
Dean Pound: "A federalist democratic polity is perfectly possible, the analytical theorist to the contrary notwithstanding."

[187] Range, Willard. *Franklin D. Roosevelt's World Order*. Athens, Ga.: University of Georgia Press, 1959. 219 pp.

[188] Reddick, Olive I. *World Organization*: *An Outline of Some Problems and Recent Proposals for Federation*. . . . Philadelphia: Women's International League for Peace and Freedom, 1941. 36 pp.

[189] Rommen, Hans. "Realism and Utopianism in World Affairs." *Review of Politics*, 6 (1944), pp. 193-215.

[190] Ryder, Katherine. "Thirteen Show the Way." *Current History*, 5 (December 28, 1943), pp. 310-13.
Model of U.S. federation is appropriate for the world.

[191] Sandburg, Carl. *The People, Yes*. New York: Harcourt, Brace, 1936. 286 pp.
"'Man will never write,'
          they said before the alphabet came
          and man at last began to write. . . .
      'Man will never make the United States of Europe
      nor later the United States of the World,
      No, you are going too far when you talk about one
      world flag for the great Family of Nations,'
          they say that now."

[192] Sharp, Walter Rice. *World Organization*: *Decentralized or Unitary*? New York: Council on Foreign Relations, American Interests in the War and in the Peace, 1944. 10 pp.

[193] Shotwell, James T. *The Great Decision*. New York: Macmillan, 1944. 268 pp.
"From now on all war will be total war and therefore the preparation to meet it will also have to be total. . . . The solution which is proposed . . . rests on the experience of history . . . it does reject as unrealistic both the do-nothing policies and half-measures of the past and those theories of world peace which at a single leap would merge the sovereign nations of today under some form of world government."

[194] Slosson, Preston. *After the War -- What*? Boston: Houghton Mifflin, 1943. 86 pp.

[195] Smuts, Jan Christiaan, et al. "Draft Pact for the Future International Authority." *International Conciliation*, 397 (February, 1944), pp. 123-65.

[196] Stassen, Harold E. "We Need a World Government." *Saturday Evening Post*, May 22, 1943.
Earliest and most explicit endorsement of world government by potential Republican presidential nominee in 1944 and 1948.

[197] Stettinius, Edward Reilly. *United Nations Will Write Charter for World Organization*. Washington: Department of State Publication No. 2320, 1945. 7 pp.
Address in New York on eve of San Francisco conference.

[198] Straight, Michael. *Make This the Last War*: *The Future of the United Nations*. New York: Harcourt, Brace, 1943. 417 pp.

World federation -- a "world New Deal" -- to be issue in 1944 politics. By *New Republic* editor.

[199] Streit, Clarence K. *World Government or Anarchy? Our Urgent Need for
World Order*. Chicago: World Citizens Association, 1939. 57 pp.
Chapters 2-3 from *Union Now*, reprinted by Anita McCormick Blaine's
group.

[200] Terry, J. William. "Federation or League." *Changing World*, 13 (April,
1941), pp. 11-12.
Criticism of a partial federal union. "If enduring peace can be attained only through an organized world community, and if the creation of such a community must await the democratization of peoples
who are without democratic traditions, enduring peace is apt to be a
long way off."

[201] Thomas, Norman. *World Federation: What Are the Difficulties?* New York:
Postwar World Council, 1942. 23 pp.

[202] --------. *What Is Our Destiny*. Garden City, N.Y.: Doubleday, 1944.
192 pp.
Gradualist.

[203] Wallace, Henry. *The Century of the Common Man*. New York: Reynal &
Hitchcock, 1943. 96 pp.
Manifesto for the "people's revolution."

[204] Welles, Sumner. *The World of the Four Freedoms*. Foreword by Nicholas
Murray Butler. New York: Columbia University Press, 1943. 18 pp.
Freedom from fear and freedom from want for the whole world.

[205] --------. *The World We Can Make*. Cambridge, Mass.: By the Trustees of
Milton Academy, 1945. 27 pp.
Cautious.

[206] --------. *Where Are We Heading?* New York: Harper & Bros., 1946. 397
pp.
Alternative drafts of Atlantic Charter, especially Churchill's, in
which Roosevelt struck out words "effective international organization."

[207] Wigmore, John H. "Constitutional Problems in the Coming World Federation." *American Bar Association Journal*, 28 (August, 1942), p. 526.
Brief exposition of principal issues of federalism: representation,
majority rule, powers of legislature and of executive, citizenship.

[208] Willkie, Wendell L. *One World*. New York: Simon & Schuster, 1943.
206 pp.
Wartime round-the-world trip, touching the Soviet Union, the United
States, and the "middle world" -- areas outside Europe that would
have major political significance after the war. Willkie called
cautiously for "international government." Phrase "One World" cap-
tured aspirations of a generation of internationalists.

[209] --------. "Our Sovereignty: Shall We Use It?" *Foreign Affairs*, 22
(April, 1944), pp. 347-61.
Sovereignty is not "something simply to be conserved" but "an active
force to be used."

²¹⁰ World Citizens Association. *The World's Destiny and the United States*:
   A Conference of Experts in International Relations. Chicago: By the
   association, 1941. 309 pp.
   See Chap. 4: "New Political Order." Culmination of private American efforts, in response to de Madariaga's "World's Design," to create a climate of opinion in the United States more favorable to post-
   war international organization. Before Pearl Harbor.

²¹¹ --------. *The World at the Crossroads*. Chicago: By the association,
   1946. 160 pp.
   Cf. Henri Bonnet.

²¹² World Government Association. *World Government*: *A Handbook for International Forums*. New York: By the association, 1942. 19 pp.

²¹³ Wright, Quincy. *A Study of War*. Chicago: University of Chicago Press,
   1942. 2 vols. Abridged ed., 1964. 451 pp.
   Definitive study. Result of project, 1926-1942.   "At millenial intervals Western civilization has made an attempt to organize itself
   as a world-empire, as a world-church, or as a world-federation, always relapsing to a balance-of-power system in the intervals."

²¹⁴ Wynner, Edith, and Lloyd, Georgia, eds. *Searchlight on Peace Plans*:
   Choose Your Road to World Government. New York: Dutton, 1944; 2nd
   ed., 1949. 532 pp.
   Handy reference work of plans to unite the nations, going back to
   Dante's *De Monarchia* (1310). First edition prepared in time for Dum-
   barton Oaks conference.

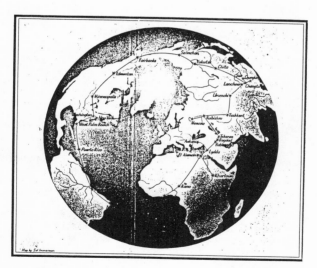

Map by Sol Immerman, in Wendell Willkie's *One World* (Simon &
Schuster, Inc., 1943). Used by permission of Simon & Schuster, Inc.

4

United Nations

The intent of this section is not to provide a comprehensive listing
of works on the United Nations, for which many other guides exist.

Works listed here deal with fundamental alternatives at the founding
of the United Nations and with proposals for its reform, including proposals of limited world government. Works by Clark and Sohn and by the Commission to Study the Organization of Peace are typical. The writings of
Evatt, Feller, Jenks, and Lie convey the perspective of the first U.N.
statesmen; those by Eagleton, Goodrich, Holcombe, Kelsen, and Mitrany contain valuable early scholarly support. The running controversy between
supporters of the new United Nations and advocates of world government
after use of atomic bombs in war can be seen in works by Eichelberger,
Evatt, McClintock, and Rothwell, among many others. Concepts of the rule
of law and its enforcement in an international context have been recurrent
themes.

Nearly half of the titles in this section deal with the review conference of 1955 called for by Article 109 of the Charter. The preponderance
of opinion at that early Cold War date (West Germany was being rearmed as
the centerpiece of NATO, and the Warsaw Pact was being drafted in response)
was that an attempt then to amend the Charter would destroy the U.N. Organization. But the number of titles indicates how seriously the matter was
explored in every country when there was constitutional provision for review. Unfortunately, Article 109 did not call for review at subsequent ten-
year periods, as Grenville Clark had suggested. Nevertheless, the Charter
has actually been amended five times -- once to enlarge the Security Council (1965), and twice to enlarge the Economic and Social Council (1965,
1973). Amendment is not impossible.

When the automatic review conference provided for in Art. 109 failed
to be convened in 1955, another occasion for U.N. reform was felt to be the
twentieth anniversary. Grenville Clark held a second Dublin conference in
1965, a third edition of *World Peace through World Law* was published, the
Chicago Committee's *Preliminary Draft of a World Constitution* was repub-
lished, and the Stanley Foundation conference proposed reform. In 1970,
Louis B. Sohn edited proposals for reform that looked ahead for twenty-five
years. Two years later, the Commission to Study the Organization of Peace
effectively disbanded.

[224] Allen, W. "U.N. Charter Review -- A U.S. View." *Journeys behind the News*, 17 (November 14, 1954), pp. 47-51.

[225] American Bar Association. "Report as to Proposals for the Organization of the Nations for Peace and Law." Chicago: ABA, 1946. 29 pp.

[226] --------. Special Committee for Peace through Law through United Nations. *Report and Recommendations*. . . . Chicago: ABA, 1947. 59 pp.

[227] --------. --------. *Report and Recommendations*. Seattle: ABA, 1948. 29 pp.

[228] American Friends Service Committee. *The Future Development of the United Nations: Some Observations on Charter Review*. New York: AFSC, 1955. 58 pp.

[229] Andersen, A. "A Danish Socialist View on a Revision of the U.N. Charter." *Socialist International Information* (London), 4 (October 2, 1954), pp. 719-22.
Address before Inter-Parliamentary Union, Vienna, 1954.

[230] Andrassy, J. "Predlog za reviziju člana 109 Povelje Ujedinjenih Naroda." *Jugoslovenska Pravo* (Beograd), 1 (1954), pp. 73-74.

[231] --------. "Revizija Povelje i kolektivne mjere." Ibid., 2 (1955), pp. 197-204.

[232] Andrews, Paul Shipman, and Meyer, Cord, Jr. "Report of the Subcommittee on United Nations Reform." *Common Cause*, 3 (December, 1949), pp. 245-52.

[233] Anglin, Douglas C. "Revision of the United Nations Charter." *University of Toronto Quarterly*, 24 (January, 1955), pp. 162-74.

[234] Anker-Ording, Aake. "Three Stages of Possible U.N. Development." *International Association*, 25 (March, 1973).
Transition to stronger U.N. specialized agencies and then to a global parliament.

[235] Arce, José. *Ahora*. Madrid: Espasa-Calpe, 1950. 293 pp.
Includes "Proyecto de reforma de la Carta de San Francisco," pp. 243-92. By Argentina's first representative to the United Nations.

[236] --------. *Right Now*. Madrid: Blass, 1951. 180 pp.
"Draft for the Amendment of the San Francisco Charter," pp. 169-80.

[237] --------. *La Carta de San Francisco: posibilidad de su revision*. Buenos Aires: Academia de Ciencias Economicas, 1958. 30 pp.

[238] Argentina. Convocation of a General Conference under Article 109 of the Charter to abolish the privilege of the veto. *Draft Resolution*. July 22, 1947. A/351.
Resolution calling for a general review conference, following up Cuba's of the year before. For discussion, see *Summary Record* (First Committee). September 19, 1947. A/BUR/SR.36.

[239] Austin, Warren R. *Strengthening the United Nations*. Washington: De-

partment of State Pub. No. 3159, International Organization and Conference Series, III.6, 1948. 6 pp.
Text of statement by Ambassador Austin to House Foreign Affairs Committee during hearings on the Vandenberg resolution, preparatory to North Atlantic Treaty, May 16, 1948.

240 --------, et al. "How I Would Change the Charter." *Rotarian* (Evanston, Ill.), 87 (October, 1955), pp. 24-29.

241 --------. "¿Como modificaria Vd. las Naciones Unidas?" *Revista rotaria* (Chicago), 45 (octubre de 1955), pp. 20-24, 32.
Symposium including Austin, Charles Malik, Lester Pearson, Carlos Romulo, and Prince Wan Waithayakon.

242 Bailey, Sydney D. *Peaceful Settlement of Disputes: Ideas and Proposals for Research.* United Nations: UNITAR (E.75.XV.PS/1), 1971. 57 pp.

243 Ball, Joseph H. "A Chance for Peace." *National Education Association Journal* (Washington), 35 (February, 1946), p. 61.
Excerpt of address by Senator Ball, urging six major changes in U.N. Charter, November 10, 1945.

244 Balladore Pallieri, G. "Gli emendamenti allo Statuto delle Nazioni Unite." *Comunità internazionalle* (Roma), 1 (April, 1946), pp. 193-201.

245 Baradei, Michael El; Franck, Thomas M.; and Trachtenberg, Robert. *The International Law Commission: The Need for a New Direction.* United Nations: UNITAR (E.81.XV.PE/1), 1981. 47 pp.

245a Baratta, Joseph P. "On the Regime of Fear." *International Year Book and Statesmen's Who's Who* (East Grinstead, 1986), pp. xii-xv.
Essay on the progress and problems of international organization, forty years after the founding of the United Nations, from a world federalist perspective.

246 Barber, H.W. "Why Revise the U.N. Charter?" *Christian Century* (Chicago), 73 (April 4, 1956), pp. 419-21.

247 Barkatt, R. "Revision of U.N. Charter." *Socialist Asia* (Rangoon), 3 (August, 1954), pp. 16-17.

248 Barnett, S.N. "Revising the U.N. Charter." *Social Education* (Washington), 19 (October, 1955), pp. 251-54.

249 Bartoš, B. "Before the Revision of the United Nations Charter." *Review of International Affairs* (Beograd), 4 (March, 1953), pp. 17-18.

250 --------. "On the Eve of the Revision of the U.N. Charter." Ibid., 5 (September, 1954), pp. 9-11.

251 --------. "The Question of Revising the Charter." Ibid., 7 (December 16, 1956), pp. 1-2. All also in French.

252 Basu Chaudhuri, Ashok Kumar. "Revision of the U.N. Charter." *Agra University Journal of Research* (Agra), 5 (January, 1957), pp. 145-54.

[253] Bauer, J. *Make the U.N. Effective for Peace.*   New York: Smith, 1952.
160 pp.

[254] Beer, M. "Dem drittem Völkerbund entgegen." *Neue Rundschau* (Berlin),
64 (1953), pp. 294-307.

[255] Berc, H.T. "Achieving Disarmament through Review of the U.N. Charter."
Chicago Bar Record, 36 (June, 1955), p. 425.

[255]a Bertrand, Maurice. *Reflections on the Reform of the United Nations.*
Geneva: U.N. Joint Inspection Unit, 1985. 85 pp. A/40/988.
Reflections on the U.N. after forty years lead to the conclusion
that the time has arrived to establish a third generation world organization.   This should not be a world government but an "economic
United Nations." Reform of the political organs of the U.N. -- the
Security Council and the General Assembly -- is now impossible, but
much could be done to rationalize and integrate its complex and decentralized economic functions, beginning with the Economic and Social Council and proceeding through the specialized agencies and
programmes of the system. The goal is to build international consensus by improved negotiation processes, then to undertake "management."

[255]b --------. *Refaire l'ONU! Un programme pour la paix.* Genève: Éditions
Zoé, 1986. 126 pp.
Extended argument for his proposal of U.N. structural reform. Empha-
sis on the historical conditions.

[256] Bess, D. "Judgment Day for the U.N." *Saturday Evening Post*, February
26, 1955, pp. 17-19 ff.

[257] Birdwood, C.B.B., baron. "Reflections on World Government." *Twentieth
Century* (London), 154 (October, 1953), pp. 269-74.

[258] Black, Joseph. "The United Nations Charter: Problems of Review and Revision." *University of Cincinnati Law Review*, 24 (Winter, 1955),
pp. 26-29.

[259] Bloomfield, Lincoln Palmer. "Charter Review: Some Pertinent Questions."
Department of State Bulletin, 31 (September 27, 1954), pp. 446-51.

[260] --------. *A World Effectively Controlled by the United Nations*: *A Preliminary Survey of One Form of a Stable Military Environment.* Washington: Special Studies Group, Institute for Defense Analysis, 1962.
38 pp.
Pentagon thinking in Kennedy administration.

[161] --------.   *The United Nations and U.S. Foreign Policy*: *A New Look at
the National Interest.* Boston: Little, Brown, 1960; rev. ed., 1967.
268 pp.

[262] --------, and Cleveland, Harlan. *Disarmament and the United Nations*:
Strategy for the United States. Princeton, N.J.: Aspen Institute
for Humanistic Studies, 1978. 47 pp.

[263] Boeg, N.V. "Review of the Charter of the United Nations." *Transactions, Grotius Society* (London), 40 (1954), pp. 5-23.

[264] Bogaert, F. "De herziening van het UNO-handvest." *Gids op maatschappelijk gebied* (Brussels), 45 (November-December, 1954), pp. 1179-83.

[265] Borisov, S. "Protiv proektov peresmotra Ustava OON." *Sovetskoe gosudarstvo i pravo* (Moskva), 6 (1955), pp. 92-98.

[266] Bradley, R. "Safe Revision of the Charter of the United Nations." *World Affairs Interpreter* (Los Angeles), 20 (Summer, 1949), pp. *190-94*.

[267] Branch, J. W., with assistance of Clark, Grenville. *1955: Year of Decision; A Survey of the Clark Proposals for Revising the United Nations Charter.* New York: Institute for International Government, 1952. 18 pp.

[268] Brindschedler, R.L. "Die Revision der Charta der Vereinigten Nationen und die Schweiz." *Zeitschrift fur schweizerisches Recht* (Basel), 73 (1954), pp. 329-59.

[269] Brockway, Fenner. "Role of the U.N.: Tightening the Brakes." *Nation*, January 1, 1955, pp. 6-7.

[270] Brown, B. H., and Johnsen, J. E. *The U.S. and the U.N.* New York: Foreign Policy Association, Headline Series, No. 107, 1954. 62 pp.

[271] --------, ed. *The U.S. Stake in the U.N.: Problems of United Nations Charter Review.* New York: Columbia University Press, 1954. 127 pp.

[272] Bulajić, M. "O pretstojećoj reviziji Povelje Ujedinjenih Nacija." *Medanarodni problemi* (Beograd), 6 (January-March, 1954), pp. 108-12.

[273] Campbell, J.R. "La revisión y el problema del veto en la Carta de la O.N.U." *Política Internacional* (Madrid), (July-September, 1954), pp. 101-19.

[274] Castren, E. "Révision de la Charte des Nations Unies." *Revue hellénique de droit international* (Athènes), 7 (janvier-mars, 1954), pp. 20-34.

[275] --------. "Revision av Förenta Nationernas stadga." *Nordisk tidsskrift for interntional ret og jus gentium* (København), 25 (1955), pp. 93-105.

[276] Catholic Association for International Peace. *The United Nations, 1945-1955: From 1945, an Appraisal; For 1955, Recommendations.* Washington: By the association, 1954. 61 pp.

[277] Chai, F. Y. *Consultation and Consensus in the Security Council.* United Nations: UNITAR (E.75.XV.PS/4), 1971. 55 pp.
     Analyzes the practice of consensus-making through consultations in the Security Council.

[278] Chatterji, M.N. "Reflections on the Amendment of the U.N. Charter." *Modern Review* (Calcutta), 6 (December, 1956), pp. 458-62.

[279] Chaudri, M.A. "Flaws in the United Nations Charter." *Pakistan Review* (Lahore), 4 (October, 1956), pp. 30-44.

[280] Chaumont, Charles. "Faut-il réviser la Charte des Nations Unies?" *Ca-*

hiers des Nations Unies (Paris), 26 (1954), pp. 4-15.

[281] Cheng, Bin. "International Law in the United Nations." *Yearbook of World Affairs, 1954* (London), 8 (1954), pp. 170-95.
On "de facto revision of the Charter."

[282] Christophides, M.   "Critique politico-juridique de la Charte des Nations Unies, suivie d'un essai de réorganisation de la communauté internationale." *Égypte contemporaine* (Le Caire), 39 (1948), pp. 389-623.

[283] Clark, Grenville, and Sohn, Louis B.   *World Peace through World Law.* Cambridge: Harvard University Press, 1958; 2nd ed., 1960; 3rd, 1966. 540 pp.
Proposes fundamental U.N. Charter reform, in effect to transform the U.N. into a minimal world government.   Most respected and influential of all such private proposals.

[284] Claude, Inis L.   "The United Nations and the Use of Force".   *International Conciliation*, 532 (1961), pp. 325-84.

[285] Cohen, B.   "Review of the U.N. Charter." *Journal of the American Association of University Women*, 48 (October, 1954), pp. 8-9.

[286] Colban, E. "United Nations Charter, 1955." *Norseman* (London), 13 (January-February, 1955), pp. 1-5.

[287] Commission to Study the Organization of Peace.   *The General International Organization: Its Framework and Functions.*   New York: Carnegie Endowment for International Peace, Division of Intercourse and Education, 1944.   585 pp.
Includes Nicholas Murray Butler, "The Hope of the World." Also the Commission's first report (1940) and fourth (1943).

[288] --------.   *Building Peace: Reports of the Commission to Study the Organization of Peace, 1939-1972.*   Metuchen, N.J.:   Scarecrow, 1973. 2 vols.
Twenty-two reports to 1972:

1.	Preliminary,	November, 1940;
2.	Transitional,	February, 1942;
3.	U.N. and Organization of Peace,	February, 1943;
4.	Fundamentals of the International Organization,	November, 1943;
5.	Security and Disarmament under the U.N.,	June, 1947;
6.	Collective Self-Defense under the U.N.,	May, 1948;
7.	Collective Security under the U.N.,	July, 1951;
8.	Regional Arrangements for Security,	June, 1953;
9.	Charter Review Conference,	March, 1955;
10.	Strengthening the United Nations,	October, 1957;
11.	Organizing Peace in the Nuclear Age,	September, 1959;
12.	Peaceful Coexistence--A New Challenge,	June, 1960;
13.	Developing the U.N.--A Revolutionary Era,	January, 1961;
14.	The U.N. Secretary General,	January, 1962;
15.	A Universal United Nations,	July, 1962;
16.	U.N., Regional Arrangements, and Free World,	July, 1963;
17.	New Dimensions for the U.N.,	May, 1966;
18.	The U.N. and Human Rights,	August, 1967;
19.	The U.N. and the Bed of the Sea,	March, 1969;
20.	The U.N.: The Next Twenty-Five Years,	November, 1969;

21. The U.N. and the Bed of the Sea II,   June, 1970;
22. The U.N. and the Human Environment,   April, 1972.

[289] --------. *Developing the United Nations*: *A Response to the Challenge of a Revolutionary Era*. New York: American Association for the United Nations, 1951.
Modest proposal. Cf. Holcombe.

[290] --------. *Strengthening the United Nations*. Arthur N. Holcombe, ed. New York: Harper, 1957.

[291] --------. *The United Nations*: *The Next Twenty-Five Years*. Louis B. Sohn, ed. Dobbs Ferry, N.Y.: Oceana, 1970.
Carefully considered proposals for modifications of Sècurity Council voting procedure, compulsory jurisdiction of International Court of Justice, etc. Not quite minimal world government.

[292] *Common Security*: *Blueprint for Survival*. The Report of the Independent Commission on Disarmanent and Security Issues. New York: Simon & Schuster, 1982. 202 pp.
Palme Commission Report. Report of independent group of former and current officials (Olaf Palme, former Swedish Prime Minister), foreign ministers, political leaders, and a high Soviet official on a way out from the arms race and the policies of deterrence. Proposals include graduated steps to achieve drastic mutual reductions of military power in Europe and eventual withdrawal of nuclear weapons. Also U.N. reform. "A doctrine of common security must replace the present expedient of mutual deterrence."

[293] Congreso Hispano-Luso-Americano de Derecho Internacional (Saõ Paulo, octubre de 1953). "Reforma de la Carta de las Naciones Unidas." *Revista peruana de derecho internacional* (Lima), 14 (1954), pp. 133-35.
Changes proposed to Arts. 2, 4, 27, and 28.

[294] Congressional Digest. "The Question of Strengthening the U.N." *Congressional Digest* (Washington), 39 (August-September, 1960), pp. 193-224.

[295] "Convegno di studi per la revisione della Carta delle Nazioni Unite." *Dritto internazionale* (Milano), 13 (1959), pp. 105-09.

[296] Conway, Edward A. "Catholics and Revision of the U.N. Charter." *America* (New York), 88 (November 29, 1952), pp. 230-32, and 89 (May 2, 1953), pp. 129-31.

[297] Corbett, Percy E. "Congress and Proposals for International Government." *International Organization* (Boston), 4 (August, 1950), pp. 383-99.

[298] Cordero Torres, J.M. "Ideas sobre la reforma de la Organizacion de las Naciones Unidas: Contribución para una mejor organizacion mundial." *Estudios internacionales y coloniales* (Madrid), 2 (1949), pp. 7-19.

[299] Cot, Pierre; Fouques-Duparc, J.; et Laugier, H. *Les Nations Unies, chantier de l'avenir*. Paris: Institut d'Étude du Développement Économique et Social, 1961. 2 vols.
"Table ronde sur la révision de la Charte des Nations Unies," II:

273-303.

[300] Courtney, K. "Reviewing the Charter." *United Nations News* (London), 9 (July-September, 1954), pp. 3-4, 28.

[301] Cousins, Norman.   "The U.N.'s Road to Survival." *United Nations World* (New York), 7 (May, 1953), pp. 38-41.

[302] --------. "What Can U.S. Do to Strengthen U.N.?" *Foreign Policy Bulletin* (New York), 34 (September 15, 1954), pp. 4, 6.

[303] Cowles, Willard B.   "Revision of the United Nations Charter and the Development of the Law." *Nebraska Law Review*, (November, 1953), pp. 35-43.

[304] Cranston, Alan. *The Killing of the Peace*. New York: Viking, 1945.   304 pp.
Running account of defeat of League of Nations in anticipation of Senate fight over United Nations.

[305] --------. "The Strengthening of the U.N. Charter." *Political Quarterly*, 18 (July-September, 1946), pp. 187-201.
Excellent survey of world government movement in U.S.

[306] Cuba. Convocation of a General Conference of Members of the United Nations under Art. 109 of the Charter. *Letter* (Belt to Sobolev). September 17, 1946. 2 pp. A/75.
Earliest request for inclusion on the General Assembly agenda of the convocation of a general review conference to eliminate the veto privilege. Cf. Argentina next year.

[307] Culbertson, Ely, and Gross, Ernest.   "Should We Re-examine the United Nations?" *American Forum of the Air* (Washington), 15 (June 8, 1952), pp. 1-11.

[308] --------. "A Two-Way Peace Plan." *New Leader* (New York), 37 (December 13, 1954), pp. 3-5.

[309] Darby, F.R.   "Fitting the Charter to a Changing World." *Institute of World Affairs*, *Proceedings* (Los Angeles), 25 (1949), pp. 131-35.
Summary of round table discussion.

[310] Davies, Clement. "United Nations Reform: Revised Charter to Safeguard Peace." *New Commonwealth Quarterly* (London), 25 (March 16, 1953), pp. 265-66.

[311] Day, B. "Should the U.N. Charter Be Changed?" *Behind the Headlines* (Toronto), 14 (January, 1955), pp. 1-16.

[312] Dean, Vera Micheles. "Reform of U.N. Ineffective without U.S.-U.S.S.R. Settlement." *Foreign Policy Bulletin* (New York), 26 (September 26, 1947), pp. 1-3.
Cf. Clark, "A Settlement with Russia," 1948.

[313] Dedijer, V.   "K problemu revizija Povelje OUN." *Naša stavarnost* (Beograd), 7 (April, 1953), pp. 22-34.

[314] --------. "Au sujet du problème de la révision de la Charte des Nations

Unies." *Revue de la politique mondiale* (Beograd), 4 (juin 16, 1953), pp. 17-20, 24.

[315] --------. "Revision of the U.N. Charter." *Socialist Asia* (Rangoon), 2 (November, 1953), pp. 6-10.

[316] Derso, [Aloysius,] and Kelen, [Emery.] *United Nations Sketchbook*: *A Cartoon History of the United Nations*. New York: Funk & Wagnalls in association with *United Nations World*, 1950.   96 pp.
Humorous view of U.N. personages in difficult first years.

[317] De Rusett, Alan. *Strengthening the Framework of Peace*: *A Study of Current Proposals for Amending, Developing, or Replacing Present International Institutions for the Maintenance of Peace*.   London: Royal Institute of International Affairs, 1950.   225 pp.

[318] --------. "Large and Small States in International Organization: Present Attitudes to the Problem of Weighted Voting." *International Affairs* (London), 30 (October, 1954), pp. 463-74.

[319] --------.   "What's Wrong with the Charter?" *Peacefinder Series* (London), 21 (1955).

[320] Diwan, P.   "Revision of the Charter of the United Nations." *Supreme Court Journal* (Madras), 19 (November, 1956), pp. 221-49.

[321] Divine, Robert A.   *Second Chance*:   *The Triumph of Internationalism in America during World War II*. New York: Atheneum, 1967.   371 pp.
Standard history of U.S. part in creation of United Nations.

[322] "Documentation of All Charter Proceedings at San Francisco." *United Nations Bulletin* (New York), 15 (November 15, 1953), pp. 446-49, 493-95.
Brief account of history of Charter review issues from San Francisco to General Assembly's eighth session, which rejected proposal to elicit views of governments on revision.   References to key events and documents.

[323] Dolivet, Louis. *The United Nations*: *A Handbook on the New World Organization*.   Preface by Trygve Lie.   New York: Farrar, Straus, 1947. 152 pp.
By the editor of *United Nations World* when there was much discussion of world government.

[324] Douglas, Paul H. "United to Enforce Peace." *Foreign Affairs* (New York), 30 (October, 1951), pp. 1-16.
Re U.N. action in Korea.

[325] Dulles, John Foster. "U.S. Constitution and U.N. Charter: An Appraisal." *Department of State Bulletin* (Washington), 29 (September 7, 1953), pp. 307-10.
Address before American Bar Association, Boston, August 26, 1953.

[326] --------.   "United Nations Charter Review." Ibid., 30 (February 1, 1954), pp. 170-73.
Statement before Senate Foreign Relations Committee, Subcommittee on Charter Review, January 18, 1954.

[327] Dworkis, Martin B. "United Nations: Suggested Reforms." *Social Education* (Washington), 13 (April, 1949), pp. 179-84; (May, 1949), pp. 223-26.

[328] Eagleton, Clyde. *International Government*. New York: Ronald, 1932; 2nd ed., 1948; 3rd, 1957. 554 pp.
By a strong supporter of the United Nations, who nevertheless saw it as a step toward world government.

[329] --------. *The Forces That Shape Our Future*. London: H. Milford, Oxford University Press, 1945. 200 pp.
James Stokes lectureship on politics.

[330] --------. "Proposals for Strengthening the United Nations." *Foreign Policy Reports* (New York), 25 (September 15, 1949), pp. 102-11.

[331] --------. "What Shall We Do with U.N.?" *World Affairs Interpreter* (Los Angeles), 25 (January, 1955), pp. 361-84.

[332] --------. "Preparation for Review of the Charter of the United Nations." *American Journal of International Law*, 49 (April, 1955), pp. 229-34.

[333] Eeckman, P. "The Domestic Jurisdiction Clause of the Charter: A Belgian View." *International Organization* (Boston), 9 (November, 1955), pp. 477-85.

[334] Eek, H. "Debatten om FN:s Stadga." *Världspolitikens Dagsfrågor* (Stockholm), 10 (1955), pp. 3-32.

[334a] Egerton, George W. "Collective Security as Political Myth: Liberal Internationalism and the League of Nations in Politics and History." *International History Review*, 5 (November, 1983), pp. 497-522.

[335] Eichelberger, Clark M. *United Nations Charter and World Government*. New York: American Association for the United Nations, 1946. 7 pp.

[336] --------. "World Government via the United Nations." American Academy of Political and Social Science *Annals* (Philadelphia), 264 (July, 1949), pp. 20-25.

[337] --------. *Organizing for Peace: A Personal History of the Founding of the United Nations*. New York: Harper & Row, 1977.
By director of American Association for the United Nations. Passes over world government movement in silence. No discussion of adequacy of U.N.

[338] Ely, R. B. "The United Nations Charter: Review and Revision." *Temple Law Quarterly*, 28 (Fall, 1954), pp. 185-98.

[339] Engel, S. "*De facto* Revision of the Charter of the United Nations." *Journal of Politics* (Gainesville, Fla), 14 (February, 1952), pp. 132-44.

[340] Engers, J.F. "De herziening van het Handvest." *Nederlands tijdschrift voor internationaal recht* (Rotterdam), 5 (Juli, 1958), pp. 299-310.
Summary in English.

[341] Epstein, William. *The Prevention of Nuclear War: A United Nations Perspective*. United Nations: UNITAR (E.84.XV.RR/30), 1984. 114 pp.
U.N. perspective on political and strategic issues.

[342] Evatt, Herbert V. "United Nations Organization versus World Government." *Free World* (New York), 11 (January, 1946), pp. 27-29.

[343] --------. *The United Nations*. Cambridge: Harvard, 1948. 154 pp.
Nine positive proposals to facilitate and improve the work of the U.N. in the future, by the Australian jurist and second president of the General Assembly.

[344] --------. *Task of the Nations*. New York: Dull, Sloan & Pearce, 1949. 279 pp.

[345] [Fabian Society.] "Should the United Nations Revise Their Charter?" *Fabian International Review* (London), 6 (September, 1954), pp. 4-5.

[346] Fahmy, I. "Modification de la Charte des Nations Unies." *Revue égyptienne de droit international* (Le Caire), 13 (1957), pp. 94-113.
Text in Arabic.

[347] Farran, C. d'O. "Proposals for United Nations Charter Revision." *International and Comparative Law Quarterly* (London), 2 (July, 1953), pp. 383-86.
Re plans of the British Parliamentary Group for World Government.

[348] Federal Union. Joint Commission on U.N. Charter Reform. *United Nations Reform: Proposals for a Federal United Nations*. London: Federal Union and Crusade for World Government, 1953. 8 pp.

[349] Feller, Abraham H. *United Nations and World Community*. Boston: Little, Brown, 1952. 153 pp.
By the general counsel of the U.N. and a close friend of Trygve Lie.

[350] Ferencz, Benjamin B. *Defining International Aggression, The Search for World Peace: A Documentary History and Analysis*. Introduction by Louis B. Sohn. Dobbs Ferry, N.Y.: Oceana, 1975. 2 vols.
In December, 1974, the U.N. General Assembly reached a consensus definition of aggression, a step long recognized as essential for effective peace keeping action. These volumes trace efforts by scholars and nations over fifty years to define international aggression, the criminal responsibility of national leaders, and appropriate punishment by the international community.

[351] --------. *An International Criminal Court, A Step toward World Peace: A Documentary History and Analysis*. Introduction by Louis B. Sohn. Dobbs Ferry, N.Y.: Oceana, 1980. 2 vols.
The U.N. is currently deliberating on a Draft Code of Offenses against the Peace and Security of Mankind. These volumns document the history of international criminal law in an effort to include in the new code aggression, genocide, apartheid, terrorism, and other universally recognized crimes against humanity. Thesis: the law of force must be replaced with the force of law.

[352] --------. *Enforcing International Law, A Way to World Peace: A Documentary History and Analysis*. Introduction by Louis B. Sohn. Dobbs Ferry, N.Y.: Oceana, 1983. 2 vols.

The enforcement of international law is documented from the Greek Amphictyonic Councils through all the major wars of history, including the Falkland war and continuing wars in the Middle East. More progress in international law enforcement has been made in the last four decades than in all previous recorded history. Final success depends on clarifying norms of international behavior, accepting binding judicial resolution of disputes, improvement of the U.N. system, general disarmament, raising an international police force, a willingness to compromise, and a will to succeed. The ultimate goal is peace with justice.

353 --------. *The Path to World Peace*: *A Brief Essay*. Washington: World Peace through Law Center, 1985. 25 pp.
Paper presented to Berlin Conference on the Law of the World, July 21-26, 1985. Shortest version of Ferencz's thought.

354 --------. *Common Sense Guide to World Peace*. Dobbs Ferry, N.Y.: Oceana, 1985. 128 pp.
Popular and fuller statement of above.

355 Finkelstein, L. S. "National Policies and Attitudes toward the United Nations." *World Politics* (New Haven), 5 (October, 1952), pp. 129-32.

356 --------. "United Nations Charter Review." *Pakistan Horizon*, 8 (March, 1955), pp. 269-75.

357 --------. "Reviewing the United Nations Charter." *International Organization*, 9 (May, 1955), pp. 213-31.

358 Fischer, Georges. "France and the Proposed Revision of the U.N. Charter." *India Quarterly* (New Delhi), 11 (October-December, 1955), pp. 365-75.

359 Fisher, E. J. "U.N. Charter Review and U.S. Sovereignty." *World Alliance News Letter*, 31 (April, 1955), pp. 4, 7.

360 Frank, Thomas M., and Munansangu, Mark M. *The New International Economic Order*: *International Law in the Making*? United Nations: UNITAR (E.81.XV.PE/6), 1982. 20 pp.

361 Friedmann, Wolfgang, et al., eds. *Transnational Law in a Changing Society*: *Essays in Honor of Philip C. Jessup*. New York: Columbia University Press, 1972. 332 pp.

362 Frye, W.R. "Should the U.N. Charter Be Revised?" *Foreign Policy Bulletin* (New York), 35 (September 15, 1955), pp. 5-6.

363 "Functionalism: The Back Road to World Government?" *War/Peace Report*, 12 (March-April, 1973), pp. 3-7.

364 Gallagher, W.C. "The Problem of the Veto in the United Nations Charter." *Chicago Bar Record*, 36 (April, 1955), pp. 325-28.

365 García Arias, Luis. "Las reformas políticas del sistema representativo en la O.N.U." *Cuaderno de Política Internacional* (Madrid), 26 (abril-junio de 1956), pp. 31-51.

[366] Gerard, F. "La réforme de la Charte de l'O.N.U." *Revue Socialiste* (Paris), 80 (October, 1954), pp. 245-54.

[367] Ghoshal, A.K. "Some Reflections on the Mode of Revision of the U.N. Charter." *Indian Journal of Political Science* (Aligarh), 15 (October-December, 1954), pp. 289-98.

[368] Gillette, G. M. "Preparing for U.N. Charter Review." *World Affairs*, 117 (Fall, 1954), pp. 67-69.

[369] --------, et al. "United Nations Charter Review." *Proceedings* of the American Society of International Law, 48 (1954), pp. 191-211.

[370] Giraud, Emile. "De l'intérêt des études relatives à une révision de la Charte des Nations Unies qui probablement n'aura pas lieu." *Revue générale de droit international publique*, 2 (avril-jun, 1955), pp. 246-69.

[371] --------. "La révision de la Charte des Nations Unies." *Recueil des cours de l'Academie de Droit International de La Haye* (Leyde), 90 (1956), pp. 307-463, pt. 2.

[372] Gjesdal, T. "Bør FN-Pakten revideres?" *Internasjonal Politikk* (Bergen), (1953), pp. 171-75. Also in *Världshorisont* (Göteborg), 7 (November, 1953), pp. 12-16.

[373] Goodrich, Leland M., and Hambro, Edvard, eds. *Charter of the United Nations*: *Commentary and Documents*. Boston: World Peace Foundation, 1946. 400 pp.

[374] --------. "The Amount of World Organization Necessary and Possible." *Yale Law Journal* (New Haven), 55 (August, 1946), pp. 950-65.

[375] --------. *The United Nations*. New York: Crowell, 1959. 419 pp.

[376] --------. *The United Nations in a Changing World*. New York: Columbia University Press, 1974. 280 pp.
By leading scholar of the United Nations.

[377] Grifalconi, John; Holmes, Alice H.; and Andrews, William S. *Three Points of View on U.N. Charter Revision*. Cambridge, Mass.: Conference on U.N. Revision, 1954. 20 pp.

[378] --------. *What Kind of Revision? A Liberal Program for U.N. Charter Change*. Chicago: American Federation of World Citizens, 1955. 5 pp.

[379] --------, and Weik, Mary H., ed. *A U.N. Charter for Man? A Collection in Digest Form of Programs Developed throughout the World to Meet the Need for United Nations Reform*. Cincinnati: American Registry of World Citizens, 1954; revised ed., 1961. 40 pp.
Twelve plans for U.N. reform, plus official disarmament plans.

[380] Gromyko, Andrei. "Nations' Interests Coincide -- Warning on Changing the Charter." *Vital Speeches*, 12 (February 15, 1946), pp. 260-62.
Address of Soviet delegate to the first General Assembly, London, January 18, 1946.

[381] Groom, A.J.R., and Taylor, Paul, eds. *Functionalism*: *Theory and Practice in International Relations*. London: University of London Press, 1975. 354 pp.
See especially Charles Pentland, "Functionalism and Theories of International Political Integration," pp. 9-24.

[382] Gross, Ernest A. "Revising the Charter: Is It Possible? Is It Wise?" *Foreign Affairs*, 32 (January, 1954), pp. 203-16.

[383] --------. "United Nations Charter Review." *Social Action*, 21 (December, 1954), pp. 5-19.

[384] Haas, Ernst B. *Beyond the Nation State*: *Functionalism and International Organization*. Stanford: Stanford University Press, 1964. 595 pp.

[385] --------. *Collective Security and the Future International System*. Denver: University of Denver Press, 1968. 117 pp.
See Chap. 4: "Global Tasks of the United Nations of the Future." A "reconciliation system" short of world government is predicted for 1985.

[386] Habicht, Max. *Proposals of World Federalists for United Nations Charter Revision*. Basavangudi, Bangalore: Indian Institute of Culture, Transaction 19, 1954. 11 pp.

[387] --------, et al. *United Nations Charter Revision*. Washington: World Peace through Law Center, 1971.

[388] Halderman, John W. *The United Nations and the Rule of Law*: *Charter Development through the Handling of International Disputes and Situations*. Dobbs Ferry, N.Y.: Oceana, 1966. 248 pp.

[389] Hambro, E. "Noen bemerkninger om revision av F.N. Pakten." *Samtiden* (Oslo), 63 (1954), pp. 331-40.

[390] Hamilton, T.J. "Atomic Pool and Charter Revision." *Freedom & Union* (Washington), 9 (February, 1954), pp. 21-22.

[391] Harper, Norman D. "Revision of the United Nations Charter: An Australian View." *India Quarterly* (New Delhi), 11 (July-September, 1955), pp. 236-47.

[392] Hauchmann, T. "Aperçu sur la révision de la Charte des Nations Unies." *Schweiz in der Völkergemeinschaft* (Glarus), 10 (April-Mai, 1955), pp. 18-20.

[393] Haviland, H.F., et al. "Improving the Policy-Making Processes." American Academy of Political and Social Science *Annals* (Philadelphia), 296 (November, 1954), pp. 106-16.

[394] Hays, Brooks, et al. "Should the United Nations Be Revised with or without Russia Now?" *Town Meeting Bulletin* (New York), 14 (May 4, 1948), pp. 3-23.
Includes Representative Hays, Ely Culbertson, Jacob Javits, and Abraham Feller.

[395] Heiss, H. "Projekte zur Reform der Satzung der Vereinten Nationen."

Juristische Blätter (Wien), 78 (February 18, 1956), pp. 95-97.

[396] Hevesy, Paul von. "Reform der Vereinten Nationen." *Aussenpolitik* (Stuttgart), 9 (Juli, 1958), pp. 441-46.

[397] Hill, Martin. *Towards Greater Order, Coherence, and Coordination in the United Nations System.* United Nations: UNITAR (E.75XV.RR.20), 1974. 115 pp.
A study of U.N. institutions and mechanisms designed to assist the international community in identifying problems and solutions for coordination.

[398] Hill, Norman Llewellyn. *International Administration.* New York: Mc-Graw Hill, 1931. 292 pp.

[399] --------. *International Organization.* New York: Harper, 1952. 627 pp.

[400] --------. *International Politics.* New York: Harper & Row, 1963. 458 pp.
Culmination of scholarship.

[401] Holcombe, Arthur N., ed. *Strengthening the United Nations.* New York: Harper, 1957. 276 pp.
Modest proposal under auspices of Commission to Study the Organization of Peace.

[402] Holland, R. "Amendment of the United Nations Charter." *Dalhousie Review* (New Brunswick), 3 (October, 1945), pp. 233-45.

[403] Holm, Torsten. "FN och världsfederalismen." *Mellanfolkligt Samarbete* (Stockholm), 19 (1949), pp. 10-16.

[404] Hoover, Herbert. "The Voice of World Experience: Reorganize U.N. without Communist Nations." *Vital Speeches*, 16 (May 15, 1950), pp. 450-52.
Was it really the "voice of experience"?

[405] Hostie, Jan F. "Reflections of a European Lawyer on Revision of the United Nations Charter." *Tulane Law Review* (New Orleans), 29 (April, 1955), pp. 473-90.

[406] Howell, J.M. "Grass-Roots International Law." American Society of International Law *Proceedings* (Washington), 52 (April, 1958), pp. 1-11, 24-26.

[407] Hoyt, Edwin C. *The Unanimity Rule in the Revision of Treaties: A Reexamination.* The Hague: Martinus Nijhoff, 1959. 264 pp.

[408] Hudson, Manley O. "The World Court -- The Next Step." *American Bar Association Journal*, 31 (September, 1945), pp. 443-45.

[409] Hudson, Richard. "Time for Mutations in the United Nations." *Bulletin of the Atomic Scientists*, 32 (November, 1976), pp. 39-43.
Argument for voting reforms in U.N. because of influx of many tiny countries into the General Assembly.

[410] --------. *The Binding Triad.* New York: Center for War/Peace Studies,

n.d., c. 1981. 5 pp.
A carefully realistic proposal, developed over 20 years, for minimum reform of the General Assembly voting system and powers (Arts. 18 and 13). Decisions would be made possible if three 2/3 majority votes could be reached: 2/3 of the member states (present and voting); a majority of the members representing 2/3 of the world's population; and a majority of the members contributing 2/3 of the regular U.N. budget. Practical demonstrations re real issues (e.g., Lebanon) have been made in a continuing series of conferences at Mohonk, N.Y.

[411] --------. *The Case for the Binding Triad*. New York: Center for War/-Peace Studies, Special Study No. 7, 1983. 30 pp.
Formal argument, with texts of amendments to Arts. 13 and 18 of the Charter, for the binding triad proposal for decision-making in the General Assembly. Includes example of resolution of Arab-Israeli conflict.

[412] Hymer, E. W. *We and the United Nations Charter*: *Should It Be Reviewed or Revised?* New York: National Federation of Business and Professional Women's Clubs, 1954. 15 pp.

[413] Iblen, V. "Revizija Povelja i Medunarodni Sud." *Zbernik Pravnog Fakulteta u Zagrebu* (Zagreb), 5 (1955), pp. 157-62.

[414] "In Defense of the Basic Principles of the United Nations." *Izvestia*, 19 (October 1, 1953), pp. 3-5.

[415] Indian Council of World Affairs. *Revision of the United Nations Charter*: *A Symposium*. New Delhi: Indian Council of World Affairs, 1954. 144 pp.

[416] International Bar Association. Committee on the Constitutional Structure of the United Nations. *Report*. New York: International Bar Association, 1954. 83 pp.

[417] Inter-Parliamentary Union. *The Problem of the Revision of the United Nations Charter*. Monaco: Inter-Parliamentary Union, 1954. 12 pp.

[418] Jackson, E. "Developing the Peaceful Functions of the United Nations." American Association of Political and Social Science *Annals* (Philadelphia), 296 (November, 1954), pp. 27-35.

[419] Jackson, S.W. "International Legislation: Discussion of Methods for Its Improvement." *American Bar Association Journal* (Chicago), 34 (March, 1948), pp. 206-09, 361.

[420] Jacob, P.E., ed. "The Future of the United Nations: Issues of Charter Revision." American Association of Political and Social Science *Annals*, 296 (November, 1954), whole issue, 237 pp.

[421] Janković, B.M. "Posterpak za reviziju Povelje Ujedinjenih Nacija." *Jugoslovenska revija za medunarodno pravo* (Beograd), 2 (1955), pp. 385-93.

[422] --------. "Verfahren zur Revision der Satzung der Vereinten Nationen." *Jahrbuch für internationales Recht* (Hamburg), 6 (1956), pp. 120-318.

[424] Jenks, C. Wilfred. *The World beyond the Charter*: *A Tentative Synthesis of Four Stages of World Organization*. London: Allen & Unwin, 1969.
Valuable perspective from within the U.N. civil service.

[425] Jessup, Philip C. *A Modern Law of Nations*. New York: Macmillan, 1948. 236 pp.
Sovereignty must be relaxed, criminal law extended. But world law now is not feasible. By U.S. ambassador at large and delegate to the U.N.

[426] --------. "Stitching the World Together." *Saturday Review*, February 1, 1964, pp. 17-19, 44.
Value of steady round of diplomatic meetings in U.N. By judge of International Court of Justice.

[427] Johnsen, Julia E., comp. *United Nations or World Government*. New York: H.W. Wilson, The Reference Shelf, Vol. 19, No. 5, 1947. 285 pp.

[428] --------. "Improving the United Nations." *Institutes and Their Publics*: *Proceedings of the International Conference of Institutes of International Affairs*. New York: Carnegie Endowment for International Peace, 1953. pp. 15-24.

[429] Johnson, D.H.N. "Reforming the United Nations." *Tablet* (London), 204 (November 13, 1954), pp. 465-66; (November 20, 1954), pp. 489-90; (November 27, 1954), pp. 513-14.

[430] Johnson, H.C., and Niemeyer, G. "Collective Security: The Validity of an Ideal." *International Organization* (Boston), 8 (February, 1954), pp. 19-35.

[431] Jovanović, B. "Predlog za reviziju člana 109 Povelje Ujedinjenih naroda." *Jugoslovenska revija za medunarodno pravo* (Beograd), 1 (1954), pp. 73-83.

[432] Joyce, James Avery, et al., eds. *Studies in Charter Revision*: *A Series of Papers by Authorities Treating of the Problems Involved in the Development of the United Nations into an Effective Instrument of World Peace*. London: Council for United Nations Charter Review, 1954. 28 pp.

[433] --------. *Revolution on East River*: *The Twilight of National Sovereignty*. New York: Abelard-Schuman, 1956. 244 pp.

[434] Kelsen, Hans. *The Law of the United Nations*: *A Critical Analysis of Its Fundamental Problems*. New York: Praeger, 1950. 903 pp.

[435] --------. "Recent Trends in the Law of the United Nations." *Social Research* (New York), 18 (June, 1951), pp. 135-51.

[436] Key, Donald M. "United States Planning for Charter Review." *Annals* of the American Academy of Political and Social Science, 296 (November, 1954), pp. 151-55.

[437] Keys, Donald F., ed. "Proposals for United Nations Reform." Paris: World Association of World Federalists, January 15, 1972. 6 pp.
Major proposal of World Federalists along Clark-Sohn lines.

⁴³⁸ --------. "The U.N. in the Looking Glass." *Transnational Perspectives*, 3 (1976), pp. 42-43.
Report of 1975 meetings of the U.N. Committee on the Charter, which considered both "strengthening the role of the organization" and "Charter review."

⁴³⁹ Kiang, Ly. "Issues in the Review of the U.N. Charter." *Free China Review* (Taiwan), 5 (October, 1955), pp. 3-16.

⁴⁴⁰ Kling, M. "Charter Revision: No Debate Now." *Nation*, January 15, 1955, pp. 46-49.

⁴⁴¹ Knecht, J. "Une tâche délicate pour l'O.N.U., une éventuelle révision de la Charte de San Francisco." *Monde diplomatique* (Paris), 1 (juin, 1954), pp. 1,

⁴⁴² Kohn, W.S. "Collective Self-Defense under a Revised United Nations Charter." *Social Research* (Albany), 22 (Summer, 1955), pp. 231-41.

⁴⁴³ Konishi, Masanobu. *La révision de la Charte des Nations Unies; vers une nouvelle organisation mondiale pour la paix.* Paris: Université de Paris, Institut des Hautes Études Internationales, 1967. 349 pp.

⁴⁴⁴ Kopal, Vladimír, and Mrázek, I. *Otázka revise Charty OSN; práce poctěna cenou Československavenské Akademie Věd za rok 1955.* Praha: Nakladatelství Československé Akademie Věd, 1957. 242 pp.

⁴⁴⁵ --------. "K pokusům o změnu postavené, struktury a dělby funkcí Rady bezpečnosti, Valného shromáždění a genéálniho tajemníka v soustavé OSN." *Pravnické štúdie* (Bratislava), 8 (1960), pp. 470-502. Summaries in Russian and French.

⁴⁴⁶ Kramer, R.L. "Die Charta der Vereinten Nationen ist revisionsbedürftig." *Berichte und Informationen des Osterreichischen Forschungsinstituts für Wirtschaft und Politik* (Salzburg), 11 (Marz 2, 1956), pp. 135-36.

⁴⁴⁷ Kraminov, D. "Zamysly Dallesa v otnoshenii OON." *Pravda* (Moskva), sentiabria 1, 1953. *Current Digest of the Soviet Press*, 5 (October 10, 1953), p. 21.

⁴⁴⁸ Krylov, C. "U.N. Charter Must Be Observed." *Izvestia* (Moscow), April 27, 1955, p. 4. *Current Digest of the Soviet Press*, 7 (June 8, 1955), pp. 15-16.

⁴⁴⁹ Kudriavtsev, V. "Za mezhdunarodnoe sotrudnichestvo." *Izvestia*, October 24, 1953.

⁴⁵⁰ Kumleben, G. "Die Vereinten Nationen nach zehn Jahren: Möglichkeiten der Revision der Charta." *Aussenpolitik* (Stuttgart), 6 (Juni, 1955), pp. 375-80.

⁴⁵¹ Lacharrière, R. de. "L'action des Nations Unies pour la sécurité et pour la paix." *Politique étrangere* (Paris), 18 (septembre-octobre, 1953), pp. 307-38.

⁴⁵² Lachs, Manfred. "Le principe de l'unanimité des grandes puissances:

fondement de la coexistence pacifique à propos du problème de la révision de la Charte des Nations Unies." *Revue progressiste de droit français* (Paris), 7 (septembre, 1954), pp. 93-98.

453 --------. "Le problème de la révision de la Charte des Nations Unies." *Revue générale de droit international publique*, 61 (janvier-mars, 1957), pp. 51-70.

454 Lefaucheux, M.H., and Lord, O.B. "Should the United Nations Be Changed?" *Western World* (Brussels), 11 (March, 1958), pp. 31-42.

455 Lehler, Ruth L. "United Nations Charter Review Conference." *Chicago Bar Record*, 36 (March, 1955), pp. 285-88.

456 Lent, Ernest S. *Supranationale politische Integration durch Stärkung der Vereinten Nationen; eine Unterschung des Programmes der Weltbewegung für einen Weltbundesstaat.* Wien: Universität, Rechts- und Staatswissenschaftliche Facultät, 1954. 250 pp.

457 Lerugar, L. "¿Gobierno para el mundo?" *Cuadernos de Política Internacional* (Madrid), 12 (octubre-diciembre de 1952), pp. 55-68.

458 "Letter from the East." *New Yorker*, December 15, 1956, pp. 43-44 ff.

459 Levin, D.B. "The Falsification of the Conception of International Law by the Bourgeois Pseudo-Science." *Sovetskoe gosudarstvo i pravo* (Moskva), 4 (1952), pp. 55-63.
Contains suggestions re Arts. 2, 11, 24, 25, and 55.

460 Liang, Yuen-li. "Prepatory Work for a Possible Revision of the United Nations Charter." *American Journal of International Law*, 48 (January, 1954), pp. 83-97.

461 Lie, Trygve. *In the Cause of Peace: Seven Years with the United Nations.* New York: Macmillan, 1954. 473 pp.
By the first Secretary General. The U.N. was developing international law toward eventual enforceable world law within a universal world society. Meanwhile, however, the U.N. remained a voluntary association of nations, not a world government.

462 Lloyd, William Bross. "The United Nations and World Federalism." *Antioch Review* (Yellow Springs, Ohio), 9 (March, 1949), pp. 16-28.

463 Lodge, Henry Cabot. "Review of the U.N. Charter." *Department of State Bulletin* (Washington), 30 (March 22, 1954), pp. 451-52.
Statement before Senate Foreign Relations Committee, Subcommittee on Charter Review, March 3, 1954. Cf. other American statements by Austin and Dulles.

464 Logue, John. *The Great Debate on Charter Reform: A Proposal for a Stronger United Nations.* Introduction by T.K. Finletter. New York: Fordham University Press, Publications of the Social Sciences, No. 2, 1955; 3rd printing, 1958. 31 pp.
Discussion of the political philosophy bearing on holding the Charter review conference of 1955, in accordance with Art. 109. Concludes that a conference would be appropriate only for *major* reform proposals. Even the world federalists' proposal was not adequate to world problems. A minimal, security proposal would too likely be

subverted by great power rivalry, to the neglect of the immense majority of mankind in the colonized world. A maximal proposal is the only one likely to be effective and even acceptable.

[465] --------, ed. *United Nations Reform and Restructure*. Villanova, Pa.: Villanova University Press, 1980. 187 pp.
Proceedings of conference on President Carter's Report on the Reform and Restructure of the U.N. System, held at Villanova, November, 1978. Contributors included Harlan Cleveland, Norman Cousins, Hans Morgenthau, Bradford Morse, Robert Muller, Louis B. Sohn, and John Stoessinger.

[466] Lohia, R. "Revision of the U.N. Charter." *Socialist Asia* (Rangoon), 2 (March, 1954), pp. 1-2.

[467] Lukens, E.C. "United Nations and World Government." *Pennsylvania Bar Association Quarterly*, 18 (January, 1947), pp. 129-37.

[468] McClintock, R.M. "The United Nations or World Government." American Academy of Political and Social Science *Annals* (Philadelphia), 262 (July, 1949), pp. 26-30.

[469] McInnis, E. "Revision of the Charter." *India Quarterly* (New Delhi), 11 (April-June, 1955), pp. 116-24.

[470] McVitty, Marion E. "Fundamental Principles of U.N. Charter Amendment." New York: United World Federalists, n.d., c. 1964. 15 pp.

[472] Maier, Franklin L. *World Peace by Covenant: The United Nations Considered as an International Organization for Securing World Peace*. New York: Exposition, 1955. 142 pp.

[473] "Manifeste de Londres, 1954: Propositions pour la révision de la Charte des Nations Unies à présenter à tous les gouvernements par l'Association Universelle des Parliamentaires pour un Gouvernement Mondial et le Mouvement Universel pour une Fédération Mondiale, adoptées à Londres en septembre 1954 par la Commission mixte des deux organisations." *Revue de droit international de sciences diplomatiques et politiques* (Genève), 32 (octobre-decembre, 1954), pp. 393-99.

[474] Manin, Philippe. *L'Organisation des Nations Unies et le maintien de la paix; le respect du consentement de l'État*. Paris: Librairie générale de droit et de jurisprudence, 1971. 343 pp.

[475] Manso, M.J. "La reforma de la Carta de la O.N.U. y el veto." *Jus de Jure Orbis* (Barcelona), 2 (15 de enero de 1954), pp. 46-57.

[476] Marcy, Carl, and Wilcox, F.O. "Congress and the United Nations." *Foreign Policy Reports* (New York), 27 (May 15, 1957), pp. 50-59.

[477] Marees van Swinderen, E. de. "De mogelijke herziening van het V.N.-Handvest. *Wordende Wereld* (s'Gravenhage), 6 (November, 1954), p. 2.

[478] Marr, C.D. "The State Department Looks at Charter Review." *Women Lawyers Journal* (New York), 41 (Summer, 1955), pp. 6-8.

[479] Marshall, George C. "Strengthening the United Nations." *Department of State Bulletin* (Washington), 18 (May 16, 1948), pp. 623-25.

Statement by Secretary of State Marshall before House Foreign Affairs Committee during first Congressional hearings on the structure of the U.N., May 5, 1948.

[480] --------. "The United Nations Charter: A Standard of Conduct among Nations." Ibid., 19 (September 26, 1948), pp. 400-01.
Address before Federal Bar Association, September 15, 1948.

[481] Martelli, George. *Experiment in World Government*:   *An Account of the United Nations Operation in the Congo, 1960-1964*. London: Johnson, 1966. 244 pp.
"The results of this, the first experiment in world government, should discourage any repetition; the United Nations should in future confine itself to genuine peacekeeping operations, in which the use of force to impose policies is excluded."

[482] Martin, Andrew, and Edwards, J.B.S. *The Changing Charter*: *A Study in the Reform of the United Nations*. London: Sylvan, David Davies Memorial Institute of International Studies, 1955. 128 pp.

[483] Marzorati, J.J. "Le socialisme et la réforme des Nations Unies." *Revue socialiste* (Paris), (novembre, 1955), pp. 363-77.

[484] M'Bow, Amadou-Mahtar. *Building the Future*. Paris: UNESCO, 1981. 258 pp.
Potential of communications technology to relieve world problems.

[485] --------. *Where the Future Begins*. Paris: UNESCO, 1982. 118 pp.
Director-General's analysis of background to UNESCO's 1984-1989 medium-term plan, including problems of the arms race, hunger, human rights, environment, science and technical progress, and human inequality.

[486] Menschaar, C.L. "Herziening VN-handvest op de lange baan geschoven." *Wordende Wereld* (s'Gravenhage), 9 (Juli, 1957), pp. 4-5.

[487] Merryman, J.H. "U.N. Charter Revision: The Case in Favor." *Nation*, January 8, 1955, pp. 27-29.

[488] Miller, F.M. "Can the Rule of Justice under Law Be Substituted for That of Force in the International Field?" *Iowa Law Review* (Iowa City), 31 (May, 1946), pp. 561-73.

[489] Mitra, B. "Regionalism and the United Nations Charter." *Economic Weekly* (Bombay), 10 (January, 1959), pp. 131-32.

[490] Mitrany, David. *A Working Peace System*: *An Argument for the Functional Development of International Organization*. London: Royal Institute of International Affairs, 1943. 56 pp.

[491] --------. *A Working Peace System*. Introduction by Hans J. Morgenthau. Chicago: Quadrangle Books, revised ed., 1966.
Contains reprint of 1943 classic on functionalism.

[492] Moe, F. "Revision of the U.N. Charter." *Socialist Asia* (Rangoon), 3 (September, 1954), pp. 29-31.

[493] Moore, A. "Revision of the United Nations Charter." *India Quarterly*

(New Delhi), 4 (April-June, 1948), pp. 133-38.

[494] Morel, G.   "La Charte des Nations Unies, doit-elle être révisée?"
Cahiers de l'Union Fédérale (Paris), (novembre, 1954), pp. 11-12.

[495] Morgenthau, Hans J.   "The New United Nations and the Revision of the
Charter." *Review of Politics* (Notre Dame, Ind.), 16 (January, 1954),
pp. 3-21.

[496] --------.   "What Can U.S. Do to Strengthen U.N.?" *Foreign Policy Bulletin* (New York), 34 (September, 1954), pp. 5-6, 15.

[497] Morozov, G.I.   "Chto skryvaetria za popytkami peresmotra Ustava OON."
Moskovskii propagandist (Moskva), 11 (1955), pp. 65-71.

[498] --------.   "O novykh planakh revizii ustava OON." *Sovetskoe gosudarstvo i pravo* (Moskva), 5 (mai, 1959), pp. 116-24.

[499] Mrázek, I.   "O změnách mezinárodních smluv a zvláště jejich revisi."
Právník (Praha), 46 (1957), pp. 148-65.

[500] Muller, Robert. *New Genesis*. New York: Doubleday, 1982. 192 pp.
By Assistant Secretary General of the U.N.   Asks why not world law,
superceding all national law?   Love is the key to overcoming violence.

[501] Munro, L.K. "Revision of the United Nations Charter." *New Zealand Law
Journal* (Wellington), 30 (September 7, 1954), pp. 271-73.

[502] Murray, Gilbert.   *From the League to U.N.*   London: Oxford University
Press, 1948.   217 pp.

[503] Muszkat, Marian. "De quelques problèmes relatifs à l'interpretation de
la Charte et aux transformations de structure des Nations Unies."
Revue hellénique de droit international, 17 (1964), pp. 240-80.

[504] Myer, H.D. "International Law Association Considers Charter Revision."
World Affairs (London), 237 (January-February, 1957), pp. 17-18.

[505] Myers, D.P.   "The Charter under Review." *World Affairs* (Washington),
119 (Spring, 1956), pp. 6-8.
Review of Wilcox and Marcy proposals.

[506] Mygatt, Tracy D.   "Charter Revision and World Federation." *Standard*
(New York), September-October, 1955, pp. 175-77.

[507] Nabliudatel' [pseud.].   "Vragi OON: Vragi mirnogo uregulirovaniia mezh-
dunarodnykh problem." *Izvestiia*, sentiabria 6, 1953, p. 6; *Current
Digest of the Soviet Press*, 5 (October 17, 1953), p. 9.

[508] Naidu, M.V.   *Alliances and Balance of Power: A Search for Conceptual
Clarity*. New Delhi: Macmillan of India, 1974; New York: St. Martin's, 1975.   306 pp.

[509] --------.   *Collective Security and the United Nations: A Definition of
the U.N. Security System*. New Delhi: Macmillan of India, 1974; New
York: St. Martins, 1975.   164 pp.

[510] Neal, Marian. "United States Attitudes towards Charter Review." *India Quarterly* (New Delhi), 11 (October-December, 1955), pp. 354-65.

[511] Newcombe, Hanna. *Review of the United Nations Charter: Six Briefs.* Ottawa: World Federalists of Canada, 1972. 61 pp.
Slightly stronger than Keys proposals, but still short of minimal world government.

[512] Nicol, Davidson, with Croke, Margaret, and Adeniran, B. *The United Nations Security Council: Towards Greater Effectiveness.* United Nations: UNITAR (E.82.XV.CR/15), 1982. 334 pp.
Proceedings of seminar with senior international officials and scholars on means to enhance effectiveness of Security Council.

[513] Nikolić, P. "Povodom eventualne revizije Povelje UN." *Archiv za pravne i društvene nauke* (Beograd), 41 (januar-mart, 1954), pp. 77-81.

[514] Ninčić, D.J. "The Balkan Alliance and the U.N. Charter." *Review of International Affairs* (Belgrad), 5 (September 16, 1954), pp. 11-12.

[515] Nova, R. del. "L'azione delle Nazioni Unite per la difesa della pace: Revisione del metodo della sicurezza collecttiva?" *Politico* (Pavia), 24 (dicembre, 1959), pp. 737-42.
Summaries in English, French, and German.

[516] Pal, K.C. "Revision of the U.N. Charter." *Indian Journal of Political Science* (Aligarh), 15 (October-December, 1954), pp. 313-26.

[517] Pałyga, E. "Wokoł rewizji Karty NZ." *Sprawy międzynarodowe* (Warszawa), 10 (pazdźiernik, 1957), pp. 43-52.

[518] Pancarci, Veli. *De la Charte des Nations Unies à une meilleure organisation du monde.* Paris: Éditions A. Pedone, 1962. 213 pp.

[519] Pappas, Anna M., ed. *Progressive Development of the Principles and Norms of International Law Relating to the New International Economic Order.* United Nations: UNITAR (A/39/504/Add.1), 1984. 122 pp.
Final comprehensive analytical study. Cf. Report of Secretary General (A/39/504).

[520] Partai Sosialis Indonesia. "Revision of U.N. Charter." *Socialist Asia* (Rangoon), 3 (July, 1954), pp. 20-22; *Socialist International Information* (London), 4 (September 4, 1954), pp. 646-49.

[521] Pechota, Vratislav. *Complementary Structures of Third-Party Settlement of International Disputes.* United Nations: UNITAR (E.75XV.PS/3), 1971. 63 pp.
Principal features of various third-party settlement procedures, their distinctive roles, sources of authority, and instrumentalities.

[522] --------. *The Quiet Approach: A Study of the Good Offices Exercised by the United Nations Secretary General.* United Nations: UNITAR (E.75.XV.PS/6), 1972. 92 pp.
Informal approaches and unofficial suggestions by the Secretary General to facilitate settlement of disputes between nations.

[523] Pelt, A. "Die Revision der Charta der Vereinten Nationen." *Vereinten*

Nationen und Oesterreich (Wien), 4 (Juni, 1955), pp. 4-6.

[524] Pennington, L.T. "Specific Proposals for U.N. Charter Revision." *World Alliance News Letter* (New York), 21 (May, 1955), pp. 4, 7.

[525] Perassi, T., e Ago, R. "Osservazioni sul problema della revisione dello Statuto delle Nazioni Unite." *Comunita internazionale* (Roma), 8 (ottobre, 1953), pp. 572-77.

[525]a Pérez de Cuéllar, Javier. *Report of the Secretary-General on the Work of the Organization.* New York: United Nations, 1985. 20 pp.
"There are two basic functions which make the United Nations an essential enterprise. The first is to provide an instrument through which a collective effort can be made to meet emergencies and deal with current problems. . . . The second function is of a more long-term nature and is related to the complex phase of political and economic development in which our world now finds itself. Throughout history there has been a natural political progression from small groups to larger ones -- from family to tribe, to town, to city, to province, to nation state. . . . We have, whether we like it or not, created a world which is in many respects one world. On some major problems affecting all humanity we have reached a global stage where interdependence is a fact of life." All of the Secretary-General's annual reports are of the greatest relevance to strengthening the United Nations.

[526] Pinder, John. *U.N. Reform*: *Proposals for Charter Amendment*. Foreword by J.E.S. Simon. London: Federal Union, 1953. 27 pp.

[527] Plaza, G. "Should the Charter Be Amended?" American Association of Political and Social Science *Annals* (Philadelphia), 246 (July, 1946), pp. 30-35.

[528] Potter, P.B. "The U.N. Charter: 1955." *American Journal of International Law* (Washington), 48 (April, 1954), pp. 275-76.

[529] Pradelle, A. de La, rapporteur. "The Present Structure of the United Nations Charter and the Direction of Desirable Changes." *International Law Association Report, 1946* (London), (1948), pp. 14-38.

[530] "Probleme einer Änderung der Charta der Vereinten Nationen: Studienkommission." *Europa-Archiv* (Frankfurt), 10 (Februar 5, 1955), pp. 7263-78.

[531] Radovanović, L.   "The Problem of U.N.O. Reform." *Review of International Affairs* (Belgrad), 12 (May 20, 1961), pp. 5-7.

[532] Raman, K. Venkata. *The Ways of the Peacemaker.* United Nations: UNITAR (E.75.XV.PS/8), 1975. 142 pp.
Establishment and operation of intermediary mechanisms practiced at the U.N.

[533] --------, ed.   *Dispute Settlement through the United Nations.*   United Nations: UNITAR (PS/10), 1977. 749 pp.
Compilation of monographs by UNITAR scholars on the procedures and mechanisms for peaceful settlement of disputes in the U.N. system.

[534] Rao, K.   "The General Conference for the Review of the Charter of the

United Nations." *Fordham Law Review* (New York), 24 (Autumn, 1955), pp. 356-68.

535 Reddy, T. Ramakrishna. *India's Policy in the United Nations.* Rutherford, N.J.: Fairleigh Dickenson University Press, 1968. 164 pp.

536 Reid, H.D. "Review of U.N. Charter." *World Affairs* (Washington), 117 (Fall, 1954), pp. 70-72.

537 "Reshit' problemy reorganizatsii OON." *Kommunist* (Moskva), 4 (mart, 1961), pp. 12-15.

538 "Revision of the United Nations Charter." *World Capitol* (New York), 1 (December, 1953), pp. 3-9.

539 "Revision of U.N. Charter: Viewpoints of Socialist Japan." *Socialist Asia* (Rangoon), 3 (June, 1954), pp. 11-14; *Socialist International Information* (London), 4 (July 10, 1954), pp. 496-500.

540 *Revizija povelju Ujedinjenih Nacija*; *documentacioni materijal.* Beograd: Institut za Medunarodnu Politiku i Privredu, 1955. 118 pp.

541 Rhyne, C.S. "Revising the Charter of the United Nations." *Wisconsin Bar Bulletin* (Madison), 27 (June, 1954), pp. 11-13.

542 Riggs, Robert E. "Overselling the U.N. Charter: Fact and Myth." *International Organization* (Boston), 14 (Spring, 1960), pp. 277-90.

543 Riorden, Virginia Lastayo. "Dulles and Charter Reform." *Young World Federalist* (Amsterdam), 4 (March, 1954), pp. 1, 3-5.

544 Roberts, John. *The Functional Approach to World Federation*: *25 Years to a Governed World.* Cincinnati: International Studies Association, March 24, 1982. 15 pp.

545 Robinson, D. "Looking to Charter Amendment." *Freedom and Union* (Washington), 9 (November, 1954), pp. 4-5.

546 Roling, B.V.A. "Some Observations on the Review of the Charter." *India Quarterly* (New Delhi), 12 (January-March, 1956), pp. 54-65.

547 Romulo, Carlos P. "Strengthening the United Nations." American Academy of Political and Social Science *Annals* (Philadelphia), 296 (November, 1954), pp. 14-19.

548 Rosenthal, A.M. "Charter Revision Put to U.N. in Paris: Little Assembly Upsets Plans of the Big Powers, Adopts Plan for Curb on Veto." *New York Times*, July 10, 1948, p. 1.

549 Rothwell, E. "United Nations or World Government." Institute of World Affairs *Proceedings*, *1947* (Los Angeles), 24 (1948), pp. 146-60.

550 Šahović, Milan. "Pitanje revizije Povelje na VIII redovnom azsedanju Generalne Skupštine UN." *Međunarodni problemi* (Beograd), 6 (januar-mart, 1954), pp. 113-15.

551 --------. "The General Assembly and the Codification and Progressive Development of International Law." *International Problems* (Belgrad),

6 (1961), pp. 87-99.

[552] Salter, Sir Arthur. *The United Nations*: *Reform, Replacement, or Supplement*? London: David Davies Memorial Institute of International Studies, 1957. 19 pp.

[553] Schachter, Oscar; Nawaz, Mahomed; and Fried, John. *Toward Wider Acceptance of United Nations Treaties*. New York: UNITAR, Arno, 1971. 190 pp.

[554] --------. *Sharing the World's Resources*. New York: Columbia University Press, 1977. 172 pp.

[555] --------, and Hellawell, Robert, eds. *Competition in International Business*: *Law and Policy on Restrictive Practices*. New York: Columbia University Press, 1981. 441 pp.

[556] Scheuner, U. "Wandlungen und Entwicklungen in der Satzung der Vereinten Nationen." *Deutsche Gessellschaft für die Vereinten Nationen, Mitteilungsblatt* (Bonn), 29 (Juni, 1960), pp. 10-14.

[557] Schlochauer, H.J. "Problems of Reviewing the United Nations Charter." *India Quarterly* (New Delhi), 12 (January-March, 1956), pp. 65-76.

[558] --------. "Bemerkungen zur Revision der Charta der Vereinten Nationen." *Zeitschrift für ausländisches öffentliches Recht und Völkerrecht* (Heidelberg), 19 (August, 1958), pp. 416-48.

[559] --------. "Quelques aspects de la révision de la Charte des Nations Unies." *Revue générale de droit international public* (Paris), 65 (janvier-mars, 1961), pp. 20-39.

[560] Schwartzenberger, G. "Review of the United Nations Charter." International Law Association *Report of Conference* (London), 46 (1955), pp. 37-192.

[561] Schwelb, Egon. "The Amending Procedure of Constitutions of International Organizations." *British Yearbook of International Law* (London), 31 (1956), pp. 49-95.

[562] --------. "Charter Review and Charter Amendment: Recent Developments." *International and Comparative Law Quarterly*, 8 (April, 1958), pp. 303-33.

[563] --------. *Charter Review and Charter Amendment*: *Recent Developments*. London: Eastern Press, 1958. 31 pp.

[564] --------. "Charter Review and Charter Amendment: Developments in 1958 and 1959." *International and Comparative Law Quarterly*, 10 (April, 1960), pp. 237-52.

[565] Scott, R.F. "Revision of the United Nations Charter: A Study of Various Approaches." *Michigan Law Review* (Ann Arbor), 53 (November, 1954), pp. 39-68.

[566] Scott, Wiliam A., and Whithey, Stephen B. *The United States and the United Nations*: *The Public View, 1945-1955*. New York: Manhattan, 1958. 314 pp.

[567] Seiter, Francis J. "Revision of the U.N. Charter: A Natural Law Approval." *DePaul Law Review* (Chicago), 4 (Spring-Summer, 1955), pp. 123-52.

[568] Sélassié, Beseat Kiflé, ed. *Consensus and Peace.* Paris: UNESCO, 1980. 231 pp.
Three approaches to the new process of *consensus* as a means to reach international decisions: institutional, interdisciplinary, intercultural.

[569] Shallchy, Mandob al-. *Les travaux des Nations Unies en vue de la révision de la Charte; application des Articles 108 et 109 de la Charte.* Tunis: Societé l'Action d'Édition et de Presse, 1967. 164 pp.

[570] Shaw, R.   "Revise the U.N. Charter." *Christian Century* (Chicago), 72 (October 5, 1955), pp. 1137-39.

[571] Shotwell, James T.   "Implementing and Amending the Charter." *International Conciliation* (New York), 416 (December, 1945), pp. 811-23.

[572] --------. *Autobiography.* Indianapolis: Bobbs-Merrill, 1961. 347 pp.
Against world government as "unrealistic." Also against European federation, for the same reason. Functionalism the way.

[573] --------. *The Faith of a Historian and Other Essays.* New York: Walker, 1964. 301 pp.

[574] "Should the United States Seek to Revise the United Nations Charter?" Institute for World Affairs *Proceedings* (Los Angeles), 29 (1954), pp. 222-25.

[575] Simon, J.E.S.   "Revise the U.N. Charter!" *New Era* (Paris), 2 (September-October, 1953), p. 10.

[576] Simoni, Arnold. *Beyond Repair: The Urgent Need for a World Organisation.* Don Mills, Ont.: Collier Macmillan Canada, 1972. 210 pp.
U.N. has failed in its declared aim to maintain peace and security, also to further economic development and to protect human rights. Since national sovereignty is the main cause, the U.N. should be reduced to a mere set of rules (e.g., prohibition of aggression), without decision-making or enforcement power.

[577] Simonius, A.   "Révision de la Charte des Nations Unies?" Association suisse pour les Nations Unies *Bulletin et documents* (Glarus), 1 (octobre, 1946), pp. 71-72.

[578] Sinha, K.N. "The Revision of the U.N. Charter." *Modern Review* (Calcutta), 89 (April, 1956), pp. 286-91.

[579] Slama, M.M. "The United Nations Charter Review." *Library Journal* (New York), 81 (July, 1956), pp. 1648-50.

[580] Soedjatmoko.   "De herziening van het Handvest der Verenigde Naties." *Nieuwe Stern* (Amsterdam), 3 (Maart, 1955), pp. 165-78.

[581] Sohn, Louis, B. "Strengthening the United Nations." *American Bar Association Journal* (Chicago), 35 (September, 1949), pp. 779-80.

582 --------. "Revision of the Charter of the United Nations." *Proceed-ings*, American Society of International Law, 48 (1954), pp. 202-05.

583 --------. "United Nations Charter Review." *Proceedings*, American Bar Association, Section on International and Comparative Law, Chicago, August 23, 1955, pp. 26-28. 1955.

584 --------. "United Nations Charter Revision and the Rule of Law: A Pro-gram for Peace." *Northwestern University Law Review*, 50 (January-February, 1956), pp. 709-25.

585 --------. *The United Nations*: *The Next Twenty-Five Years*. Dobbs Fer-ry, N.Y.: Oceana, 1970. 263 pp.
Carefully considered proposals for modifications of Security Council voting procedure, compulsory jurisdiction of International Court of Justice, etc. Not quite minimal world government.

586 --------, et al. *Modernizing the Security Council*: *Special Report*. New York: Commission to Study the Organization of Peace, 1974. 22 pp.

587 Soltan, H. "Amendment de la Charte des Nations Unies." *Revue egyp-tienne de droit international* (Le Caire), 8 (1952), pp. 1-10.

588 Sørensen, Max. "Debatten om Revision af de Forenede Nationer's Pagt." *Økonomi og politik* (København), 27 (oktober-december, 1953), pp. 307-17.

589 Stafford, R. H. "U.N. Charter Review: A Question of Timing." *World Alliance News Letter*, 31 (April, 1955), pp. 3, 7.

590 Stanley, C. Maxwell. "Why Support Charter Review?" *Young World Feder-alist*, 2 (March, 1955), pp. 9-11.

591 Stanley Foundation Conference Statement. "The United Nations of 1975." *Saturday Review*, July 24, 1965, pp. 34-37.
Proposals for U.N. Charter reform signed by fourteen distinguished statesmen, including two former presidents of the U.N. General As-sembly, Carlos P. Romulo and Zafrulla Khan. On 20th anniversary of U.N.

592 Stromberg, Roland N. "Collective Security." In Alexander DeConde, ed., *The Encyclopedia of American Foreign Policy*: *Studies of the Princi-pal Movements and Ideas* (New York: Scribners, 1978, 3 vols.), I:124-33.
Masterful on origin of League of Nations and inadequacy of collec-tive security. Closes with call for world government.

593 Sukijasvocić, M. "Revizija Povelje i definicija napada." *Jugosloven-ska revija za međunarodno pravo* (Beograd), 2 (1955), pp. 204-09.

594 Taft, Robert A. "Revise Charter of the United Nations!" *Commercial and Financial Chronicle* (New York), 170 (November 3, 1949), pp. 1790-91.

595 Talmadge, I.D.W. "Reviewing the U.N. Charter, and a Look at the Rus-sians at the San Francisco Meeting." Institute of Social Studies *Bulletin* (New York), 3 (Fall, 1955), pp. 30-32.

[596] Tarazi, S. "The Risks of Revision: Appraisal of United Nations Prepa-
rations for Charter Review." American Association of Political and
Social Science *Annals* (Philadelphia), 296 (November, 1954), pp. 140-
46.

[597] --------. "Quelques réflexions sur la révision de la Charte des Nations
Unies." *Revue de droit international pour le Moyen-Orient* (Paris),
4 (août, 1955), pp. 350-58.

[598] Theiler, E. "A Carta das Nações Unidas e a sua reforma." *Boletim da
Sociedade Brasileira de Direito Internacional* (Rio de Janeiro), 13
(janeiro-dezembro, 1957), pp. 103-70.

[599] Thompson, K.W. "The Charter of the United Nations: Realities and Review." American Bar Association *Proceedings* (Chicago), (August 23,
1955), pp. 29-35.

[600] Tito, Josip Broz. "Govor na svećanoj sednici oba doma indiskog parla-
menta, 21.XII.1954." *Borba* (Beograd), decembar 22, 1954, p. 3.

[601] Trope, S.H. "Strengthening the U.N. Charter." *New York Herald Tribune*,
September 18, 1953, p. 14.
Re third conference of Parliamentarians for World Government, Copen-
hagen, 1953.

[602] Tsoutsos, A.G. "Le principe de la légalité dans l'ordre juridique international -- à propos d'une révision de la Charte." *Revue hellénique de droit international* (Athènes), 7 (janvier-mars, 1954), pp.
35-44.

[603] Tugwell, R.G. "Can the United Nations Become a World Government?" *Common Cause* (Chicago), 2 (February, 1949), pp. 244-51.

[604] Unden, O. "Revision of the U.N. Charter." *Socialist Asia* (Rangoon), 2
(January, 1954), pp. 5-7.

[605] *UNESCO Yearbook on Peace and Conflict Studies*. Paris: UNESCO, 1980- ,
annual.
New approaches to study of war, from psychological, social, political, economic, military, philosophical, statistical, and diplomatic
points of view.   Also new approaches to study of peace and conflict
resolution: non-violence, civilian-based defense, disarmament,
UNESCO, regional and international institution building.

[606] UNESCO. *The Concept of International Organization*. Paris: UNESCO,
1981. 245 pp.

[607] United Nations Association of Great Britain and Northern Ireland. "Revision of U.N. Charter." *World Affairs* (Wellington), 8 (September,
1953), pp. 5-10.

[608] --------. *Operation S.U.N. to Strengthen the United Nations*.   London:
United Nations Association, 1957. 28 pp.

[609] "United Nations Charter Review." *Current Notes on International Affairs*
(Canberra), 25 (January, 1954), pp. 35-42.

[610] "United Nations Charter Revision." Catholic Association for Interna-

tional Peace *News* (Washington), 15 (April, 1954), pp. 1-9.

[611] "United Nations Takes First Step to Review Charter: British Government's Attitude Has Changed." *World Affairs* (London), 231 (January-
February, 1956), pp. 9-10.

[612] *The United Nations Conference on International Organization, San Francisco, California, April 25 - June 26, 1945:   Selected Documents.*
Washington: Department of State Publication 2490, Conference Series
83, 1946. 991 pp.
Proceedings during final drafting of the Charter at San Francisco.
China and fourteen small nations all expressed willingness to limit
national sovereignty.

[613] United Nations, General Assembly. Committee on Arrangements for a Conference for the Purpose of Reviewing the Charter. *Report.*   19 June
1957.   2 pp.   A/3593.   General Assembly Official Records (GAOR),
12th sess., Annexes vol. 1, agenda item 22.
Article 109, para. 3, provides that a general conference for the review of the Charter should be held no later than the tenth annual
session of the General Assembly, if so decided by a majority of the
Assembly and by any seven members of the Security Council.   On 21
November 1955, the Assembly decided that such a conference should be
held, if it could be conducted under auspicious international circumstances "at an appropriate time" (A/Res.992). It appointed the
above committee consisting of all the members of the U.N. to consider, in consultation with the Secretary General,   the question of
fixing a time and place for the conference, its organization and
procedures, and requested him to report to the twelfth session of
the Assembly.   At meetings held in 1957, 1959,   1961,   1962,   1963,
1965,   and 1967, the committee decided the time was not appropriate
for a review of the Charter and recommended that the fixing of a
date for a review conference be postponed.   No meetings of the committee have been held since 1967 (A/AC.81/-).   For records, see:
A/4199, 8 Sept. 1959, GAOR, 14th sess., Annexes, item 22, 2 pp.
A/4877, 18 Sept. 1961, GAOR, 16th sess., Annexes, item 18, 2 pp.
A/5193, 14 Sept. 1962, GAOR, 17th sess., Annexes, item 21, 2 pp.
A/5487, 4 Sept. 1963, GAOR, 18th sess., Annexes, item 21, 11 pp.
A/5987, 22 Sept. 1965, GAOR, 20th sess., Annexes, item 26, 1 p.
A/6865, 18 Oct. 1967, GAOR, 22nd sess., Annexes, item 26, 1 p.
For summary records and documents, see A/AC.81/SR.1-13.

[614] --------. Request for the inclusion of an additional item in the agenda of the 24th session. Establishment of a Special Committee to consider suggestions for revising the Charter of the United Nations.
Letter of Colombia to President of the General Assembly, 21 November
1969. 4 pp. A/7659.

[615] --------. Sixth Committee. Need to consider suggestions regarding the
review of the Charter of the United Nations. Agenda item 107 (XXIV).
Report. 11 December 1969. 4 pp. A/7870.

[616] --------. --------. Need to consider suggestions regarding the review
of the Charter of the United Nations. Agenda item 88 (XXV). *Report.*
9 December 1970. 5 pp. A/8219.

[617] --------. Special Committee on the Rationalization of the Procedures
and Organization of the General Assembly. *Report.* 1971. 219 pp.

A/8426.   GAOR, 26th sess., 26th sup.

[618] --------.   Need to consider suggestions regarding the review of the
Charter of the United Nations.   *Report* of the Secretary General,
transmitting comments of Governments.   22 August 1972.   53 pp.
A/8746 and Addenda 1, 2, and 3.
Official report of opinions of governments on Charter review.
U.S.S.R. opposed, U.S. without opinion.

[619] --------.   Strengthening the role of the United Nations with regard to
the maintenance and consolidation of international peace and securi-
ty, the development of cooperation among all nations, and the promo-
tion of the rules of international law in relations between states.
Report of the Secretary General,   including replies from Member
States.   25 October 1973.   26 pp.   A/9128.
See also subsequent reports:
A/9695, 16 Oct. 1974,
A/10255, 10 Oct. 1975.

[620] --------.   Strengthening the role of the United Nations with regard to
the maintenance and consolidation of international peace and security. . . . *Letter* of Romania of 31 October 1975.   3 November 1975.
16 pp. A/C.6/437.

[621] --------.   Special Committee on the Charter of the United Nations and
on the Strengthening of the Role of the Organization. *Report*. 1977.
248 pp. A/32/33. GAOR, 32nd sess., 33rd sup.
For subsequent reports of this continuing committee, see:
A/33/33, 1978, GAOR, 33rd sess., 33rd sup. 103 pp.
A/34/33, 1979, GAOR, 34th sess., 33rd sup. 152 pp.
A/35/33, 1980, GAOR, 35th sess., 33rd sup. 108 pp.
A/36/33, 1981, GAOR, 36th sess., 33rd sup. 93 pp.
A/37/33, 1982, GAOR, 37th sess., 33rd sup. 83 pp.
A/38/33, 1983, GAOR, 38th sess., 33rd sup. 40 pp.
A/39/33, 1984, GAOR, 39th sess., 33rd sup. 43 pp.
A/40/33, 1985, GAOR, 40th sess., 33rd sup. 59 pp.

[622] U.S. Chamber of Commerce. Committee on International Political and Social Problems.   *The United Nations and World Government*: *A Factual
Study*. Washington: Chamber of Commerce, 1950. 50 pp.

[623] U.S. Congress, Senate. Committee on Foreign Relations, Subcommittee on
the United Nations Charter.   "Revision of the United Nations Charter." Washington: Report No. 2501, 1950.

[624] --------. *Final Report*. 84th Cong., 2nd sess. Washington: Report No.
1797, 1956.   37 pp.

[625] U.S. Department of State, "Uniting for Peace." Washington: State Department Publication 4035, International Organizations and Conference Series III, 64, December, 1950.
Secretary Acheson's speech to U.N. of September 20, 1950, John Foster Dulles' of October 9, etc.

[626] Visscher, C. de.   "La conférence de révision de la Charte des Nations
Unies: Article 109 de la Charte." *Friedens-Warte* (Basel), 53 (1955),
pp. 37-46.

[627] Vite, A.A. "La nueva organización internacional de las Naciones Unidas y sus organismos especializados." *Revista del Colegio Nacional Vicente Rocafuerte* (Guayaquil), 60 (septiembre de 1950), pp. 31-74, esp. 55-56.

[628] Wainhouse, D. "Charter Review as a Means of Strengthening the U.N." *Department of State Bulletin* (Washington), 31 (August 30, 1954), pp. 296-99.

[629] --------. "Some Problems of Charter Review." Ibid., 31 (November 15, 1954), pp. 737-42.

[630] Walters, F.P. "U.N. Reform: Responsibility at the Centre." *International Relations* (London), 1 (October, 1957), pp. 339-48.

[631] Weik, Mary H. *Let's Talk It Over*! A *Handbook for Discussion Groups on U.N. Charter Reform.* Cincinnati, Ohio: American Federation of World Citizens, 1955. 57 pp.

[632] White, Thomas R., and Ransom, William L. "What Can United Nations Do for Majority Action?" *American Bar Association Journal* (Chicago), 33 (August, 1947), pp. 756-59.

[633] --------. "How to Amend the United Nations Charter: A Proposal for Strengthening World Law." Ibid., 37 (June, 1951), pp. 431-33.

[634] White, W.S. "Sixteen Senators Press for U.N. Revision: Russia Challenged to Accept Veto Limit and Arms Curb of Face United Lineup." *New York Times*, April 13, 1948, pp. 1, 11.

[635] "Why They Attack the Charter." *New Times* (Moscow), 41 (October 10, 1953), pp. 5-10.

[636] Wilcox, Francis O. "How the United Nations Charter Has Developed." American Academy of Political and Social Science *Annals* (Philadelphia), 296 (November, 1954), pp. 1-13.

[637] --------, and Marcy, Carl M. *Proposals for Change in the United Nations.* Washington: Brookings Institution, 1955; 2nd ed., 1963. 537 pp.
Critical appraisal of proposals for Charter reform. See review by D.P. Myers.

[638] Wilcox, R.B. "Prospects for United Nations Charter Review." *Chicago Bar Record*, 37 (November, 1955), p. 75.

[639] Wiley, A. "The Senate and the Review of the United Nations Charter." American Academy of Political and Social Science *Annals* (Philadelphia), 296 (November, 1954), pp. 156-62.

[640] Winterhager, Eva Marie. "Die Revision von Grundungsvertragen internationaler und supernationaler Organisationen." Frankfurt am Main: 1963. 87 pp.

[641] Woetzel, Robert K. *The Nuremberg Trials in International Law.* London: Stevens, 1960; New York: Praeger, 1960, 2nd ed., 1962. 287 pp.

[642] --------. *The Philosophy of Freedom.* Dobbs Ferry, N.Y.: Oceana, 1966;

Allahabad: Indian Universities Press, 1966.   200 pp.
Western democratic theory adapted to circumstances of present day
Third World societies. With a discussion at the Center for the Study
of Democratic Institutions.

643 --------, with Stone, Julius. *Toward a Feasible International Criminal
Court*. Foreword by Charles S. Rhyne.   Geneva: World Peace through
Law Center, 1970. 325 pp.

644 Wofford, Harris. "Revision of the U.N. Charter and Trends in U.S. Foreign Policy." *Socialist Asia* (Rangoon), 2 (January, 1954), pp. 1-5.

645 World Movement for World Federal Government. "Proposals for U.N. Charter Revision as Adopted at . . . Copenhagen, 1954 . . . and Approved
at the WMWFG Congress, London, September, 1954." *World Federalist*
(Amsterdam), 3 (November, 1954), pp. 3-4.

646 --------. "Report of Seventh Congress of World Movement for World Federal Government in Association with World Association of Parliamentarians for World Government." Ibid., 4 (August-September, 1955),
pp. 1-11.

647 World Parliament Association. *Proposals to Endow the U.N. with Powers
to Maintain World Peace*. 1959
Proposals by Max Habicht, Louis B. Sohn, and Robert Silkin.

648 Wright, Quincy.   "Making the United Nations Work." *Review of Politics*
(Notre Dame), 8 (October, 1946), pp. 528-32.

649 --------, et al.   "Should the United Nations Be Revised?" *University
of Chicago Round Table*, 714 (December 2, 1951), pp. 1-26.
Radio discussion by Wright, Brunson MacChesney, and Walter Johnson.
Includes Paul H. Douglas, "United to Enforce Peace."

650 --------. "Attitude of the American Association for the United Nations
on a Charter Review Conference."   American Society of International
Law *Proceedings, 1954* (Washington), (1954), pp. 206-10.

651 --------.   "Human Rights and Charter Revision." American Academy of
Political and Social Science *Annals* (Philadelphia), 296 (November,
1954), pp. 46-55.

652 Wynner, Edith.   *World Federal Government in Maximum Terms*:   *Proposals
for United Nations Charter Reform*.   Afton, N.Y.:   Fedonat Press,
1954.
Maximal world government to be achieved by a peoples' convention,
despite opposition by national governments.

653 Yakemtchouk, R.O.   "La sécurité collective et la sécurité regionale."
Revue de droit international, de sciences diplomatiques et politiques* (Genève), 32 (juillet-septembre, 1954), pp. 241-61.

654 --------.   "Vers la révision de la Charte de l'O.N.U.?" *Revue politique et parlementaire* (Paris), 220 (octobre, 1956), pp. 146-54.

655 Yepes, J.M.   "La reforma de la Carta de las Naciones Unidas y el derecho internacional americano." *Universitas* (Bogotá), 6 (1954), pp.
47-70.

[656] Yokota, Kisaburo, and Tomoo, Otaka.   "Japan and the United Nations: A Study of National Policy and Public Attitudes of Japan toward the United Nations."   *India Quarterly* (New Delhi),   11 (January-March, 1955), pp. 3-15.

[657] Younger, Kenneth. "United Nations Charter Review: A British Opinion." *India Quarterly*, 11 (April-June, 1955), pp. 105-16.

[658] Zacklin, Ralph.   *The Amendment of the Constitutive Instruments of the United Nations and Specialized Agencies.*   Leyden: Sijthoff, 1968. 216 pp.

[659] Zhukov, Yuri.   "What Is Behind the Plan to Revise the U.N.   Charter?" *Pravda* (Moscow), May 11, 1948.

[660] Zoller, Elisabeth. *Peacetime Unilateral Remedies*: *An Analysis of Countermeasures*. Ardsley-on-Hudson, N.Y.:   Transnational Publishers, 1984. 224 pp.
Examines to what extent a state is entitled to take the law into its own hands when its interests have been violated by other nations. Reviews whole issue of coercion of states as currently practiced within the international community.

[661] --------. *Enforcing International Law through U.S. Legislation.* Ardsley-on-Hudson, N.Y.: Transnational Publishers, 1985.   224 pp. Examines the legal means by which U.S. citizens can obtain redress in U.S. courts or public agencies for injuries caused them by foreign states; reviews the means by which foreign states and nationals can defend themselves from U.S. international sanctions such as import restrictions or freezing of assets.   Evaluates the adequacy of the imaginative U.S. enforcing legislation with respect to its two goals: to obtain reparation for damages caused to American interests, or to compel foreign nations to abide by fundamental international obligations.

Ramon Gordon cartoon, in I. A. Richards, *Nations and Peace*, 1947, 1974.
Used by permission of Simon & Schuster, Inc.

5

International Control
of Atomic Energy

The international control of atomic energy -- a policy advocated by the atomic scientists immediately after Hiroshima and a policy of the United States from late 1945 to early 1948 -- had implications for world federation. Grenville Clark explained that abolishing the veto in atomic energy cases, as provided for in the U.S. plan, was not enough. The U.N. General Assembly, Security Council, and World Court had to be transformed into the legislative, executive, and judicial branches of a limited world government to make the control of atomic energy really work. The U.S. plan (also called the Baruch plan) was effectively defeated by the end of 1946, when the nuclear arms race started in earnest. Nevertheless, the U.S. initiative -- and a corresponding Soviet proposal -- led to the formation of the U.N. Disarmament Commission in 1952 and to the series of U.N. Disarmament Committees, Conferences, and the Campaign since that time. Other consequences were the formation of the International Atomic Energy Agency in 1956, and the signing of the Partial Test Ban Treaty in 1963.

Typical atomic scientists' literature can be seen in Masters and Way, *One World or None*. Note the article by Einstein in this work. Other works by those atomic scientists who advocated world government, in addition to the international control of atomic energy, can be found in the next section, on world federation.

Failure of the Baruch Plan has had such enormous consequences for the peace of the world that it has been the subject of many historical studies.

[669] Acheson, Dean, and Lilienthal, David E., et al. *A Report on the International Control of Atomic Energy*. Washington: Department of State Publication 2498, March 16, 1946.
Original U.S. proposal for the international control of atomic energy. Implications for international organization: ". . . in attempting to solve [the problem of atomic energy], new patterns of cooperative effort could be established which would be capable of extension to other fields, and which might make a contribution toward the gradual achievement of a greater sense of community among the peoples of the world" (p. 3). Also: ". . . in the very fact of cooperative effort among the nations of the world rests the hope we rightly hold for solving the problem of war itself" (p. 47).

[670] Allen, James S. *Atomic Imperialism: The State, Monopoly, and the Bomb*. New York: International Publishers, 1952. 288 pp.
CPUSA view.

[671] Association of Los Alamos Scientists. *Our Atomic World*. Albuquerque: University of New Mexico Press, March, 1946.
Atomic scientists at the bomb assembly plant called for ultimate world government.

[672] Baratta, Joseph Preston. "Was the Baruch Plan a Proposal of World Government?" *International History Review*, 7 (November, 1985), pp. 592-621.
The Baruch plan was the nearest approach to a world government proposal by the United States; a full proposal could have been more "fair" to the Russians, who, in the circumstances of 1946 probably still would have rejected it, but at least they would not have been alarmed by the deceptiveness of the plan actually offered; and the story of the failure to make the plan a complete world government proposal casts a sidelight on the origins of the Cold War, and offers some guidance for a way out of the present nuclear arms race.

[673] Baruch, Bernard M. *Baruch: The Public Years*. New York: Holt, Rinehart & Winston, 1960. 431 pp
Candid on "diminution of sovereignty" necessary for international control of atomic energy.

[674] _____. *United States Atomic Energy Proposals*. Washington, D.C.: State Department Publication 2560, n.d., post June 14, 1946. 12 pp.
Baruch's historic speech.

[675] Bernstein, Barton J. "The Quest for Security: American Foreign Policy and International Control of Atomic Energy, 1942-1946." *Journal of American History*, 60 (March, 1974), pp. 1003-44.
"Neither the United States nor the Soviet Union was prepared in 1945 or 1946 to take the risks that the other power required for agreement."

[676] Bernstein, George A. "Control of Atomic Energy by the United Nations." *Antioch Review*, (Winter, 1946-1947), p. 488.

[677] Blackett, P.M.S. *The Atom and the Charter*. London: Fabian, 1946. 11 pp.

[678] _____. *Fear, War, and the Bomb: Military and Political Consequences of Atomic Energy*. New York: McGraw-Hill, Whittlesey, 1948. 244 pp.

Reviewed failure of talks in U.N. Atomic Energy Commission, warning of long war with atomic bombs.

[679] Bohr, Niels. "Open Letter to the United Nations." *Science*, 112 (July, 1950), pp. 1-6.

[680] Bradley, David. *No Place to Hide*. Boston: Little, Brown, 1948. 182 pp.
Eyewitness to Bikini tests gave early warning about radioactivity.

[681] Bratt, Eyvind. *Förenta Nationerna och atomvapnet*. Stockholm: Utrikespolitiska Institutet, 1948. 32 pp.

[682] Briggs, Herbert W. "World Government and the Control of Atomic Energy." *Annals*, American Academy of Political and Social Science, 249 (January, 1947), pp. 42-53.

[683] British Atomic Scientists Association. "Memorandum to United Nations Atomic Energy Association." London: University College, mimeographed, May 22, 1946. 14 pp.

[684] Brodie, Bernard, ed. *The Absolute Weapon*: *Atomic Power and World Order*. New York: Harcourt Brace, 1946. 214 pp.
Earliest formulation of deterrence theory -- alternative to world government.

[685] --------. "The Atomic Dilemma." *Annals*, American Academy of Political and Social Science, 249 (January, 1947), pp. 32-41.
World government would not necessarily eliminate the danger of war.

[686] Bush, Vannevar. *Modern Arms and Free Men*. New York: Simon & Schuster, 1949. 273 pp.
Atom bombs are not imminent in warfare on any big scale.

[687] Carnegie Endowment for International Peace. "The Control of Atomic Energy: Proposals before the United Nations Atomic Energy Commission and Unofficial Plans." *International Conciliation*, 423 (September, 1946), pp. 308-438.

[688] --------. Committee on Atomic Energy. *Utilization and Control of Atomic Energy*: *A Draft Convention Prepared by the Legal Subcommittee in Consultation with Other Legal, Political, and Scientific Experts*. New York: CEIP, 1946. 40 pp.

[689] --------. --------. *Conference on Problems of War and Peace in the Atomic Age*. New York: CEIP, 1946. 212 pp.
Includes contributions by the Federation of Atomic Scientists and the Commission to Study the Organization of Peace.

[690] Clark, Grenville. "An Atomic Energy Authority and World Government." Letter to the Editor. *New York Times*, June 23, 1946.
Clark's analysis of the Baruch Plan as the "entering wedge" for "world government."

[691] --------. "U.N. Voting." Letter to the Editor. *New York Times*, August 18, 1946.
Clark's disappointment with the rigid negotiation of the Baruch Plan.

[692] Culbertson, Ely.   "Atomic Power and World Peace." *Common Sense*, 14
    (December, 1945), pp. 3-7.
    The adequate political solution to problems of atomic energy cannot
    be the U.N. Charter nor a federal world government, but a "federa-
    tive alliance."

[693] Davidson, Maurice P.   "International Aspects of Atomic Energy." New
    York: New York Committee on Atomic Information, Committee on Law
    and Legislation, mimeographed, 1951. 19 pp.

[694] Delcoigne, Georges, et Rubinstein, G. *Non-proliferation des armes nuc-
    léaires et systèmes de contrôle*.   Bruxelles: Université Libre, In-
    stitut de Sociologie Solvay, Études de science politique, 1970. 214
    pp.

[695] Gerber, Larry G. "The Baruch Plan and the Origins of the Cold War."
    Diplomatic History, 6 (Winter, 1982), pp. 69-95.
    Able review of literature.

[696] Gideonse, Henry D.; Fosdick, Raymond B.; Ogburn, William F.; and Schu-
    man, Frederick L. *The Politics of Atomic Energy*. New York: Wood-
    row Wilson Foundation, 1946. 56 pp.

[697] Golovin, I. N. *I. V. Kurchatov: A Socialist-Realist Biography of the
    Soviet Nuclear Scientist*.   Translated by William H. Doughterty.
    Bloomington, Ind.: Selbstverlag Press, 1968. 99 pp.
    History of Russian atomic bomb project. It started in May, 1942, in
    Kazan.   Crash program began after "atomic blackmail" began, in Au-
    gust, 1945.   First sustained chain-reaction a few days before the
    critical vote on the Baruch Plan at the end of 1946.   First Russian
    test, August 29, 1949.

[698] Gormly, James L.   "The Washington Declaration and the 'Poor Relation':
    Anglo-American Atomic Diplomacy, 1945-1946." *Diplomatic History*, 8
    (Spring, 1984), pp. 125-43.
    Diplomatic account of Truman-Attlee-King Declaration and Moscow
    Declaration of 1945, ushering in negotiations on the international
    control of atomic energy. U.S. "simply wanted to retain her exist-
    ing monopoly." Failure to establish international control was "hu-
    manity's greatest and final failure."

[699] Hartley, Livingston. *Atomic Key to the Future.   Implications of the
    United States Proposals for the International Control of Atomic En-
    ergy*.   Washington: National Committee on Atomic Information, 1946.
    14 pp.

[700] Hecht, Selig. *Explaining the Atom*. New York: Viking, 1947. 205 pp.
    Note Epilogue: "The Future."

[701] Herken, Gregg. *The Winning Weapon: The Atomic Bomb in the Cold War,
    1945-1950*. New York: Knopf, 1980. 425 pp.
    Bomb was used *both* to defeat Japan and to exert diplomatic pressure
    on Russia.   American monopoly a hollow threat (12 A-bombs by 1947).
    U.S. policy led not to security and prestige, but to arms race, ten-
    sions, and loss of civil liberties.

[702] Hewlett, Richard G., and Anderson, Oscar E., Jr.   *A History of the*

United States Atomic Energy Commission. University Park, Pa.: Penn-
sylvania State University Press, 1962.   2 vols.   Vol. I: *The New
World, 1939-1946*.
Official history, including Baruch Plan.

[703] Infield, Leopold. *Atomic Energy and World Government*. Toronto: Canadian Institute of International Affairs, Vol. 6, No. 4., 1946.   20
pp.

[704] Jungk, Robert.   *Brighter than 1000 Suns*:   *The Personal History of the
Atomic Scientists*. New York: Harcourt, Brace, 1958.   350 pp.
Cf. Alice Kimball Smith.

[705] *K peregovoram mezhdu pravitel'stvom SSSR i pravitel'stvom SShA po atomnoi probleme*. [Concerning the U.S.S.R.-U.S.A. negotiations on atomic energy.] Moskva: Gospoletizdat, 1954.   55 pp.

[706] "Last Chance to Avoid Atomic Destruction." *Look*,   March 5,   1946,   pp.
19-33.
Popular exposition of argument for world government.   Illustrated.

[707] Lawrence, William L. *Dawn over Zero*: *The Story of the Atomic Bomb*. New
York: Knopf, 1946.   274 pp.
Eye witness to New Mexico test and Nagasaki bombing.

[708] --------. *The Hell Bomb*. New York: Knopf, 1951.   198 pp.
"We have had it dinned into our ears for so long that there is no
defense against the atomic bomb, and that the only choice confronting us is 'one world or none,' without anyone taking the trouble to
challenge those two pernicious catch phrases, that we have accepted them as gospel truth. . . ."

[709] Lieberman, Joseph I.   *The Scorpion and the Tarantula*: *The Struggle to
Control Atomic Weapons, 1945-1949*. Boston: Houghton Mifflin, 1970.
460 pp.
"This is the story of a disastrous failure of statecraft. . . .   In
the guilt and responsibility for this epic failure, the United
States shares equally with the Soviet Union."

[710] Lippmann, Walter.   "The International Control of Atomic Energy." In
Masters and Way, *One World or None*, pp. 66-75.
Rare pro-world government opinion by this national commentator.

[712] McBride, James H.   *The Test Ban Treaty*:   *Military, Technological, and
Political Implications*. Chicago: Henry Regnery, 1967.   197 pp.

[713] McNight, Allan. *Atomic Safeguards*: *A Study in International Verification*. United Nations: UNITAR (E.75.XV.ST/5), 1971.   301 pp.
A case study of the International Atomic Energy Agency and an analysis of the methods for verification of treaty obligations. Emphasis
on administration rather than politics.

[714] Masters, Dexter, and Way, Katharine, eds. *One World or None*. New York:
McGraw Hill, 1946.   79 pp.
Contributors: Einstein, Philip Morrison, Harlow Shapley, J. Robert
Oppenheimer, Walter Lippman, etc.   Timely, major statement by the
Federation of American Scientists.

[715] Milhaud, Edgard. *Pour la liberation de la crainte*: *deux amendments a la Charte*: *controle atomique et limitation du droit de veto*. Neuchatel: La Baconniere, 1947. 96 pp.

[716] Muszkat, Marian. *Atomnaia energiia i bor'ba za mir*. Perevod s pol'-skogo. [Nuclear energy and the struggle for peace.] Moskva: Izdat. Inostr. Liter., 1951. 358 pp.

[717] Nogee, Joseph L. *Soviet Policy towards International Control of Atomic Energy*. Notre Dame: Notre Dame University Press, 1961. 306 pp.
Based on available Soviet sources. "To the Kremlin, non-Soviet intrusion into the Soviet industrial structure constituted a far greater threat to its long-term stability and survival than an atomic arms race."

[718] Osborn, Frederick. *Atomic Impasse, 1948*. Washington: U.S. Department of State, No. 14, September, 1948. 48 pp.
Speeches by U.S. representative to U.N. AEC at end of negotiations.

[719] Rabinowitch, Eugene, ed. *Minutes to Midnight*: *The International Control of Atomic Energy*. Chicago: Bulletin of the Atomic Scientists, 1950. 128 pp.
Documents and commentary.

[720] Rhyne, Charles S., et al. *Law-Making Activities of the International Atomic Energy Agency*. Washington: World Association of Lawyers, 1976. 76 pp.

[721] Romulo, Carlos P. Address to General Assembly, December 13, 1946. *United Nations Official Records*, General Assembly, 1st sess., 2nd part, Meeting 61, pp. 1247-53, Microprint.
Historic speech on defeat of Baruch Plan and of Grenville Clark's first efforts for U.N. reform. Marks turn of nations from United Nations to national programs of military defense.

[722] Rose, David J., and Lester, Richard K. "Nuclear Power, Nuclear Weapons, and International Stability." *Scientific American*, 238 (April, 1978), pp. 45-57.
"International institution building" (strengthened International Atomic Energy Agency in U.N.) recommended for next decade.

[723] Rosenbloom, Morris V. *Peace through Strength*: *Bernard Baruch and a Blueprint for Security*. Forword by Eleanor Roosevelt. New York: Farrar, Straus, & Young, 1953. 325 pp.
Deterrence the alternative to international control of atomic energy.

[724] Royal Institute of International Affairs. *Atomic Energy*: *Its International Implications*. London: Chatham House, 1948, 128 pp.

[725] Schweitzer, Albert. *Peace or Atomic War*? New York: Holt, 1958. 47 pp.
Three radio broadcasts from Oslo, April 28-30, 1958.

[726] Sethna, M.J. *International Legal Controls and Sanctions Concerning the Production and Use of Atomic Energy*. Bombay: Kothari McDuneil, 1966. 144 pp.

[727] Sherwin, Martin J. *A World Destroyed*: *The Atomic Bomb and the Grand Alliance*. New York: Knopf, 1975. 315 pp.
Parallels Hewlett. "To comprehend the relationship between atomic energy and diplomatic policies that developed during the war, the bomb must be seen as both scientists and policymakers saw it before Hiroshima: as a possible means of controlling the postwar course of world affairs."

[728] Shils, Edward A. *The Atomic Bomb in World Politics*. London: National Peace Council, Peace Aims Pamphlet No. 45, 1948. 79 pp.

[729] --------. "The Failure of the UNAEC: An Interpretation." *Bulletin of the Atomic Scientists*, 4 (July, 1948), pp. 205-10.

[730] Shotwell, James T. "The Control of Atomic Energy and a New International World." In his *Autobiography* (Indianapolis: Bobbs-Merrill, 1961), pp. 319-30.

[731] Smith, Alice Kimball. "Behind the Decision to Use the Atomic Bomb: Chicago, 1944-1945." *Bulletin of the Atomic Scientists*, 14 (October, 1958), pp. 289-93.
Early scientific proposals, such as the Jeffries Report (November 18, 1944), for a post-war international atomic energy control organization.

[732] --------. *A Peril and a Hope*: *The Scientists' Movement in America*. Cambridge: Massachusetts Institute of Technology Press, 1971. 591 pp.
Standard history of the atomic scientists movement. Failure to achieve international control.

[733] Smith, Thomas Vernor. *Atomic Power and Moral Faith*. Claremont, Calif.: Claremont College, 1946. 21 pp.

[734] Smyth, Henry DeWolf. *Atomic Energy for Military Purposes*: *The Official Report on the Development of the Atomic Bomb under the Auspices of the United States Government, 1940-1945*. Princeton: Princeton University Press, 1945. 306 pp.
Released immediately after bombings of Hiroshima and Nagasaki. No secrets.

[735] Social Science Research Council, Committee on Social and Economic Aspects of Atomic Energy. *Public Reaction to the Atomic Bomb and World Affairs*: *A Nationwide Survey of Attitudes and Information*. Ithaca: Cornell University Press, 1947. 310 pp.

[736] Società italiana per l'organizzazione internazionale. *Enti nucleari internazionali: statuti e documenti*. Padova: CEDAM, 1959. 249 pp.

[737] Spanier, John W., and Nogee, Joseph L. *The Politics of Disarmament*: *A Study in Soviet-American Gamesmanship*. New York: Praeger, 1962. 226 pp.
Baruch Plan considered. Preferred approach was between "utopian" and "realist" schools.

[738] Stimson, Henry L. "The Bomb and the Opportunity." *Harpers*, March, 1946, p. 204.
"By its sole possession of the bomb, at least for the present, the

United danger of atomic destruction.) is removed depends on whether we and other nations move fairly quickly, and with frank transparency of purpose, toward the goal of uniting all men of good will against the appalling threat to man's very existence."

[739] --------. "The Atomic Bomb and Peace with Russia." *Bulletin of the Atomic Scientists*, 4 (August, 1948), pp. 237-44.
"We cannot have world government or atomic control by wishing for them, and we cannot have them, in any meaningful sense, without Russia."

[740] Teller, Edward. "Comments on the 'Draft of a World Constitution.'" *Bulletin of the Atomic Scientists*, 4 (July, 1948), p. 204.
Teller did not urge building the H-bomb until hopes for world government were dashed. Russian A-bomb test in August, 1949, was last straw.

[741] United Nations, Atomic Energy Commission. Findings and Recommendations. *First report* to the Security Council. 31 December 1946. 90 pp. AEC/18/Rev.1. AECOR, 1st sess.

[742] --------. Proceedings. *Second report* to the Security Council. 17 September 1947. 105 pp. AEC/26. AECOR, 2nd sess.

[743] --------. *Third report* to the Security Council. 25 May 1948. 60 pp. AEC/31. AECOR, 2nd sess.

[744] --------. International control of atomic energy and the prohibition of atomic weapons. *Recommendations*. 24 August 1949. 75 pp. AEC/-C.1/77/Rev.2. AECOR, 4th sess., suppl. 1.

[745] --------. International control of atomic energy. *Interim Report* on the consultations of the six permanent members. 24 October 1949. 72 pp. A/1045.

[746] --------. International control of atomic energy and the prohibition of atomic weapons. *Recommendations*. 1949. 90 pp. AEC/C.1/77/Rev.1.

[747] United Nations, Disarmament Commission. *First report*. 29 May 1952. 6 pp. DC/11.
Marks first involvement of Disarmament Commission with questions of atomic energy.

[748] --------. *Second report*. 13 October 1952. 206 pp. DC/20.

[749] United Nations, General Assembly. Ad Hoc Political Committee. International control of atomic energy. *Report*. 19 November 1949. 6 pp. A/1119.

[750] --------. First Committee. Principles governing the general regulation and reduction of armaments. *Report*. 13 December 1946. 6 pp. A/267. GAOR, 1st sess., part 2, plenary, annex 73.

[751] --------. --------. International control of atomic energy. *Resolution*. 23 November 1949. 1 p. A/1251. GAOR, 4th sess., res. 299.
Request that U.N. AEC continue its consultations despite deadlock in talks. Acceptance of A/1119.

752 --------. --------_. Regulation, limitation, and balanced reduction of all armed forces and all armaments. *Report*. 22 December 1951. 17 pp. A/2025. GAOR, 6th sess.

753 --------. --------. Regulation, limitation, and balanced reduction of all armed forces and all armaments. *Resolution*. 8 April 1953. 1 p. A/2361/Add.1. GAOR, 7th sess., suppl. 20A, res. 704.

754 U.S. Department of State. *The International Control of Atomic Energy*: *The First Report of the U.N. Atomic Energy Commission to the Security Council, December 31, 1946*. Washington: Department of State Publication 2737, 1947. 101 pp.

755 -------- . . . . *Second Report . . . September 11, 1947*. Publication 2932, 1947. 106 pp.

756 -------- . . . . *Third Report . . . May 17, 1948*. Publication 3179, 1948. 78 pp.

757 --------. *International Control of Atomic Energy*: *Growth of a Policy*. Washington: Department of State Publication 2702, 1947. 281 pp.

758 --------. "International Control of Atomic Energy: Policy at the Crossroads." Washington: Department of State Publication 3161, June, 1948. 251 pp.
State Department account of Baruch Plan negotiations. Russia to blame.

759 Walker, Sydnor H. *The First One Hundred Days of the Atomic Age, August 6 - November 15, 1945*: *Compilation of Current Opinion upon Political and International Implications of the Atomic Bomb*. New York: Woodrow Wilson Foundation, 1946. 72 pp.

760 Waton, Harry. *The Atomic Bomb and the United Nations*. Brooklyn: Spinoza Institute of America, 1950. 9 pp.

761 Wiener, Norbert. "A Scientist Rebels." *Atlantic*, December, 1946, p. 46.
Eloquent refusal to participate in the development of intercontinental ballistic missiles, already under way at defeat of Baruch Plan. In effect, a call for atomic scientists to refuse to participate in the nuclear arms race.

762 Wimperis, H.E. *World Power and Atomic Energy*: *The Impact on International Relations*. London: Constable, 1946. 86 pp.

763 Wood, Alex. "Notes on the Course of Negotiations for Control of Atomic Energy." In *Two Worlds in Focus*: *Studies of the Cold War* (London: National Peace Council, 1950), pp. 111-33.

764 Woodward, E. L. *Some Political Consequences of the Atomic Bomb*. New York: Oxford University Press, 1946. 30 pp.

765 Wright, Quincy. "Draft for a Convention on Atomic Energy." *Bulletin of the Atomic Scientists*, 1 (April, 1946), pp. 11-13.
Perhaps the most workable plan without compromising national sovereignty in the inept way of the Baruch Plan.

6

Universal Federation—
U.S. & Canada to 1955

In the United States, the years before 1947 were particularly fertile for world federalism. Both elements of a great crisis were present -- a heady sense of opportunity after the Allied victory and the miracles of production and of science achieved during the war, and also a sense of great danger, particularly from the use of atomic energy in war. The atomic scientists raised the cry, "One World or None!" Lawyers, judges, one or two Supreme Court Justices, university presidents, deans of law schools, prominent professors, teachers, journalists, a few businessmen, some Senators, Congressmen, and former and future officials of the executive branch discussed seriously the possibility and necessity of establishing a world federation. There was a similar movement in Europe, though hampered and delayed by wartime destruction.

The world federalist movement struggled against the policies of the United States and the Soviet Union at the beginning of the Cold War, until the Korean War and McCarthyism effectively ended the popular movement. A few works such as G. A. Borgese's *Foundations of the World Republic*, long in preparation and bearing the marks of the struggle, appeared in the years thereafter. The year 1955 may be taken as a convenient dividing point.

Here will be found thoughtful and timely proposals as well as fundamental criticism.

Proposals include those of atomic scientists, Borgese and the Chicago Committee, Brown, Clark, Cousins, Cranston, Culbertson, Einstein, Finletter, Holliday, Holt, Meyer, Muste, Reves, Taylor, Wallace, White, Wofford, and Wynner. Some more discursive, late, and reflective works are useful, including those by Barr, Buchanan, Schuman, and Wofford. The collection entitled *Foundations for World Order* is particularly valuable.

Criticism came from Austin, Brinton, Burnham, Deutsch, Dulles (Alan and John Foster), Eagleton, Eichelberger, Jessup, Mangone, Morgenthau, Niebuhr, Kamp, Pelcovitz, Welles, Wright, and the Yale symposium of 1949. A lively debate took place in the *American Bar Association Journal*.

The collection of national constitutions by Amos Peaslee is of interest. The times after the Second World War, and even more during the period of decolonialization, lent themselves to the creation of new sovereignties. Each act of statecraft provided a precedent for the creation of a world federal state. Fifteen new constitutions were written in the period. New

states were created in Israel, West and East Germany, India, Pakistan,
Burma, and Indonesia.   The constitutions of France, Italy, West Germany,
and Holland were given language explicitly permitting limitations of sovereignty for the purpose of participating in a regional or world federation.   The constitution of Japan renounced war as a sovereign right of the
nation. Some twenty nations, to date, have placed such limitations on their
claimed legal independence: Belgium, Congo, Costa Rica, Denmark, Federal
Republic of Germany, France, Greece, Ireland, Italy, Japan, Luxembourg,
Netherlands, Philippines, Portugal, Rwanda, Singapore, Spain, Switzerland,
Yugoslavia, and Zaire. An effort to amend the U.S. Constitution to similar
effect failed (1950), as one can see in the works of Andrews, Dean, Lloyd,
and Skewes-Cox.

Major themes discussed here include the continuing U.N.-world government controversy, the need for U.S. leadership in all projects to strength-
en the U.N., the nature of law on the world level (it must reach individuals), the degree of world community so far attained, the realism/idealism
dichotomy, the political conditions necessary for a more perfect union, and
the nuclear threat. By 1955, most authors had turned aside from the drafting of model world constitutions and other ideal plans (Grenville Clark
excepted),   and were concentrating on exploring the preconditions necessary
for world union.

OPERATION CROSSROADS

Lute Pease cartoon, in *Newark Evening News* on June 11, 1949. Used by
permission of Media General, Inc.

775 "A Federal World Government Now?" *Congressional Digest*,   27 (August-
     September, 1948), pp. 193-224.
     Pro and con discussion for revising the United Nations into a feder-
     al world government.

776 Alsberg, Henry G.   *Let's Talk about the Peace*.   New York: Hastings,
     1945.   324 pp.

777 Aly, Bower, ed. *World Organization*. Committee on Debate Materials and
     Interstate Cooperation, National University Extension Association.
     Columbia, Mo.: Lucas, 1942.
     High school debate topic, 1942-1943.

778 --------. *World Government*. Columbia, Mo.: Artcraft, 1948. 2 vols.
     High school debate topic, 1948-1949.

779 --------. *International Organization*. Columbia, Mo.: Artcraft, 1952.
     High school debate topic, 1952-1953.

780 American Friends Service Committee. *American-Russian Relations*: *Some
     Constructive Considerations*. Report of a Working Party of the Exec-
     utive Board of the AFSC. Dittoed, n.d., ante June 23, 1946.
     Quaker approach.

781 --------. *The United States and the Soviet Union*. Philadelphia: AFSC,
     1949.

782 --------. *Steps to Peace*: *A Quaker View of U.S. Foreign Policy*. Phil-
     adelphia: AFSC, 1951. 64 pp.
     The AFSC never went so far as to advocate world government.

783 Andrews, Burton.   "Amending the Constitution to Provide for Participa-
     tion in a World Government." *Albany Law Review*, 14 (June, 1950),
     pp. 12548.
     Re debate over "necessity" of a U.S. Constitutional Amendment.

784 Armstrong, Hamilton Fish.   "Coalition for Peace." *Foreign Affairs*, 27
     (October, 1948), pp. 1-16.
     Comment on federalist movement by editor.

785 Armstrong, O. K.   "Grassroots Crusader." *Reader's Digest*, May, 1946,
     pp. 45-49.
     Robert Lee Humber's campaign in state legislatures to get resolu-
     tions favoring world federation.   Eventually, 21 states passed such
     resolutions.

786 Association of Oak Ridge Engineers and Scientists.   World Government
     Committee, Norton Gerber, chairman. *Primer for Peace*: *World Govern-
     ment for the Atomic Age*; *Presenting the Results of a Study*.   Oak
     Ridge, Tenn.: By the Committee, 1947. 62 pp.
     Most explicit advocacy of world government by any of the atomic sci-
     entists' organizations.

787 Austin, Warren R. "A Warning on World Government." *Harpers*, May, 1949,
     pp. 93-97. Answer to Bowles.

788 Barnard, Chester I. *On Planning for World Government*. New York: Con-
     ference on Science, Philosophy, and Religion in Their Relation to

the Democratic Way of Life, No. 4, 1944, pp. 825-58.

[789] Barr, Stringfellow. *Final Report on the Pocono Conference.* New York: Foundation for World Government, 1948. 8 pp.

[790] --------. *The Pilgrimage of Western Man.* New York: Harcourt, Brace, 1949. 369 pp.
Historical quest for unity since the Reformation.

[791] --------. *Let's Join the Human Race.* Chicago: University of Chicago Press, 1950. 30 pp.
Demands of the colonized and undeveloped peoples.

[792] --------. *Citizens of the World.* Garden City, N.Y., 1952. 285 pp.
Last production of Foundation for World Government.

[793] Beard, Charles A. *The Enduring Federalist.* New York: Doubleday, 1948. 391 pp.
World federation on model of United States. Cf. Van Doren.

[794] Benoit-Smullyan, Emile.   "An American Foreign Policy for Survival." *Ethics*, 56 (July, 1946), pp. 280-90.
Minimal world government.

[795] Bernier, Robert. *L'autorite politique internationale et la souveraine-te des etats*; *fondements philosophiques de l'ordre politique.* Mont-real: Institut Social Populaire, 1951. 201 pp.

[796] Bernstein, George A.   "World Government -- Progress Report." *Nation*, June, 1948, pp. 628-30, 660-62.
Concise and able survey.

[798] Bete, Channing L. *Cops or Corpses*: *World Law vs. World War.*   Green-field, Mass.: Newell Pond Press, 1948. 40 pp.
Minimal world government presented by cartoon poster type penwork.

[799] Bigman, Stanley K.   "The 'New Internationalism' under Attack." *Public Opinion Quarterly*, 14 (Summer, 1950), pp. 235-61.
Findings of Columbia University's study of opposition to world gov-ernment.

[800] Billington, Ray Allen; Loewenberg, Bert James; and Brockunier, Samuel Hugh. *The United States*: *American Democracy in World Perspective.* New York: Rinehart, 1947. 894 pp.
Argument for a new history, placing the American struggle for free-dom and social and economic justice within a similar struggle throughout the world.

[801] "Blueprint for Survival: World Constitution." *New Republic*, April 12, 1948, p. 7.
Review of Chicago Committee's "Preliminary Draft of a World Consti-tution." Cf. Teller, Culbertson, and Farmer.

[802] Bolté, Charles. *The New Veteran.* New York: Reynal & Hitchcock, 1945. 212 pp.
By chairman of American Veterans Committee when new veterans group was considering world government.

[803] Borden, William L. *There Will Be No Time*: *The Revolution in Strategy*. New York: Macmillan, 1946. 225 pp.

[804] --------. *Constitution for a World Federal Government*. Trenton, N.J.: By the author, 1949.

[805] Borgese, Elizabeth Mann. "Why a Maximalist Constitution?" *Bulletin of the Atomic Scientists*, 4 (July, 1948), pp. 7-12.
A minimalist constitution is unworkable even to keep the peace and would be unacceptable to the bulk of humanity.

[806] Borgese, Giuseppe Antonio. *Foundations of the World Republic*. Chicago: University of Chicago Press, 1953. 328 pp.
"The era of humanity has not begun, but the age of nations has ended." By the leading spirit of the Chicago Committee to Frame a World Constitution. Exposition of world government as an idea rooted in history and literature. Fullest explanation of *justice*, which, as the purpose of a good world government, distinguishes maximal pro- posals from minimal.

[807] Bowles, Chester. "World Government -- Yes, But. . . ." *Harpers*, March, 1949, pp. 21-27.
By the Governor of Connecticut. U.S. must take initiative to trans- form U.N. into an effective security organization.

[808] Bowman, Isaiah. *Is an International Society Possible?* New York: Na- tional Industrial Conference Board, 1947. 15 pp.

[809] Bozjak, Nikola. *Peace on Earth*: . . . *One Constitution for All Mankind*. San Pedro, Calif.: By the author, 1946. 56 pp.

[810] Branch, John W., with assistance of Clark, Grenville. *1955, Year of Decision*: *A Survey of the Clark Proposals for Revising the United Nations Charter*. New York: Institute for International Government, 1952. 18 pp.
Anticipation of Charter review conference in 1955 provided for in Art. 109. Follow-up to Clark's *A Plan for Peace*.

[811] Briggs, Herbert Whittaker. "Power Politics and International Organi- zation." *American Journal of International Law*, 39 (1945), pp. 664- 79.

[812] --------. "The Problem of World Government." Ibid. 41 (1947), pp. 108- 12.
Answer to Finletter. World state must evolve gradually, cannot be created overnight.

[813] --------. "International Law, World Government, and the Role of Law." *American Bar Association Journal*, 33 (July, 1947), pp. 680-83.

[814] Brinton, Crane. *From Many, One*. Cambridge: Harvard University Press, 1948. 126 pp.
Opposition to world government. "I think that there will be another general war and that the human race will survive it."

[815] Brown, Harrison. *Must Destruction Be Our Destiny?* *A Scientist Speaks as a Citizen*. New York: Simon & Schuster, 1946. 158 pp.
Major atomic scientist's statement. Atomic bomb makes world govern-

ment necessary.

816 _____. *The Challenge of Man's Future*. New York: Viking, 1954. 290
pp.
Three future possibilities: reversion to agrarian existence (if war
continues), centralized and collectivized industrial society, or
free industrial society in which human beings can live in reasonable
harmony with their environment.

817 Brownfield, William. "A Candle in the Wind." Ohio Junior Chamber of
Commerce, dittoed, 1949. 17 pp.
By the president of the Ohio Jaycees and vice-chairman of the U.S.
Jaycee International Relations Committee. Pro world law. Concludes
with Jaycee creed: "We believe that the brotherhood of man tran-
scends the sovereignty of nations, that economic justice can best be
won by free men through free enterprise, that government should be
of laws and not of men, that earth's great treasure lies in human
personality, and that service to humanity is the best work of life."

818 Buchanan, Scott. *Essay in Politics*. New York: Philosophical Library,
1953. 236 pp.
Response to Representative Reginald Bolling's challenge to Buchanan
to prepare "a sketch of an American policy, both domestic and foreign, that would lead the country towards, rather than away from, a
good world government." Result was so abstruse that Einstein gave
up by page 40. Cf. Warburg.

819 Burnham, James. *The Struggle for the World*. New York: John Day, 1947.
248 pp.
The disillusioned Trotskyite proposed a U.S. world empire.

820 Carney, Fred S., et al. *An Appeal to Reason: The Case for a Peoples'
World Constitutional Convention*. Chicago: By World Republic, n.d.,
c. February, 1947. 24 pp.
The World Republic boys' manifesto in response to Clifton Fadiman's
challenge to write a modern version of Tom Paine's "The Crisis."

821 Chesterton, Arthur K. *The Menace of World Government*. Willowdale,
Ont.: League of Empire Loyalists, National Federation of Christian
Laymen, 1955. 14 pp.
Cf. Kamp.

822 Chevalier, S. "A World Community or a World State?" *Vital Speeches*,
13 (March 1, 1947), pp. 309-18.

823 Cittadini, Nicola. *The World Economic Government: Scientific Solution
for Lasting Peace and Growing Welfare*. New York: Nelson, 1946. 45
pp.

824 Clark, Grenville. "A New World Order -- The American Lawyer's Role."
Indiana Law Journal, 19 (July, 1944), pp. 289-300.
Clark's first published proposal of limited world government.

825 _____. "The Dumbarton Oaks Proposals -- An Analysis." *American Bar
Association Journal*, 30 (December, 1944), pp. 667-73.
Clark's fundamental critique of the proposed U.N. Charter and his
call for a "World Constitutional Convention" to draft a more adequate one.

826 --------. "The Dublin Declaration." Address before the Harvard Faculty Club. *World Affairs*, 108 (December, 1945), pp. 265-72.
Explanation of call, after use of the atomic bomb, for federal world
government in place of the United Nations.

827 --------; Cranston, Alan; and Mahony, Thomas H. Dublin Conference Com-
mittee. *Proposals for Amendment of the United Nations Charter*:   A
Petition to the General Assembly of the United Nations.   New York:
Council for Limited World Government, February 1, 1946.   19 pp.
In Clark Papers.

828 --------. "An Atomic Energy Authority and World Government." Letter
to the Editor. *New York Times*, June 23, 1946.
Clark's analysis of the Baruch Plan as the "entering wedge" for
"world government."

829 --------. "U.N. Voting." Letter to the Editor.   *New York Times*, August
18, 1946.
Clark's disappointment with the rigid negotiation of the Baruch
Plan.

830 --------. "Let's Amend the Charter." *Yankee*, December, 1946, p. 25.
Facing Warren R. Austin, "Let's Not Amend the Charter."

831 --------. "World Government -- What It Would Mean." *Look*, January 21,
1947, p. 96.
The editors translated Clark's arguments into a cartoon strip.

832 --------. "Is the US Imperialistic? Is the USSR Imperialistic?" *The
Christian Register* (Unitarian), September, 1947, pp. 341-42.
Yes. Cf. similar replies in same issue by Wayne Morse, Raymond Gram
Swing, and Henry Wallace.

833 --------. *A Show-Down with Ourselves*.   St. Louis: Plaza Bank, 1948.
10 pp.
Address to New York Bar on a general East-West settlement.

834 --------. "A Settlement with Russia -- Its Necessity for World Order."
Address at the Association of the Bar of New York, February 7, 1948.
In Clark Papers.
A general East-West settlement to reverse the Cold War and make pos-
sible an agreement on disarmament and U.N. reform.

835 --------. "Settlement with Russia." *Yankee*, May, 1948, pp. 29-31, 44-
45.
Reduced version of privately printed address to New York Bar Association. Cf. Dulles.

836 --------. *A Plan for Peace*. New York: Harper & Bros., 1950. 83 pp.
First in the genre of warnings on nuclear war, with the difference
that Clark proposed a realistic solution of steps toward world federation.

837 --------, and Sohn, Louis B. *Peace through Disarmament and Charter Revision*: *Detailed Proposals for Revision of the United Nations Charter*. Dublin, N.H.: By the authors, 1953. 149 pp. *Supplement*. 1956.
121 pp.

Preliminary draft of *World Peace through World Law*. Cf. Reno.

838 --------. *Essentials for Genuine Peace*. New York: Institute for International Government, n.d., c. 1955. 8 pp.
Twelve propositions for genuine peace.

839 --------. *Disarmament and World Law*. Concord, N.H.: United World Federalists of New Hampshire, 1955. 12 pp.
Fundamentals: law forbidding violence, police to deter violations, judicial and quasi-judicial tribunals, and disarmament.

841 Committee to Frame a World Constitution. Robert M. Hutchins, president; G.A. Borgese, secretary. "Preliminary Draft of a World Constitution." *Common Cause*, 1 (March, 1948). pp. 1-40. Reprinted as *A Constitution for the World* by the Center for the Study of Democratic Institutions, Santa Barbara, Calif., 1965. 112 pp.
Model world constitution. Maximalist. The problem of representation is ingeniously solved through a system of regional electoral districts that conform to the civilizations. Its preamble, list of powers, tribune of the people to protect minorities, and constitutional checks and balances are of particular interest.

842 --------. *Documents 1-150, 1945-1948*. Microfilm, Department of Photoduplication, Regenstein Library, University of Chicago. 4500 pp.
"World Federalist Papers." Analyses, draft constitutions, transcripts of proceedings. The proceedings of discussions between Hutchins, Borgese, Mortimer Adler, Richard McKeon, Reinhold Niebuhr, and Rexford Tugwell are modern dialogues not unlike Plato's.

843 Compton, A.H. "Atomic Power in War and Peace." *Saturday Review of Literature*, October 27, 1945, pp. 18 ff.
World government is now inevitable.

844 Conway, Edward A. "Catholics and World Federation." *America*, 80 (December 4, 1948), pp. 231-33.
Cautious extrapolation of Pope's endorsement of European federation.

845 Cook, Thomas I. "Theoretical Foundations of World Government." *The Review of Politics*, 12 (January, 1950), pp. 20-55.
Minimum world government, being repressive, would command no loyalty from its citizens.

846 Corbett, Percy Elwood. "World Government -- In Whose Time?" *International Affairs* (London), 25 (October, 1949), pp. 426-33.

847 --------. *World Government Proposals before Congress*. New Haven: Yale Institute of International Studies, Memo No. 34, 1950. 22 pp.

848 --------. "Congress and Proposals for International Government." *International Organization*, 4 (1950), pp. 383-99.

849 --------. *The Individual and World Society*. Princeton: Center for Research on World Political Institutions, Pub. 2, 1953. 59 pp.
Deals with difficulty that "international or supra-national institutions cannot be strong unless they attract considerable loyalty, and yet loyalty is very hard to attract unless an institution is already strong." Functionalism.

850 Cornell, Julien. *New World Primer*.   New York: New Directions, 1947.
174 pp.
U.N. doomed to fail; world government (on U.S. and English models)
the "logical climax" of history.

851 Cousins, Norman. "Modern Man Is Obsolete." *Saturday Review of Literature*, August 18, 1945, pp. 5-9.
Written the night after Hiroshima. Gave impetus to popular movement
for world government.

852 --------. *Modern Man Is Obsolete*. New York: Viking, 1945. 59 pp.

853 --------. "Don't Resign from the Human Race." *Saturday Review of Literature*, August 7, 1948, pp. 6-11.
"The only price [man] has to pay for his survival is decision." Re-
affirmation of ideal at time of Berlin blockade and seemingly imminent world war.

854 --------. "As 1960 Sees Us." *Saturday Review of Literature*, August 5,
1950.
Late plug for World Federalists' Senate resolution, SCR-56, at crisis of Korean War.

855 --------. *Who Speaks for Man?* New York: Macmillan, 1953. 318 pp.

856 Cranston, Alan. "The Strengthening of the U.N. Charter." *Political
Quarterly*, 18 (July-September, 1946), pp. 187-201.
Excellent survey of world government movement in U.S.

857 --------. "What about World Government?" *New Republic*, May 22, 1950,
p. 16.

858 Culbertson, Ely. *Summary of the World Federation Plan*: An Outline of
a Practical and Detailed Plan for World Settlement. Garden City,
N.Y.: Doubleday, Doran, 1943. 78 pp.
Culbertson's first proposal of his Quota Force Plan. Really a balance of scheme.

859 --------. *Total Peace*: What Makes Wars and How to Organize Peace.
Garden City, N.Y.: Doubleday, Doran, 1943. 344 pp.
Elaboration of Quota Force Plan.

860 --------. *Must We Fight Russia?* Philadelphia: Winston, 1946. 62 pp.
Armed league from "Stop Russia" viewpoint.

861 --------. "ABC Plan for World Peace." *Reader's Digest*, June, 1948,
pp. 82-88.
Last version of his deceptive plan. One of "world government" resolutions before Congress.

862 --------. "The Preliminary Draft of a World Constitution." *Indiana
Law Journal*, 24 (Summer, 1949), pp. 474-82.
Includes reply by Elizabeth Mann Borgese, pp. 483-88.

863 Cultural and Scientific Conference for World Peace. *Speaking of Peace*.
New York: National Council of the Arts, Sciences, and Professions,
1949. 152 pp.
Edited report on the controversial Cultural and Scientific Confer-

ence for World Peace, attended by Harlow Shapley, Dimitri Shostako-
vitch and others, held in New York, March 25-27, 1949.

864 Davenport, Russell W. "The Ordeal of Wendell Willkie." *Atlantic Monthly*, November, 1945, pp. 67-73.
"The real objectives of One World lie far ahead of us. . . ."

865 Dean, W.T., Jr. "World Government and the Consitution of the United
States." *California Law Review* (Berkeley), 38 (August, 1950), pp.
452-77.
Constitutional implications of both U.N. Charter and a world constitution.

866 Deutsch, Karl W. *Political Community at the International Level: Problems of Definition and Measurement*. Princeton: Princeton University Press, 1953. 71 pp.
Cf. Wright, *World Community*.

867 Dolivet, Louis. "Primer for World Government." *Free World*, November,
1945, pp. 21-23.
Proposal to transform General Assembly into a world parliament, then
to abolish veto. Report on Dublin conference in same issue. By future editor of *United Nations World*.

868 Dulles, Alan W. Foreign Policy Association, *The United Nations*, Headline Series, No. 59, September-October, 1946, pp. 84-90.
"Russia is by no means the sole obstacle. There is no indication
that American public opinion, for example, would approve the establishment of a superstate, or permit American membership in it. In
other words, time -- a long time -- will be needed before world government is politically feasible."

869 Dulles, John Foster. "The General Assembly." *Foreign Affairs*, 24 (October, 1945), pp. 1-11.
"Of course, anyone who is free to disregard realities and to act
only in the realm of theory can write a 'better' Charter. A reasonably intelligent schoolboy could do that. The task of statesmanship, however, is to relate theory to reality."

870 --------. "Not War, Not Peace." Address before the Foreign Policy Association of New York, January 17, 1948. 11 pp.
Antagonist to Clark on proposed general East-West settlement.

871 --------. *War or Peace*. New York: Macmillan, 1950. 274 pp.
Approved federation in theory; regarded it as impractical in 1950.

872 Eagleton, Clyde. "The Demand for World Government." *American Journal
of International Law*, 40 (April, 1946), pp. 390-94.

873 --------. "World Government Discussion in the United States." *London
Quarterly of World Affairs*, 12 (1946), pp. 251-58.

874 --------. "The Beam in Our Own Eye." *Harpers*, June, 1946, pp. 481-85.
By an author of the U.N. Charter who was critical later of its inadequacies and of U.S. unilateralism.

875 Eichelberger, Clark M. *The United Nations Charter and World Government*. New York: American Association for the United Nations, 1948.

7 pp.
The U.N. can become a dynamic organization if advocates of world
government would support it, not sabotage it.

[876] --------. "World Government via the United Nations." *Annals* of the
American Association of Political and Social Science (Philadelphia),
264 (July, 1949), pp. 20-25.

[877] *Einstein on Peace*.   Nathan, Otto, and Norden, Heinz, eds.   New York:
Schocken, 1960. 704 pp.
Einstein's clear and courageous views on world government.

[878] Einstein, Albert.   As told to Raymond Swing.   "Einstein on the Atomic
Bomb." *Atlantic Monthly*, November, 1945, pp. 43-45.
Proposal of tripartite agreement to establish world government.
Answered by Welles.

[879] --------. *Only Then Shall We Find Courage*.   Chicago: Emergency Committee of the Atomic Scientists, 1947. 7 pp.
Main educational product of the Emergency Committee in first year;
175,000 copies distributed.   Reprinted in Linus Pauling's *No More
War!*

[880] --------. "The Military Mentality." *The American Scholar*, Summer,
1947, pp. 353-54.
Answer to Louis N. Ridenour's quietist article in the Spring issue.

[881] --------. "To the General Assembly of the United Nations." *United Nations World*, October, 1947, pp. 13-14.
Only world government proposal to elicit a considered response from
Russia.   See "Open Letter to Dr.   Einstein from Four Soviet Scientists." *Bulletin of the Atomic Scientists*, 4 (February, 1948), pp.
34, 37-38.

[882] --------. *Out of My Later Years*.   New York: Philosophical Library,
1950. 282 pp.
Several chapters deal with world federation.

[883] Eisenhower, Dwight D. *Crusade in Europe*.   Garden City, N.Y.: Doubleday, 1948. 559 pp.
Plain remarks on "limited, federated world government," p. 459 et
seq.

[884] Evatt, Herbert V. "United Nations Organization vs. World Government."
Free World, 2 (January, 1946), pp. 27-29.
The leader of the small nations against the veto at San Francisco
argued that world federation is not feasible because nations are un-
willing to surrender their right to self-government.   Talk now of
world federation diverts attention from the only available world
organization, the U.N.

[885] Farmer, Fyke. "The World Constitution." *Tennessee Law Review*, 20
(June, 1949), pp. 790-93.
Review of "Preliminary Draft of a World Constitution." Cf. Culbert-
son.

[886] --------. *Plan for the Representation of the people of the United
States in World Constitutional Assembly at Geneva, 1950*. Nashville:

By the author, 1949. 13 pp.
Peoples' convention. Farmer and two others were actually elected by
Tennessee.

887   Farrar, Shelton. *A World without War -- It Can Be Done*. New York: Kane,
1951. 98

888   Finer, Herman. *America's Destiny*. New York: Macmillan, 1947. 407 pp.
World government cannot be attained peacefully.

889   Finletter, Thomas K. "Timetable for World Government." *Atlantic Month-*
ly, March, 1946, pp. 43-60.
By brains of Americans United for World Government.   No gradual way
to world government.

890   --------. "Air Power and World Peace." *Atlantic*, April, 1948, pp. 25-
28.
Air power only an interim method.   By Truman's Secretary of the Air
Force (1949).

891   Fischer, Louis.   "Peaceable Answer to the Russian Challenge: Broadest
Possible World Government,   Fullest Possible World Democracy." *Com-*
mentary, July, 1946, pp. 20-32.
By former Slavophile and future biographer of Gandhi.

892   *Foundations for World Order*. Denver: University of Denver Press, 1949.
174 pp.
Contains thoughtful essays on the historical foundations (E.L. Woodward), scientific foundations (J. Robert Oppenheimer), moral foundations (E.H. Carr), constitutional foundations (Robert M. Hutchins),
and others.

893   French, Raleigh L. *Plans for a World Republic*.   Boston: Christopher,
1947. 116 pp.
Christian speculation.

894   Friedrich, Carl J. *Inevitable Peace*.   Cambridge: Harvard University
Press, 1948. 294 pp.
Kant's argument shows that world government is inevitable.

895   Garrett, Ray, Jr. "A World Constitution: Analysis of the Draft by the
Hutchins Committee." *American Bar Association Journal*,   34 (July,
1948), pp. 563-66, 640.
"Members of this Committee have worked on the assumption that the
people of the world will not let a world government do anything less
than all of what it should do."

896   Gideonse, Harry D., et al. *The Politics of Atomic Energy*.   New York:
Woodrow Wilson Foundation, March, 1946. 56 pp.
Includes Frederick L. Schuman, "Toward the World State."

897   Goldwin, Robert A., ed. *Readings in World Politics*. Chicago: American Foundation for Political Education, 1951. 3 vols.
Fundamental reading materials for a discussion program in world politics.   Sections on state and individual,   democracy, communism,
causes of war, balance of power, power politics, domination or empire, international law, and world government. Readings under the
last category include selections from Lord Lothian, Robert M. Hutch-

ins, Nathan Pelcovitz, and Grenville Clark.

[898] Grifalconi, John, and Weik, Mary H., ed. *A U.N. Charter for Man? A Collection in Digest Form of Programs Developed throughout the World to Meet the Need for United Nations Reform.* Cincinnati: American Registry of World Citizens, 1954; revised ed., 1961. 40 pp.
Twelve plans for U.N. reform, plus official disarmament plan.

[899] Guérard, Albert. "World Comes of Age." *Nation*, April 29, 1946, pp. 457-59.
Answer to Neibuhr.

[900] Guetzkow, Harold S. *Multiple Loyalties: Theoretical Approach to a Problem in International Organization.* Princeton: Publication of Center for Research on World Political Institutions, Woodrow Wilson School of Public and International Affairs, No. 4, 1955. 62 pp.

[901] Hall, Arnold H. *The Science of World Government and a Charter.* Boston: Plimpton, 2nd ed., 1944. 16 pp.

[902] Hammarskjöld, Dag. "The Value of Knowledge: Finding a Middle Road between Disorganization and World Government." *Vital Speeches* (New York), 21 (November 15, 1954), pp. 838-40.

[903] Harley, John Eugene. *Woodrow Wilson Still Lives: His World Ideals Triumphant.* Los Angeles: Center for International Understanding, 1944. 193 pp.

[904] Hart, Hornell. *Can World Government Be Predicted by Mathematics?* Durham, N.C.: Duke University Press, 1944. 16 pp.

[905] --------, et al, eds. *Toward a Consensus for World Law and Order.* Durham, N.C.: Duke University Press, November, 1949.
Survey of various proposed alternatives for U.S. foreign policy: United Nations, Streit's Atlantic Union, Culberson plan, United World Federalists' plan, Chicago constitution, peoples' convention in Geneva in 1950, American world empire, preventive war, Wallace's policy, Quaker proposals, pacifism.

[906] Hennessy, Bernard.   "A Case Study of Intra-Pressure Group Conflicts: The United World Federalists." *Journal of Politics*, 16 (1954), pp. 76-95.
Arrest and decline of the group in the 1950s was partly due to internal difficulties.

[907] Hersey, John. *Hiroshima.* New York: Knopf, 1946. 118 pp.
Timely account of effect of bomb on six innocent people. Warning of nuclear war.

[908] Hessler, William H. "World Government: Minimal, Medial, Maximal." *The Reporter*, 3 (November 21, 1950), p. 17.

[909] Hile, George D. *Outlawing War: Supposititious Speech of B. Franklin.* Cleveland: By the author, 1937. 47 pp.
Draft maximal world constitution, emphasizing economic problems (depth of Depression), in response to disappointing Washington Naval Conference of 1924. No long lost work of Benjamin Franklin on world government.

[910] Hobbs, C. "A Federal World Government." *Christian Science Monitor*, April 22, 1947, ed. page.

[911] --------. "Revision of the U.N. Charter." Ibid., November 28, 1953, ed. page.

[912] Hogan, Willard N. *A Study of the Proposals for Supra-National Government*. Unpublished staff study. Washington: Brookings Institution, November, 1953.

[913] Holcombe, Arthur N. *Our More Perfect Union*. Cambridge: Harvard University Press, 1950. 460 pp.
       Exceptional political scientist who supported world federation.

[914] Holliday, W. T. "Our Final Choice." *Reader's Digest*, January, 1948, pp. 1-6.
       Lead article -- said to have reached more people about world government than any other.

[915] --------. *Our Number One Job*: *World Peace*. Cleveland, Ohio: Publications Office, Standand Oil Co. of Ohio, 1948. 27 pp.
       Fuller pamphlet excerpted in *Reader's Digest*. Holliday, as president of Standard Oil, had the honor of being the highest ranking capitalist in the world government movement.

[916] --------. "World Law or World Anarchy." *American Bar Association Journal*, 35 (August, 1949), pp. 641-44, 711-12.
       The editor in the same issue was more skeptical.

[917] Holm, James Noble, and Kent, Robert L. *How to Debate Successfully, Illustrated by Federal World Government*. Portland, Me.: J.M. Walch, 1947. 146 pp.
       College debate topic, 1947-1948.

[918] Holman, Frank E. "World Government No Answer to America's Desire for Peace." *American Bar Association Journal*, 32 (October, 1946), pp. 642-44.

[919] Holt, George C. "The Conference on World Government." *Journal of Higher Education*, 17 (May, 1946), pp. 227-35.
       Brief report on Rollins College Conference of March, 1946.

[920] Holt, Hamilton, and Holt, George C., eds. "World Government: A Symposium." *World Affairs*, 109 (June, 1946), pp. 83-122.
       Contains "Appeal to the Peoples of the World" and full report of Rollins College Conference on World Government.

[921] Hughan, Jessie W. *New Leagues for Old*: *Blueprints or Foundations*? New York: Plowshare Press, n.d., ca. 1945. 32 pp.
       By author of *A Study of International Government* (New York: Crowell, 1923).

[922] Hughes, H. Stuart. *An Essay for Our Times*. New York: Knopf, 1949. 196 pp.
       Investigation of philosophical crisis of Western civilization, in which struggle between Russia and America is only one aspect.

[923] Hutchins,   Robert M.   "The Constitutional Foundations of World Order."
      Common Cause, 1 (December, 1947), pp. 201-08.
      Bold statement   marking failure of   national leadership to   take the
      initiative for necessary world federation.

[924] --------. *St. Thomas and the World State*.   Milwaukee: Marquette Uni-
      versity Press, 1949. 53 pp.
      Lecture before Aristotelian Society. "What is indicated, therefore,
      is a clear call for world government on the part of the Church."

[925] Hutchinson, Paul. "World Government -- Or Else!" Six editorials. *Chris-
      tian Century*, January-May, 1948, passim.
      World government as a "moral cause" to bring forth all the powers of
      organized religion. One of the most vigorous expressions of support
      from the churches.

[926] Huxley, Aldous. "Bridges to One World." *Tomorrow*, November, 1947, pp.
      12-15.

[927] Huxley, Thomas H., and Huxley, Julian. *Touchstone for Ethics*. New York:
      Harper & Bros., 1947. 257 pp.
      Argues from biological point of view for world unity.

[928] Javits, Benjamin. *Peace by Investment*.   New York: Funk and Wagnalls,
      1950. 242 pp.
      A $2 trillion, 50-year aid program to "buy the peace by investing in
      people."

[929] Jessup, John K. "World Government." *Life*, June 21, 1948, pp. 49-56.
      Excellent photo spread on the movement -- primarily United World
      Federalists and the Chicago Committee to Frame a World Constitution.

[930] Jessup, Philip C.   *The International Problem of Governing Mankind*.
      Claremont, Calif.:   Claremont College, 1947. 63 pp.
      "The danger of war is so terrible and so acute in this atom-split-
      ting age that we are forced to take the risk of too much rather than
      too little international control of sovereignty. . . .   The idea of
      international solidarity and of a world community is growing. I see
      no evidence that it has yet grown to the point which would make pos-
      sible the adoption and operation of a world constitution which . . .
      is the final and not the preliminary stage in the development of a
      political community."

[931] Johnsen, Julia E., comp. *United Nations or World Government*. New York:
      H.W. Wilson, The Reference Shelf, Vol. 19, No. 5, 1947. 285 pp.

[932] --------. *Federal World Government*. New York: H.W. Wilson, The Refer-
      ence Shelf, Vol. 20, No. 5, 1948. 280 pp.
      Austin, Lie, Eichelberger replaced Reves, Cousins, Holliday in the
      1947 volume.

[933] Junior Chamber of Commerce. "World Government." *Future*, August, 1948.
      Whole issue.

[934] Kahler, Erich. "The Reality of Utopia." *American Scholar*, 15 (Spring,
      1946), pp. 167-79
      The utopians are those who believe peace can be based on strength,
      not law. By a member of the Chicago Committee.

[935] Kamp, Joseph P. *We Must Abolish the United States*.   New York: Consti-
       tutional Education League, 1950. 168 pp.
       Not for sincere and responsible opponents of world federation.

[936] Koestler, Arthur. *Insight and Outlook*:   *An Inquiry into the Common
       Foundations of Science, Art, and Social Ethics*. New York: Macmil-
       lan, 1949. 434 pp.
       The drive for social self-transcendence may yet overcome mankind's
       egoism and bring about a world of peace under federal world govern-
       ment.

[937] Kohn, Hans. *The World Must Federate! Isolation vs. Cooperation*.   New
       York: Press of the Woolly Whale, 1940. 30 pp.

[938] --------. *The Idea of Nationalism*:   *A Study of Its Origin and Back-
       ground*. New York: Macmillan, 1951.

[939] Kornhauser, Samuel J. "World Government under Law." *American Bar Asso-
       ciation Journal*, 33 (June, 1947), pp. 563-66, 636-41.
       William L. Ransom, ed.: ". . . the issues are too great and too im-
       portant for any American lawyer to exclude from his reading and his
       thinking." Cf. Ranney in same issue.

[940] Kirchway, Freda.   "One World or None." *Nation*, August 18, 1945, pp.
       149-50.

[941] Knudson, Albert C. *The Philosophy of War and Peace*. New York: Abing-
       don-Cokesbury, 1947. 22 pp
       By Boston University dean of theology.   World federation necessary
       for peace.

[942] Kreps, Theodore J. "Toward a World Economy." *Annals*, American Academy
       of Political and Social Science, 257 (May, 1948), pp. 157-74.
       World economics.

[943] Laski, Harold. "The Crisis in Our Civilization." *Foreign Affairs*, 26
       (October, 1947), pp. 36-51.
       World government must be based on peoples, not nation states.   In
       same issue with Stimson's article.

[944] Lent, Ernest S.   *The Basic Mistake of the United World Federalists*.
       East Patterson, N.J.: By the author, 1952. 44 pp.

[945] --------. "The Development of United World Federalist Thought and Pol-
       icy." *International Organization*, 9 (1955), pp. 486-501.
       Review of organization, leaders, strategy, ideas, and programs.

[946] Levi, Werner. *Fundamentals of World Organization*. Minneapolis: Uni-
       versity of Minnesota Press, 1950. 232 pp.
       Investigation of "human foundations" of international organization.

[947] Lewis, E.R. "Are We Ready for a World State?" *Yale Review*, 35 (1946),
       pp. 491-501.

[948] Lilienthal, Alfred M. *Which Way to World Government?* New York: For-
       eign Policy Association, Headline Series, No. 83, 1950. 62 pp.
       Guide to world government organizations, chiefly in U.S.

[949] Lindsey, R.H. "Europe and the World Citizenship Movement." *American Perspective*, 4 (Spring, 1950), pp. 215-22.
Significance of the Garry Davis phenomenon.

[950] Lindstrom, Ralph G. "The World Federalist and Three Laws of Peace." *Los Angeles Bar Bulletin*, 24 (August, 1949), p. 362.
By leader of United World Federalists in Southern California.

[951] Linowitz, S. "Is World Government Feasible?" *American Bar Association Journal*, 36 (July, 1950), pp. 531-32.
Reply to W. T. Holliday.

[952] Lippmann, Walter. *The Cold War*. New York: Harper & Bros., 1947.   62 pp.

[953] --------. "The Rivalry of Nations." *Atlantic*, February, 1948, pp. 17-20.
Notes cycle in American history: isolationism,   belated and unprepared intervention, crusading spirit, faith in a supranational order and eternal peace,   disappointment,   isolationism again,   and so on. Concludes that, for an effective foreign policy, Americans should accept conflict between states as normal and should abandon distrust of power politics, diplomacy, and spheres of interest.

[954] Lloyd, William Bross, Jr. *Constitutional Action for Peace*.   Hinsdale, Ill.: Henry Regnery, 1947. 25 pp.
Outlined need for Constitutional convention and described Wisconsin campaign of 1946, much in advance of United World Federalists' California campaign.

[955] --------.   "The United Nations and World Federalism." *Antioch Review*, 9 (March, 1949), pp. 16-28.
By leader of Campaign for World Government.

[956] --------. *Town Meeting for America*: *How Citizens Can Set the Course for United States - World Relations*.   New York: Island Press Cooperative, 1951. 84 pp.
Lloyd's summation of his Campaign for World Government convictions.

[957] Logue, John. "Ambassador Kennan and Professor Mitrany." *World Frontiers*, 2 (Winter, 1952-53), pp. 27-32.
Kennan's national interest is just "selfishness made respectable"; Mitrany's functionalism is just the old diplomacy dressed up as a gradual approach to world government.   Until the public is educated to see the necessity for world government, they will never support world statesmanship nor delegate effective powers to a world organization.

[958] Lukens, E.C.   "United Nations and World Government." *Pennsylvania Bar Association Quarterly*, 18 (January, 1947), pp. 129-37.

[959] McClintock, R.M.   "The United Nations or World Government." American Academy of Political and Social Science *Annals*, 262 (July, 1949), pp. 26-30.

[960] McDougal, Myres S., and Leighton, Gertrude C. K. "The Rights of Man in the World Community: Constitutional Illusions versus Rational Ac-

tion." *Law and Contemporary Problems*, 14 (Summer, 1949), pp. 490-536.
Symposium on International Human Rights, Duke University Law School.
Position of U.N. Human Rights Commission.

[961] MacIver, R. M. *The Web of Government*. New York: Macmillan, 1947. 498 pp.
"A profound study of the growth of government. . . ."

[962] McKeon, Richard P. "Economic, Political and Moral Communities in the World Society." *Ethics*, 57 (January, 1947), pp. 79-91.
Another answer to Niebuhr by member of Chicago Committee.

[963] MacLeish, Archibald. "The People's Peace." *Atlantic Monthly*, July, 1947, pp. 54-58.
Not law, but encouragement of international understanding toward a world community, must lay the groundwork of peace.

[964] Macmahon, Arthur W., ed. *Federalism*: *Mature and Emergent*. Garden City, N.Y.: Doubleday, 1955. 557 pp.
Scholarly compendium under auspices of College of Europe.

[965] Mangone, Gerard J. *The Idea and Practice of World Government*. New York: Columbia University Press, 1951. 278 pp.
Theoretical. Not confined to postwar years.

[966] Manion, Clarence. *The Key to Peace*. Chicago: Heritage Foundation, 1950.
"Principles of Americanism opposed to world government."

[967] Masters, Dexter, and Way, Katharine, eds. *One World or None*. Foreword by Niels Bohr, Introduction by A.H. Compton. New York: McGraw Hill, 1946. 79 pp.
Contributors: Einstein, Philip Morrison, Harlow Shapley, J. Robert Oppenheimer, Walter Lippman, etc. Timely, major statement by the Federation of American Scientists.

[968] Mebane, Alexander D. *Wither Must I Fly? A Key to Current Plans for a Warless World Order*. New York: Mimeographed, 1949. 40 pp.
Mebane was an organic chemist, who wrote this report for the Association of New York Scientists, World Government Study Group.

[969] Metz, H. "World Government Movement held 'Weakening' to U.N." *Christian Science Monitor*, February 27, 1950, p. 4.

[970] Meyer, Cord, Jr. "A Serviceman Looks at the Peace." *Atlantic*, September, 1945, pp. 43-48.
The United Nations is all we have won from the war.

[971] --------. *Peace or Anarchy*. Boston: Little, Brown, 1947. 233 pp.
Strong argument from atomic fear by the first President of United World Federalists.

[972] --------. "We Must Have World Government Now." *Scholastic*, 53 (October 20, 1948), pp. 10-11.

[973] --------. "A Plea for World Government." *Annals* of the American Academy of Political and Social Science, 264 (July, 1949), pp. 6-13.

[974] --------, and Brinton, Crane. *World Government -- Necessity or Utopia?* Toronto: Canadian Association for Adult Education, 1949. 16 pp.

[975] --------_, and Hamilton, T.J.   "World Government and U.N.: A Debate." *New York Times Magazine*, February 26, 1950, pp. 11, 16, 18.

[976] --------. "Danger and Opportunity." *The Progressive*, 14 (August, 1950), p. 8.

[977] Miller, F.M. "Can the Rule of Justice under Law Be Substituted for That of Force in the International Field?" *Iowa Law Review*, 31 (May, 1946), pp. 561-73.

[978] Mitrany, David. *A Working Peace System: An Argument for the Functional Development of International Organization*. London: Royal Institute of International Affairs, 1943. 56 pp.
Original publication of the theory of functionalism.

[979] --------. "The Functional Approach to World Organization." *International Affairs*, 24 (July, 1948), pp. 350-63.
Practical critique of federalism.

[980] Morgenthau, Hans J. *Politics among Nations: The Struggle for Power and Peace*. New York: Knopf, 1948; many eds. 489 pp.
"Our analysis of the problem of domestic peace has shown that the argument of the advocates of the world state is unanswerable: There can be no permanent international peace without a state coextensive with the confines of the political world."

[981] --------. "The Problem of Sovereignty Reconsidered." *Columbia Law Review*, 48 (April, 1948), pp. 341-65.

[982] --------. "The Twilight of International Morality." *Ethics*, 57 (January, 1948), pp. 79-99.
Loyalty to supranational ethics in conflict with national moral demands is less possible now than in early 19th century.

[983] Mount Holyoke College. Institute on the United Nations. *How Can We the People Achieve a Just Peace?* South Hadley, Mass.: Mount Holyoke College, 1949. 251 pp.

[984] Mowrer, Edgar Ansel. *The Nightmare of American Foreign Policy*. New York: Knopf, 1948. 283 pp.
Present policy inadequate to ensure peace. By leading political commentator.

[985] --------. *Challenge and Decision*. New York: McGraw-Hill, 1950. 291 pp.
Anti-Communist minimalist proposal.

[986] Mumford, Lewis. "Atom Bomb: 'Miracle' or Catastrophe?" *Air Affairs*, July, 1948, pp. 326-45.
Proposal of one-year armistice leading to transformation of the U.N. into a world government. U.S. should reverse its "negative and arbitrary" policy to take lead.

[987] --------. *Atomic War -- The Way Out*. London: National Peace Council,

Peace Aims Pamphlet No. 46, 1948. 19 pp.
"If today we had political leadership in Washington, capable of moving along the lines that Grenville Clark, Albert Einstein, G.A. Borgese, Arnold Toynbee and men of similar stature in the same camp have indicated, would Russia be able to withhold cooperation?"

[988] --------. *In the Name of Sanity*. New York: Harcourt, Brace, 1954. 244 pp.
"The aim of this book is to give fresh insight -- and with that insight hope and courage -- to those who are disquieted by the violence and irrationality of our times."

[989] Muste, A. J. *Not by Might*. New York: Harper & Bros., 1947. 227 pp.
Pacifist policy convincingly argued.

[990] Nash, Vernon. *It Must Be Done Again*. New York: Federal Union, 1940. 48 pp.
Based on John Fiske's *Critical Period of American History*.

[991] --------. *Yes, But --: Questions and Answers about a Federal World Government*. New York: World Federalists, U.S.A., 1946. 34 pp.
Reprinted many times.

[993] --------. *The World Must Be Governed*. New York: Harper & Bros., 1949. 206 pp.
By the popular United World Federalists speaker.

[994] Nathan, Otto, and Norden, Heinz, eds. *Einstein on Peace*. New York: Schocken, 1960. 704 pp.
Einstein's clear views.

[995] Neumann, R.G. "World Federation: An Illusion." *American Perspective*, 3 (October, 1949), pp. 265-71.
Federation not now feasible; other steps proposed.

[996] Niebuhr, Reinhold. *The Children of Light and the Children of Darkness*. New York: Scribners, 1944; reprint ed., 1972. 190 pp.
Classic on realism-idealism dichotomy.

[997] --------. "The Myth of World Government." *Nation*, March 16, 1946, pp. 312-14.
Article in which Niebuhr explained his leaving the Chicago Committee to Frame a World Constitution. World community must precede world law. Law has little role to create community.

[998] --------. "They All Fear America." *Christian Century*, (August 20, 1947), pp. 993-94.
In a world war, America would stand alone.

[999] --------. "The Illusion of World Government." *Foreign Affairs*, 27 (April, 1949), pp. 379-88.
World is not yet enough of a community to support a government.

[1000] Northrop, F.S.C. *The Meeting of East and West: An Inquiry Concerning Human Understanding*. New York: Macmillan, 1946. 531 pp.
By professor of philosophy at Yale. A "great, difficult, and important book."

1001 --------, ed. *Ideological Differences and World Order*: *Studies in the Philosophy and Science of the World's Cultures*. New Haven: Yale University Press, 1949. 486 pp.
Includes Roscoe Pound, "Toward a New *Jus Gentium*."

1002 --------.   *The Taming of the Nations*:   *A Study in the Cultural Bases of International Policy*. New York: Macmillan, 1952. 362 pp.

1003 Oliver, L. Stauffer. "World Government Inevitable." *Temple Law Quarterly*, 24 (July, 1950), pp. 7-26.
By Philadelphia judge.

1004 Olson, Martin O. *World Peace Ideology*: *A Detailed Program for a Compulsory World Government*. New York: William-Frederick Press, 1951. 27 pp.

1005 Orwell, George. *1984*. New York: Harcourt, Brace, 1949. 314 pp.
Not really an anti-world government book, but rather one that draws out the implications of a world divided into West, East, and Third.

1006 Osborn, Fairfield. *Our Plundered Planet*. Boston: Little, Brown, 1948. 217 pp.
Early environmentalism.

1007 Page, Kirby. *Now Is the Time to Prevent a Third World War*. La Habra, Calif.: By the author, 1946. 123 pp.

1008 Parker, John J.   *The American Constitution and World Order Based on Law*.   New York: Association of the Bar of the City of New York, 1953.   25 pp.
Benjamin N. Cardozo lecture. By Chief Judge, U.S. Court of Appeals, Fourth District.   Support for United Nations as step toward world federal government.

1009 Parmelee, Maurice. *Geo-Economic Regionalism and World Federation*. New York: Exposition Press, 1949. 137 pp.
Proposed regional federations, as did the Committee to Frame a World Constitution, but on a quite different delineation.

1010 Peaslee, Amos J. *United Nations Government*. New York: Justice House, 1945.   183 pp.
Wartime speeches on problems of world government.

1011 --------.   *Constitutions of Nations*.   Concord, N.H.:   Rumford, 1950; 2nd ed., 1956; 3rd. 1968. 3 vols.
Texts of eighty-six national constitutions; reference for world constitutions.   The constitutions of France (1946),   Italy (1947), West Germany (1949), and the Netherlands (1952) all contained language permitting limitations of sovereignt for participation in a regional or world government. Cf.   Blaustein and Flanz (1979), in next section.

1012 Peck, George T. "Drafting a World Constitution." *New York Herald Tribune*, Forum section (X), November 3, 1946, p. 32.

1013 Pei, Mario Andrew. *The American Road to Peace*: *A Constitution for the World*. New York: S.F. Vanni, 1945. 168 pp.

[1014] Pelcovits, N.A. "World Government Now?" *Harpers*, November, 1946, pp. 396-403.
U.S. State Department view just before announcement of containment policy.

[1015] Perry, Ralph Barton. *One World in the Making*. New York: Current Books, 1945. 275 pp.
Lectures before the Lowell Institute.

[1016] Posen, Daniel Q.   *I Have Been to the Village*.   Ann Arbor, Mich.: Edwards Bros., 1948. 151 pp.
North Dakota physicist's odyssey in behalf of international control of atomic energy and world government.

[1017] Pratt, Eliot.   "World Federalists." *United Nations World*, September, 1948, pp. 36-38.

[1018] "Preview of the War We Did Not Want." *Colliers*,   October 27, 1951. Whole issue.
Warning to Kremlin that its effort to enslave mankind is leading directly to World War III, in which U.S. will occupy U.S.S.R. under aegis of U.N.

[1019] Progressive Party. *A Fact Book for Wallace-Taylor Workers*. New York: n.d., post July 25, 1948. 49 pp.
Sections on Cold War and world government.

[1020] Pyzel, Robert.   *The Task That Lies Before Us*: *A Counter-Proposal for the Charter of the United Nations*. New York: J.M. Barrett, 1946. 68 pp.

[1021] Quarles, James.   "E Pluribus Unum: 1946 Model." *World Affairs*, 109 (September, 1946), pp. 181-85.
Deplorable lack of realism in minds of world government advocates.

[1022] Rabinowitch, Eugene.   "Scientists and World Government." *Bulletin of the Atomic Scientists*, 2 (December, 1947), pp. 345-46.
Regret that atomic scientists did not press earlier for world government.

[1023] Ranney, John C. "The Bases of American Federalism." *William and Mary Quarterly*, 3 (Third Series, 1946), pp. 1-35.
Articles of Confederation were an important step to U.S. federal union; U.N. is a similar step, which cannot be hurried, to world union.

[1024] --------.   "World Federalism." *American Bar Association Journal*, 33 (June, 1947), pp. 567-70, 641-42.
U.S. federal analogy is misapplied.

[1025] Reno, Robert H., ed.   *A Digest of Peace through Disarmament and Charter Revision by Grenville Clark and Louis B. Sohn*.   Concord, N.H.: By the author, 1953. 83 pp.

[1026] Reves, Emery. *A Democratic Manifesto*. New York: Random House, 1942. 144 pp.
Precursor to *Anatomy of Peace*.

1027 --------. *The Anatomy of Peace*. New York: Harper & Bros., 1945. 275 pp.
Powerful argument against national sovereignty.   There is no freedom without law, no national independence without world law. Probably the most popular book on world government.

1028 --------.   "The Anatomy of Peace." *Reader's Digest*, December, 1945, pp. 123-35; January, 1946, pp. 145-60.

1029 --------. "World Government *Is* the First Step." *Reader's Digest*, February, 1946, pp. 109-17.

1030 --------. "World Government vs. United Nations." *Free World*, 11 and 12 (June, July, August, 1946), pp. 21 ff.
A Round Table discussion.   For world government as the only means adequate to establish permanent peace: Reves and Merle Miller; for the U.N., if constantly strengthened: Max Ascoli, Max Lerner, and Michael Straight.

1031 Rich, S. Grover. *The Movement for World Government*.   Salt Lake City: University of Utah, Institute of Government, April, 1951. 18 pp.
Suscinct survey of arguments.   Since technically one world is coming, we must work for political union but start with current realities of nations.

1032 Richards, I. A. *Nations and Peace*. New York: Simon & Schuster, 1947. 159 pp.
Written in Basic English (vocabulary of 850 words) and cleverly illustrated.

1033 Rider, Fremont.   *The Great Dilemma of World Organization*.   New York: Reynal & Hitchcock, 1946. 85 pp.
On problem of representation.

1034 Robinson, Donald Fay. *A People's World*: *A Plan for World Government*. Cooperstown, N.Y.: Freeman's Journal, 1944. 31 pp.

1035 Rollins College Institute on World Government.   *An Appeal to the Peoples of the World*. Winter Park, Fla.: Rollins College, July, 1946. 6 pp.

1036 Roper, Elmo. "American Attitudes on World Organization." *Public Opinion Quarterly*, 17 (Winter, 1953-54), pp. 405-42.

1037 Rougement, Denis de. *The Last Trump*. New York: Doubleday, 1947. 151 pp.
Wry irony on the hates and passions against world government.

1038 Rudd, Herbert Finley. *Uniting the Nations*: *A Method of Balanced Representation*.   Durham, N.H.: University of New Hampshire Extension Service, 1944. 23 pp.
Colleague of Grenville Clark.   Influential on Clark's scheme of weighted representation.

1039 Rusk, Dean.   *Universal, Regional, and Bilateral Patterns of International Organization*. Washington: Department of State Publication 3828, 1950.
Statement before Senate Foreign Relations Committee, February 15,

1950.

1040 Schiffer, Walter. *The Legal Community of Mankind*: *A Critical Analy-*
      sis of the Modern Concept of World Organization.   New York: Colum-
      bia University Press, 1954; 2nd ed., Greenwood, 1972. 367 pp.

1041 Schilpp, Paul A.   "Millions Now Living Will Die -- Unless." *Motive*,
      March, 1948, pp. 5-7.

1042 Schorr, Daniel L.   "Federalists of 22 Nations Urge World Government."
      Christian Science Monitor, September 25, 1948, p. 2.

1043 Schuman, Frederick L.   "The Dilemma of the Peace Seekers." *American*
      Political Science Review, 39 (February, 1945), pp. 12-30.
      Choice between world imperium and world government.

1044 --------.   "Towards the World State." *Scientific Monthly*, 63 (July,
      1946), p. 10.

1045 --------. *The Commonwealth of Man*: *An Inquiry into Power Politics and*
      World Government. New York: Knopf, 1952. 494 pp.
      One of the last Foundation for World Government products. Cf. books
      by Barr, Buchanan, and Wofford.

1046 Schwimmer, Rosika, and Lloyd, Lola Maverick.   *Chaos*, *War*, *or a New*
      World Order: *What We Must Do to Establish the All-Inclusive*, *Non-*
      Military, *Democratic Federation of Nations*.   Chicago: By the au-
      thors, 1924; enlarged ed., 1942. 8 pp.
      Draft world constitution (no police forces),   to be written in a
      peoples' convention if national governments fail to act. Pacifist.

1047 Sellin, Thorsten, ed.   "World Government." *Annals*, American Academy
      of Political and Social Science, 264 (July, 1949).   200 pp.
      Symposium, with contributions by Cord Meyer and leading scholars.

1048 Shotwell, James T.   "The United Nations: Strengthening World Govern-
      ment."

1049 "Should the United States Support a Federal Union of All Nations?"
      Congressional Digest, 31 (August-September, 1952), pp. 193-224.
      Also on continued support for the United Nations and on Atlantic
      Union.

1050 Shub, Anatole, ed. *The New Leader*: *Alternatives to the H-Bomb*. Bos-
      ton: Beacon, 1955. 124 pp.
      Symposium organized by *New Leader* magazine.   Contributors: Lewis
      Mumford, Chester Bowles, Norman Thomas, Hans Kohn, Salvador de
      Madariaga, P. Rieff, Michael Karpovich, Eugene Rabinowitch, W.A.
      Harriman.

1051 Skewes-Cox, Bennet.   *The United Nations from League to Government*:
      Problems of Amending the Charter into a World Federal Constitution.
      Enid, Okla.: Phillips Science Press, 1965. 189 pp.
      Reprint, with new prologue and epilogue, of 1947 study. Anticipates
      Clark and Sohn's plan, but concludes Charter reform is impractical.
      Author later was active in California for passage of state resolu-
      tion calling for U.S. Constitutional amendment convention to enable
      U.S. participation in a world government.

[1052] Smith, R. H.   "One World or None: The Need for World Law." *American Bar Association Journal*, 32 (May, 1946), pp. 292-94.
Atomic scientists' influence.

[1053] Social Science Foundation of the University of Denver. *Foundations for World Order*.   Denver: University of Denver Press, 1949.   174 pp.
Contains Hutchins' "Constitutional Foundations of World Order."

[1054] Sohn, Louis B., ed.   *Cases and Other Materials on World Law*.   Brooklyn: Foundation Press, 1950. 1363 pp.
Materials, mostly from the early United Nations' era and the most vigorous period of the world government movement, used in Sohn's course on world organization taught at Harvard Law since 1946.

[1055] --------. *Studies in Federalism [and] Foreign Affairs*.   Harvard University, School of Law, 1952. 57 pp.

[1056] --------.   "Revision of the Charter of the United Nations." *Proceedings*, American Society of International Law, 48 (1954), pp. 202-05.

[1057] --------.   "United Nations Charter Review." *Proceedings*, American Bar Association, Section on International and Comparative Law, Chicago, August 23, 1955, pp. 26-28.   1955.

[1058] --------.   "United Nations Charter Revision and the Rule of Law: A Program for Peace." *Northwestern University Law Review*, 50 (January-February, 1956), pp. 709-25.

[1059] --------, ed. *Cases on United Nations Law*. Brooklyn: Foundation Press, 1956; 2nd ed., 1967. 1086 pp.
Complements his earlier volume on world law.

[1060] Sorokin, Pitirim A. *The Reconstruction of Humanity*.   Boston: Beacon, 1948.   247 pp.
Human nature to be made altruistic; world government a "quack cure for war."

[1061] Sprading, Charles T.   *The World State Craze*.   Los Angeles: Wetzel, 1954.   109 pp.
Cf. Kamp.

[1062] Stevenson, Adlai. *Call to Greatness*. New York: 1954.   110 pp.

[1063] Stimson, Henry L. "The Challenge to Americans." *Foreign Affairs*, 26 (October, 1947), pp. 5-14.
"Lasting peace and freedom cannot be achieved until the world finds a way to the necessary government of the whole." Corrective to Kennan's "X" article.

[1064] Stowe, Leland. *While Time Remains*. New York: Knopf, 1946.   379 pp.
Part V: "The Road to World Citizenship."

[1065] --------. *Target: You*. New York: Knopf, 1949.   288 pp.
Last chapter: "The Other Defense: World Government through World Law."

[1066] Streit, Clarence. *World Government or Anarchy? Our Urgent Need for World Order*. Chicago: World Citizens Association, 1939. 57 pp. Chapters 2 and 3 of *Union Now*.

[1067] Swing, Raymond Gram. *In the Name of Sanity*. New York: Harper, 1946. 116 pp.
Contains his 1945-46 radio broadcasts on the implications of atomic energy for world government.

[1068] "Symposium on World Organization." *Yale Law Journal*, 55 (August, 1946), whole issue.
". . . To attempt to establish world government before the conditions necessary to its success exist may well . . . hasten the division of the world into two irreconcilably opposed and hostile groups." Articles by Leland Goodrich, Harold Lasswell, Hans Morgenthau, Quincy Wright, and others.

[1069] Szilard, Leo. "Calling for a Crusade." *Bulletin of the Atomic Scientists*, 3 (April-May, 1947), pp. 102-06, 125.
With apparent deadlock over Baruch Plan, Szilard and other atomic scientists now called for general world government.

[1070] Tait, Edwin Edgar. *Blueprint of a World Government, with Delegated Authority Designed to Prevent Wars, Maintain Peace among Nations, and Assure Economic Security to All People*. Pittsburgh: Smith Bros., 1945. 41 pp.

[1071] Taylor, Edmond. *Richer by Asia*. Boston: Houghton Mifflin, 1947. 431 pp.
Book which raised consciousness of American movement to importance of undeveloped world. Gandhi's relevance.

[1072] Taylor, Glen H. "Why a World Republic?" *Free World*, December, 1945, pp. 26-31.
Senator Taylor's explanation for introducing his first resolution for a world republic (October, 1945).

[1073] Thomas, Elbert D. *This Nation under God*. New York: Harper & Bros., 1950. 210 pp.
By Utah Senator who sponsored the world federalist resolution.

[1074] Thomas, Norman. *Appeal to the Nations*. New York: Henry Holt, 1947. 175 pp.
"His program differs little from that of the United States Government."

[1075] Tugwell, Rexford Guy. "Can the United Nations Become a World Government?" *Common Cause*, 2 (February, 1949), pp. 244-51.

[1076] --------. *A Chronicle of Jeopardy, 1945-1955*. Chicago: University of Chicago Press, 1955. 488 pp.
By the former New Deal administrator and member of the Committee to Frame a World Constitution. Hasty.

[1077] Ulman, Ruth. *Federal World Government*. University Debaters' Annual, 1947-1948. New York: H.W. Wilson, 1948. Vol. 35.
College debate topic, 1947-1948 academic year.

1078 United World Federalists. *One World -- or None!* New York: UWF, 1950.
41 pp.
"Peace is now a fighting word. . . . But let's be sure we're fighting for Federation!" With the Korean War, UWF began using federalist slogans as weapons of the Cold War.

1079 University of Chicago Round Table. *The Making of World Government.*
Round Table, 451 (November 10, 1946). 21 pp.
Mortimer Adler, G. A. Borgese, and Rexford G. Tugwell on the Com-
mittee to Frame a World Constitution.

1080 --------. *What Are the Steps to World Government?* Chicago: Round
Table, 499 (October 12, 1947). 25 pp.
Discussion between Henry Usborne, Louis Gottschalk, and G.A. Bor-
gese on American crusade for a peoples' convention.

1081 --------. *The Problem of World Government.* Chicago: Round Table,
524 (April 4, 1948). 29 pp.
Radio discussion between Jawaharlal Nehru, Wellington Koo, and Robert M. Hutchins on Asian views of world government.

1082 Urey, Harold C. "The Atom and Humanity." *Science,* 102 (November 2,
1945), p. 435.
"We are inevitably led to the conclusion that a superior world government of some kind possessing adequate power to maintain the
peace and with the various divisions of the world relatively disarmed, is the only way out."

1083 --------. "The Paramount Problem of 1949." *Air Affairs,* 2 (Winter,
1949), pp. 461-76.

1084 --------. "The Case for World Government." *Christian Century,* 66
(June 28, 1949), pp. 785-86.
World government is inevitable and necessary.

1085 U.S. Chamber of Commerce. Committee on International Political and
Social Problems. *The United Nations and World Government.* Washington: Chamber of Commerce, 1950. 50 pp.
A "factual and non-propaganda study," from a practical policy point
of view, with respect to the state and national legislation for
creating a world government of the time.

1086 Van Doren, Carl. *The Great Rehearsal: The Story of the Making and Ra-
tifying of the Constitution of the United States.* New York: Viking,
1948. 336 pp.
"The situation [in 1787-1789] was, in any number of respects which
can be seen at a glance, much like that of the sovereign states of
the United Nations in 1948." Cf. Nash and Jensen.

1087 --------, and Lippmann, Walter. "World Federation: Is It a Practical
Goal?" *American Scholar,* 17 (July, 1948), pp. 347-52.
Continued in October issue.

1088 Vogt, William. *Road to Survival.* New York: William Sloan, 1948. 335
pp.
Early environmentalism.

1089 Wallace, Henry A. *Toward World Peace.* New York: Reynal & Hitchcock,

1948. 121 pp.
Progressive Party campaign statement.

1090 --------. "Toward World Federation." *New Republic*, February 23, 1948,
p. 10.

1091 Warburg, James P. *Put Yourself in Marshall's Place*. New York: Simon
& Schuster, 1948. 93 pp.
Without condoning Russian actions, Warburg argued that American actions were calculated to irritate and alarm the Soviet Union.   He
urged the United States to "break the vicious circle" to initiate a
process of transforming the U.N. into a world government.

1092 --------. *Last Call for Common Sense*.   New York: Harcourt, Brace,
1949. 311 pp.

1093 --------. *Faith, Purpose and Power*: *A Plea for a Positive Policy*.
New York: Farrar, Straus, 1950. 180 pp.
Realistic proposal for a positive U.S. policy of world federation
in place of anti-Communism.   By prominent New York banker and commentator on national policy. Cf. Buchanan.

1094 Watch Tower Bible and Tract Society. *One World, One Government*. Brooklyn: International Bible Students Association, 1944. 31 pp.
Opinion of Jehovah's Witnesses.

1095 Welles, Sumner. "The Atomic Bomb and World Government." *Atlantic*,
January, 1946, pp. 39-42.
Welles' answer to Einstein's article in the November issue.   "How
can fears and suspicions be ended until the nations, and particularly the Big Three, work together within the United Nations Organization and thus little by little discover by actual proof that
there exists no valid reason for their fears and suspicions?"

1096 Wheelwright, Robert. *Cats 'n' Clover 'n' Town Meeting*.   Illustrated
by Andrew Wyeth. 1947. 15 pp.
Colloquial soliloquy on the "Younited Nashuns."

1097 White, E. B. "World Government and Peace." New York: New Yorker,
1945. 17 pp.
Pamphlet of *New Yorker* editorials, precursor to *The Wild Flag*.

1098 --------. *The Wild Flag*. Boston: Houghton Mifflin, 1946. 188 pp.
"The most appalling thing in the world that I know of is world government, except the lack of it."   A slim book written with good
humor and intelligence.

1099 White, Thomas R. "If 'Two Worlds':   What Can United Nations Do for
Majority Action?" *American Bar Association Journal*, 33 (August,
1947), pp. 756-59.
Includes reply by William L. Ransom. White was for an organization
of states-members (not representatives of peoples); Ransom, for a
U.N. without Russia (no world government).

1100 Wilkin, Robert N. "World Order: Law and Justice or Power and Force?"
American Bar Association Journal, 33 (1947), pp. 18-21.

1101 --------. "What Are We Fighting For? Judicial Order -- The Real Is-

sue." *American Bar Association Journal*, 37 (February, 1951), p. 111.
By Cincinnati judge and world federalist at time of Korean War.

1102 Wilson, Duncan, and Wilson, Elizabeth. *Federation and World Order*. Introduction by C.E.M. Joad. Toronto: Nelson, 1939. 184 pp.

1103 Winant, Clinton D. *A People's Peace*. Washington: By the author, June, 1945. 15 pp.

1104 Wofford, Harris, Jr. *It's Up to Us*: *Federal World Government in Our Time*. New York: Harcourt, Brace, 1946. 146 pp.
Story of Student Federalists by its founder.

1105 --------. "Road to the World Republic." *Common Cause*, 2 (August, 1948), pp. 23-28.
Classic argument for forming a world federalist political party.

1106 --------, and Wofford, Clare. *India Afire*. New York: John Day, 1951. 343 pp.
Gandhi's movement of nonviolence the model for the world government movement.

1107 Women's International League for Peace and Freedom. *SOS for 'One World.'* Philadelphia, WILPF, 1947. 15 pp.
By rival of DAR.

1108 "World Government." *Life*, June 21, 1948, pp. 49-56.
Photo account of movement at height.

1109 Wright, Quincy, ed. *The World Community*. Chicago: University of Chicago Press, 1948. 323 pp.
Contemporary scholarly thought on the "community" issue.

1110 Wynner, Edith, and Lloyd, Georgia, eds. *Searchlight on Peace Plans*: *Choose Your Road to World Government*. New York: E. P. Dutton, 1944; 2nd ed., 1949. 607 pp.
Handy reference work of plans to unite the nations, going back to Dante's *De Monarchia* (1310). First edition prepared in time for Dumbarton Oaks conference. Cf. Hemblen, Hirsch, Marriott, Paullin.

1111 --------. *World Federal Government in Maximum Terms*: *Proposals for United Nations Charter Reform*. Afton, N.Y.: Fedonat Press, 1954. 84 pp.
Maximal world government to be achieved, despite opposition by national governments, by a peoples' convention.

1112 Ziff, William B. *The Gentlemen Talk of Peace*. New York: Macmillan, 1944. 530 pp.

1113 --------. *Two Worlds*: *A Realistic Approach to the Problem of Keeping the Peace*. New York: Harper & Bros., 1946. 335 pp.
See last two chapters.

1114 Zoll, Allen A. *Should Americans Be Against World Government*? New York: National Council for American Education, 1950. 23 pp.

7

Universal Federation—
U.S. & Canada after 1955

After 1955, the major events for world federalists were the publication of Clark and Sohn's *World Peace through World Law* (1958), the debate about general and complete disarmament to which it contributed following Khruschev's disarmament proposal in 1959 and Eisenhower's positive response, the McCloy-Zorin agreement on the principles for the negotiation of general and complete disarmament in 1961, and the Law of the Sea conference of 1969-1982.

Writers who have discussed the issues of *World Peace through World Law* include Clark, Dugan, Gardner, Hollins, Kahn, Larsen, Lusky, McClure, Rhyne, Sohn, and the Russians Boganov and Tunkin (in Russian section).

Some account of the McCloy-Zorin agreement is found in Hollins and Price.

Works on the Law of the Sea include those by Elizabeth Mann Borgese Buzan, Laursen, Logue, and Wertenbaker.

During these difficult years, a number of new figures appeared who restated the fundamental doctrines of world federalism: Breitner, Caplow, Douglas, Glossop, Kindleberger, Stanley, Millard, Pauling, and Wagar. Perhaps the Catholic bishops belong in this group.

Continuing figures include: Andrews, Brown, Clark, Cousins, Holcombe, Hutchins, Isely, Reves, and Wynner. Works by the Canadian peace researchers, Hanna and Alan Newcombe, are also included here.

Criticism has concentrated on the fundamental preconditions necessary for the rule of world law. There has been an undertone of contempt for "utopianism" and for neglect of "reality." Federalist literature was less and less read by makers of American foreign policy. Critics include: Beitz, Bloomfield, Deutsch, Dyson, Haas, Kahn, Levi, Mangone, Meyer, Schell, Shafer, and Wright.

By 1975, the very terms "world federalism" and "world government" had dropped out of common usage. There was a new sense of public powerlessness in the air. Robert Heilbroner's book marks the mood. In stark federalist terms, the abandonment of hope in the rule of law meant the acceptance of the inevitability of war. One group, however, who were rooted in the world federalist movement but were willing to explore alternatives between these theoretical poles were the scholars centered around Saul Mendlovitz and Richard A. Falk. They developed around 1965 the new field of "world order" studies (see subsequent section).

The new themes were the steadily greater threat of nuclear war, the need for disarmament *under law*, the neglect of even the international law already existing, the decline of the communism-capitalism dispute (the real one is national vs. world sovereignty), and the strength of nationalism. By the 1980s, the federalist movement was visibly aging and in decline, while national politics remained fixed in what were originally described as temporary or expedient measures of military deterrence.

"The question is, how fast can YOU work?"
   —*copyright 1950 by Herblock in The Washington Post* on February 10, 1950
Used by permission of HERBLOCK CARTOONS.

[1124] Abbott, Lawrence. *World Federalism*: *What? Why? How?* Washington:
World Federalists Association, n.d., c. 1975. 51 pp.
Current pamphlet and guide to movement. Updates Nash, *Yes, But* --.

[1125] Alcock, Norman. "Time to Reconsider Clark and Sohn." *Peace Research*
(Dundas, Ontario), 11 (January, 1979), pp. 37-46.

[1126] --------, and Simoni, Arnold.   *Peacemakers Association of Nations*.
Huntsville, Canada: Canadian Peace Research Institute, 1983.

[1127] American Bar Association.   Section on International and Comparative
Law. *Report on the Self-Judging Aspect of the United States' Domestic Jurisdiction Reservation to Its Adherence to the Statute of
the International Court of Justice.*   Chicago, ABA, August, 1959.
108 pp.
Basic survey of the pros and cons of U.S. participation in the
World Court. Recommended repeal of the Connally amendment.

[1128] --------. Special Committee on World Peace through Law. *The Rule of
Law among Nations*:   *Digest and Proceedings of Regional Conferences
of Lawyers.* Washington: ABA, 1959. 61 pp.

[1129] --------. *World Peace through Law*: *Editorial Comment*.   Washington:
ABA, 1959. 2 vols.
Comment on Clark-Sohn plan and others.

[1130] --------. --------.   *Report on the Connally Amendment*.   Washington:
ABA, August, 1960. 40 pp.
Recommended repeal (with two dissents).

[1131] --------. Standing Committee on Peace through Law through the United
Nations. *Report on the Connally Amendment*. Washington: ABA, August, 1960. 12 pp.
Conclusion: lacking guidelines to the distinction between "domestic" and "international," the United States should not repeal. Dis-
sent by Arthur Dean.

[1132] --------. Special Committee on World Peace through Law. *The Rule of
Law in the World*. Washington: 1960. 20 pp.
Compilation of quotations.

[1133] --------. --------. *World Peace through the Rule of Law*: *Four Years
of Progress and a Program for the Future.* Washington: ABA, 1963.
31 pp.

[1134] --------. --------. *World Peace through Law*: *The Athens World Conference.* St. Paul, Minn.: West, 1964. 874 pp.
After the Clark-Sohn plan was published, a Special Committee on
World Peace through Law was formed in the American Bar Association,
under the chairmanship of Charles S. Rhyne.   Conferences were held
throughout the U.S. and then the world. The Athens conference of
1963 attracted lawyers from over 100 nations.   Work continues to
this day at the World Peace through Law Center in Washington.

[1135] Andrews, Paul Shipman. "Blueprint for a Peaceful World." *Current History*, 29 (August, 1960), pp. 75-81.

[1136] Bantell, John F. "Grenville Clark and the Founding of the United Na-

tions: The Failure of World Federalism." *Peace and Change* (Kent, Ohio), 10 (Fall-Winter, 1984), pp. 97-116.
Close study of Clark's role in period of 1939-1945. "In retrospect, Clark's attempt to guide American foreign policy toward support of 'genuine' world government may seem quixotic.   But Clark, although something of an innocent in foreign affairs, was no impractical visionary."

[1137] Baratta, Joseph P. *Grenville Clark, World Federalist*.   Amsterdam: Institute for Global Policy Studies, Occasional Paper No. 3, 1985.   47 pp.
The great world political factor in the future, Clark thought, would not be nuclear war but the dead end of deterrence policy. The fundamental alternative would be a policy of strengthening the United Nations by transforming it into a limited, federal world government, with powers to enact and enforce law. Clark maintained four principles for U.N. reform: (1) universal membership, (2) weighted representation in the world legislature, (3) powers limited to peace and security, and (4) a transition through negotiated agreement. His distinguished career is sketched in order to demonstrate his realism, timeliness, and practical wisdom.

[1138] Beitz, Charles R. *Political Theory and International Relations*. Princeton: Princeton University Press, 1979. 212 pp.
Argument that neither the Hobbesian state of nature nor the traditional alternative of the morality of states adequately describes modern international realities. Third view is that of international normative political theory, which Beitz calls "cosmopolitan."

[1139] Benoit, Emile, and Boulding, Kenneth, eds. *Disarmament and the Economy*. New York: Harper & Row, 1963. 310 pp.
Symposium on "an economic equivalent of defense." Demonstration that the economic problems of disarming are soluble.

[1140] Beres, Louis René. "Examining the Logic of World Federal Government." *Publius*, 4 (Summer, 1974), pp. 75-87.
Most federalists neglect the realities of power.   Their writing is generally superficial and "enthusiastic." "As a result, large numbers of people have been diverted from a variety of potentially more productive courses to international order."

[1141] --------. "Steps toward a New Planetary Identity." *Bulletin of the Atomic Scientists*, 37 (February, 1981), pp. 43-47.
World is moving inexorably toward nuclear war, by design or accident. Three steps are necessary to prevent nuclear destruction: (1) aroused consciousness of peril ("credible deterrence" and "peace through strength" are myths); (2) reversal of nuclear arms competition (return to minimum deterrence, arms control treaties, decreased arms spending, comprehensive test ban); (3) implementation of promising plans for world order reform.

[1142] Blaisdell, Donald C. *International Organization*.   New York: Ronald, 1966. 531 pp.

[1143] Blaustein, Albert P., and Flanz, Gisbert H. *Constitutions of the Countries of the World*. Dobbs Ferry, N.Y.: Oceana, 1971-   . 18 binders (loose-leaf; updateable).
Contains chronology, current text, and bibliography. Supercedes

Peaslee.

1144 Bloomfield, Lincoln P. "The United States, the United Nations, and the
Creation of Community." *International Organization*, 14 (1960), pp.
503-13.
"Debate on strategy to achieve world government has almost com-
pletely ignored the first truth that world order is dependent upon
some minimal consensus on common global problems." Functionalism.

1145 --------. "Arms Control and World Government." *World Politics*, 14
(July, 1962), pp. 633-45.
Great problem is not drafting Charter changes but reaching political consensus. Article marks revival of interest by arms control
experts in world government.

1146 Bogardus, Emory S. *Toward a World Community*. Los Angeles: University
of Southern California Press, 1964. 101 pp.
What ordinary people can do.

1147 Borgese, Elizabeth Mann. *The Ocean Regime: A Suggested Statute for
the Peaceful Uses of the High Seas and the Sea Bed beyond the Limits of National Jurisdiction*. Santa Barbara, Calif.: Center for
the Study of Democratic Institutions, Occasional Paper, 1968. 40
pp.
Work marking transition from world law to law of the sea.

1148 --------. "World Communities." *Center Magazine*, 4 (September-October, 1971), pp. 10-18.
Suggests system, parallel to U.N., of world communities dealing
with transnational interests: oceans, health, science, universities. Functionalism.

1149 --------. *Pacem in Maribus*. New York: Dodd, Mead, 1972. 382 pp.

1150 --------. "An Open Letter to the U.N. Charter Review Committee." *Center Report*, June, 1975, pp. 26-27.
Political pressure for revision comes from new nations. Agreements
on world order for the seas and outer space would prepare way for
general U.N. reform.

1151 --------. *The Drama of the Oceans*. New York: Abrams, 1975. 258 pp.
"This [regional and global ocean management] does not require the
establishment of a world state or a superstate or the relinquishing
of sovereignty. Such a notion is rooted in the static, land-based
concept of division -- even opposition -- between the part and the
whole. . . . The dynamic environment of the oceans imposes, instead, an organic concept of integration in which the part grows as
the whole grows. Thus, there is no surrender of sovereignty. On
the contrary, the growth of international community (the whole)
fosters the growth of national sovereignty (the part)."

1152 --------, and Krieger, David, eds. *The Tides of Change: Peace, Pollution, and the Potential of the Oceans*. New York: Mason, Charter,
1975. 357 pp.
Papers and projects of Pacem in Maribus in preparation for the U.N.
conference on the Law of the Sea.

1153 --------. "The Law of the Sea." *Scientific American*, 248 (March,

1983), pp. 42-49.
In December, 1982, 119 nations signed the U.N. Convention on the Law of the Sea.   Ratification is pending.   Doctrine of freedom of the seas has been replaced by that of the common heritage of mankind.

¹¹⁵⁴ Breitner, Thomas. *World Constitution*: *A Study on the Legal Framework of a World Federation*. Berkeley, Calif.: Monographs on World Government, Series A, No. 1, 1963. 40 pp.

¹¹⁵⁵ Brennan, Donald G., ed.   *Arms Control, Disarmament, and National Security*. New York: Braziller, 1961. 475 pp.
Handbook of varied intellectual and technical approaches. Includes commentary by four European experts.

¹¹⁵⁶ Brown, Harrison, and Real, James. *Community of Fear*.   Santa Barbara, Calif.: Center for the Study of Democratic Institutions, 1960. 40 pp.
Continuation of deterrence policy will result either in nuclear war or in regimentation of American life on grounds of military necessity. Cf. Millis below, in Center series.

¹¹⁵⁷ --------. "Learning to Live in a Technological Society: Toward a World Community." *Bulletin of the Atomic Scientists*, 35 (October, 1979), pp. 23-27.
World government is the goal,   but four technical problems inhibit progress: nuclear confrontation, national economic inequality, competition over scarce materials, and trade barriers.   All could be reduced by rich countries if they would cooperate in their own interests.

¹¹⁵⁸ Bundy, McGeorge.   "After the Deluge, the Covenant." *Saturday Review*, August 24, 1974, pp. 18-20.
Imaginative reconstruction of history of next 50 years from perspective of 2024. A World Nuclear Authority, World Food Commission, and World Population Court will be established along the lines of limited world government, but the nation states will remain largely intact.

¹¹⁵⁹ Buzan, Barry. *Seabed Politics*. New York: Praeger, 1976. 311 pp.
History of U.N. Law of the Sea Conference.   Analyzes the political factors by which "active international jurisdiction and supervision" has developed over the seabed against the claims of states.

¹¹⁶⁰ Campaign for U.N.   U.N. Reform. *A Program to Reform and Restructure the U.N. System*. Wayne, N.J.: n.d., ca. 1982. 17 pp.

¹¹⁶¹ Caplow, Theodore. *A Feasibility Study of World Government*. Occasional Paper 13, Stanley Foundation, 1977. 28 pp.
By University of Virginia sociologist.   A mature and sophisticated argument.

¹¹⁶² Chase, Stuart.   "One World or None." *Bulletin of the Atomic Scientists*, 31 (December, 1975), p. 5.
Sovereign state is unworkable, yet political leaders remain sunk in its traditions.   Need is for world agencies to administer disarmament, energy, food, finance, pollution, oceans, air traffic, and satellites.   Much depends on leadership "both honest and intelli-

gent" to guide nations into the "realities of the Atomic Age."

[1163] Clark, Grenville, and Sohn, Louis B. *World Peace through World Law.*
Cambridge: Harvard University Press, 1958; 2nd ed.,   1960; 3rd,
1966. 540 pp.
Probably the most respected and most influential of all volumes on
world government.   Proposes fundamental U.N. Charter reform with
facing texts and commentary.   Less minimalist than   earlier Clark
proposals.

[1164] ----------.   "World Order: The Need for a Bold New Approach." *Annals*
of the American Academy of Political and Social Science, 336 (July,
1961), pp. 134-62.

[1165] ----------, and ----------.   *Draft of a Proposed Treaty Establishing a
World Disarmament and World Development Organization within the
Framework of the United Nations.*   Dublin, N.H.:   By the authors,
1962. 122 pp.
Later incorporated into third edition of *World Peace through World
Law.*

[1166] ----------.   "The Need for Total Disarmament under Enforceable World
Law." *Current History*, 47 (August, 1964), pp. 93-96, 115.
Peace has not been achieved, not for lack of desire, but for lack
of understanding.   It is not enough to reduce national armaments.
Their security and political functions must be replaced by enforceable world law, as in any community.   Hence limited world government.

[1167] ---------- et al.   *Declaration of the Second Dublin Conference.*   Concord, N.H.: Grenville Clark Institute, 1965. 7 pp.

[1168] ----------, and -------. *Introduction to World Peace through World Law.*
Introductory essay and notes on resources by Robert Woito.   Chicago: World without War, 1984. 102 pp.
Revised by Sohn in 1973 and 1983.   Best and most recent brief discussion of the issues raised by their proposal.

[1169] *Common Security*:   *Blueprint for Survival.* The Report of the Independent Commission on Disarmament and Security Issues. New York: Simon
& Schuster, 1982. 202 pp.
Palme Commission Report. Report of independent group of former and
current officials (Olaf Palme, former Swedish Prime Minister), foreign ministers, political leaders, and a high Soviet official on a
way out from the arms race and the policies of deterrence.   Proposals include graduated steps to achieve drastic mutual reductions
of military power in Europe and eventual withdrawal of nuclear weapons. Also U.N. reform.   "A doctrine of common security must replace the present expedient of mutual deterrence."

[1170] Cousins, Norman. *In Place of Folly.* New York: Washington Square, 1961.
224 pp.
'"The enemy is not solely the unfettered sovereign national state,
violating the natural rights of man and jeopardizing his natural
environment. . . . The enemy is a man who not only believes in his
own helplessness but actually worships it.   His main article of
faith is that there are mammoth forces at work which the individual
cannot possibly comprehend, much less alter or direct.   And so he

expends vast energies in attempting to convince other people that there is nothing they can do."

1171 --------. "What Is World Law?" *Saturday Review*, August 14, 1965, pp. 24-25.
Idea of world law is very simple, but creating it presents many practical difficulties. World law must be enforceable yet not be tyrannical.

1172 --------. "The Second Dublin Declaration." *Saturday Review*, December 11, 1965, p. 28.
Renewed call for world federation. "Peace means more than the temporary absence of major war in an armed world. Genuine peace requires enforceable law, order and justice. In short, peace requires government."

1173 --------. "Prophecy and Pessimism." *Saturday Review*, August 24, 1974, pp. 6-7.
Current doomsday prophecies, based on present trends of tangible facts, are indeed discouraging. But history is also moved by intangibles. One of these is the sometimes heroic way human beings respond to crisis.

1174 --------. "Litany for Mankind." *Transnational Perspectives*, 6, 4 (1980), p. 14.
"I am a single cell in a body of four billion cells. . . . Human unity is the fulfillment of diversity. It is the harmony of opposites."

1175 --------, and Clifford, J. Garry, eds. *Memoirs of a Man*: *Grenville Clark*. New York: Norton, 1975. 319 pp.
Reminiscences by Clark's friends, who convey some of his wise and distinguished character. To explain his public service as a private citizen, Clark liked to quote Lincoln: "The people will save the government, if the government itself will do its part only indifferently well."

1176 Davis, Garry. *The World Is My Country*: *The Adventures of a World Citizen*. New York: Putnam, 1961. 254 pp.
Retrospective on his 1948-1949 affair.

1177 --------. *World Government, Ready or Not!* Sorrento, Me.: Juniper Ledge, 1984. 402 pp.

1178 Deutsch, Karl. *Nationalism and Its Alternatives*. New York: Knopf, 1969. 200 pp.
Subjects of needed research.

1179 Dougherty, James E. *Security through World Law and World Government*: *Myth or Reality?* Philadelphia: Foreign Policy Research Institute, Monograph Series, No. 15, 1974. 64 pp.

1180 Douglas, William O. *The Rule of Law in World Affairs*. Santa Barbara, Calif.: Center for the Study of Democratic Institutions, 1961. 32 pp.
Reflections on the transition between absolute national sovereignty and the rule of world law. The U.N. is doing what Lincoln advised the governor of Missouri to do in a similar period of breakdown of

law and order: build majorities concerned about mutual security in every community by holding neighborhood meetings where all will pledge to cease harassing others.   War is intolerable; the rule of law is our only alternative.

[1181] --------. *Towards a Global Federalism*. New York: New York University Press, 1968. 177 pp.
By the Supreme Court Justice. Best course is further development of internationalism in 19th century sense rather than immediate world federation.

[1182] --------. "The Rule of Law in World Affairs." *Center Report*, February, 1976, pp. 14-17.
International law already exists.   What is needed is the will to apply it.

[1183] Dreifuss, Kurt. "Creative World Government." Chicago: Society for a World Service Authority, mimeographed, July, 1964.

[1184] Dugan, Maire. "Social Conflict Theory and World Order." *Transnational Perspectives*, 3 (1976), pp. 8-10, 23.
Critique of Clark-Sohn plan according to social science conflict theory.   Even with world community, homogeneity, and transnational popular relations, which have yet to develop, there would still not be perfect peace.

[1185] Dyson, Freeman. *Weapons and Hope*. New York: Harper & Row, 1984.   340 pp.
Explicitly rejects world government from security concepts because it is not "modest and devoid of utopian and universalistic pretensions." Of the remaining concepts -- assured destruction, limited nuclear war, counterforce, nonviolent resistance, defense unlimited, and live-and-let-live (detargetting existing nuclear weapons) -- Dyson selects the last as offering the most hope.

[1186] Ehrenzeller, Thomas P. *Solar Man*. Winona, Minn.: Apollo Books, 1985.   251 pp.

[1187] Etzioni, Amitai. "The Dialectics of Supranational Unification." *American Political Science Review*, 56 (December, 1962), pp. 927-35.
Analyzes structure of complex organizations and considers possible future direction of processes of supranational unification.

[1188] --------. *The Hard Way to Peace*: *A New Strategy*. New York: Collier, 1962.   285 pp.
Regional groupings can facilitate the process of global consensus formation.

[1189] --------. *Winning without War*.   Garden City: Doubleday, 1964.   271 pp.

[1190] --------. *Political Unification*: *A Comparative Study of Leaders and Forces*. New York: Holt, Reinhart & Winston, 1965. 346 pp.
Sociological study of regional polities for light they may shed on the task of establishing a global state.

[1191] --------, and Wenglinsky, Martin, eds. *War and Its Prevention*.   New York: Harper & Row, 1970. 308 pp.

Wide-ranging sociological studies.

[1191]a Forsberg, Randall.   "The Freeze and Beyond: Confining the Military
to Defense as a Route to Disarmament." *World Policy*, 1 (Winter,
1984), pp. 285-318.
Seven steps to peace: (1) U.S.-U.S.S.R. nuclear weapons freeze;
(2) end of large-scale military intervention by North in South; (3)
fifty percent cut in nuclear and conventional forces of NATO, Warsaw Pact, China, Japan; (4) greater development assistance to Third
World and improved negotiation structures for U.N.; (5) abolition
of military alliances and limitation of military forces to border
defense; (6) abolition of all nuclear weapons; (7) general and complete disarmament under effective international control.

[1192] Friedmann, Wolfgang, et al., eds. *Transnational Law in a Changing Society*: *Essays in Honor of Philip C. Jessup*.   New York: Columbia
University Press, 1972. 332 pp.

[1193] Friedrich, Carl J. *Man and His Government*:   *An Empirical Theory of
Politics*. New York: McGraw-Hill, 1963. 737 pp.
"A federal system, then, is a particular kind of constitutional order. The function it is supposed to serve is to restrain the powers
wielded by the inclusive community, as well as those of the communities included within it. It is . . . a kind of division or sepa-
ration of powers, but applied on a spatial basis."

[1194] --------. *Trends of Federalism in Theory and Practice*. New York: Praeger, 1968.   193 pp.
Argues that federalism is best understood not as a static structure
(a division of powers), but as a historical process of community
cooperation or joint decision making on common problems.   The process may proceed in the direction either of integration of communities, or of differentiation.   Functions of the components are as
important as structures of the whole.   Some eleven federal systems
in particular flux are examined (e.g., Canada, India, United Europe).

[1195] Fromm, Erich. *May Man Prevail*: *An Inquiry into the Facts and Fictions
of Foreign Policy*. Garden City, N.Y.: Doubleday, 1961. 252 pp.
In this psychoanalyst's view, much of what passes for political
thinking, East and West, is really pathological.   Both Russia and
America have interests primarily in peace and not in world domination. Progress could be made if leaders regarded each other as rational men with whom negotiation is possible.

[1196] --------. *The Anatomy of Human Destructiveness*. New York: Holt, Reinhart & Winston, 1973. Cf. Reves.

[1197] Fuchs, Lawrence H. "Nations in the Future: Organization for Survival."
Western Political Quarterly, 9 (1956), pp. 11-20.
Governments do not come into existence "gradually" but at "decisive
moments." In 1945, nations were far more ready for world government than since.

[1198] Fuson, Ben W. "Unearthly Nation." *Fellowship*, March, 1964, p. 12 ff.
Account of Dr. Hugh Schonfield's mondcivitan movement, a variant on
the idea of world citizens.

[1199] Galt, Tom. *Peace and War*: *Man Made*. Boston: Beacon, 1962.   138 pp.
Survey. Cf. Wynner, Hemblen, etc.

[1200] Gardner, Richard N.   *United Nations Procedures and Power Realities*:
The International Apportionment Problem.   Address of Deputy Assistant Secretary of State for International Organizational Affairs to
American Society of International Law, April 23, 1965.   *Congressional Record*, 111:9458-61.
Official consideration of U.N. voting reforms due to greatly in-
creased voting power of Third World in General Assembly: weighted
representation, dual voting, bicameralism, committees with selected
representation, informal relations with U.N. secretariat, and conciliation.

[1201] --------, ed. *Blueprint for Peace*. New York: McGraw-Hill, 1966.   404
pp.
Proposals of prominent Americans to White House Conference on International Cooperation.

[1202] --------, and Millikan, Max F., eds. *The Global Partnership*: *International Agencies and Economic Development*.   New York: Praeger,
1968. 498 pp.

[1203] Glossop, Ronald J. *Confronting War*:   *An Examination of Humanity's
Most Pressing Problem*. Jefferson, N.C.: McFarland, 1983.   290 pp.
By a professor of philosophy. Fruit of two courses: "The Problem
of War and Peace" and "Global Problems and Human Survival." Comprehensive and fundamental. Non-doctrinaire. Ends with chapter on
world government.

[1204] Gompert, D.; Mandelbaum, M.; Garwin, R.L.; and Banton, J. H.   *Nuclear
Weapons and World Politics*: *Alternatives for the Future*. New York:
McGraw-Hill, 1977.   360 pp.
Council on Foreign Relations publication.

[1205] Green, Lucile, and Yudell, Esther, eds.   *The Worried Woman's Guide to
Peace through World Law*.   Piedmont, Calif.:   Northern California
Women for Peace, 1965. 100 pp.
Cf. Waskow, *The Worried Man's Guide*. . . .

[1206] Haas, Ernest B.   *Beyond the Nation State*: *Functionalism and International Organization*.   Stanford: Stanford University Press, 1968.
595 pp.

[1207] --------.   *Collective Security and the Future International System*.
Denver: University of Denver Press, 1968.   117 pp.
See Chap. 4: "Global Tasks and the United Nations of the Future."
A "reconciliation system" short of world federation is predicted
for 1985.

[1208] Handrahan, John R. *It Is Coming*: *On World Representative Government*.
New York: Comet Press, 1959. 74 pp.
A "Reflection Book."

[1209] Heilbroner, Robert L. *An Inquiry into the Human Prospect*.   New York:
Norton, 1974. 150 pp.
Neither socialism nor capitalism is equipped to meet the challenges
of war, the arms race, overpopulation, pollution, misuse of techno-

logy, and alienation of the young. "Is there hope for man?"

1210 Hevesy, Paul de. *The Unification of the World*: *Proposals of a Diplo-
matist*. New York: Pergamon Press, 1966. 356 pp.
Economic factors for world union.

1211 Hoffman, Walter. *Improving the U.N.'s Peacekeeping Capacity*.   Wayne,
N.J.: Center for U.N. Reform Education, U.N. Reform Monograph No.
1, n.d., c. 1983. 8 pp.

1212 --------. *Improving U.N. Dispute Settlement Machinery*.   Wayne, N.J.:
CURE, U.N. Reform Monograph No. 2, 1984. 25 pp.

1213 Holcombe, Arthur N.   *Organizing Peace in the Nuclear Age*.   New York:
New York University Press, 1959. 245 pp.
Eleventh report of Commission to Study the Organization of Peace.

1214 --------. *A Strategy of Peace in a Changing World*.   Cambridge: Harvard University Press, 1967. 332 pp.
Collection of late articles, mostly re Edwin Ginn, founder of the
World Peace Foundation and an advocate of world government.   Ripe
wisdom.

1215 Hollins, Elizabeth Jay, ed.   *Peace Is Possible*:   *A Reader for Laymen*.
New York: Grossman, 1966. 339 pp.

1216 Hollins, Harry B., ed. *Current Disarmament Proposals*. New York: Institute for International Order, World Law Fund, 1964. 195 pp.
Texts of agreements and draft treaties on disarmament such as the
McCloy-Zorin accord of 1961.   Continuation of Grenville Clark's
work.

1217 --------. *The World Law Fund*: *A Statement of Purpose*. New York: WLF,
1966. 12 pp.

1218 Hudgens, Tom A. *Let's Abolish War*. Denver, Colo.: BILR Corp., 1985.
66 pp.
Lead pamphlet of L.A.W. membership campaign.

1219 Hudson, Richard. *The Binding Triad*.   New York: Center for War/Peace
Studies, n.d., c. 1981. 5 pp.
A carefully realistic proposal, developed over 20 years, for minimum reform of the General Assembly voting system and powers (Arts.
18 and 13). Decisions would be made possible if three 2/3 majority
votes could be reached: 2/3 of the member states (present and voting); a majority of the members representing 2/3 of the world's
population; and a majority of the members contributing 2/3 of the
regular U.N. budget. Practical demonstrations re real issues (e.g.,
Lebanon) have been made in a continuing series of conferences at
Mohonk, N.Y.

1220 --------. *The Case for the Binding Triad*. New York: Center for War/-
Peace Studies, Special Study No. 7, 1983. 30 pp.
Formal argument, with texts of amendments to Arts. 13 and 18 of the
Charter, for the binding triad proposal for decision-making in the
General Assembly.   Includes example of resolution of Arab-Israeli
conflict.

[1221] Hutchins, Robert M. *Two Faces of Federalism*: *An Outline of an Argument about Pluralism, Unity, and Law*. Santa Barbara, Calif.: Center for the Study of Democratic Institutions, Fund for the Republic, 1961. 126 pp.
Reconsiderations.

[1222] *International Political Communities*: *An Anthology*. Garden City, N.Y.: Doubleday, 1966. 512 pp.
Regionalism.

[1223] Isely, Philip, et al. *A Constitution for the Federation of Earth*. Lakewood, Colo.: World Constitution and Parliament Association, 1977. 56 pp.
Maximalist draft. Adopted by members of the association at Innsbruck, Austria, June, 1977. Isely claims only remaining step is ratification. He has developed considerable interest among parliamentarians and citizens outside the United States. The constitution has interesting features, for example, three legislative houses -- of peoples, nations, and counsellors. Grenville Clark would say this is a formula for paralysis.

[1224] James, Preston E. *One World Divided*. New York: Blaisdell, 1964; 2nd ed., 1974; 3rd, 1980. 482 pp.
Study of geographical impact of industrial and democratic revolutions. Analysis re habitat, population, economic development, and political organization. Eleven "culture regions" distinguished. No prediction of early unification. Opening line of first and second editions was, "All men are brothers." By third edition, text had been transformed into a slick college geography text.

[1225] Johnson, Andrew Nissen. *Enforceable World Peace*: *Thoughts of a Diplomat*. Minneapolis: Burgess, 1973. 156 pp.

[1226] Joyce, James Avery. *The Story of International Cooperation*. Foreword by U Thant. New York: Franklin Watts, 1964. 258 pp.
Survey from Greek Olympic Games, Roman Empire, Renaissance, voyages of discovery, wars of rising nation states, and international organization in the 19th and 20th centuries.

[1227] Kahn, Herman. "World Government vs. Thermonuclear War." *War/Peace Report*, March, 1963, pp. 3-7.
Critique of Clark and Sohn's *World Peace through World Law*. Danger of world dictatorship. Reply by Clark in April issue. Rejoinder by Kahn in May.

[1228] --------, and Wiener, Anthony J. *The Year 2000*: *A Framework for Speculation on the Next Thirty-three Years*. New York: Macmillan, 1967. 431 pp.
World federal government considered "in the very long run." Probably will not be possible except by Atlantic Union or war or crisis.

[1228]a Kaiser, Karl. "Transnational Politics: Toward a Theory of Multinational Politics." *International Organization*, 25 (Autumn, 1971), pp. 790-817.

[1229] Kaplan, Morton A., ed. *Isolation or Interdependence? Today's Choices for Tomorrow's World*. New York: Free Press, 1975. 254 pp.

Conference papers at Center for Policy Study, University of Chicago, April, 1974.

1230 Kelman, Herbert C., ed. *International Behavior*. New York: Holt, Reinhart, 1965.
Major study of alternatives to warfare by Society for the Psychological Study of Social Issues.

1231 Kennedy, John F. *Let Us Call a Truce to Terror*. Address before the U.N. General Assembly, September 25, 1961. Washington: Department of State Pub. 7282, International Organization and Conference Series 23, 1961. 23 pp.
President's speech proposing general and complete disarmament.

1232 --------. *Toward a Strategy of Peace*. Address at American University, June 10, 1963. Washington: Arms Control and Disarmament Agency Pub. 17, 1963. 17 pp.
America's weapons are designed to deter, not to be used. Meanwhile, peace depends on a gradual evolution of human institutions in all countries.

1233 --------. *A Step toward Peace*: *Report to the People on the Nuclear Test Ban Treaty*. Radio and Television address of July 26, 1963. Washington: Arms Control and Disarmament Agency Pub. 16, 1963. 20 pp.
Includes text of historic treaty.

1234 --------. *New Opportunities in the Search for Peace*. Address to the U.N. General Assembly, September 20, 1963. Washington: Department of State Pub. 7595, General Foreign Policy Series 189, 1963. 20 pp.
Review of U.S. foreign policy with respect to ultimate peaceful cooperation.

1235 Keys, Donald F. *The New Federalists*. Washington: World Federalist Education Fund, n.d., c. 1973. 14 pp.
Federalism has progressed beyond its legalistic (world peace through world law) and populist (peoples' convention) beginnings. It is now very like functionalism, with the addition of the vision of an ultimate political step to inauguarate the rule of law. For now, it concentrates on cooperation with kindred organizations, like the United Nations Association and Planetary Citizens.

1236 --------, and Laszlo, Ervin, eds. *Disarmament. The Human Factor*. Proceedings of a Colloquium on the Societal Context for Disarmament, Sponsored by UNITAR and Planetary Citizens and Held at the United Nations. New York: 1978. 164 pp.

1237 --------. *Earth at Omega*: *Passage to Planetization*. Introduction by Norman Cousins. Boston: Branden, 1982; 2nd ed., 1985. 117 pp.

1238 Kiang, John. *One World*: *The Approach to Permanent Peace on Earth and the General Happiness of Mankind*; *A Popular Manifesto with Scholarly Annotations*. Notre Dame, Ind.: One World, 1984. 633 pp.

1239 Larson, Arthur.   "Development of a World Rule of Law." *Social Education*, 26 (November, 1962), pp. 390-96.
Rule of world law would settle both legal and political disputes.

Law is not maintenance of status quo but framework for orderly change. Diplomacy is becoming obsolete because of unacceptability of war. A defense of the Clark-Sohn plan. Condemned by Bogdanov.

1240 --------, ed. Forword by U Thant. *A Warless World*: *Problems and Opportunities of a Disarmed World under Law*. New York: McGraw-Hill, 1963. 209 pp.
Essays by Louis B. Sohn, Arnold Toynbee, Walter Millis, Arthur Larson, Kenneth Boulding, Hubert Humphrey, Grenville Clark, Margaret Mead, William E. Hocking, and James Wadsworth. Appendix on Russian ideas.

1241 Lens, Sidney. "World Government Reconsidered." *Nation*, September 17, 1983, pp. 201-04.
By senior editor of *The Progressive*. Recent argument in the popular press that world government is necessary to prevent war; the main problem now is the transition. Negative reply by Richard Falk and others to effect that the transition implies agreement on world disarmament, dissolution of the American and Soviet empires, the advent of democracy in communist states and of equality of distribution in capitalist ones. But if these conditions were met, what need any more would there be for world government?

1242 Lentz, Theodore F., ed. *Towards a Science of Peace*: *Turning Point in Human Destiny*. Foreword by Julian Huxley. New York: Bookman, 1955. 194 pp.

1243 --------, ed. *Humatriotism*: *Human Interest in Peace and Survival*. St. Louis, Mo.: Futures, 1976. 255 pp.
Loyalty to humanity as a whole must be developed like love of country or patriotism.

1244 Levi, Werner. "On the Causes of Peace." *Journal of Conflict Resolution*, 8 (March, 1964), pp. 23-35.
Government is the cause, but before world government can be established a world normative order will have to develop. Nationalism will be supplanted only as habits, emotions, and material satisfactions are derived from the international society now forming.

1245 Levine, Robert A. *World Government and the Current Policies of the Nations*. Santa Monica, Calif.: RAND Corporation, Report P-2932, 1964. 19 pp.

1246 Lloyd, William Bross, Jr. *Waging Peace*: *The Swiss Experience*. Foreword by Quincy Wright; Preface by William E. Rappard. Washington: Public Affairs Press, 1958. 101 pp.
Discusses analogy of three Swiss cantons that were made neutrals with the *duty* of conciliating the Protestant and Catholic cantons during the Reformation. Today, certain nations could be designated "peacemakers," with the duty to mediate conflicts and to enforce decisions by recourse to their military forces.

1247 --------. *Peace Requires Peacemakers*. Santa Barbara, Calif.: Center for the Study of Democratic Institutions, 1964. 48 pp.

1248 Logue, John. "The Great Debate on Charter Reform: A Proposal for a Stronger United Nations." *Publications of the Social Sciences*, No. 2. New York: Fordham University Press, 1955; 3rd printing, 1958.

Discussion of the political philosophy bearing on holding the Charter review conference of 1955, in accordance with Art. 109.   Concludes that a conference would be appropriate only for *major* reform proposals.   Even the world federalists' proposal was not adequate to world problems.   A minimal, security proposal would too likely be subverted by great power rivalry, to the neglect of the immense majority of mankind in the colonized world.   A maximal proposal is the only one likely to be effective and even acceptable.

1249   --------.   "Challenge in the United Nations." *Commonweal*, July 20, 1956, pp. 387-90.
"We cannot win the battle of competitive coexistence unless we are more consistently on the side of principle." Call for creative U.S. leadership in the U.N., as the pro-West majority began slipping away with the admission of sixteen new states.

1250   --------, ed.   *The Fate of the Oceans.* Villanova, Pa.: Villanova University Press, 1972. 237 pp.
Conference proceedings. Papers by Elizabeth Mann Borgese and others.

1251   --------, ed.   *United Nations Reform and Restructure.* Villanova, Pa.: Villanova University Press, 1980.
Proceedings of conference on President Carter's Report on the Reform and Restructure of the U.N. System, held at Villanova, November, 1978. Contributors included Harlan Cleveland, Norman Cousins, Hans Morgenthau, Bradford Morse, Robert Muller, Louis B. Sohn, and John Stoessinger.

1252   --------.   "The Revenge of John Selden: The Draft Convention on the Law of the Sea in the Light of Hugo Grotius' Mare Liberum." *Grotiana*, New Series, 3 (1982), pp. 27-56.
The recent Law of the Sea convention was not a victory for the common heritage of mankind, but for "ocean nationalists."

1253   Lusky, Louis.   "Peace -- the Presence of Justice." *The Humanist*, 17 (1957), pp. 195-209.
Until the world population is more homogeneous, people will not willingly submit to majority rule.

1254   --------.   "Four Problems in Law-Making for Peace." *Political Science Quarterly*, 80 (September, 1965), pp. 341-56.
Critique of Clark-Sohn proposals, first on grounds that they are not maximal enough (do not provide mechanisms for solution of economic and political conflicts at root of war), then not sufficiently minimal (would have too much legislative and police powers).

1255   McClure, Wallace.   *World Legal Order: Possible Contributions by the People of the United States.* Chapel Hill: University of North Carolina Press, 1960. 366 pp.
Proposal for a Constitutional amendment or Supreme Court decision to give treaties (international law) precedence over national law. Step toward world law. By professor at World Rule of Law Center at Duke University.

1256   MacDougall, Curtis D.   *Gideon's Army.* New York: Marzani & Munsell, 1965. 3 vols.
Pioneering history of Wallace's 1948 Progressive Party campaign. The Party platform had a strong world government plank written by

Scott Buchanan, with the assistance of R. G. Tugwell, Frederick L. Schuman, and Wallace himself.

1257 McVitty, Marion E.   "A Comparison and Evaluation of Current Disarmament Proposals as of March 1,   1964." New York: World Law Fund, 1964. 43 pp.
By United World Federalists' long time U.N. observer.

1258 McWhinney, Edward.   *Federal Constitution-Making for a Multi-National World*. Leyden: Sijthoff, 1966. 150 pp.
Prepared under auspices of the American Society of International Law.   Begins not with a given ideal federal system, but with the political community conditions necessary first.   Expert discussion of classical federalism, the limited variety in the U.S., plural models in Europe, the "export" type in the Third World, "bicultural" constitutionalism in Canada, the British Commonwealth, and world federalism. Cf. American Committee on United Europe.

1259 Mally, Gerhard.   *Interdependence*: *The European-American Connection in the Global Context*.   Lexington, Mass.:   Atlantic Council for the United States, Lexington Books, 1976. 229 pp.

1260 Mangone, Gerald J.   "The Fallacy of World Federalism." *Current History*, 29 (September, 1960), pp. 163-68.
Community to precede law. Cf. Andrews.

1261 Melman, Seymour, ed. *Disarmament*: *Its Politics and Economics*.   Boston: American Academy of Arts and Sciences, 1962. 398 pp.
Papers on U.S. and U.S.S.R. proposals for general and complete disarmament, inspection, enforcement, economic effects, conversion, and the political process.

1262 Meyer, Cord, Jr.   *Facing Reality*:   *From World Federalism to the CIA*. New York: Harper, 1980. 433 pp.
Mostly a defense of his subsequent career in the CIA.   *One* chapter on federalism.   Other chapters give Meyer's version of the CIA's subversion of the National Student Association, revealed in 1967. The World Federalists, apparently, were not similarly subverted.

1263 Millard, Everett Lee. *Freedom in a Federal World*. Dobbs Ferry, N.Y.: Oceana, 1959; 5th ed., 1969. 224 pp.
Proposes an assembly of peoples in the United Nations. Written with *elan* by the editor of *One World*, a newsletter of the movement that succeeded *World Government News*.

1264 Miller, Lynn H.   *Organizing Mankind*: *An Analysis of Contempory International Organization*.   John C. Bollens, consulting ed.   Boston: Holbrook, 1972. 365 pp.

1265 Millis, Walter. *A World without War*.   Santa Barbara, Calif.: Center for the Study of Democratic Institutions, 1961. 72 pp.
Argument that, assuming war is abolished, a viable international order is possible and practicable. Cf. *Permanent Peace* below and Brown, *Community of Fear*, above in Center series.

1266 --------.   *Permanent Peace*.   Santa Barbara, Calif.:   Center for the Study of Democratic Institutions, 1961. 31 pp.
Deals with transition to an international order without war.

[1267] --------, and Real, James. *The Abolition of War*.   New York: Macmillan, 1963.   217 pp.

[1268] Mills, C.   Wright.   *The Causes of World War III*.   New York: Simon &
Schuster, 1958.   172 pp.
Bold critique of the personalities and social conditions behind the
Cold War. Includes chapters on "crackpot realism" and the "politics
of peace." By the iconoclastic author of *The Power Elite*.

[1269] Monnet, Jean. *Memoirs*. Trans. by Richard Mayne.   Intro.   by George
Ball. Garden City, N.Y.:   Doubleday, 1978.   544 pp.
"Have I said clearly enough that the Community we have created is
not an end in itself?   It is a process of change, continuing that
same process which in an earlier period of history produced our
national forms of life. Like our provinces in the past, our nations
today must learn to live together under common rules and institutions freely arrived at.   The sovereign nations of the past can no
longer solve the problems of the present: they cannot ensure their
own progress or control their future.   And the Community itself is
only a stage on the way to the organized world of tomorrow."

[1269]a Moore, Wilbert E.   "Global Sociology: The World as a Singular System" and "The Utility of Utopias." In Wilbert E. Moore, ed., *Order
and Change*:   Essays in Comparative Sociology (New   York: Wiley,
1967).

[1270] Mowrer, Edgar Ansel, and Mowrer, Lilian T.   *Umano and the Price of
Lasting Peace*. New York: Philosophical Library, 1973.   158 pp.
On the Italian philosopher's "positive science of government."

[1271] National Conference of Catholic Bishops.   *The Challenge of Peace*:
God's Promise and Our Response. Boston: U.S. Catholic Conference,
1983.   87 pp.
Bishops' Pastoral Letter. "Looking ahead to the long and productive
future of humanity for which we all hope, we feel that a more inclusive and final solution is needed [to the problem of nuclear
war]. We speak here of the truly effective international authority
for which Pope John XXIII ardently longed in *Peace on Earth*, and of
which Pope Paul VI spoke to the United Nations on his visit there
in 1965. The hope for such a structure is not unrealistic, because
the point has been reached where public opinion sees clearly that,
with the massive weaponry of the present, war is no longer viable.
There *is* a substitute for war."

[1272] Newcombe, Hanna. *Design for a Better World*. Lanham, Md.:   University
Press of America, 1983.   362 pp.

[1273] --------. *Alternative International Security Systems*.   Dundas, Ontario: Peace Research Institute-Dundas, 1983.   29 pp.

[1274] --------, and Newcombe, Alan. "World Community on Your Doorstep: Citizen Taxes for the U.N., Mundialization and Town-Twinning as a Way
to Peace." In Charney, Israel, *Strategies against Violence*:   Design for Non-violent Change*. 17 pp.
Survey of mundialization movement (declaration of cities and towns
as world territories) in Europe, Japan, and North America.

1275 --------, and Newcombe, Alan. *A World Policy for Canadians*. Brief to
     Canadian House of Commons Committee on External Affairs, April,
     1971.   Dundas, Ont.:   Canadian Peace Research Institute, Mimeo-
     graphed, 1971. 21 pp.
     Recommendations for Canadian foreign policy on U.N. Charter revi-
     sion, submission to World Court, admission of China and all states
     to U.N., increased foreign aid, international police force, East-
     West alliances, voting with Scandinavian bloc rather than West in
     U.N.

1276 --------. "Comparison of World Order Schemes." *Journal of World Peace*,
     2 (Fall, 1985), pp. 1-11.
     Sixteen recent proposals of world government are compared.

1277 Niebuhr, Reinhold; Brown, Harrison; Douglas, William O., et al.   *A
     World without War*. New York: Washington Square, 1961. 182 pp.
     Four pamphlets from the Center for the Study of Democratic Institu-
     tions on the changed nature of war "which neither we nor the Rus-
     sians can win."

1278 O'Grady, Olivia Marie.   *The Beasts of the Apocalypse*:   *A Commentary
     Based on Events in the Warp and Woof of Two Thousand Years of His-
     tory, Bringing into Focus the Pattern of Contemporary Movements to
     Establish a World Government*.   Benicia, Calif.:   O'Grady Publica-
     tions, 1959. 427 pp.

1279 Organski, A.F.K.   *World Politics*.   New York: Knopf, 1958; 2nd ed.,
     1968.   509 pp.

1280 Paterson, Thomas G, ed.   *Cold War Critics*:   *Alternatives to American
     Foreign Policy in the Truman Years*.   Chicago: Quadrangle Books,
     1971. 313 pp.
     Critics included Grenville Clark, Leo Szilard, Albert Einstein, A.
     J. Muste, and Vito Marcantonio.

1281 Pauling, Linus. *No More War!* New York: Dodd, Mead, 1958. 254 pp.
     Danger of nuclear war, need for international agreements, in apoca-
     lyptic style of early atomic scientists.

1282 Pearson, Lester B.   "Beyond the Nation State." *Saturday Review*, Feb-
     ruary 15, 1969, pp. 24-27, 54.
     Steps are urgently needed to create a world community superior to
     sovereign states.   United Kingdom is proof that a viable political
     structure can include differing national societies. By retired Ca-
     nadian Prime Minister.

1283 Plischke, Elmer, ed.   *Systems of Integrating the International Commun-
     ity*. Princeton: Van Nostrand, 1964. 198 pp.
     Papers at symposium under auspices of Department of Government and
     Politics at the University of Maryland, December, 1962.

1284 Price, Charles C.   "The Case for Disarmament: Some Personal Reflec-
     tions on the United States and Disarmament." *Annals*, American Aca-
     demy of Political and Social Science, 469 (September, 1983), pp.
     144-54.
     Authoritative account of the McCloy-Zorin accord of 1961 and its
     historical context. Closest approach to a general agreement on dis-
     armament.

[1285] Reves, Emery. "Introspection." *World Federalist*, July, 1963, pp. 37-38.
Another brave call for formation of a world federalist political party. Lobbying with existing parties has achieved nothing. Time to enter political struggle for power. Today in all countries, the difference between socialism and capitalism is becoming blurred; only significant difference is between maintenance of national sovereignty and creation of world sovereignty.

[1286] --------. "Why Waste Time Discussing Disarmament?" *Look*, March 28, 1961, pp. 67-72.
The real issue is peace, not disarmament. Current discussion of disarmament exactly parallels that of the 1920s and '30s: if we achieved a treaty abolishing nuclear and heavy conventional weapons, like the former limitations on the calibre of naval guns and the tonnage of capital ships, can it really be supposed that the leaders of sovereign powers would not still find cause for distrust? Would they not revert to rearmament in the vital interest of national defense? Peace between conflicting groups of men has never been possible until some sovereign power, some sovereign source of law, has been set up *above* the clashing social units. The problem of peace now is to create the statesmanship and the popular will to establish a common, democratic world state with powers to rule by law.

[1287] Romanoff, Alexis Lawrence. *One World Federation*. Ithaca, N.Y.: Ithaca Heritage Books (Cornell Campus Store), 1978. 151 pp.
The ideal cast into verse. Not written in spirit of the *Federalist Papers*.

[1288] Roosevelt, Elliott. *The Conservators*. New York: Arbor House, 1983. 416 pp.
Recent argument by FDR's son for a "planetary supragovernment."

[1289] Russett, Bruce M. *Trends in World Politics: Government in the Modern World*. New York: Macmillan, 1965. 156 pp.

[1290] Schell, Jonathan. *The Fate of the Earth*. New York: Knopf, 1982. 244 pp.
Concludes that a "global political revolution" is needed to solve the problem of nuclear war, but leaves the solution "to others." Never actually uses the words "world government."

[1291] --------. *The Abolition*. New York: Knopf, 1984. 173 pp.
Sequel to *The Fate of the Earth*. Here Schell openly and fairly considers world government as the fundamental alternative to deterrence, yet comes up with a third alternative that is basically an early warning system like that of the Acheson-Lilienthal plan for the international control of atomic energy (1946).

[1292] Schoenfeld, Charles G. "International Law, Nationalism, and the Sense of Self: A Psychoanalytic Inquiry." *Journal of Psychiatry and the Law*, 2 (1974), pp. 303-12.

[1293] --------. *Psychoanalysis Applied to the Law*. Port Washington, N.Y.: Associated Faculty Press, 1984. 196 pp.
Chapter 7, "International Law and Peace," contains an analysis of

sovereignty as a regression to the infantile (3-4 month old) "stage of non-diferentiation" between child and mother, and of nationalism as the neurotic suppression of inevitable thoughts of "separation-individuation." Author doubts that world government could satisfy these psychic needs, but he misunderstands it as mere disarmament or pacifism.

[1294] Shafer, Boyd C. *Nationalism: Its Nature and Interpreters*. Washington: American Historical Association, Pamphlet 701, 1959, 1976. 58 pp.
". . . If there is to be at any future time a truly international authority or world state above the nation, that international or world government will have to evolve somewhat as national governments did."

[1295] --------. *Faces of Nationalism: New Realities and Old Myths*. New York: 1972. 535 pp.
Leading study of nationalism.

[1296] --------. "Webs of Common Interests: Nationalism, Internationalism, and Peace." *Historian*, 36 (1974), pp. 403-33.

[1297] --------. *Nationalism and Internationalism: Belonging*. Melbourne, Fla.: Krieger, 1982. 278 pp.
"Internationalism, with its promise of world community, is an unfulfilled dream."

[1298] Sheehan, William. *Stop Global Drift*. Santa Barbara, Calif.: Center for the Future, 1978. 131 pp.

[1299] Singer, Joel David, and Small, Melvin. *Resort to Arms: International and Civil Wars, 1816-1980*. Beverly Hills, Calif.: Sage Publications, 1982. 373 pp.
Cf. Wright's *Study of War*.

[1300] Smoker, Paul. "A Preliminary Empirical Study of a International Integrative Subsystem." *International Association*, 7 (November, 1965). Study of rate of increase of international organizations from 1870 to 1960. Some 1,529 such organizations were counted. Rate declined only during two world wars and again by 1960. Measure of world integration.

[1301] Sohn, Louis B, ed. *Cases on United Nations Law*. Brooklyn: Foundation Press, 1956; 2nd ed., 1967. 1086 pp.
Complements his earlier volume on world law.

[1302] --------. "United Nations Charter Revision and the Rule of Law: A Program for Peace." *Northwestern University Law Review*, 50 (January-February, 1956), pp. 700-25.

[1303] --------. "The Authority of the United Nations to Establish and Maintain a Permanent United Nations Force." *American Journal of International Law*, 52 (April, 1958), pp. 229-40.

[1304] --------. "Preamble to a Global Constitution." *Saturday Review*, May 21, 1960, pp. 22-23, 50.
Review of Wallace McClure's *World Legal Order*. "This book is to some extent a political tract of a kind that flourished in the author's favored period -- the early days of the United States. But

we are living in revolutionary times and we need again this kind of partisan writing, fighting valiantly for a great and noble cause."

[1305] --------. "Adjudication and Enforcement in Arms Control." *Daedalus*, 89 (Fall, 1960), pp. 879-91.

[1306] --------. "Manley O. Hudson -- Obituary." *American Journal of Comparative Law*, 9 (1960), p. 334.

[1307] --------. "The Role of International Institutions as Conflict Adjusting Agencies." *University of Chicago Law Review*, 28 (Winter, 1961) pp. 205-57.

[1308] --------. "Security through Disarmament." *Nation*, February 25, 1961, pp. 159-63.

[1309] --------. "Disarmament Is Not Enough." Lecture, Cornell University, March 16, 1962.

[1310] --------. "The Role of International Law in International Relations." Lecture, U.S. Army War College, October 16, 1962.

[1311] --------. "The Many Faces of International Law." *American Journal of International Law*, 57 (October, 1963), pp. 867-70.

[1312] --------. "How to Achieve United States Security and a Free World." Speech, Meeting of United World Federalists, May 10, 1964.

[1313] --------. "Expulsion or Forced Withdrawal from an International Organization." *Harvard Law Review* (Cambridge), 77 (June, 1964), pp. 1381-1425.

[1314] --------. "Compulsory Jurisdiction of the International Court of Justice." Conference Paper, International Law Association, Tokyo, August 17, 1964.

[1315] --------. "Basic Problems of Disarmament." *Notre Dame Lawyer*, 41 (1965), pp. 133-51.

[1316] --------, et al. *Report for Presentation at the White House Conference on International Cooperation*. Washington: National Citizens' Commission on International Cooperation, Committee on Human Rights, 1965. 24 pp.

[1317] --------. "World Peace through World Law -- Dream or Reality?" *Royalton Review*, 3 (1968), pp. 101-10.
Law alone is insufficient to ensure a peaceful world. Governing institutions, too, are necessary: world executive, judiciary, police forces, and disarmament program.

[1317]a --------. "The Growth of the Science of International Organizations." In Karl Deutsch and Stanley Hoffmann, eds., *The Relevance of International Law* (Cambridge, Mass.: Schenkman, 1968), pp. 251-69.

[1318] --------, and Buergenthal, T. *International Protection of Human Rights*. Indianapolis: Bobbs-Merrill, 1973. 1402 pp.

[1319] --------. "Settlement of Disputes Arising out of the Law of the Sea

Convention." *San Diego Law Review*, 12 (April, 1975), pp. 495-517.

1320 --------.   "Due Process in the United Nations." *American Journal of International Law*, 69 (July, 1975), pp. 620-22.

1321 --------. "The Human Rights Law of the Charter." *Texas International Law Journal*, 12 (Spring-Summer, 1977), pp. 129-40.

1322 --------. "Conflict Management and the Oceans." New York: International Peace Academy, 1977.

1323 --------.   "World Peace through World Law Twenty Years Later." Address to Peace Research Summer School, Carleton University, Ottawa, Ontario, August, 1978.
Nearest approach to official action came in 1975.   Weighted voting has given way to increases in members of the Security Council. Eventual popular election of representatives to General Assembly seems likely to favor dictatorships (monolithic delegations) and probably should be dropped.   There has been more progress in human rights and economic organization than proposed.   Bulk remains un-achieved.

1324 --------.   "Disarmament and International Security." *Transnational Perspectives*, 5 (1979), pp. 6-9.
Account of initiatives by Secretary of State Christian Herter and President Kennedy, also of the McCloy-Zorin agreement. Complements Price.

1325 --------.   "The Improvement of the U.N. Machinery on Human Rights." *International Studies Quarterly*, 23 (June, 1979), pp. 184-215.

1326 Solomon, Jack. *Complete Handbook on World Government*.   Chicago: National Debate Research Co., 1960. 214 pp.
Cf. Aly, Holm, et al.

1327 Somerville, John. "World Authority: Realities and Illusions." *Ethics*, 74 (October, 1965), pp. 33-46.
Radically different ideologies can coexist (Catholics and Protes-tants, Christians and Moslems), once each learns that the other is a decent competitor and not a criminal conspirator. Capitalists and Communists do not yet so regard each other.

1328 Speer, James P. "Hans Morgenthau and the World State." *World Politics*, 20 (1968), pp. 207-77.
Critique of Morgenthau's abandonment of the argument for world government in *Politics among Nations* just at the point where the argument should lead to action. Instead, Morgenthau reverted to a plea for wise diplomacy.

1329 Stanley, C. Maxwell. *Waging Peace*: *A Businessman Looks at United States Foreign Policy*. New York: Macmillan, 1959. 256 pp.
By a president of United World Federalists, who later founded the Stanley Foundation for the study of international relations.   He also published *World Press Review* to build greater international consciousness in the U.S.

1330 --------. *Managing Global Problems*: *A Guide to Survival*. Muscatine, Iowa: Stanley Foundation, 1981. 286 pp.

Comprehensive proposals offered within a strategy for solving global problems by national means, while fostering creation of political and economic institutions endowed with extra-national and supra-national authority.

1331 Stromberg, Roland N. "Collective Security," in Alexander DeConde, ed.,
The Encyclopedia of American Foreign Policy: *Studies of the Principal Movements and Ideas*. New York: Scribners, 1978. 3 vols. I:124-
33.
Masterful on origin of League of Nations and inadequacy of collective security. Closes with call for world government.

1332 Swaab, Maurice. *The Final Solution*: *Neither Communism nor Capitalism,
But a New Concept of Universal Self-Government by Mandatory Individual Participation*. New York: Mediator's, 1973. 129 pp.

1333 Swing, Raymond Gram. *Good Evening*! *A Professional Memoir*. New York:
Harcourt, Brace, & World, 1964. 311 pp.
Only complement to *In the Name of Sanity*. Swing, like other advo-
cates in later years, passed rapidly over his federalist period.

1334 Tugwell, Rexford Guy. *Model for a New Consitution*. Santa Barbara,
Calif.: Center for the Study of Democratic Institutions, 1970. 160
pp.
Model new constitution for the *United States*. Shows influence of
Chicago world constitution.

1335 Van Slyck, Philip. *Peace*: *The Control of National Power*. Preface by
Herbert H. Humphrey. Boston: Beacon, 1964. 186 pp.
"A guide for the concerned citizen on problems of disarmament and
strengthening of the United Nations." A production of the Fund for
Education Concerning World Peace through World Law.

1336 Wadsworth, James J. *The Price of Peace*. New York: Praeger, 1962. 127
pp.
By former U.S. disarmament negotiator. Argument for new initiatives
that would seem more trustworthy to the Soviets.

1337 Wagar, W. Warren. *H. G. Wells and the World State*. New Haven, Conn.:
Yale University Press, 1961. 301 pp.
"Deals ably with the central idea that colored all of Well's work
from 1900 on."

1338 --------. *The City of Man*: *Prophecies of a World Civilization in 20th
Century Thought*. Boston: Houghton Mifflin, 1963. 310 pp.
Emotion and analysis alone will not produce peace; prophecy is
needed. Attempt is made to synthesize visions of Toynbee, Mumford,
de Chardin, and others.

1339 --------. "Toward the City of Man." *Center Magazine*, 1 (September,
1968), pp. 33-41.
A new world culture is developing.   Martyrs and heroes will bring
about a new world order. "All institutions are simply ideas trans-
planted into will and action."

1340 --------. *Building the City of Man*: *Outlines of a World Civilization*.
New York: Grossman, 1971. 180 pp.
New attitudes, ideology, and religion based on global orientation,

world solidarity, and loyalty to all mankind are needed in order to make possible the substitution of law for violence.

[1341] Warburg, James. *Disarmament*: *The Challenge of the Nineteen Sixties*. New York: Doubleday, 1961. 288 pp.
Disarmament is possible only if security is provided by a limited world government.

[1342] --------. *The United States in the Postwar World*: *A Critical Apprai-sal*. London: Gollancz, 1966. 255 pp.

[1343] Ward, Barbara. *Nationalism and Ideology*. New York: Norton, 1966. 125 pp.
Plea for internationalism and peace.

[1344] Waskow, Arthur I. *The Worried Man's Guide to World Peace*. Garden City, N.Y.: Doubleday, 1963. 219 pp.
A guide for those who ask, "What can I do?" Cf. Green, *The Worried Woman's Guide*.

[1345] Weik, Mary H. "The Search for World Community." *Journal of Human Re-lations*, 4 (Winter, 1956), pp. 9-34.
Support for U.N. Charter reform.

[1346] Weizsacker, Carl Friedrich von.   "A Central World Political Organiza-tion Is Essential." *Center Report*, June, 1975, pp. 6-7.
World federal government is essential in long term. In short term, we should support detente and Third World development. Pessimistic. "The securing of world peace sets mankind a clearly defined task, a task clearly beyond its current political social system. . . ."

[1347] Wertenbaker, William. "The Law of the Sea." *New Yorker*, August 1, 1983, pp. 38-65; August 8, 1983, pp. 56-83.
In nine years of meetings of the last conference on the Law of the Sea, a vote was never taken. Consensus was developed to reach the historic agreement on December 10, 1982.

[1348] Weston, Burns, ed. *Toward Nuclear Disarmament and Global Security*: *A Search for Alternatives*. Boulder, Colo.: Westview Press, 1984. 746 pp.

[1349] Woito, Robert. *To End War*: *A New Approach to International Conflict*. New York: Pilgrim, 1967; 6th ed., 1982. 755 pp.
Extensive guide to the arguments, ideas, context, and lines of ac-tion for creating a world without war, under law.

[1350] Wooley, Wesley T., Jr. "The Quest for Permanent Peace -- American Su-pra-nationalism, 1945-1947." *Historian*, 35 (1972), pp. 18-31.
Views of federalists and other critics of U.N. Charter: Norman Cou-sins, Robert M. Hutchins, Emery Reves, Clarence Streit, Raymond Swing, James Burnham, Ely Culbertson, and William Ziff.

[1351] World Federalists of Canada. Heinrich, Dieter, presentor. *The Common Security Alternative*: *Canadian Strategies to Transform the War Sys-tem*. A Brief for Submission to the Joint Committee on Canada's In-ternational Relations, December, 1985. Ottawa: WFC, 1985. 26 pp.
Formal proposal for a common security policy. Argument that worsen-ing global crises require world political cooperation, which can be

realized by a policy of common security, replacing that of national security. The transition policy -- maintaining military deterrence while developing a new "total orientation" -- is also defined.

[1352] Wright, Quincy. *The Role of International Law in the Elimination of War*. New York: Oceana, 1961. 119 pp.
Emphasizes the functional differences between rules designed to insure order (must be clear and precise) and principles of administration and justice (should be less positive and more equitable).

[1353] --------; Evan, William M.; and Deutsch, Morton, eds. *Preventing World War III: Some Proposals*. New York: Simon & Schuster, 1962. 460 pp.
Papers on stopping the arms race, reducing international tensions, and building a world society.

[1354] --------. "The Foundations of a Universal International System." *Notre Dame Lawyer*, 44 (April, 1969), pp. 527-47.
Of six proposed alternatives to present state of international relations, strengthening the U.N. and expanding international law alone is possible and likely to contribute to peace within the next generation.

[1355] Wynner, Edith. *Pac-Planoj "lau la Karto."* [Peace Plans a la Carte.] Chicago: Campaign for World Government, n.d., c. 1955. 8 pp.
Pri Mond-Federacio.

[1356] --------. "Noah, the Flood, and World Government." *The Humanist*, July-August, 1975, pp. 24-27.
When warned, Noah acted. We do not. Time for radical, unofficial, popular action.

[1357] Yost, Charles W. "World Peace Is Possible." *World Magazine*, September 12, 1972, pp. 17-21.
By former U.S. ambassador to U.N. Argues U.N. must become a global federation to avoid world disaster. Problem is that great powers continue to act unilaterally in own immediate interests rather than cooperatively in long term interests through U.N.

[1358] Zimmerman, Carle C. "Convergence of the Major Human Family Systems during the Space Age." In Edward A. Tiryakian, ed., *Sociological Theory, Values, and Socio-Cultural Change* (New York: Harper & Row, 1967).

8

U.S. Congressional Hearings and Official Reports

The world federalist movement succeeded in getting federalist resolutions passed in twenty-one states. About ten resolutions were introduced in Congress. The effort in Congress was led by Representatives
Walter Judd (R., Minn.) and Brooks Hays (D., Ark.), and by Senators Glen
Taylor (D., Idaho), Charles Tobey (R., N.H.), Estes Kefauver (D., Tenn.),
and John Sparkman (D., Ala.). The United World Federalist resolution of
1949 was co-sponsored by 111 Representatives (Judd-Hays, HCR-64) and 21
Senators (Tobey, SCR-56). These co-sponsors included Abraham Ribicoff,
Christian Herter, John F. Kennedy, Gerald Ford, Mike Mansfield, Peter Rodi-
no, Jacob Javits, and Henry Jackson, Senators Herbert Humphrey, Wayne
Morse, and Claude Pepper. Senator J. William Fulbright co-sponsored the
Atlantic Union resolution. Richard M. Nixon, when a Congressman in 1947 and
1948, co-sponsored several similar resolutions. None of these later famous
figures, however, took an active part in pressing for the legislation. But
they reflect the times.

The official reports listed here contain basic documents on the founding of the United Nations, the international control of atomic energy, and
the world federalist resolutions. There were hearings in the House in 1948
and 1949 and in the Senate in 1950. In diplomatic terms, the hearings were
used as occasions to build support for the North Atlantic Treaty and for
the very strained interpretation made of Art. 51 of the U.N. Charter. Nevertheless, the reports are invaluable sources for top-level discussion of
world federalism.

United World Federalists concentrated most of their energy on defeat-
ing the Atlantic Union resolution in order to uphold the principle of universality. The Korean War then set the whole movement back. Thereafter,
important hearings were held on Charter revision in 1955 and on proposals
for calling a Charter review conference in the 1970s, but political leadership was lacking.

[1367] *Foreign Relations of the United States, 1944*, vol. 1: General. Washington: Department of State Publication 8138, 1966. 1526 pp.
Establishment of international organization for the maintenance of peace and security, Dumbarton Oaks, etc.

[1368] *Foreign Relations of the United States, 1945*, vol. 1: General: The United Nations. Washington: Department of State Publication 8294, 1967. 1611 pp.
Dumbarton Oaks and San Francisco conferences.

[1369] *Foreign Relations of the United States, 1946*, vol. 1: General: The United Nations. Washington: Department of State Publication 8573, 1972. 1544 pp.
Baruch Plan, Military Staff Committee, arms control, development of international law.

[1370] *Postwar Foreign Policy Preparation, 1939-1945*. Washington: Department of State Publication 3580, 1949. 726 pp.
Official consideration of problems and possibilities of postwar international organization. Cordell Hull's elaborate study.

[1371] *The United Nations Conference on International Organization, San Francisco, California, April 25 - June 26, 1945: Selected Documents*. Washington: Department of State Publication 2490, Conference Series 83, 1946. 991 pp.
Proceedings during final drafting of the Charter at San Francisco. China, France, and fifteen small nations all expressed willingness to limit national sovereignty. Cf. pp. 665, 693-98.

[1372] U.S. Congress, Senate.   *Debate on the U.N. Participation Act*. 79th Cong., 1st sess., November 26, 1945. *Congressional Record*, 91: 10,971-75.
Comments by Senators Connally, Vandenberg, Taylor, Ball, and Fullbright on the Dublin Declaration and on Taylor's bill to create a World Republic.

[1373] U.S. Congress, Senate. Committee on Foreign Relations. *Revision of United Nations Charter*. Executive Hearings, 80th Cong., 2nd sess., April 20, 1948. Senate Library Vol. S.3093, Tab 1.   In "Executive Sessions of the Senate Foreign Relations Committee" (Historical Series), vol. 1, pp. 257-61. SupDocs No. Y4.F76/2:Ex3/2/v.1.
Earliest known formal consideration of inadequacy of U.N. Hearings released 1976.

[1374] U.S. Congress, Senate. Committee on Foreign Relations. *The Vandenberg Resolution*. Executive Hearings, 80th Cong., 2nd sess., May 11-19, 1948. Senate Library Vol. S.2464.   In "The Vandenberg Resolution and the North Atlantic Treaty" (Historical Series), pp. 3-38. SupDocs No. Y4.F76/2:V28.
Consideration of how to treat U.N.   on enactment of North Atlantic Treaty. Hearings released 1973.

[1375] U.S. Congress, House of Representatives. Committee on Foreign Affairs. *Structure of the United Nations and the Relations of the United States to the United Nations*. Hearings, 80th Cong., 2nd sess., May 4-14, 1948. House Library Vol. H-1210, Tab 1, Microfiche. SupDocs No. Y4.F76/1:Un34/3. 591 pp.
First Congressional hearings on world federalist resolutions (used

to prepare way for North Atlantic Treaty).

[1376] U.S. Congress, House of Representatives. Committee on Foreign Affairs. *To Seek Development of the United Nations into a World Federation.* Hearings on HCR-64 and Related Pending Resolutions, 81st Cong., 1st sess., October 12-13, 1949. House Library Vol. H.1269, Tab 10, Microfiche. SupDocs No. Y4.F76/1:Un34/5. 292 pp.
Hearings primarily on United World Federalists' and Atlantic Union resolutions.

[1377] U.S. Congress, Senate. Subcommittee of the Committee on Foreign Relations. *Revision of the United Nations Charter.* Hearings on Resolutions Relative to Revision of the United Nations Charter, Atlantic Union, World Federation, etc., 81st Cong., 2nd sess., February 2-20, 1950. Senate Library Vol. S.944, Tab 5, Microfiche. SupDocs No. Y4.F76/2:Un35/2. 808 pp.
Senate hearings at which State Department quashed all world federalist resolutions.

[1377]a U.S. Congress, Senate. Committee on Foreign Relations, Subcommittee on the United Nations Charter. "Revision of the United Nations Charter." Washington: Report No. 2501, 1950.

[1378] U.S. Congress, Senate. Committee on Foreign Relations. *Review of the United Nations Charter.* Hearings on U.S. Participation in Charter Review Conference of 1955 (Art. 109), Parts 1-7, 83rd Cong., 2nd sess., January 18 - July 10, 1954. Senate Library Vol. S.1103, Tab 6, Microfiche. SupDocs No. Y4.F76/2:Un35/3/pts.1-7. 902 pp.
Parts 8-13, 84th Cong., 1st sess., March 17 - May 3, 1955. Senate Library Vol. S.1137, Tab 1, Microfiche. SupDocs No. Y4.F76/2:-Un35/3/pts.8-13. 2065 pp.
Hearings held in selected cities across the country on U.N. Charter revision, in accordance with the review conference provided for in Art. 109 for 1955.

[1378]a U.S. Congress, Senate. Committee on Foreign Relations, Subcommittee on the United Nations Charter. *Final Report.* 84 Cong., 2nd sess. Washington: Report No. 1797, 1956. 37 pp.

[1379] U.S. Congress, Senate. Committee on Foreign Relations. *Compulsory Jurisdiction and the International Court of Justice.* Hearings, 86th Cong., 2nd sess., January 27 and February 17, 1960. Senate Library Vol. S.1387, Tab 3, Microfiche. SupDocs No. Y4.F76/2:In8/-11/960. 520 pp.
Statements on all facets of the Connally amendment.

[1380] U.S. Congress, Senate. Committee on Foreign Relations. *United Nations Charter Amendments.* Hearings before the Committee, 89th Cong., 1st sess., April 28-29, 1965. Senate Library Vol. S.1678, Tab 1, Microfiche. SupDocs No. Y4.F76/2:Un35/13. 138 pp.
Amendments increasing the number of nations in the Security Council to 15, and of those in the Economic and Social Council to 27.

[1381] U.S. Congress, House of Representatives. Committee on Foreign Affairs. *United Nations Twenty-Fifth Anniversary.* Hearings in Review of Performance, Operations, and Future Goals, 91st Cong., 2nd sess., Part 1, February 18 - March 5, 1970. House Library Vol. H.2483, Tab 6. SupDocs No. Y4.F76/1:Un34/13. Part 2, April 21 - August 6, 1970.

House Library Vol.   H.2550, Tab 1.   SupDocs No.   Y4.F76/1:Un34/13/-pt.2. 565 pp.
Problem areas in U.N., failure of U.N. to deal with Vietnam War, relative usefulness in peacekeeping operations, ocean regime, alternatives to U.N., measures to strengthen it, elections of U.N. representatives, place of U.N. in U.S. policy.

[1382] --------. *United Nations Charter Review Conference.* Hearings on Resolutions Urging Such Conference Be Held, 92nd Cong., 2nd sess., April 27 - May 1, 1972. House Library Vol. H.2744, Tab 9. CIS No. H381-43. SupDocs No. Y4.F76/1:Un34/19. 72 pp.
Hearings on renewed resolutions favoring a U.N. Charter review conference, one of which called for establishment of a commission on U.S. participation in the U.N.

[1383] --------. *United Nations Charter Review Conference.* Hearings on Resolutions Urging Such Conference Be Held, 94th Cong., 1st sess., July 17, 1975. House Library Vol. H.3201, Tab 6. CIS No. H381-61. SupDocs No. Y4.In8/16:Un35/2. 63 pp.
Hearings on HCR-206, calling on the President to direct the State Department to propose changes in the Charter or procedural changes.

[1384] U.S. Congress, Senate. Committee on Foreign Relations. *Reform of the United Nations: An Analysis of the President's Proposals and Their Comparison with Proposals of Other Countries.* Report by Carol A. Capps et al., Analyzing the President's Recommendations of March, 1978, for Reform of the U.N., 96th Cong., 1st sess., October 26, 1979. Senate Library Vol. S.3647, Tab 2. CIS No. S382-40. Sup-Docs No. Y4.F76/2:Un35/39.
Proposals for strengthening U.N. peacekeeping capabilities, modifying Security Council voting and veto powers, coordinating human rights programs, revising members' financial assessments, and restructuring technical assistance programs.

9

Universal Federation—
Great Britain

The British have had nearly as strong a world federalist movement as the Americans, ever since Federal Union (not the same as Streit's organization of the same name) was founded in 1939. Before the war, the British were particularly receptive to ideas of supranational union, since their own government seemed unable to stop the rise of Hitler. A climate of opinion was created favorable to Churchill's offer of union with France on June 16, 1940, on the eve of her defeat by Nazi Germany. British victory in war by 1945, however, restored much of the people's faith in King and Parliament. Nevertheless, after the war, the British keenly felt their peril between the two giants of America and Russia, they sensed their Empire slipping away, and they regretted the passing of their historic role as balancer in European politics. They naturally tended to think of the British Commonwealth as a model for the world. They also had just established their first socialist government and were relatively stable politically with respect to communism, unlike, say, France. So in many ways they were well placed to undertake an initiative for world federation.

After a U.S. rebuff to a speech by Foreign Minister Ernest Bevin, Henry Usborne, a young Labour MP, decided to lead an unofficial crusade for world federal government. His proposal was to hold a peoples' convention in Geneva by 1950. He failed to make much headway against the politics of the Cold War, but in the 1950s his group, the British Parliamentary Group for World Government, continued to uphold the ideal. The group included such MPs as Lords Beveridge, Boyd-Orr, and Merthyr, and Clement Davies, I.J. Pitman, and Arthur Henderson. They created the "parliamentary approach," by which members of national parliaments (or Congress) will take the initiative for world federation. The parliamentary approach has led to the formation of the World Association of Parliamentarians for World Government and most recently to Parliamentarians for World Order.

Other notable British authors include Curtis, Mitrany, Boyd-Orr, Toynbee, and H.G. Wells (a virtual prophet of the world state). Geoffrey Barraclough can be seen as continuing Toynbee's view that, in the twentieth century, world history, not national history, is the proper context for politics. E. H. Carr provides a valuable critical voice. He was much more of a moderate about the realist/idealist dichotomy than is sometimes remembered. Bertrand Russell, who once at the height of Cold War tension in 1948 advocated use of atomic weapons to compel Russia to accept world government, provides a warning that even philosophers can sometimes be carried away by war hysteria. The movement for world federation is always in danger of gliding into one for world empire.

[1394] Alder, Vera Stanley. *Humanity Comes of Age*: *A Study of Individual and World Fulfillment*. London: Dakers, 1950. 212 pp.
Survey of the "conditions which are drawing a suffering humanity into a deep and subconscious brotherhood, whose results should swing the public will inevitably into the balance for a unified world under a coherent central organisation." Religious.

[1395] Bailey, Gerald. *Towards a New International Order*: *League and Federation*. London: National Peace Council, Peace Aims Pamphlet No. 1, 1940. 10 pp.
Address to annual meeting of Women's International League.

[1396] Barraclough, Geoffrey. *An Introduction to Contemporary History*.   New York: Basic Books, 1964. 272 pp.
Contemporary age (1890-present) is universal.   Euro- or Atlantic-centered history is inadequate.

[1397] --------, ed. *The Times Atlas of World History*. Maplewood, N.J.: Hammond, 1978. 360 pp.
Note Section 7: "The Age of Global Civilisation."

[1398] Bennett, D.C.T. *Freedom from War*. London: Pilot, 1945. 81 pp.

[1399] Beveridge, Sir William. *Peace by Federation*? London: Federal Tracts No. 1, Federal Union, 1940. 35 pp.

[1400] --------. *The Price of Peace*. New York: Norton, 1945. 160 pp.
By most prestigious member of Usborne's group.

[1401] Bevin, Ernest.   Speech on "World Law" in Debate on Foreign Affairs. House of Commons, *Hansard's Parliamentary Debates*,   November 23, 1945, H.C. 416, cols. 759-87.
"I am willing to sit with anybody, of any nation, to try to devise a franchise or a constitution -- just as other great countries have done -- for a world assembly . . . with a limited objective -- the objective of peace. . . . It would be a world law with a world judiciary to interpret it, with a world police to enforce it, with the decision of the people in their own votes resting in their own hands, irrespective of race or creed, as the great world sovereign elected authority which would hold in its care the destinies of the world."   Highest British pronouncement in favor of limited world government. Response to atomic energy.

[1403] Boyd-Orr, John, baron. "Food: The World Situation." *Fellowship*, November, 1947.

[1404] --------. *Food*: *The Foundation of World Unity*.   London: National Peace Council, Towards World Government, No. 1, 1948. 20 pp.
Boyd-Orr, the first director of the U.N. Food and Agriculture Organization, resigned in 1948 in protest against the U.N.'s inability to be "above politics in supplying the world's basic need for food. Thereafter he worked for world government.

[1405] -------. *Science, Politics, and Peace*: *Lecture Delivered on the Occasion of the Award of the Nobel Peace Prize of 1949*.   London: National Peace Council, 1949. 24 pp.

[1406] --------. *Economic and Political Problems of the Atomic Age*. Birmingham: Birmingham and Midland Institute, 1953. 19 pp.

1407 --------. "Ethics for the Atomic Age." *Monthly Record* (London), 60
(April, 1955).

1408 --------. *As I Recall*. London: MacGibbon & Kee, 1966. 290 pp.
Memoirs putting into perspective his work for world government.

1409 Brailsford, Henry Noel. *The Federal Idea*. London: Federal Union,
1940. 15 pp.

1410 British Parliamentary Group for World Government. McAllister, Gilbert,
ed. *First Report of World Parliamentary Conference on World Government*. London: 1951. 121 pp.

1411 --------.   *The Case for World Government*: *The 1952 Manifesto*.   London: House of Commons, 1952. 14 pp.

1412 --------. --------.   *World Government*: *The Report of the Second London Parliamentary Conference, September 20-26, 1952*. London: World
Association of Parliamentarians for World Government, 1953. 187 pp.

1413 --------. --------.   *Report of the Third Parliamentary Conference on
World Government* (*Copenhagen*).   London: World Association of Parliamentarians for World Government, 1953. 140 pp.

1414 --------. --------. *World*: *A Report of the Fourth Parliamentary Conference on World Government*. London: 1955.

1415 --------. *Parliamentary Path to Peace . . . 1947-1955*. London: 1955;
revised ed., 1958. 38 pp.
Continuation of Henry Usborne's group. Members included Lords Beveridge, Boyd-Orr, and Merthyr, and Messrs. Clement Davies, I.J.
Pitman, and Arthur Henderson.

1416 Buler-Murphey, Basil. *Safety of Our Future*: *World Federation*. Foreword by Lord Boyd-Orr. Melbourne: Robertson & Mullens, 1957.   184
pp.

1417 Carr, Edward Hallett. *The Twenty Years' Crisis, 1919-1939*: *An Introduction to the Study of International Relations*. London: Macmillan, 1940. 312 pp.
Fundamental for conflict of realism and utopianism (idealism) in
world politics.   Both needed in theory and found in fact.   Model
for international conciliation is the reconciliation of labor and
capital -- sacrifices are needed, then legislation can follow.
"World federation" is an "elegant superstructure" that must wait
until "some progress has been made in digging the foundations."

1418 --------, and de Madariaga, Salvadore. *The Future of International
Government*. London: National Peace Council, Peace Aims Pamphlet
No. 4, 1941. 24 pp.

1419 --------. *Nationalism and After*. London: Macmillan, 1945. 74 pp.

1420 Chaning-Pearce, M., ed. *Federal Union*: *A Symposium*. London: Cape,
1940. 336 pp.

1421 --------, et al.   "The Basic Principles of Federalism." *New Common-wealth Quarterly*, 6 (1941), pp. 163-232.

1422 Cherry, Jack, and Walker, E.   *The Disunited Nations*: *A Protest and a Plan*.   London: Hastings National Liberal Organisation, To Set You Thinking Series, No. 4, 1957. 72 pp.

1423 Chesterton, Arthur K.   *The Menace of World Government*.   Willowdale, Ont.: League of Empire Loyalists, National Federation of Christian Laymen, 1955. 14 pp.
Cf. Kamp.

1424 Cohen, L. Jonathan. *The Principles of World Citizenship*. Oxford: Basil Blackwell, 1954.   103 pp
Philosophical contribution. "If [anyone] objects that there can be no world sovereign state without a uniform world ideology and there-fore urges instead a regional federation of like-minded nations, he can be shown adequate evidence that such an ideology is not needed and that policies for regional federation have nothing to do with world government."

1425 Colombos, C. John.   "The Shape of Things to Come: The Organisation and Functions of the Future International Authority." *Grotius Society Problems of Peace and War*, 30 (1945), pp. 83-118.

1426 Curry, W. B.   *The Case for Federal Union*.   Hammondsworth, Middlesex: Penguin, November, 1939. 213 pp.
Equivalent in England to Streit's *Union Now*.

1427 Curtis, Lionel. *Civitas Dei*. London: Macmillan, 1934-1937. 3 vols. Curtis introduced the term "commonwealth" (*res publica*) for "em-pire," founded the *Round Table* and the Royal Institute for Interna-tional Affairs, and directed the Institute of Pacific Relations. *Civitas Dei* was the most important of his many works. In its broad historical vision, search for a coherent principle of politics, and clear advocacy of world federation, it is comparable to the work of H. G. Wells or Arnold Toynbee.

1428 --------. *World Order (Civitas Dei)*. Forward by A. Lawrence Lowell. New York: Oxford University Press, 1939. 985 pp.
American edition. See Book IV, Chap. 7.

1429 --------. *Decision*. London: Oxford, Milford, 1941. 76 pp.

1430 --------. *Decision and Action*. London: Oxford, Milford, 1942.   114 pp.

1431 --------. *Towards a World Order*. London: National Peace Council, Peace Aims Phamphlet No. 17, 1942. 48 pp.

1432 --------. *Faith and Works*: *A World Safe for Small Nations*.   Intro-duction by Sir William Beveridge. London: Oxford, Milford, 1943. 120 pp.

1433 --------. *The Way to Peace*. London: Oxford, Milford, 1944. 98 pp.

1434 --------. *World War*: *Its Cause and Cure*. London: Oxford, Milford, 1945. 274 pp.

[1435] --------. *World War: Its Cause and Cure*; *The Problem Reconsidered in the Light of Atomic Energy*. New York: Putnams, 2nd ed. 1946. 274 pp.
Proposes U.N. General Assembly be transformed into a federal world parliament, with representation weighted by taxable capacity.

[1436] --------. *The Master Key to Peace*. London: Oxford, 1947. 28 pp.

[1437] --------. *World Revolution in the Cause of Peace*. Foreword by Owen J. Roberts. New York: Macmillan, 1949. 135 pp.

[1438] --------. *The Open Road to Freedom*. London: Oxford, Blackwell, 1950. 78 pp.
Minimal world government.

[1439] Dana, Charles A., and Farncombe, A.E. *World Government -- Shall Britain Participate?* London: British-American Council for World Government Organisation, 1944. 48 pp.

[1440] Davies, David, baron. *The Seven Pillars of Peace*. London: Longmans, Green, 1945. 149 pp.
Hope that Big Four in United Nations would become nucleus of necessary world government. By leading British scholar on international relations.

[1441] De Rusett, Alan. *Strengthening the Framework of Peace: A Study of Current Proposals for Amending, Developing, or Replacing Present International Institutions for the Maintenance of Peace*. London: Royal Institute of International Affairs, 1950. 225 pp.

[1442] Dexter, Lewis A. "Some Neglected Aspects of 'Federalism.'" *New Commonwealth Quarterly*, 5 (1939), pp. 244-47.

[1443] Dobson, Dennis. *The Birth of a World People: The Provisional Constitution of the Commonwealth of World Citizens*. Introduction by Hugh J. Schonfield. London: By the author, 1956. 59 pp.
Formal attempt to create a legal community of World Citizens. Not a blueprint for world government but an effort to strengthen world community preparatory to it.

[1444] Eagleton, Clyde. "The League of Nations and Federal Union." *New Commonwealth Quarterly*, 5 (1939), pp. 119-30.

[1445] --------. "World Government Discussion in the United States." *London Quarterly of World Affairs*, 12 (1946), pp. 251-58.

[1446] Earle, Edward Mead. "H.G. Wells: British Patriot in Search of a World State." *World Politics*, 2 (January, 1950), pp. 181-208.

[1447] Ewing, A.C. *The Individual, the State, and World Government*. New York: Macmillan, 1947. 322 pp.
The Cambridge philosopher "discusses rationally the chief general political principles at issue in the world today."

[1448] Fawcett, Charles Bungay. *The Bases of a World Commonwealth*. London: Watts, 1941; 2nd ed., 1943. 179 pp.

[1450] Federal Union. Joint Commission on U.N. Charter Reform. *United Nations Reform*: *Proposals for a Federal United Nations*. London: Federal Union and Crusade for World Government, 1953. 8 pp.

[1451] *Federation*: *Peace Aim -- War Weapon*. London: Federal Union, 1942. 15 pp.

[1452] Federn, Robert. *Peace, Prosperity, International Order*. London: Williams & Norgate, 1945. 168 pp.

[1453] Freeman, Peter. *The Government of the World*. Madras, India: Adyar Library, 1952. 60 pp.
Reprint from book, *Where Theosophy and Science Meet* (1952).

[1454] Frost, Richard Aylme. *The British Commonwealth and the World*. London: Royal Institute of International Affairs, 1945. 74 pp.
Discussions at the British Commonwealth Relations Conference, London, February 1945.

[1455] Garnett, James C.M. *World Unity*. London: Oxford University Press, Milford, 1939. 32 pp.

[1456] Gladwyn Jebb, H.M., baron. *Memoirs*. London: Weidenfeld & Nicolson, 1972. 422 pp.
English view of great conferences at Dumbarton Oaks and San Francisco. Clement Attlee a "world government man."

[1457] Glover, Edward. *War, Sadism and Pacifism*: *Further Essays on Group Psychology and War*. London: Allen & Unwin, 1946. 292 pp.
Revised and expanded edition of book first published in 1933. Psychoanalytic study of war. Cf. Ranyard West.

[1458] Greaves, H.R.G. *Federal Union in Practice*. London: Allen & Unwin, 1940. 135 pp.

[1459] Greenidge, C.W.W. "The British Caribbean Federation." *World Affairs*, 4 (July, 1950), pp. 321-34.
Background on proposal for federation of British West Indies.

[1460] Habicht, Max. *The Power of an International Judge to Give a Decision ex aequo et bono*. London: New Commonwealth Institute, 1935. 86 pp.

[1461] Hackett, Ian J. *The Spring of Civilisation*. London: Campaign for Earth Federation, 9 Grange Park W5, 1973.

[1462] Harris, Errol E. *Survival of Political Man*: *A Study of the Principles of International Order*. Johannesburg: University of Witwatersrand, 1950. 225 pp.

[1463] --------. *Annihilation and Utopia*: *The Principles of International Politics*. London: Allen & Unwin, 1966. 331 pp.
Philosophical analysis of the ideological conflict between East and West. Discusses the legal principles of world order, the conditions of world community, democracy, communism, and their reconciliation. Concludes with an account of the stages by which an effective world authority might be brought into being.

[1464] Hart, Norman J., et al. *Basis of Federalism*:   *A Symposium*.   Paris:
World Student Federalists, 1949. 67 pp.

[1465] Hayek, F. A. von. "Economic Conditions of Inter-State Federalism." *New
Commonwealth Quarterly*, 5 (1939), pp. 131-49.

[1466] Hinsley, Francis H. *Power and the Pursuit of Peace*:   *Theory and Practice in the History of Relations between States*.   Cambridge: Cambridge University Press, 1963. 416 pp.
Federalism (centralized international organization) was character-
istic of peace plans from Dante to the Enlightenment, then it was
superseded by confederalism. But failure of confederalism from the
times of the Hague conferences and the world wars has created need
for new principles. Cf. Carr, Osgood.

[1467] Hoyland, John S.   *Federate or Perish*.   London: Federal Union, 1944.
202 pp.

[1467]a Huddleston, John. *The Earth Is But One Country*. London: Baha'i Publishing Trust, 1976; 2nd ed., 1980. 185 pp.
"The purpose of this book is to show how the Baha'i Faith meets the
needs of mankind today, and how it is building up what is believed
will be a new world-wide civilization in which all peoples can live
together in justice, harmony, and peace.   The emphasis is on the
practical means to this end as well as on the dream."

[1468] Huxley, Aldous. "Bridges to One World." *Tomorrow*, November, 1947, pp.
12-15.

[1469] Jacks, Lawrence P. *The Idea of a World Community*.   London: National
Peace Council, Towards World Government, No. 2, 1949. 19 pp.

[1470] Jackson, Barbara (Ward), Lady. *The West at Bay*. New York: W.W. Norton, 1948. 288 pp.
Cold War politics.

[1471] --------. *Policy for the West*. New York: W. W. Norton, 1950.   317
pp.
Saw "ultimate necessity" of world government but progress toward
that goal as "evolutionary,   functional," and regional.   Atlantic
union the preferred next step.

[1472] --------. *Spaceship Earth*. London: Hamish Hamilton, 1966. 152 pp.
Economic interdependence is moving the earth toward "the intimacy,
the fellowship, and the vulnerability of a spaceship." Late argument for the existence of world community.

[1473] --------.   *Nationalism and Ideology*.   New York: Norton, 1966.   125
pp.
"Young people off to the Peace Corps, worker priests in the slums
of Paris, young Komsomols volunteering for schools in the Arctic,
nuns in Calcutta giving starving beggars off the streets a decent
death -- the examples are world-wide.   They make up pockets of a
new elite who are so far beyond our angry nationalisms that, like
the just men of the Talmudic legend, their profound humanity may
well hold up the rooftrees of heaven for all mankind."

[1474] Joad, C.E.M. *The Philosophy of Federal Union*. Federal Tracts No. 5.

London: Macmillan, 1941. 40 pp.

[1475] --------. *Conditions of Survival*: *Federal Union*. London: Federal
Union, 1946. 24 pp.

[1476] --------. "World vs. Regional Federation." *New Statesman and Nation*,
36 (November 27, 1948), pp. 459-60.

[1477] Johnstone, Robert. *The Lost World*: *Does It Exist*? Gerrard's Cross:
Colin Smythe, 1978. 152 pp.
Search for a new religion being born in our times in response to
patriotism, which Toynbee saw as the successor religion to Christi-
anity in the Western world. Critique of nationalism; argument for
world federation on spiritual grounds.

[1478] Joyce, James Avery, ed. *World Organisation*: *Federal or Functional?*
A Round Table Discussion. London: C.A. Watts, 1945. 54 pp.
Comment on Mitrany's *A Working Peace System*, by Patrick Ransome,
George Catlin, Edvard Hambro, C.B. Purdom, J.A. Joyce, H.G. Wells,
and David Mitrany, February 5, 1944.

[1479] --------. *World in the Making*: *The Story of International Cooperation*. New York: Schuman, 1953. 159 pp.

[1480] --------. *Revolution on East River*: *The Twilight of National Sovereignty*. New York: Abelard-Schuman, 1956. 244 pp.

[1481] --------. *The Story of International Cooperation*. Foreword by U Thant.
New York: Franklin Watts, 1964. 258 pp.
Survey from Greek Olympic Games, Roman Empire, Renaissance, voyages
of discovery, wars of rising nation states, and international organization in the 19th and 20th centuries.

[1482] --------. *The New Politics of Human Rights*. London: Macmillan, 1978.
305 pp.

[1483] Keen, Frank Noel. "World Legislation." Grotius Society, *Problems of
Peace and War*, 16 (1931), pp. 1-12.

[1484] --------. *Crossing the Rubicon*: *Or the Passage from the Rule of Force
to the Rule of Law among Nations*. Birmingham: Cornish, 1939. 60
pp.

[1485] --------. "The Future Development of International Law." Grotius Society, *Problems of Peace and War*, 29 (1944), pp. 35-50.

[1486] --------. *The Abolition of War*. London: David Davies Memorial Institute of International Studies, 1955. 54 pp.
International arbitration.

[1487] Keeton, George W. "Federalism and World Order." *New Commonwealth
Quarterly*, 5 (1939), pp. 6-10.

[1488] --------, ed. *The Path to Peace*: *A Debate*. London: Institute for
World Affairs, Pitman, 1945. 114 pp.
Articles from the institute's *Law Journal*, 1944-1945.

[1489] Killby, J.K. "World Federation -- through U.N.?" *United Nations News*

(London), 5 (May-June, 1950), pp. 13-15.

[1490] Kindleberger, Charles P. "Systems of International Economic Organization." In David P. Calleo, ed., *Money and the Coming World Order*
(New York: New York University Press, Lehrman, 1976), pp. 15-39.
"In political terms, the provision of the world public good of stability is best provided, if not by a world government, by a system
of rules." Such substitute systems, however, readily "break down."
Recent economic thinking on necessity for world government.

[1491] Kohr, Leopold. *The Breakdown of Nations*.   London: Routledge & Kegan
Paul, 1957. 244 pp.
Anti-world government. A world of small states is best, but it may
pass through a stage of universal empire, possibly American.

[1491a] Laski, Harold J. *Reflections on the Revolution of Our Time*. New York:
Viking, 1943. 419 pp.
Replies to Gilbert Murray on abrogating national sovereignty.

[1492] Law, Richard. *Return from Utopia*. London: Faber & Faber, 1950. 206
pp.
By prominent Cabinet member. Criticism of the "easy utopia" of
world federation after start of the Korean War. The Communist challenge was *not* to sacrifice liberty in order to survive.

[1492a] Layton, Christopher. *One Europe*: *One World*; *A First Exploration of
Europe's Potential Contribution to World Order*. London: The Journal of World Trade Law in association with the Federal Trust for
Education and Research, 1986. 70 pp.
"This essay is inspired by the belief that the time has come for a
united Europe to take up its responsibilities for working for a
more united world." Masterful exploration of Europe's contribution
to a "world governance system that works."

[1493] Layton, Walter T. baron. *The British Commonwealth and World Order*.
London: News Chronicle, 1944. 19 pp.

[1494] Lewis, Sulwyn. *Towards International Cooperation*.   Oxford: Pergamon,
1966. 327 pp.
Eight components of modern nationalism (e.g., self-determination)
have to find substitutes in internationalism.

[1495] Livingstone, Dame Adelaide. *The Peace Ballot*. London: Gollancz, 1935.
64 pp.
Lord Cecil's unofficial Peace Ballot of 1934, in which 11,000,000
people voted to support the League of Nations. Model for Usborne's
proposed peoples' convention of 1950.

[1496] Lord, Mia. *The Practical Way to End Wars and Other World Crises*: *The
Case for World Federal Government*. London: Association of World
Federalists, L.A. Cousins, 1977. 31 pp.

[1497] Lothian, Philip Henry, 11th marquess of. *Pacifism Is Not Enough*: *Nor
Patriotism Either*. Preface by William Beveridge. London: Oxford
University Press, 1935; 2nd ed., 1941). 57 pp.
Classic of world federalism. Lothian was a colleague of Lionel
Curtis.

[1498] Luard, D. Evan T.   *Nationality and Wealth*: *A Study in World Government*. London: Oxford University Press, 1964. 370 pp.

[1499] --------. *Types of International Society*. New York: Free Press, 1976.

[1500] Lugard, Frederick J.D. *Federal Union and the Colonies*. Federal Tracts No. 7. London: Macmillan, 1941. 32 pp.

[1501] McAllister, Gilbert, ed. *The Bomb*: *Challenge and Answer*. London: Batsford, 1955. 160 pp.
      Includes views of Bertrand Russell, Lord Beveridge, and Henry Usborne.

[1502] MacKay, R.W.G. *Britain in Wonderland*. London: Gollancz, 1948.   222 pp.

[1503] Marriott, John A.R. *Commonwealth or Anarchy*? *A Survey of Projects of Peace from the Sixteenth to the Twentieth Century*. London: Allan, 1937. 227 pp.

[1504] Martelli, George.   *Experiment in World Government*: *An Account of the United Nations Operation in the Congo, 1960-1964*. London: Johnson, 1966. 244 pp.
      "The results of this, the first experiment in world government, should discourage any repetition; the United Nations should in future confine itself to genuine peacekeeping operations,   in which the use of force to impose policies is excluded."

[1505] Merthyr, Lord.   "Speech on the Inadequacies of the Charter," June 28, 1950.   House of Lords, *Hansard's Parliamentary Debates*, H.L.   167, cols. 1189-90.

[1506] Mitrany, David. *The Progress of International Government*. New Haven: Yale University Press, 1933. 176 pp.

[1507] --------. *A Working Peace System*: *An Argument for the Functional Development of International Organisation*. London: Royal Institute of International Affairs, 1943. 56 pp.

[1508] --------.   *The Road to Security*.   London: National Peace Council, Peace Aims Pamphlet No. 29, 1944. 20 pp.

[1509] --------.   "The Functional Approach to World Organisation." *International Affairs* (London), 24 (July, 1948), pp. 350-63.

[1510] --------, and Garnett, Maxwell. *World Unity and the Nations*. London: National Peace Council, Towards World Government, No. 3, February, 1950. 16 pp.
      "Government without the foundation of any active functioning society would be either a mere policeman or a tyrant."

[1511] --------. *A Working Peace System*. Introduction by Hans J. Morgenthau. Chicago: Quadrangle Books, revised ed., 1966. 221 pp.
      Contains reprint of 1943 classic on functionalism.

[1512] Myrdal, Gunnar. *Realities and Illusions in Regard to Inter-Governmental Organisations*. London: Oxford University Press, 1955. 28 pp.

[1513] *One World*: *A Study Handbook*.   London: National Adult School Union, 1963.   240 pp.
"World government can only rest securely upon the unity of mankind in basic matters. How far and in what form can we anticipate this? What reasonable hope is there of a world community,   its members citizens of a world free from war and free from want?" A book of readings on unification issues, such as the U.N., variety in democratic governments, India, Russia, China, women, environment, labor, and religion.

[1514] Orme, Dennis F.   *A Christian Manifesto for Our Land*.   Bristol: Federation for World Peace and Unification, 1975.   22 pp.

[1515] Orwell, George.   "Wells, Hitler, and the World State."   In *Critical Essays* (London: Secker & Warburg, 1946).   Reprinted in U.S. as *Dickens, Dali and Others* (New York: Reynal & Hitchcock, 1946), pp. 115-23.
"All sensible men for decades past have been substantially in agreement with what Mr. Wells says; but sensible men have no power and, in too many cases, no disposition to sacrifice themselves."

[1516] Pearson, Lester B.   "Beyond the Nation State." *Saturday Review*, February 15, 1969, pp. 24-27, 54.
Steps are urgently needed to create a world community superior to sovereign states.   United Kingdom is proof that a viable political structure can include differing national societies. By retired Canadian Prime Minister.

[1517] Pinder, John.   *U.N. Reform*: *Proposals for Charter Amendment*.   London: Federal Union, 1953.   27 pp.

[1518] Pritt, Denis N.   *Federal Illusion? An Examination of the Proposals for Federal Union*.   London: Muller, 1940.   152 pp.
"Federation or attempted federation of groups of states with no real predisposition to union, such as is involved in the proposals for Federal Union, contain no genuine peace-making qualities. . . . [Peace] must be won, and can only be won, by eliminating the causes of war by Socialism and by Socialism alone."

[1519] Quanjer, Johan H.   *One World*, *One Truth*.   London: By the author, 1964. 89 pp.
Religious (Christian) speculation on world government. "There will be endless international conferences which will come to nothing until the two powers realize there is a third way out.   The third force is a combination of the basic ideas of both democracy and communism."

[1520] Ransome, Patrick, ed.   *Studies in Federal Planning*. London: Macmillan, 1943.   363 pp.
Articles by Lord Lothian, K.C. Wheare, C.E.M. Joad, George Catlin, K. Zilliacus, and others, first written for the Federal Union Research Institute and published in the Federal Tracts series.

[1521] Robbins, Lionel, baron.   *Economic Planning and International Order*. London: Macmillan, 1937; 2nd ed., 1972.

[1521]a --------.   *The Economic Causes of War*.   London: Cape, 1939.   124 pp.

[1522] --------. *Economic Aspects of Federation*. London: Federal Tracts No. 2, 1941. 32 pp.

[1523] --------. *Autobiography of an Economist*. London: Macmillan, St. Martin's Press, 1971. 301 pp.
Argued in favor of federalism, but came to see it as "unrealistic" for his generation. When "the intense proselytizing zeal of the totalitarian powers" burns itself out, then may come a time for more comprehensive unions. "As things are, men would fight not to join such a union, rather than to join it."

[1524] Roberts, John. *Twenty-Five Years to a Governed World*. London: Association of World Federalists, 1975. 15 pp.

[1525] --------. *Disarmament Is Not Enough*. London: Association of World Federalists, 1979. 15 pp.

[1575a] --------, and Mayne, Richard. *The Pioneers: A History of Federal Union*. London: Federal Trust for Education and Research, Macmillan, 1986.

[1526] Russell, Bertrand. *Towards World Government*. London: New Commonwealth, 1948.
Mankind cannot long survive unless great wars are prevented.

[1527] --------. "How World Government Can Be Achieved." *New Leader*, 31 (March, 6, 1948), pp. 8-9.
Article in which Russell called for use of force to establish world government, if negotiations should fail.

[1528] --------. "World Government: By Force or Consent?" *New Leader*, 31 (September 4, 1948), pp. 8-9.

[1529] --------. "Only World Government Can Prevent the War Nobody Can Win." *Bulletin of the Atomic Scientists*, 14 (September, 1958), pp. 259-61.
Nuclear test ban, disengagement in Central Europe, and federal world government are necessary.

[1530] --------. *Has Man a Future*? New York: Simon & Schuster, 1962. 128 pp.
A world government, since it would have no external enemies, would not be able to invoke the motive of defending the homeland in order to build loyalty to the union.

[1531] Schonfield, Hugh J. *By What Authority*. London: Herbert Joseph, 1945. 175 pp.
Peace through federation. By distinguished Jewish scholar, diplomat, and later founder of Mondcivitan Republic (1959).

[1532] Seed, Philip. *The Psychological Problem of Disarmament*. London: Housmans, 1966. 74 pp.
Addresses problem why men and nations cannot do what their self-interests demand. Cause is "psychological dissociation" (hope of peace and friendship dissociated from toughness necessary for development of nuclear weapons).

[1533] Segall, Jeffrey, et al. *Proposal for a U.N. Second Assembly*. London:

By the authors, 1985.
Modifications to Art. 22 would permit beginnings of a popularly representative second house with recommendatory powers.

[1534] Thomas, David. *Y ddinasyddiaeth fawr*. Wrecsam, Wales: Hughes, 1938. 200 pp.
Intellectual cooperation, international federation, and internationalism. In Welsh.

[1535] Toynbee, Arnold J. *A Study of History*, abridgement of vols. I-VI by D.C. Somervell. New York: Oxford University Press, 1947. 617 pp. Vols. I-X, 1957. 2 vols.
Work of great relevance for proposal of world government, which Toynbee supported.

[1536] --------. "The International Outlook." *International Affairs*, 23 (October, 1947), pp. 463-76.
Political issue is not whether, but which way the world will be unified.

[1537] --------. *Civilization on Trial*. New York: Oxford University Press, 1948. 263 pp.
Contains "The Unification of the World and the Change in Historical Perspective," "The Dwarfing of Europe," "The International Outlook," and "Civilization on Trial."

[1538] --------. *The World and the West*. New York: Oxford University Press, 1953. 99 pp.
Chapter I useful for understanding Russians.

[1539] --------. *America and the World Revolution*. New York: Oxford University Press, 1962. 231 pp.
Part II useful for understanding Americans.

[1540] --------. *Change and Habit: The Challenge of Our Time*. New York: Oxford University Press, 1966. 240 pp.
Toynbee's later views on whether a world-wide state is feasible. It is, technically; but our political habits are opposed. They can be changed and probably will be, under the pressure of social change or death. Some kind of world government will exist by 2000.

[1541] Usborne, Henry. *Towards World Government: The Role of Great Britain*. London: National Peace Council, 1946. 12 pp.
Exposition of resolution to be introduced in House of Commons (January, 1947).

[1542] --------, et al. *Crusade for World Government: The Plan in Outline*. London: The British Parliamentary Committee of the Crusade for World Government, n.d., c. August, 1947. 13 pp.
Pamphlet that launched the movement for a peoples' convention in Geneva, 1950.

[1543] --------. "The Crusade for World Government." *Bulletin of the Atomic Scientists*, 3 (December, 1947), pp. 359-60.

[1544] --------; Beveridge, Lord; Russell, Bertrand; and Haddow, Alexander. *The Bomb: Challenge and Answer*. London: Batsford, 1955. 160 pp. Reviewed in *Bulletin of the Atomic Scientists*, 12 (May, 1956), p.

184.
Plea for world federalism from four points of view: threat of nuclear weapons, threat of war in general, disarmament, and communications.

[1545] --------. *A Warning and a Way Round*: *The Case for a Minimal Federation of Nations*. By the author, 1980. 169 pp.
Reflections on the history of the world government movement through
the barren times after 1951, with a proposal for a "mini-fed" of
nations other than the "three Giants" (America, Russia, China), as
a way remaining to initiate world federation. Alternative is holo-
caust.

[1546] --------. *Prescription for Peace*: *The Case for a Minimal and Neutral
Federation of Middle-World Nations* (*'Minifed'*).   Totterdown, Eve-
sham: By the author, 1985. 120 pp.
Usborne's mature summation of his views on federalism. He proposes,
as a practical next step, a federal union of Third World nations.
This would not include the United States and hence be a threat to
the Soviet Union, like Atlantic Union, nor would it merely consist
of Europe, like European Union, and still be too small and weak
between the two giants. Book is endorsed by the British Parliamentary Group for World Government.

[1548] Van Meerhaeche, M. *International Economic Institutions*. London: Longmans, 1966. 404 pp.

[1549] Wells, H.G. *Anticipations of the Reaction of Mechanical and Scientific Progress upon Human Life and Thought*. London: Chapman & Hall,
1902. 318 pp.
"The suggestion is powerful, the conclusion is hard to resist, that
through whatever disorders of danger and conflict, whatever centuries of misunderstanding and bloodshed, men may still have to pass,
this process nevertheless aims finally and will attain to the establishment of one world-state at peace within itself."

[1550] --------. *The Idea of a League of Nations*. Boston: Atlantic Monthly
Press, 1919. 44 pp.
With Lord Grey, Lord Bryce, Gilbert Murray, Lionel Curtis, and
others, Wells founded the League of Free Nations Association.

[1551] --------. "The Next Stage in History" (Book 9) in *The Outline of History*. New York: Macmillan, 1920. 2 vols.
See especially Chap. 41: "Man's Coming of Age. The Probable Struggle for the Unification of the World into One Community of Knowledge and Will. . . How a Federal World Government May Come About.
. . ." Suppressed in 1949 Postgate edition.

[1552] --------.   *The Shape of Things to Come*.   New York: Macmillan, 1933.
431 pp.
Wells' most explicit and imaginative work on world government.

[1553] --------. *The New World Order*. New York: Knopf, 1940. 191 pp.
World federal union of socialist democracies.

[1554] --------.   *Phoenix*: *A Summary of the Inescapable Conditions of World
Reorganisation*. London: Secker & Warburg, 1942. 192 pp.
Wells' last work on the world state. For studies, see Earle, Wagar,

and Orwell.

1555 West, Ranyard. *Psychology and World Order*. New York: Pelican, 1945.
      125 pp.
      One of a handful of books that penetrates through the confusions of
      modern politics to its underlying psychology.   Contains a chapter
      on the psychological conditions for world order and world govern-
      ment. Cf. Fromm.

1556 Wheare, K.C.   *Federal Government*.   London: Oxford University Press,
      1946; 4th ed., 1963.   266 pp.
      Defined federalism as the division of powers such that the general
      and regional governments are each coordinate and independent. Also
      emphasized political factors, particularly defense, among the con-
      ditions for uniting federally. Classic theory. Cf. Friedrich and
      Deutsch.

1557 Whyte, Lancelot Law. *Everyman Looks Forward*.   London: Cresset, 1946.
      86 pp.

1558 Williams, John E. *A New Charter for the United Nations*. Bushey, Herts,
      England: World Union Press, 1965. 78 pp.

1559 Wilson, Duncan, and Wilson, Elizabeth.   *Federation and World Order*.
      Introduction by C.E.M.   Joad.   London: Nelson & Sons, 1939.   184
      pp.
      Comparative study of how federations work in the United States,
      Canada,   and Australia.   "In the education of the public, there
      should be two main subjects: first,   the history of past attempts
      at international organisation, with a view to discerning where they
      have failed and what is the heritage which we still have from them
      and may still use; secondly, the ultimate aims towards which we
      should direct and coordinate such existing organisations as may
      still appear serviceable [to] the type of world order which we hope
      to achieve. This book attempts to provide some historical data for
      the consideration of one type of possible world order, namely, an
      International Federation."

1560 Wood, Hugh McKinnon.   "Legal Relations between Individuals and a World
      Organisation of States." *Grotius Society Problems of Peace and War*,
      30 (1945), pp. 141-64.

1561 Woodward, E. L. *Some Political Consequences of the Atomic Bomb*.   New
      York: Oxford University Press, 1946. 20 pp.

1562 Wootton, Barbara.   "Economic Problems of Federal Union." *New Common-*
      wealth Quarterly, 5 (1939), pp. 150-56.

1563 --------. *Socialism and Federation*.   London: Federal Tracts No. 6,
      1941. 32 pp.

1564 Young, Sir George. *Federalism and Freedom*: *Plan the Peace to Win the*
      War. London: Oxford University Press, 1941. 204 pp.
      Argument for a federation to meet the challenge of Nazi Germany
      after a year of war. "Association between Capitalism and Communism
      in a European Union will be a better insurance against internecine
      or international war than any armed security."

10

British Parliamentary Debates

[1574] Great Britain, Parliament, House of Commons. *Debate on the Address to the King.* Program and Policy of the Labour Government, August 16, 1945. Hansard's Parliamentary Debates, H.C. 413, cols. 70-133.
Initial response to use of atomic bombs.

[1575] --------. *Debate on Ratification of United Nations Charter*, August 22-23, 1945. Hansard's Parliamentary Debates, H.C. 413, cols. 659-755, 861-950.
Includes Clement Attlee on the responsibilities of the great powers and on the protections for the small in the U.N. Charter, Anthony Eden on the improvements of the Charter over the League Covenant, and Ernest Bevin on the time it will take to create a world state.

[1576] --------. *Debate on Foreign Affairs*, November 22-23, 1945. Hansard's Parliamentary Debates, H.C. 416, cols. 601-714, 759-846.
Debate on international control of atomic energy. Includes Attlee on international "lawlessness" (col. 608), Eden on "abating our present ideas of sovereignty" (col. 613), Bevin on "world law" (cols. 781-87), and Henry Usborne on world government (cols. 678-82).

[1577] --------. *Debate on the Address to the King.* Program and Policy of the Labour Government, November 12, 1946. Hansard's Parliamentary Debates, H.C. 430, cols. 9-44.
Includes Henry Usborne's proposal of a Labour policy in favor of world government. Critical comments by Winston Churchill; cautious defense by Clement Attlee.

[1578] --------. *Debate on the Address to the King*, October 28, 1948. Hansard's Parliamentary Debates, H.C. 457, cols. 224-377.
Includes Henry Usborne on world government (cols. 332-36).

[1579] --------. *World Government*, July 28, 1950. Hansard's Parliamentary Debates, H.C. 478, cols. 913-944.
Speeches of Henry Usborne, Clement Davies, I.J. Pitman, et al. in response to the Korean War.

11

Universal Federation—
Continental Europe

The French have had a small, divided, and vigorous federalist movement. They have been activists and theoreticians, closely connected to the
real problems of uniting nations, particularly in Europe. Their statesmen
have been leaders of the movement to unite Europe (see subsequent section).
Those listed here have been more concerned with world citizenship, mundialization (declaration of towns as world territories ready to accept world
law), and world federation, which they express by the term *mondialisme*.

Thinkers and activists from many other European countries are represented here, notably: Denmark, Norway, Sweden, Belgium, Netherlands, West
Germany, Czechoslovakia, Austria, Hungary, Poland, Spain, Portugal, Switzerland, Italy, Yugoslavia, Romania, Greece, and Turkey. The Portuguese scholar, Nicolas Socrate Politis, writing in the darkest days of the Second
World War, clearly came to grips with the great problem of the twentieth
century -- the synthesis of order and liberty. Before the end of the war,
there was much courageous thought about a Central European federation,
which might have precluded the communist satellite system, or might still
do so. The Swiss, especially during the war, lent their presses to discussion of European and world federation, and they continue to hold up the
model of Switzerland for the world. By 1950, twenty-one nations had federalist organizations that were members of the World Movement for World Federal Government (now the World Association of World Federalists).

The Club of Rome probably represents the best recent European thinking
on world issues without going so far as to propose world federation. Authors include: Meadows, Mesarovic, Tinbergen, Gabor, Laszlo, de Montbrial,
Botkin, Guernier, Giarini, Peccei, Saint-Geours, and Schaff. The independent Brandt and Palme reports are of particular current interest.

[1589] Aarse, S. *Naciísmo kaj Esperantismo*. [Nationalism and the Idea of Esperanto.] Laroque Timbaut, France, 47340: Cercle esperantiste de l'Agenais, 1981. 73 pp.

[1590] Adrian, A. H., et al. *La bataille de la paix, les chances du fédéralisme*. Paris: Éditions du Monde nouveau, 1947. 319 pp.

[1592] Ambrosini, Gaspare. *Sovranità degli stati e comunità internazionale*. Roma: Banco di Roma, 1956. 40 pp.

[1593] Anker-Ording, Aake. "Three Stages of Possible U.N. Development." *International Association*, 25 (1973).

[1594] Aron, Raymond. *Peace and War: A Theory of International Relations*. Garden City, N.Y.: Doubleday, 1966; abridged ed., 1973.
Broad and deeply conceived study of international relations. Aron searched for some realistic alternative to a balance of nuclear power or a world federation with power to coerce states. The Clark-Sohn plan, while intellectually elegant, was politically unacceptable at the present stage of history.

[1595] Aron, Robert, and Marc, Alexandre. *Principes du fédéralisme*.   Paris: Le Portulan, 1948. 147 pp.
Integral federalism.

[1596] Balicki, Jan. *Dyskryminacja rasowa w świetle prawa międzynarodowego*. [Racial Discrimination in the Light of International Law.] Warzawa: Ossolineum, 1972. 294 pp.

[1597] Baudin, Louis.   "France and International Economic Policy." *International Affairs*, 22 (April, 1946), pp. 187-98.
Regional economic and political federation desireable as steps toward universal federation.

[1598] Belilos, Léon. *Unir les hommes*. Paris: La Colombe, 1956.
Regional then world federation.

[1599] Bendix, Karen S. *Vi og verdenskatastrofen: Generalopgør med tider og tilstande*. København: Nyt nordisk forlag, 1946. 40 pp.

[1600] Beneš, Edvard. *Future of the Small Nations and the Idea of Federation*. New York: Czechoslovak Information Service, 1942. 11 pp.
Speech at Foreign Press Association luncheon.

[1601] --------. *Towards a Lasting Peace*.   New York: Czechoslovak Information Service, 1942. 42 pp.
Three wartime speeches, including one above.

[1602] Berhanou, Dinke. *A Model for World Government*.   Milan: R. Bellini, 1973. 157 pp.

[1603] Betchov, Robert. *The Year of the Spiatnik*.   Dundas, Ont.: Canadian Peace Research Institute, 1975. 278 pp.
Contemporary novel on the establishment of world federation after limited use of nuclear weapons.   More politically articulate than General Sir John Hackett's *The Third World War* (1978).   Contains annex of a "Pact for a World Authority."

1604 Bobbio, Norberto.   "Orientamenti federalistici nei paesi anglo-sasso-
      ni." Comunità internazionale, 1 (1946), pp. 542-53.

1605 Bodmer, Walter.   Das Postulat des Weltstaates: Eine rechtstheore-
      tische Untersuchung. Zürich: Juris-Verlag, 1952.

1606 Bos, Maarten, ed.   The Present State of International Law.   Kluwer,
      Deventer: Maarten Bros., 1973. 392 pp.
      Includes Louis B. Sohn, "The Development of the Charter of the
      United Nations."

1607 Botkin, James W.; Elmandjra, Mahdi; and Malitza, Mircea. No Limits to
      Learning: Bridging the Human Gap; A Report to the Club of Rome.
      New York: Oxford, 1979. 159 pp.

1608 Bourgeois, Jerry; Diedisheim, Jean; Predine, Jean; Marchand, Guy; and
      Wellhoff, Roger. "World Federalism." Translated by John Roberts
      and Gerry Grant. In Mundialist Summa: One World of Reason (Paris:
      Club Humaniste, 1977), pp. 47-67.
      Recent French thought on federalism.

1609 Bourquin, Maurice. Vers une nouvelle société des nations. Neuchâtel:
      Éditions de la Baconnière, 1945. 280 pp.

1610 Brandt Commission. Common Crisis North-South: A Program for Survival.
      Cambridge, Mass.: MIT Press, 1980. 304 pp.
      Report of independent group of international statesman and leaders
      on the urgent problems of inequality in the world and the failure
      of its economic system. The industrialized world must recognize its
      mutual interests with the developing countries if mankind is to
      survive. Proposals include a new approach to international finance
      and development of the world monetary system. "This is a political
      report, and it deals with world problems politically, calling on
      all countries to make an imaginative response." Cf. Palme Report,
      Common Security.

1611 --------. Common Crisis North-South: Cooperation for World Recovery.
      Cambridge, Mass.: MIT Press, 1983. 184 pp.

1612 Brenda, Julien. "Pour un governement mondial." Fontaine, 7 (avril,
      1946), pp. 611-26.

1613 Brent, Abraham Rodrigues. Federatie van de wereld.   Inleidend woord
      door Lord Beveridge. Leiden: H.E. Stenfert Kroese, 1950. 148 pp.

1614 Breuer, B. Armand. Testverallam vilagallum.   Budapest: Vajna es Bo-
      kor, 1947. 39 pp.

1615 Briemont, Georges. Où est l'utopie? Fédéralisme mondiale, assemblée
      des peuples, états souverains, ère atomique, Garry Davis, etc. Ni-
      velle, Belgique: Havaux, 1950. 128 pp.

1616 Brugmans, Hendrik. Panorama de la pensée fédéraliste.   Avant-propos
      de Robert Aron. Paris: La Colombe, 1956. 155 pp.

1617 --------, and Duclos, Pierre. Le fédéralisme contemporain: critières,
      institutions, perspectives. Leyde: Sythoff, 1963. 191 pp.
      Integral federalism.

1618 --------. *La pensée politique du fédéralisme.* Leyde: Sythoff, 1969.
144 pp.

1619 Burns, Edward M.   "The American Ideal of a World Republic." In *Geist
einer freien Gesellschaft* (Heidelberg: Quelle & Meyer, 1962), pp.
122-61.

1620 Buron, Robert.   *Demain la politique, réflection pour une autre société.* Paris: Denoël, 1970. 253 pp.

1621 Carbone, Carlo.   *L'uomo e la comunità internazionale.* Roma: Domaini,
1957. 145 pp.

1622 Carr, E.H., et al.   *Nations ou fédéralisme.* Paris: Plon, 1946.   278
pp.

1623 Casteilla, André, ed.   *Somme mondialiste.* Paris: Club Humaniste, 1975.
3 vols.
Collection of over 100 articles by world citizens and world federalists. Compendium of movement, especially in France, to date.

1624 --------, ed.   *Mundialist Summa: One World of Reason.*   Paris: Club
Humaniste, 1977. 150 pp.
Vol. I of above. For Vol. II, see Roberts.

1625 --------. *Les princes ou du pouvoir.* Paris: Club Humaniste, 1977.

1626 Châtillon, André H.   *Le vrai problème de la paix: comment transformer
notre système économique et social; étude préliminaire.* Lausanne:
Éditions du Chêne vert, 1951. 102 pp.

1627 Clarin, Anders.   *Handbok for världsfederalister organisation.*   Stockholm: Pro vero, Seelig, 1967. 64 pp.

1628 Clark, Grenville, och Sohn, Louis B.   *Världsfred genom världslag.*
Trans. by Hans Blix. Stockholm: P.A. Norstedt, 1960. 483 pp.

1629 -------- og --------.   *Verdensfred gjennom verdenslov.* Oversatt etter
annen, reviderte utg. av Torkel Opsahl. Oslo: Grundt Tanum, 1960.
372 pp.

1630 -------- et --------.   *La paix par le droit mondial.* Trad. par Francis
Gerard; préface de Paul Geouffre de la Pradelle.   Paris: Presses
universitaires de France, 1961. 545 pp.

1631 -------- und --------.   *Frieden durch ein neues Weltrecht: die notwen-
dige Umgestaltung der Vereinten Nationen.* Deutsch übersetzt von
Claus Weiss. Frankfurt am Main: Metzner, 1961. 611 pp.

1632 -------- y --------.   *La paz por el derecho mundial.* Traduccion por
Enrique Jardi. Barcelona: Bosch, 1961. 440 pp.

1633 -------- en --------.   *Wereldvrede door wereldrecht.* Vertaald door mr.
W.M. Peletier. Haarlem: H.D. Tjeenk Willink, 1961. 412 pp.

1634 Committee to Frame a World Constitution.   *Projet de constitution mondiale.* Préface de Thomas Mann. Paris: Nagel, 1949. 91 pp.

[1635] --------. *Disegno preliminare di costituzione mondiale, proposto e firmato da Roberto Hutchins et al.* Con una presentazione di Pierro Calamandrei. Unica traduzione di Elio Gianturco. Milano: Mondadori, 1949. 147 pp.

[1636] --------. *Ist eine Weltregierung möglich? Vorentwurf einer Weltverfassung.* Vorgeschlagen und unterzeichnet von Robert M. Hutchins et al. Die deutsche Übersetzung wurde von Prof. Friedrich Glum redigiert. Frankfurt am Main: S. Fischer, 1951. 150 pp.

[1637] *Common Crisis North—South: A Program for Survival.* The Report of the Independent Commission on International Development Issues. Cambridge, Mass.: MIT Press, 1980. 304 pp.
Brandt Commission Report 1. Report of independent group of international statesman and leaders on the urgent problems of inequality in the world and the failure of its economic system. The industrialized world must recognize its mutual interests with the developing countries if mankind is to survive. Proposalsinclude a new approach to international finance and development of the world monetary system. "This is a political report, and it deals with world problems politically, calling on all countries to make an imaginative response." Cf. Palme Report, *Common Security*.

[1638] *Common Security: Blueprint for Survival.* The Report of the Independent Commission on Disarmanent and Security Issues. New York: Simon & Schuster, 1982. 202 pp.
Palme Commission Report. Report of independent group of former and current officials (Olaf Palme, former Swedish Prime Minister), foreign ministers, political leaders, and a high Soviet official on a way out from the arms race and the policies of deterrence. Proposals include graduated steps to achieve drastic mutual reductions of military power in Europe and eventual withdrawal of nuclear weapons. Also U.N. reform. "A doctrine of common security must replace the present expedient of mutual deterrence."

[1638]a Corsetti, Renato, ed. *Diskriminacio.* Rotterdam: Universala Esperanto-Asocio, 1984.
Deals with issue of discrimination.

[1639] Cousins, Norman. *Atomen och manniskan.* [Modern Man Is Obsolete.] Stockholm: Bonnier, 1946. 80 pp.

[1640] Creyghton, J. H. C. *Emergency World Government.* The Hague: Movement for Political World Union, 1971. 28 pp.
Transition schema to world government.

[1641] --------. "World Federalism and the World Union Movement." *World Union*, December, 1971, pp. 82-87.
Nations will never agree to delegate sovereignty to a world federal government. The people must exercise their own sovereignty. Most recent exponent of the radical approach via a peoples' convention.

[1642] Diedisheim, Jean. *Les patries, vers une mutation du mode de penser.* Neuchâtel: Éditions de la Baconnière, 1967. 166 pp.

[1643] Duclos, Pierre. *L'évolution des rapports politiques depuis 1750 (liberté, integration, unité).* Préface de B. Mirkine-Guetzevitch et M.

Prelot. Paris: Presses universitaires de France, 1950. 344 pp.

[1644] Een Verden. *Een verden eller ingen.* Udg. af Foreningen Een Verden under redaktion af Svend-Age Hestoft. København: Samlerens forlag, 1949. 23 pp.

[1645] Elgström, Lenah. "Världsregeringen -- en kvinnotanke." *Mellanfolkligt Samarbete*, 17 (1947), pp. 108-13.
Tribute to work of Rosika Schwimmer.

[1646] Enander, Mauriz, et al., eds. *Riktlinjer för en världsfederation, ett inlägg i diskussionen om världens framtid.* Stockholm: Natur och Kultur, 1945. 280 pp.
Articles by Alf Ahlberg, Gunnar Andersson, Allan Degerman, et al. Wartime Swedish thought on the need for a federation of humanity necessitated by national interdependence.

[1647] --------. "Världsregering eller världskaos?" *Mellanfolkligt Samarbete*, 17 (1947), pp. 145-48.
Background on World Movement for World Federal Government.

[1648] Ermacora, Felix. *Allemeine Staatslehre: vom Nationalstaat zum Weltstaat.* Berlin: Duncker und Humblot, 1970. 2 vols.

[1649] Evans, Archibald. *Workers' Rights Are Human Rights: A Guide for International Standards.* IDOC International, 1981.

[1650] --------. *Towards a New International Order: A World Federalist Proposal.* Amsterdam: World Association of World Federalists, 1982. 96 pp.
Federalist policy as the U.N., the specialized agencies, national governments, and a broad public turn their efforts toward creating a new international economic order.

[1651] --------. *Les fédéralistes mondiaux et le nouvel ordre international.* Amsterdam: World Association of World Federalists, 1983.

[1652] Faes, Émile. *L'État mondial d'une confédération humaine, propositions constructives de la vie pour la vie.* Mulhouse, Haut-Rhin: Braun-Seiffer, 1948. 212 pp.

[1653] Frankl, Paul. *Weltregierung.* Leiden: H. E. Stenfert Kroese, 1948. 302 pp.
U.N. to be reformed with a popular Assembly and national Senate.

[1654] Gabor, Dennis, et al. *Beyond the Age of Waste [Fourth Report to Club of Rome].* New York: Oxford, 1978; 2nd ed., 1981. 237 pp.
Options if science and technology are used wisely.

[1655] Gandolphe, Maurice. *Système de paix et de securité mondiale: universalisme exécutoire, paix organique, équilibre vital, droit des hommes.* Intro. de A. de La Pradelle. Paris: Éditions inter-nationales, 1949. 138 pp.

[1656] Gasser, Adolf. *Gemeindefreihet als Rettung Europas: Grundlinien einer ethischen Geschichtsauffassung.* Basel: Verlag Bücherfreunde, 1947. 266 pp.

1658 Gérard, Francis. *Vers l'unité fédérale du monde, espoir ou utopie?*
     Paris: Denoël, 1971. 248 pp.

1659 Giarini, Orio. *Road Maps to the Future: Dialog on Wealth and Welfare*;
     An Alternative View of World Capital Formation. Report to the Club
     of Rome. Oxford: Pergamon, 1980. 386 pp.

1660 Gostoli, Antonio. *Per una migliore organizzazione del mondo*. Milano:
     Gastaldi, 1950.

1661 Gozard, Gilles. *Après la guerre total, la paix total*. Paris: Édi-
     tions Medicis, 1945. 116 pp.

1662 Gramsci, Antonio. *Letters from Prison*. Selected, translated, and in-
     troduced by Lynne Lawner. New York: Harper & Row, 1973. 292 pp.
     A transitional figure for Marxism.   Gramsci attempted to accommo-
     date Marxism to the facts of the failure of capitalism to collapse
     due to its internal contradictions, the fragility of proletarian
     internationalism, and the rise of totalitarianism in place of so-
     cialist hopes, especially in the Soviet Union. He granted that the
     ideological superstructure of thought and culture has as much in-
     fluence on history as the economic substructure -- a unified con-
     cept expressed in his term, "hegemony." His works are full of im-
     plications for an international political movement connecting East
     and West. There is a large recent secondary literature.

1663 --------. *The Modern Prince and Other Writings*. New York: Interna-
     tional Publishers, 1957. 192 pp.

1664 Guernier, Eugène Leonard. *La paix, oeuvre de l'esprit*. Paris: Édi-
     tions de l'Épargne, 1965. 304 pp.

1665 Guernier, Maurice. *Tiers Monde, trois quarts du monde*. Rapport au
     Club de Rome. Paris: Dunod, 1980. 153 pp.

1666 Guerrero, José G. *L'ordre international: hier, aujourd'hui, demain*.
     Genève: Neuchâtel, 1945. 176 pp.

1667 --------. *World Union or Federation for Peace*. Geneva: By the au-
     thor, 1947. 54 pp.
     Proposal for a federal U.N. charter, by a former League official.
     Chapter III of above work.

1668 Guerry, Émile Maurice. *The Popes and World Government*. Forward by
     Paul Émile Cardinal Léger; trans. by Gregory J. Roettger. Balti-
     more: Helicon, 1964. 254 pp.

1668a Haase, Martin, ed. *Monda ekonomio*. Rotterdam: World Esperanto
     Youth Organization, 1981.
     Report of a seminar on the New International Economic Order.

1669 Habicht, Max. *Post-War Treaties for the Pacific Settlement of Inter-
     national Disputes*. Cambridge, Mass.: Harvard University Press,
     1931. 1109 pp.

1670 -------- . *The Power of an International Judge to Give a Decision* ex
     aequo et bono. London: New Commonwealth Institute, 1935. 86 pp.

[1671] --------.   "Disarmament and World Federalism."   Lecture at the Institute of Mundialist Studies, Chateau de La Lambertie,   France,   Summer, 1978.
By professor of law at University of Zurich.   The first step in solving global problems like nuclear arms is to understand them. The problem is not only to ban the weapon, but to preserve control, even during times of grave international disputes.   Control implies monitoring, compulsory judicial determination of fact, and enforcement. These functions require a world state.   Switzerland provides a model. So do Clark and Sohn.

[1672] --------.   "The Human Right to Peace." Lecture at the Institute of Mundialist Studies, Summer, 1979.
The U.N. Declaration of Human Rights, including Article 28 on the Right to International Order, is not positive law but a social program to be carried out. The peace program is not being carried out, apparently because the general public (in the West) does not really believe it is possible to abolish war and hence is worth spending money on it.   Four model world constitutions show the way.

[1673] --------.   "National Sovereignty and Peace." Lecture at the Institute of Mundialist Studies, Summer, 1980.
The doctrine of national sovereignty is the cause of continuing wars since 1945.   It is outmoded in the atomic age, when soldiers go off to defend wife and children,   only to return home unable to find them. Swiss constitution is a model for the necessary restriction -- not abolition -- of sovereignty.   Majority rule is necessary to disarm and abolish war.

[1674] --------.   "World Peace through a New World Law." Lecture at the Institute of Mundialist Studies, Summer, 1981.
Fundamental propositions of world federalism; for example, "World peace can only come when the rule of unanimity in international relations has been discarded, and law and order are imposed independently of the consent of the parties."

[1675] --------.   *The Abolition of War*:   *Autobiographical Notes of a World Federalist and a Selection of His Papers on Peace and World Federalism*. Paris: Club Humaniste, 1985.   250 pp.

[1676] Haegler, Rolf Paul. *Histoire et idéologie du mondialisme*.   Zürich: Europa Verlag A. G., 1972.   252 pp.
A history not only of the European mundialization movement but also of the world government movement in general. Includes bibliography.

[1677] Haesaerts, Paul. *L'état mondiale, essai de synthèse politique*. Bruxelles: Jaric, 1948.   451 pp.

[1678] Hennessy, Jean. *Diplomatique nouvelle et fédéralisme*. Paris: Société des éditions "La Caravelle," 1942.   148 pp.

[1679] Heraud, Guy, et Béguelin, Roland. *Europa-Jura, 150ème anniversaire du Congrès de Vienne*. Delemont: Rassemblement jurassien, 1965.   171 pp.

[1680] Hermann, J.-M. "De Garry Davis à James Burnham: Citoyens du monde ou vassaux de l'empire?" *Cahiers internationaux*, 1 (novembre, 1949), pp. 15-30.

[1681] Heyman, Aage. *An Attempt to Define Laws and Regulations for a Common-wealth of Nations*. Hellerup, Denmark: O. Tellers, 1949. 27 pp.

[1682] Heyting, W. J. "The Organization of Post-War Peace." *Transactions of the Grotius Society*, 30 (1944), pp. 209-38.

[1683] Hitler, Adolf. *My New Order*. Edited with commentary by Raoul de Roussey de Sales. New York: Reynal, 1941. 1008 pp.
Last attempt to establish a wider order in Europe, or the world, by force. The very opposite of what federalists aim to do by nonviolence.

[1684] Holm, Torsten. *FN och världsfederalismen*. Stockholm: Informationsbyran Mellanfolkligt Samarbete for Fred, 1949. 16 pp.

[1685] --------. *Den demokratiska världens organisationsproblem: idéer och riktningar i den världspolitiska debatten*. Stockholm: Kooperativa förbundets bokförlag, 1952. 32 pp.

[1686] Ingrim, Robert. *Bündnis oder Krieg*. Munich: Verlag neues Abendland, 1955. 163 pp.

[1687] Jaspers, Karl. "Empire universel ou ordre mondial." Translated from the German. *Table Ronde*, 25 (January, 1950), pp. 26-37.

[1688] John XXIII, Pope. *Pacem in Terris*. Encyclical letter addressed to all mankind, Rome, April 11, 1963.   Boston: St. Paul Editions, 1963. 61 pp.
"The universal common good poses problems of world-wide dimensions which cannot be adequately solved except by the efforts of a public authority endowed with a wideness of powers, structure and means of the same porportions: that is, of public authority which is in a position to operate in an effective manner on a world-wide basis."

[1689] Jünger, Ernst. *Der Weltstaat: Organismus und Organisation*. Stuttgart: E. Klett, 1960. 75 pp.

[1690] Kant, Immanuel. *Idea for a Universal History from a Cosmopolitan Point of View*. Koenigsberg: 1784; Berlin: Prussian Academy, 1912. Eighth thesis: "The history of mankind can be seen, in the large, as the realization of Nature's secret plan to bring forth a perfectly constituted state as the only condition in which the capacities of mankind can be fully developed, and also bring forth that external relation among states which is perfectly adequate to this end."

[1691] --------. *Perpetual Peace*. Koenigsberg: 1795; Berlin: Prussian Academy, 1912.
Second definitive article: "The law of nations shall be founded on a federation of free states." Classic argument for law in place of lawless freedom.

[1692] King, Janice C., and King, R.G. *Manifesto for Individual Secession into World Community*.   Paris: Crosby Continental Editions, 1948. 101 pp.

[1693] Knös, Gunnar. *Wereld federatie van alle landen met nationale ontwa-*

pening en internationale politiemacht: *vier radiolezingen*. Utrecht: W. de Haan, 1946. 29 pp.

[1694] Korowicz, Marek Stanislaw. *Organisations internationales et souveraineté des états membres*.   Texte élarge d'un cours à l'Institute des hautes études internationales de l'Université de Paris. Paris: A. Pedone, 1961. 349 pp.

[1695] Kremser, Rudolf. *Staat und Überstaat*: *ein Streifzug durch Utopie und Wirklichkeit*. Vienna: Wancura-Verlag, 1949. 136 pp.

[1696] Landheer, B., et al., eds. *World Society*: *How Is an Effective and Desirable World Order Possible?*   The Hague: Martinus Nijhoff, 1971. 211 pp.

[1696a] Lapenna, Ivo. *Aktualaj problemoj de la nuntempa internacia vivo*. [Current Problems of Today's International Life.] Rotterdam: By the author, 1952.
Deals with the concept of international law, human rights, forms of international organization, and the United Nations.

[1696b] --------; Lins, Ulrich; kaj Carlevaro, Tazio; eds. *Esperanto en perspektivo*: *Faktoj kaj analizoj pri la Internacia Lingvo*. London kaj Rotterdam: Universala Esperanto-Asocio, 1974.
Chapter 22 deals with the question of a common language in international institutions.

[1697] Larmeroux, Jean. *Les État-Unis du monde*. Paris: J. & R. Sennac, 1946. 62 pp.
By first president of the World Movement for World Federal Government.

[1698] --------. *Los estados unidos del mundo*. Valencia: Fomento de Cultura Editiones, 1952. 102 pp.

[1699] Laszlo, Ervin, et al. *Goals for Mankind*: *A [Fifth] Report to the Club of Rome on the New Horizons of Global Community*. New York: Dutton, 1977. 434 pp.
Exposition of goals held throughout the world as guides to future action.   "The achievement of world solidarity is the great imperative of our era."

[1700] --------. *The Inner Limits of Mankind*: *Heretical Reflections on Today's Values, Culture, and Politics*. Toronto: Pergamon, 1978. 78 pp.

[1701] --------, and Keys, Donald, eds. *Disarmament: The Human Factor*. Toronto: Pergamon, 1981. 164 pp.

[1702] Laursen, Finn. *Federalism and World Order*: *Compendium I*.   Copenhagen: World Federalist Youth, 1970. 110 pp. *Compendium II*. 1972. 155 pp.
Guide to sources and major events of federalist movement.

[1703] --------, et al. *Federalism and Non-Alignment*: *Report on the Joint Seminar of the Union of Yugoslav Youth and World Federalist Youth, April 10-16, 1972*. Copenhagen: World Federalist Youth, 1972. 137 pp.

Valuable papers on federalism in the West and in Yugoslavia. A bridge between the federal systems of East and West?

[1704] --------. "Security versus Access to Resources: Explaining a Decade of U.S. Ocean Policy." *World Politics*, 34 (January, 1982), pp. 197-229.

[1704]a --------, ed. *Toward a New International Marine Order*. The Hague: Martinus Nijhoff, 1982. 198 pp.
Proceedings of the New International Order Youth seminar held in Amsterdam. Review of Law of the Sea conference (UNCLOS III).

[1704]b --------. *Superpower at Sea*: *U.S. Ocean Policy*. New York: Praeger, 1983. 209 pp.
On U.S. maritime law at time of fateful U.S. rejection of the Law of the Sea treaty.

[1704]c --------. *Federalist Theory and World Order*. Amsterdam: Institute for Global Policy Studies, Occasional Paper No. 4, 1986. 29 pp.
Review of concept of federalism (process, integration, amalgamation, bargain), then the world federalist argument and strategy (peoples' convention, U.N. reform, functionalism, peace activism). Policy suggestions for a modernized world federalist movement are made. Federalists should remain federalists, but should become more familiar with current trends in theory (just world order) and practice (European integration, United Nations, New International Economic Order, peace movement). Research and activism needs particular focus on the process of change.

[1705] Lecharlier, Joseph. *Évolution mondiale par la raison, l'équité, la justice: plus jamais de guerre*. Jette-Bruxelles: Par l'auteur, 1950. 48 pp.

[1706] Ledermann, László. "L'abaissement des frontières économiques par le moyen de la fédération: expériences historiques et perspectives d'avenir." *Friedenswarte*, 44 (1944), pp. 221-33.

[1707] --------. *Les précurseurs de l'organisation internationale*. Neuchâtel: La Baconnière, 1945. 178 pp.

[1708] --------. *Fédération internationale: idées d'hier, possibilités de demain*. Neuchâtel: La Baconnière, 1950. 170 pp.

[1709] Leibholz, Gerhard. "Zum Begriff der Supernationalitat." In Université de Genève, Faculté de droit, *Recueil d'études de droit international en hommage à Paul Guggenheim* (Genève: En vente à la Librairie de l'Université, 1968), pp. 814-24.

[1710] Lent, Ernest S. *Supranationale politische Integration Stärkung der Vereinten Nationen: eine Untersuchung des Programmes der Weltbewegung für einen Weltbundesstaat*. Wien: Universität, Rechts- und Staats-wissenschaftliche Facultät, 1954. 261 pp.

[1711] Luca, Pietro de. *La sovranità degli stati nella comunità dei popoli*. Padova: CEDAM, 1956. 258 pp.

[1712] Lütem, İlhan. *Federal Bir Dünya Nizamı Tasarıları*. Ankara: Güncy Matbaacılik ve Gazetecilik, 1950. 150 pp.

By member of Turkish Group for the Protection and Safeguarding of Human Rights and Fundamental Freedoms.

[1713] Madariaga, Salvador de. *The World's Design*.   London: Allen & Unwin, 1938. 291 pp.

[1714] --------. *World Government*: *Dream or Necessity?* London: H. Joseph, World Unity Booklet No. 1, 1946. 28 pp.
Madariaga was Spanish delegate to the League of Nations, director of the Disarmament Section from 1922 to 1928, and later ambassador to Washington and Paris. As the League broke up, he established a "World Foundation," which was one of the roots of the (American) Commission to Study the Organization of Peace.

[1715] Man, Henri de. *Au delà du nationalisme, vers un gouvernement mondial*. Genève: Les Éditions du Cheval ailé, 1946. 320 pp.

[1716] Marc, Alexandre. *A hauteur d'homme, la révolution fédéraliste*. Paris: Éditions "Je sers," 1948. 240 pp.

[1717] --------. *Civilisation en sursis*. Paris: La Colombe, 1955. 314 pp.

[1718] --------. *Europe, terre décisive*. Paris: La Colombe, 1959. 162 pp.

[1719] --------. *L'Europe dans le monde*. Paris: Payot, 1965. 238 pp.
Integral federalism by a former leader of the World Movement for World Federal Government.

[1720] --------, et al. *La révolution fédéraliste*.   Paris: Presse d'Europe, 1969. 254 pp.

[1721] Marçais, Henri. *Destruction atomique ou gouvernement mondial*: *discours aux élus du peuple français par Henri Marçais et ses camarades*. Paris: Citoyens du monde, 1950. 96 pp.

[1722] Marchand, Guy. *Un ou Zero*: *le monde sera mondialiste ou ne sera plus*. Paris: Club Humaniste, 1973. 179 pp.

[1723] --------. *Eins oder Null*: *Abriss des Mundialismus*. Paris: Club Humaniste, 1977.

[1724] --------. "Draft of a World Constitution." In *Mundialist Summa* (Paris: Club Humaniste, 1977), pp. 75-78.
A national senate and popular house (weighted by education) are provided. Also councils of wise men, of human rights and duties, of social and economic concerns, and of minorities.

[1725] Marcic, René. *Ernst Jüngers Rechtsentwurf zum Weltstaat*.   München: Pustet, 1966. 32 p
Antrittsvorlesung, gehalten am 19 Nov. 1964.

[1725]a Marinov, Hristo, ed. *Ekofuturo*.   Sofia: Bulgara Esperanto-Asocio, 1984.
Chapters on the environment, natural resources, and energy.

[1726] Maritain, Jacques. *Man and the State*. Chicago: University of Chicago Press, 1951. 219 pp.
Proposed a "supreme advisory council . . . endowed with unquestion-

able moral authority" instead of a world government. Cf. A.C. Ewing.

[1727] Markus, Joseph. *Grandes puissances -- petites nations et le problème de l'organisation internationale.* Neuchâtel: Éditions de la Baconnière, 1947. 236 pp.

[1728] Mayeux, Marie Rose. *Organisation supranationale de la paix*: contribution à l'étude de la pensée pontificale au XIXe et au XXe siècle. Paris: Éditions ouvrières, 1948. 272 pp.

[1729] Meadows, Dennis L., et al. *The Limits to Growth*: A Report for the Club of Rome's Project on the Predicament of Mankind. New York: New American Library, Signet, 1972. 205 pp.
Growth has become an obsession, which is running into the limits of the planet.

[1730] Mesarovic, Mihajlo, and Pestel, Eduard. *Mankind at the Turning Point*: Second Report to the Club of Rome. New York: Dutton, 1974. 210 pp.
Planning techniques to break out of the trap of crisis management and the politics of expediency.

[1731] Meulen, Jacob ter. *Der Gedanke der internationalen Organisation in seiner Entwicklung.* The Hague: Nijhoff, 1917-1940. 2 vols.
History of international organization, 1300-1889.

[1732] --------. *La paix mondiale par le mondialisme.* Bruxelles: Vanderlinden, 1956.

[1733] Mignot, Henri. *Fictions et réalites democratiques, l'union fédérale ou la guerre.* Le Puy-en-Velay: Les Cahiers du nouvel humanisme, 1951. 196 pp.

[1734] Modigliani, Edoardo, and Berardi, Andrea. *L'Organizzazione della pace, dal punto di vista giuridico.* Verona: M. Lecce, 1947. 82 pp.

[1735] Monnet, Jean. *Memoires.* Paris: Fayard, 1976. 642 pp.

[1736] Montbrial, Thierry de. *Energie, le compte à rebours.* Rapport au Club de Rome. Paris: J.C. Lattes, 1978. 317 pp.

[1737] Mouravieff, Boris. *Le problème de l'autorité super-étatique.* Neuchâtel: La Baconnière, 1950. 133 pp.
L'Évolution du monde et des idées.

[1738] Muszkat, Marian. "De quelques problèmes relatifs à l'interpretation de la Charte et aux transformations de structure des Nations Unies." *Revue hellénique de droit international*, 17 (1964), pp. 240-80.

[1739] Myrdal, Gunnar. *Realities and Illusions in Regard to Inter-Governmental Organisations.* London: Oxford University Press, 1955. 28 pp.

[1740] Olivetti, Adriano. *L'Ordine politico delle comunità dello Stato secundo le leggi dello spirito.* Rome: Edizioni di Comunità, 1946. 387 pp.

[1741] Orlando, Vittorio Emanuele. "I presupposti giuridici di una federazione di Stati." In *Studi di diritto pubblico in onore de Oreste Ranelletti* (Padova: Cedam, 1930), 2 vols. II: 149-73.

[1742] Otlet, Paul. *Constitution mondiale de la société des nations, le nouveau droit des gens.* Genève: Édition Atar S.A., 1917; Paris: Éditions G. Cres, 1917. 253 pp.

[1743] Palme Commission Report. *Common Security: Blueprint for Survival.* The Report of the Independent Commission on Disarmanent and Security Issues. New York: Simon & Schuster, 1982. 202 pp.
Report of independent group of former and current officials (Olaf Palme, former Swedish Prime Minister), foreign ministers, political leaders, and a high Soviet official on a way out from the arms race and the policies of deterrence. Proposals include graduated steps to achieve drastic mutual reductions of military power in Europe and eventual withdrawal of nuclear weapons. Also U.N. reform. "A doctrine of common security must replace the present expedient of mutual deterrence."

[1744] Peccei, Aurelio. *One Hundred Pages for the Future.* Reflections of the President of the Club of Rome. New York: Pergamon, 1981. 191 pp.

[1745] Périllier, Louis. *Demain, le gouvernement mondiale?* Paris: Jean Grassin, Idées présentes 14, 1974. 239 pp.

[1746] --------. *La patrie planetaire: à problèmes mondiaux, solutions mondiaux.* Paris: Éditions Robert Laffont, 1976. 240 pp.

[1747] --------, and Tur, Jean-Jacques L. *Le mondialisme.* Paris: PUF, 1977. 126 pp.

[1748] --------. *Le contrôle, clé du desarmement.* Paris: Club Humaniste, 1980. 190 pp.

[1749] Petrucci, Luigi. *La federazione universale dei popoli e il conflitto nucleare: il confronto diretto.* Firenze: Il fauno, 1974. 169 pp.

[1750] Picard, Roger. *L'unité européenne par l'intercitoyenneté.* Paris: Éditions SPID, 1949. 117 pp.

[1751] Polak, Martin W. *A Short Path to World Peace.* Trans. by A.V. Zimmernian. Hilversum, Netherlands: C. de Boer, 1960. 95 pp.

[1752] Polish Freedom Movement. *Independence and Democracy: Charter of the Free Man.* London: 1948. 7 pp.

[1753] Politis, Nicolas Socrate. *Le grand problème du XXe siècle, la syntèse de l'ordre et de la liberté.* Lisboa: Faculdade de Direito da Universidade de Lisboa, 1942. 166 pp.

[1754] Poznański, Czeslaw. *Federacja . . . ale jaka?* [Federation -- What Kind?] London: Kolin, 1941. 53 pp.

[1755] Prawitz, Jan. *Världsplanering for fred.* Stockholm: Centralförbundet Folk och försvar, 1969. 58 pp.

[1755]a Privat, Edmond. *Interpopola konduto.* Budapest: Literatura Mondo,

1935.
On world problems and the role of international organizations.

[1755]b --------. *Federala sperto*. 1958.
On federalism in the U.S., Switzerland, and the United Nations.

[1756] Proudhon, Pierre-Joseph. *Du principe fédératif*. 1863. Précédé d'études
sur le fédéralisme par G. Scelle, J.-L. Puech, et Th. Ruyssen.
Paris: Librairie Marcel Rivière et Cie., 1959. 607 pp.
To Proudhon, Europe was still too big for a confederation. He over-
looked American federalism. It has been said that had he known the
Federalist Papers, he would have entitled his book, *Du Principe
anti-fédératif*. Nevertheless, he was first to develop a purely rational concept of federalism. Link to Rousseau.

[1757] Quesnel, Louis. *Le sens de l'histoire, essai de prospective politique*.
Paris: Buchet-Chastel, 1967. 213 pp.

[1758] Raclet, Jean Emmanuel. *Préfiguration de gouvernement général du monde
en l'an 2000*. Paris: La Pensée universelle, 1973. 123 pp.

[1759] Rappard, William E. "Du fédéralisme international." *L'esprit international*, année 14, no. 53 (1940), pp. 3-22.

[1760] Riggs, Robert Edwon, and Mykletun, Jostein I. *Beyond Functionalism:
Attitudes toward International Organization in Norway and the United States*. Minneapolis: University of Minnesota Press, 1979. 224
pp.

[1760]a Ripka, Hubert. *Las pequeñas y las grandes naciones: condiciones para
una nueva organización internacional*. Mexico, D.F.: Ediciones la-
tino-americanas del Instituto panamericano de bibliografiz y docu-
mentación, 1945. 104 pp.

[1761] Risse, Heinz. *Chaos oder Einheit als Ende der menschlichen Geschichte*.
Stuttgart: Mittelbach, 1949.

[1762] Roberts, John, ed. *Mundialist Summa: A World of Hope*.   Paris: Club
Humaniste, 1980. 142 pp.

[1763] Saint-Geours, Jean. *L'imperatif de cooperation Nord-Sud, la synergie
des mondes*. Paris: Dunod, 1981. 124 pp.

[1764] Saint-Jean, C. "L'organisation de la paix et la principe fédératif."
Cahiers du monde nouveau, 2 (fevrier, 1946), pp. 1222-34.

[1765] Sauer, Ernst. *Souveranität und Solidarität; ein Beitrag zur völker-
rechtlichen Wertlehre*. Göttingen: "Musterschmidt," 1954. 174 pp.

[1766] Schaff, Adam, and Friedrichs, Gunter. *Microelectronics and Society
for Better or Worse*. Report to Club of Rome. New York: Pergamon,
1982. 353 pp.

[1767] Schelle, Georges. "'Union' versus 'League.'" *New Commonwealth Quarterly*, 5 (1939), pp. 204-15.

[1768] --------. "Le fédéralisme et l'Union française." *Revue politique et
parliamentaire*, 50 (mars, 1948), pp. 217-29.

Federation is only solution to France's colonial problem.

[1769] Schmid, Emil A.   "Abbau der Zölle mehr auf weltweitföderalistischen, denn auf europäisch zentralistischen Wege; eine wirtschaftliche Gemeinschaft freier Nationen." Zürich: Thomas-Verlag, 1958.   86 pp.

[1770] Schmitt, Carl.   "La unidad del mundo." *Prólogo general a la colección por Florentino Pérez Embid.*   Madrid: Ateneo, Colección "O crece o muere," no. 1, 1951.   37 pp.

[1771] Schwarzenberger, Georg. *Civitas Maxima?*   Tübingen: Mohr, 1973.   45 pp.

[1772] Secrétan, Jacques.   "Nations Unies, ou federalisme?   Deux heures de cours." Paris: Recueil Sirey, 1958.   86 pp.

[1773] Shotwell, James T. *La grande décision.*   Tr. par Roger Picard.   New York: Brentano's, 1945.

[1774] Silva, Raymond. *Au service de la paix, l'idée fédéraliste.*   Neuchâtel: La Baconnière, 1943; 2nd ed., 1944.   237 pp.

[1775] --------.   "Autour de trois congrès: le fédéralisme en marche." *Cahiers du monde nouveau*, 4 (janvier, 1948), pp. 75-84.
Substantial report on Montreux congresses in 1947.

[1776] Suchy, Juliusz, and Łychowski, Tadeusz. *Organizacje międzynarodowe.* Warszawa: Pánstwowe Wydawnictwo Naukowe, 1954.   245 pp.

[1777] Szerer, Mieczyslaw. *Federacje a przyszłość Polski.*   London: King & Staples, 1942.   52 pp.

[1778] Tammes, A.J.P.   "Theorie en systematiek van het federalisme." *Études internationales*, 1 (janvier, 1948), pp. 27-43.

[1779] Tinbergen, Jan. *Shaping the World Economy: Suggestions for an International Economic Policy.* New York: Twentieth Century Fund, 1962. 330 pp.

[1780] --------. *Lessons from the Past.* Amsterdam: Elsevier, 1963. 131 pp.

[1781] --------, et al. *Reshaping the International Order [RIO]: A [Third] Report to the Club of Rome.* New York: Dutton, 1976.   325 pp.
Principles and measures that must be adopted if a more just and equitable -- and presumably more peaceful -- world society is to evolve.

[1782] Truyol y Serra, Antonio. *Genèse et fondements spirituels de l'idée d'une communauté universelle, de la* civitas maxima *stoïcienne à la* civitas gentium *moderne.*   Lisboa: Universidad de Lisboa, 1958. 147 pp.
Long historical view from antiquity to modern times.

[1782]a Ulatowska, Elizabeth A. *Handbook for Effective Global Action.* Bussum and Amsterdam: Global Lobby and World Association of World Federalists, 1985; 2nd ed., 1986.   160 pp.
Action guidelines for organizations seeking to influence national

governments on global issues. Special focus on building public con-
stituency and national support for the Five Continent Peace Initiative, Palme and Brandt reports, New International Economic Order,
strengthening the United Nations, and peace work. Practical.

[1783] Ulliet, Yves Arnaud. *Le mondialisme contre la guerre*. Préface de Robert Sarrazac. Paris: En vente à la technique du livre, 1950. 252
pp.

[1784] Utrikespolitiska institutet, Stockholm. *Peace and Security after the
Second World War*: *A Swedish Contribution to the Subject*. Uppsala:
Swedish Institute of International Affairs, 1945. 191 pp.

[1785] Van Oven, Aleida. *Wereldorganisatie, Wenschelijkheid en Mogeljkheid*.
s'Gravenhage: Nijhoff, 1948. 556 pp.

[1786] Vedovato, Giuseppe. "Progetti di organizzazione internazionale nel
medio evo." *Comunità internazionale*, 1 (1946), pp. 401-11.

[1787] --------. *La comunità internazionale, evoluzione e compiti*. Firenze:
Sansoni, 1950. 286 pp.

[1788] Warin, Charles. *Une monnaie pour un nouvel ordre économique mondial*.
Paris: Club Humaniste, 1982.

[1789] Wehberg, Hans. "Zum gegenwärtigen Stande des Problems einer künftigen
Weltorganisation." *Friedenswarte*, 43 (1943), pp. 205-20.

[1790] Wilbrandt, Robert. *Aufbruch zum Weltbundesstaat*. Stuttgart: F. Mittelbach, 1947. 80 pp.

[1791] World Association of World Federalists. "Tokyo Proclamation" and "Towards a New World Order: Statement of Policy." *Transnational Perspectives*, 6 (1980), pp. 10-17.
The 18th congress of WAWF issued a new statement of policy. It
called for a new international order, supported by all nations, for
the peaceful settlement of disputes, achievement of general and
complete disarmament, fair distribution of the world's resources,
protection of the environment, responsible management of the common
heritage of mankind, satisfaction of needs, and human rights. New
emphasis was placed on world citizenship.

[1792] --------. *Proposals for the Reform and Development of the United Nations*. Chicago and Amsterdam: World Association of World Federalists, Task Force to Strengthen the United Nations (SUN), 1985. 12
pp.
Fifteen-point proposal incorporating more than 50 suggestions for
strengthening the U.N. Some involve Charter amendment, others not.
Includes sections on peaceful settlement of disputes, the World
Court, U.N. peacekeeping operations, arms control, U.N. financing,
Security Council and General Assembly voting reforms, human rights,
a new economic order, world trade, law of the sea, environmental
protection, population, terrorism, disaster relief, and world government.

[1793] World Council for the People's World Convention. *Gemeinschaft der
Weltbürger in Deutschland*: *Weltbürger, Völkerkonvent, Weltrecht*:
ein Appell an alle. Baden-Baden: By the council, 1951. 36 pp.

German effort in behalf of Henry Usborne's people's convention.

[1794] World Movement for World Federal Government.   "Montreux Declaration."
August 23, 1947.   In *Stop War*:   *The Montreux Conference* (London:
British Branch of WMWFG, 1948), pp. 8-9.
Founding document of the international federalist movement   -- the
World Movement and   its successor,   the World Association of World
Federalists.

[1795] --------. "Luxembourg Declaration." September 11, 1948. *Common Cause*
(Chicago), 2 (November, 1948), pp. 122-24.

[1796] Youth and Student Division, World Association of World Federalists.
World Peace through World Economy. Assen, Netherlands: Van Gorcum,
1968.   147 pp.
Discusses neglected point of world economic reform as a precondi-
tion to world federation.   Includes papers by Jan Tinbergen, Amitai
Etzioni, and others.

[1797] Zenkl, Petr. *T.G. Masaryk and the Idea of European and World Federation*.   Translated from the Czech by Vlasta Vraz.   Chicago: Czech
National Council of America, 1955.   63 pp.

[1798] Ziccardi, P.   "Federalismo, societarismo e regionalismo nella societa
internazionale." *Comunità internazionale*, 4 (gennaio, 1949), pp.
59-80.

12

Universal Federation—
Third World

The world federalist movement has not been restricted to North America
and Europe. Writers far removed from the "West" (though of course influenced by it) have written on uniting the world through the rule of law.
Japan, India, and Mexico have produced the most federalist works, but soli-
tary authors have discussed the subject in Costa Rica, Guatemala, Cuba, the
Dominican Republic, Ecuador, Colombia, Venezuela, Brasil, Peru, Bolivia,
Paraguay, Uruguay, Chile, Argentina, Tunisia, Nigeria, Mozambique, South
Africa, Egypt, Israel, Iran, Pakistan, China, Korea, Philippines, Indone-
sia, Australia, and New Zealand.

Regional approaches have been strong in Latin America, reflecting her
needs and the history of Pan-Americanism. The Japanese, at time of writing,
have the strongest federalist organizations outside the U.S. and Europe,
perhaps because of their experience at Hiroshima and Nagasaki and their un-
usual dependence on foreign trade. The Indians, in keeping with their long
history, offer a unique religious perspective on a union of humanity.

The great opportunity to bring the colonized peoples of the world into
a world federation, instead of into a congeries of national states on the
European pattern, came at the close of World War II. No event has given
more lease on life to nationalism. Nevertheless, a number of new regional
organizations attest to the need for greater unity: the Organization of
American States, the Central American Common Market, the Organization of
African Unity, the Arab League, the Association of South-East Asian Nations,
the Non-Aligned Movement, and, of course, the Organization of Petroleum Ex-
porting Countries.

For geographical reasons, countries outside North America and Europe
have been put under the heading of the Third World, though that term does
not strictly include Japan, Israel, South Africa, Australia, and New Zealand.

[1808] Alvarez Faller, F. J.   *Tendencias hacia una federación internacional*.
Mesones, Mexico: Costa-Amic, 1963. 144 pp.
Survey of international organization from Bolivar's Congress of
Panama to the Council of Europe.   Hope for eventual world federa-
tion.

[1809] Arce, José.   *Ahora*. Madrid: Espasa-Calpe, 1950. 293 pp.
Includes "Proyecto de reforma de la Carta de San Francisco," pp.
243-92. By Argentina's first representative to the United Nations.

[1810] --------. *Right Now*. Madrid: Blass, 1951. 180 pp.
"Personally, I think we should revise the Charter RIGHT NOW, immediately, and that by trying to do so, we shall not increase in the
slightest the dangers of the present situation. On the contrary, I
think we should improve the situation,   that we would remove the
danger of war." Annex contains suggested revisions of the Charter.
The veto would be eliminated, in favor of a 8/11 majority rule.
"Draft for the Amendment of the San Francisco Charter," pp. 169-80.

[1811] --------. "La Carta de San Francisco: posibilidad de su revision."
Buenos Aires: Academia de Ciencias Economicas, 1958. 30 pp.

[1812] Avalos Pérez, Jesus.   *Union de estados soberanos*:   *Un proyecto para
futuro*. Mexico: Universidad Nacional, 1943. 80 pp.
Cf. Padilla.

[1813] Ayusawa, Iwao. *The Road to World Federation*. Tokyo: Sekai Rempō Kensetsu Dōmei, 1966.
Includes review of Clark-Sohn plan.

[1813]a Bahá'í Universal House of Justice. *The Promise of World Peace*. Haifa:
Bahá'í World Center, October, 1985. 21 pp.
"For the first time in history the dream of peace on earth is within the reach of the nations. Indeed, peace is the next stage in the
evolution of this planet. Humanity has the choice of reaching peace
after unimaginable catastrophes or achieving it by an act of will.
. . .   Banning particular weapons will not remove the root causes
of war.   Neither can the massive dislocation in the affairs of humanity be resolved through the settlement of specific conflicts. A
genuine universal framework must be adopted. . . . World order can
be founded only on the consciousness of the oneness of mankind. But
the achievement of such an order requires several stages, ultimately leading to the establishment of a world commonwealth."

[1814] Bhalerao, M. R. *A Plea, Urgent Entreaty, for World Government*. Lash-
kar, India: Gwalior, 1950. 20 pp.

[1815] Blanco Gaspar, Vicente.   *El voto ponderado*.   Madrid: Instituto Hispano-Luso-Americano de Derecho Internacional, 1981. 228 pp.

[1816] Buber, Martin. *Paths in Utopia*. Boston: Beacon, 1949. 152 pp.
Offered to Stringfellow Barr important fragments of a "world mind."

[1817] Buler-Murphey, Basil. *Safety of Our Future*: *World Federation*. Foreword by Lord Boyd-Orr. Melbourne: Robertson & Mullens, 1957.   184
pp.

[1818] Chaudhuri, Sanjib.   *A Constitution for World Government*.   Calcutta:

Bhupal Chandra Dutta Art Press, 1950. 246 pp.
Recommended by Prime Minister Nehru's sister, Madame Pandit, ambassador of India to the U.N.

[1819] --------. *Steps to World Federal Government through a Constitution for World Government Placed before the United Nations.* Calcutta: By the author, 1950. 12 pp.

[1820] --------. *Steps for the Formation of the First Parliament of the World.* Calcutta: World Constitution Office, 1952. 4 pp.

[1821] Clark, Grenville, and Sohn, Louis B. *Mashru' jadīd lil-salim al-alami.* [A New Plan for World Peace.] Arabic trans. by Mahmud al-Shanayti; introduction by Butrus Butrus-Ghali. Qahirah: Dar al-Ma'arifah, 1961. 115 pp.

[1822] --------. *No Genuine Peace without Enforceable World Law: Answers to Fourteen Questions Relating to World Peace Submitted by Iwao Ayusawa.* Dublin: By the author, 1963. 19 pp.

[1823] --------, --------, kongchŏ. *Syegyepŏp e ŭhan syegye pyŏnghwa.* Trans. by Chong-su Kim and Sŭng-hŏn Yi. Seoul: Popmunsa, 1968. 347 pp.

[1824] Conference of Non-Members of the United Nations. *Declaration.* Tokyo: May, 1954. 5 pp.
On the United Nations, world government, control of atomic energy, and ending the Vietnam War.

[1825] Dai 7 kai sekai rempō heiwa sokushin shukyosha taikai jumukyoku, ed. *Sekai rempō o 21 seiki made-ni: Sekai rempō shukyosha Kameoka taikai hōkokusho.* [World federation in the 21st century: Report of the Kameoka convention of religious world federalists.] Kameoka-shi: Hoeisha, 1976. 275 pp.

[1826] Dev, Shankar. *One World, One Government.* New Delhi: All India Association of World Federalists, 1974. 96 pp.

[1827] Dhungyal, Tulasi Prashad. *The Way to World Peace.* Babaras: Khadananda Prasad, 1952. 41 pp.

[1828] Disandro, Carlos A. *El gobierno mundial y las tensiones de la sinarquia.* Mar del Plata: Editorial Montonera, 1971. 19 pp.

[1829] Donoso Velasco, José Ignacio. *La carta fundamental de las naciones.* Quito: Imp. "Bona Spes," 1949. 27 pp.

[1830] Effendi, Shoghi. *Call to the Nations.* Haifa: Bahá'í World Center, 1977. 69 pp.
"A world federal system, ruling the whole earth and exercising unchallengeable authority over its unimaginably vast resources, blending and embodying the ideals of both the East and the West, liberated from the curse of war and its miseries, and bent on the exploitation of all the available sources of energy on the surface of the planet, a system in which Force is made the servant of Justice, whose life is sustained by its universal recognition of one God and by its allegiance to one common Revelation -- such is the goal towards which humanity, impelled by the unifying forces of life, is moving" (1936). The Bahá'í religion is the only one to

express belief in world federal government.

1830a --------. *The World Order of Bahá'u'lláh*. Wilmette, Ill.: National
Spiritual Assembly of the Bahá'ís in the United States, 1938; 2nd
ed., 1955; 3rd, 1974. 234 pp.

1831 Escarcega Peraza, Florencio, ed. *Un gobierno mundial*. Mexico: Impreso
en Editorial Universo, 1968. 174 pp.

1832 Espaillat de la Mota, Francisco.   *Teorís del estado terráqueo*.   New
York: Mayans, 1944. 241 pp.

1833 --------. *The Superstate*. New York: Hobson, 1947. 35 pp.

1834 Fairbank, John King, ed. *The Chinese World Order: Traditional China's
Foreign Relations*. Cambridge: Harvard University Press, 1968. 416
pp.
See especially John K. Fairbank, "A Preliminary Framework," pp. 3-
14, and Benjamin I. Schwartz, "The Chinese Perception of World Order, Past and Present," pp. 276-88.

1835 Fattāḥī, Hurmuz.   *Rāhī barā-yi ta'mīn-i sa'ādat va āsāyīsh-i bashar*.
[Mankind's Welfare, Peace, and Prosperity: Offered to the Adherents
of World Federal Government.] Teheran?: By the author, 1967.   99
pp.

1836 Fernández-Hidalgo, M. N.   *La union mundial; estudio sobre la revolu-
cion del futuro*.   Mexico: Costa-Ami Instituto Autónome de Desar-
rollo y Planeación Economica, Colección ciencias sociales, 12, 1974.
350 pp.

1836a Fernández-Menendez, Manuel.   *El hombre en su camino*; *La homo sur sia
vojo*. Montevideo: La Bona Semisto, 1965.
Bilingual volume on the United Nations, UNESCO, and human rights.

1837 Fernández Rodríquez, Lorenzo. *Código universal eterno*.   Pitrufquen,
Chile: By the author, 1955. 168 pp.

1838 Finkelstein, L. S.   "United Nations Charter Review." *Pakistan Horizon*, 8 (March, 1955), pp. 269-75.

1839 Frydman, Maurice.   *The World Federation and the August Resolution of
the Indian National Congress*. Aundh: Aundh Publishing Trust, World
Federation Library, 1944. 33 pp.

1840 García Arias, Luís. *La universalidad y la igualdad en la organización
internacional: ante la reforma de la Carta de las N.U.*   La Paz:
Universidad Mayor de San Andrés, Escuela de Derecho y Ciencias Políticas, Cuaderno 13, 1953. 26 pp.

1841 García Rivera, Armando. *Cosmocracía*. Lima: By the author, 1947. 158
pp.

1842 Ghose, Aurobindo. *The Ideal of Human Unity*. New York: Dutton, 1950;
revised ed., 1953. 400 pp.

1843 --------. *The Human Cycle: The Ideal of Human Unity, War and Self-
determination*. Pondicherry: Sri Aurobindo Ashram, International

Center of Education Collection, vol. 9, 1962.   912 pp.

[1844] Goetz, Hermann. *Commonwealth of Tomorrow*. Forword by Sir R.P. Masa-
ni. Allahabad: Indian Periodicals, 1944. 181 pp.

[1845] Gutiérrez y Sánchez, Gustavo. *La carta magna de la comunidad de las
naciones*. La Habana: Editorial "Lex," 1945. 589 pp.
Cuban views on developing the U.N. Charter, 1944.

[1846] Hitaka, Ikki. *Sekai rempō sengen*. [Declaration of World Federation.]
Tokyo?: 1950. 156 pp.

[1847] Holmes, John Wendell. *Beyond Nationalism*: *Democratic Federation or
Fascist Imperialism?* Melbourne: Queensland Branch of Australian
Institute of International Relations, 1942.

[1848] Hoyland, John S. *Gandhi and World Government*.   London: Crusade for
World Government, n.d., c. March, 1948. 23 pp.
"We must aim at a family of independent World States, which necessarily rules out all internal armies. . . .   If by India's efforts
such world federation . . . is brought into being, the hope of the
Kingdom of God may legitimately be entertained" (*Harijan*, July 13,
1947).

[1849] Hussein, Ahmed. *al-Ummah al-Insaniyah*. [The Human Nation.] Qahirah:
National Press, 1966. 474 pp.

[1850] Inagaki, Morikatsu. *Sekai rempō kempō*. [World Federal Constitution.]
Draft Proposal and Explanation of a World Federal Constitution and
of a Less-than-World [Partial] Federal Constitution. Tokyo: By the
author, 1965. 139 pp.
Model constitutions, analyses of arguments, and personal recollec-
tions.

[1851] --------. *Jinrui to bōryoku*. [Mankind and Violence.]   Tokyo: Mokutaku
shobō, 1971. 75 pp.
The problem of war in the 20th century.

[1852] --------. *Jinrui no unmei*. [Destiny of Humanity.]   Tokyo: Mokutaku-
sha, 1978. 190 pp.
Human evolution and social progress by the 20th century. The Japanese concept of. law versus the Western concept.

[1853] --------. *Ningen kenkyū*. [Study of Man.]   Tokyo: Motakushobō, 1980.
69 pp.
Industrialization and its unnaturalness.

[1854] Japanese Research Committee. "World Federal Constitution." *Evolution*,
1980.

[1855] Kartus, Sidney. *Aurobindo*: *Prophet of Human Unity*.   San Francisco:
Cultural Integration Fellowship, 1961. 37 pp.

[1856] Kiek, Edward S. *The International Jungle and the Way Out!* Kent Town,
Australia: Kent, 1944. 15 pp.

[1857] Kim, Samuel S. *The Maoist Image of World Order*. Princeton: Occasional Paper No. 5, World Order Studies Program, Center of Internation-

al Studies,   Woodrow Wilson School   of Public and International Affairs, 1977.   57 pp.
Cf. Goodman.

1858 Level Osuna, Bernardo.   *Una posición frente al nuevo order jurídico internacional.*   Mérida: Universidad de los Andes, Facultad de Derecho, 1965.   301 pp.

1859 Levontin, A.V.   *The Myth of International Security: A Juridical and Critical Analysis.*   Jerusalem: Magnes, 1957.   346 pp.
"Our state system is at the end of its tether.   International relations are laden with a sense of   doom.   There is a genuine feeling that things cannot long continue as they are. . . .   This is not a study of world government,   but of   the necessity for world government."

1860 Lin Mou-sheng.   "Toward World   Organization."   *Contemporary China*,   3 (May 31, 1943),   pp.
Text of address at Institute for Post-War Planning,   Temple University.   Plan for a federal U.N. pact after the war.

1861 Lin Yu-tang. *T'i hsiao chieh fei.*   [Between Tears and Laughter.]   1943; reprinted, Freeport, N.Y.:   Books for Libraries, 1972.   216 pp.
World politics; China in World War II.

1862 Li Yu-ying.   "Federalism and World Confederation."   *Free World*, 4 (December, 1942), p. 231.

1863 Lopez Moctezuma y Escobedo, Carlos.   *Hacia una estructura jurídica de América Latina.*   Mexico: Universidad Nacional Autónoma de Mexico, 1967.   177 pp.
Thesis for licenciatura en derecho.   Regionalism.

1864 Madhavtirtha, Swami.   *One World Government based on Field Theory.*   Ahmedabad: By the author, 1954.   124 pp.

1865 Mahabharati, Alokananda.   *The Master's World   Union Scheme: Being a Scheme of   World Federation on the   Basis of the Fatherhood   of God and the Brotherhood of Man. . . .*   Amrit Mandir: Bamai P.O., Arunachal Mission, India, 1921.   250 pp.
Scheme of Thakur Dayananda, a Sunnyasin [Suni?]; presented by A.M., his disciple.

1866 Martín, Antonio Edmundo.   *El estado federativo universel.*   Ciudad Trujillo, Dominican Republic: Impr. Montalvo, 1943.   128 pp.

1867 Masel,   Segismundo.   *Anteproyecto de transformación   de la O.N.U.   en confederación mundial de las naciones con gobierno universal poseedor exclusivo de las armas bélicas.*   Buenos Aires: Editorial La Voz del Mundo, 1973.   15 pp.

1868 Matilla,   Alfredo.   *Proceso historico del internacionalismo.*   Cuidad Trujillo, D.R.:   1944.   237 pp.

1869 Matsumura, Mohei.   *Zetsumetsu sensō dai-teigen.*   [A grand proposal for abolishing wars.]   Tokyo: Sobunsha, 1983.   384 pp.

1870 M'Bow, Amadou Mahtar.   "An Age of Solidarity or an Age of Barbarism."

Unesco Courier, February, 1975, pp. 19-20.
Choice confronting man is that between social and economic justice,
on the one hand, and ruin and desolation on the other. By the director-general of UNESCO.

1871 Melo, Roque Gadelha de. *Um governo mundial e o problema da guerra e
      da paz*. Bahia, Salvador: Livraria Progresso, Estante de sociolo-
      gia e política, 7, 1952. 148 pp.

1872 Mendonça, Gentil de Carvalho. *O estado internacional*.   Recife: Tese
      para a Faculdade de Direito do Recife, 1943. 74 pp.

1873 Miyakawa, Sadayoshi. *Sekai rempō kaigi ni tsukaishite*. [Memoir of My
      Attendance at a World Federation Convention.] Tokyo?: 1954.   250
      pp.
      Report on the third conference of the World Association of Parlia-
      mentarians for World Government, Copenhagen, 1953.   Includes Japan-
      ese version of Chicago Committee's *Preliminary Draft of a World
      Constitution*.

1874 Miyoshi, Yasuyuki. *Sekai-teki ni kurutte iru kokubō-ron*: *Sekai renpō
      sosetsu no seiji-teki purosesu*. [The bankrupt international theory
      of military defense: A political process of founding world federa-
      tion.] Tokyo: Keiso shobo, 1982. 346 pp.

1875 Mizuki, Sotaro. *Sekai seifu to kenpō*.   [World Government and Consti-
      tutional Law.] Tokyo: Yushindo, 1974.

1876 Montórfano, Victor. *La política que viene y su relación con "la atom-
      íca."* Asunción: Editorial Guarania, 1948-   . Vol. I.

1877 Movimiento pro Federacion Americana. *A Plan for Peace: An American
      Federation, a European Federation, and an Asiatic Federation Coor-
      dinated in One World Organization (a Modified United Nations Organ-
      ization)*. Bogotá: Edificio Crane, "El Grafico," 1951. 38 pp.
      The idea of federation misused to "eliminate the political power of
      Communism." John Foster Dulles is quoted for the American federa-
      tion, Paul Reynaud for the European, and Carlos P. Romulo for the
      Asiatic.

1878 Mullick, Uditendu Prakash. *One World, One State: United Nations and
      World Government*. Calcutta: By the author on behalf of M.S. Banga
      Saraswati Prakasanalaya, 1978. 102 pp.

1879 Orzabal Quintana, Arturo. *América Latina y el imperativo de un mundo
      sin guerra*. Mexico: Costa-Amic, 1963. 122 pp.

1880 Ozaki, Sakae. *Shin kokuren kōsō*: *Dai 3 ji sekai taisen kara chikyū o
      sukuu*. [A conception of a new United Nations: How to save the
      earth from a third world war.] Tokyo: Sekkasha, 1983. 203 pp.

1881 Padilla, Ezequiel. *Paz permanente y democracia internacional*. Mexico:
      Departamento de Información para el Extranjero, Serie cultural, 9,
      1944. 20 pp.
      By Mexican foreign minister. "Enduring Peace cannot be established
      without first creating the juridical status that will maintain it.
      Those who contend that war is a result of anarchy in international
      relations, are right."

[1882] Park, No-Yong. *The White Man's Peace*: *An Oriental View of Our Attempts at Making World Peace*. Boston: Meador, 1948. 252 pp.

[1883] Patel, Satyavrata Ramdas. *World Constitutional Law and Practice*: *Major Constitutions and Governments*. Delhi: Vikas, 1970. 495 pp.

[1884] Pimentel, A. Fonseca. *Democratic World Government and the United Nations*. Brasilia: Escopo Editora, 1979; 2nd ed., 1980. 158 pp. By retired Brasilian official. The U.N. must become a world government.

[1885] Pinheiro de Vasconcellos, Henrique. *The World State or the New Order of Common Sense*. Foreword by Clovis Bevilacque. Rio de Janeiro: Grafica Olimpica, 1944. 239 pp. Project of world federation elaborated by Brasilian diplomat.

[1886] Porté, Alfred S. *L'ordre mondial de l'avenir*. Le Caire: R. Schinder, 1945. 46 pp. In French, English, and Arabic.

[1887] Pratap, Mahendra. *To U.S.S.R.*: *A Friendly Communication*. Brindaban, India: 1947. 13 pp.

[1888] --------. *World Federation with Unity of Religions and the Economic System of One Joint Family*. Brindaban: World Federation, 1952. 68 pp.

[1889] Radhakrishnan, Sarvepalli. *Is This Peace?* Bombay: Hind Kitabs, 1945. 74 pp. Limited world government needed.

[1890] Rajagopal, V. *League of the Peoples, India and Abroad*. Madras: Vavilla, 1952. 31 pp.

[1891] Raúl Atria, B., ed. *Variables políticas de la integración andina*. Instituto de Ciencia Política, Universidad Católica de Chile, Ediciones Nueva Universidad, Vicerrectoría de Communicaciones, 1974. 358 pp. Papers at seminar on Andean integration, Santiago, July, 1973.

[1892] Ray, Parimal. *Sāmrājya-bistāra, svādhīnatā-samgrāma o āntarjātika sangha*. [Imperialism, Freedom, International Organization.] Dacca?: 1963. 148 pp.

[1893] Reddy, T. Ramakrishna. *India's Policy in the United Nations*. Rutherford, N.J.: Fairleigh Dickenson University Press, 1968. 164 pp.

[1894] Relgis, Eugen. *Cosmometápolis*. Versión española por Eloy Muñiz. Montevideo, Uruguay: Editiones "Humanidad," 1950. 142 pp.

[1895] Rosser, John H. *World Charter*: *A Constitution for the Post-War World*. Brisbane: Morcoms, 1943. 58 pp.

[1896] Sakaguchi, Saburo. *Chikyū seifu no seiritsu*: *40 okunin no heiwa to kōfuku no jitsugen*. [Establishment of planetary government: Realization of happiness and peace of four billion people.] Tokyo: Kenyu-kan, 1982. 240 pp.

1897 --------. *Gendai bunmei no kaibō*: *Sekai kiki to nihon no chie*. [Anatomy of present civilization: World crisis and Japanese wisdom.] Tokyo: Kenyukan, 1982. 285 pp.

1898 Salayan, Abdul Wahib. *Perdamaian dari abad ke abad*. Djakarta: 1969. 112 pp.

1899 Salvat, Augustin. *Reflexiones sobre el ideal ecuménico, el panamericanismo y la post-guerra*. Mexico: Escuela nacional de jurisprudencia de la Universidad nacional autónomia de Mexico, 1944. 113 pp. Tesis para optar al grado de licenciado en derecho.

1900 Sampaio Doria, Antonio de. *O imperio do mundo e as Nações unidas*. Sao Paulo, Brasil: Limonad, 1962. 126 pp.

1901 Santís Durán, Augusto. *Democracia mundial, el camino hacia la paz*. Guatemala: By the author, 1949. 67 pp.

1902 Sekai Rempō Kensetsu Domei, ed. *Sekai rempō undō 20 nen shi*. [Twenty years history of the world federalist movement.] Tokyo: 1969. 615 pp.

1903 Suter, Keith. *A New International Order*: *Proposals for Making a Better World*. North Ryde, New South Wales: World Association of World Federalists, 1981. 100 pp.
Contains brief explanations and evaluations of the United Nations, proposals for U.N. reform, world federalism, world peace throught world law, regionalism, and various current federalist organizations.

1904 Swami, T.V.M. *A Thesis on One-World Government Scheme*: *Mankind Is One Family*. Thiruvaiyaru, India: 1953. 11 pp.
First published in the *Illustrated Weekly of India*, January 13, 1952, as "Wanted: A Society of World Citizenship, a Solution for World Peace."

1906 Tabata, Shigejirō. *Sekai seifu no shisō*. [Thought on World Government.] Tokyo: Iwanami shoten, 1950. 253 pp.
Contains Chicago Committee's *Preliminary Draft of a World Constitution*. Cf. Miyakawa.

1907 Takada, Yasuma. *Sekai shakai ron*. [The world society.] Tokyo: Chugai shuppan, Sekai keizai koza dai 1 kan, 1947. 280 pp.
By a prominent Japanese economist. Last chapter on the way to a world state.

1908 Tanaka, Seimei. *Sekai rempō*: *Sono shisō to undō*. [World federation: Ideology and movement.] Toyko: Heibonsha, 1974. 385 pp.
Excellent book in Japanese. Comprehensive and informative.

1909 Tanaka, Teruo. *Sekai renpō ga yattekuru*. [World federation is just around the corner.] Tokyo: Senbunsha, 1985. 239 pp.

1910 Tanikawa, Tetsuzō. *Sekai rempō no kosō*. [Transition to World Federation.] 1977. 198 pp.
Series: Kōdansha gakujutsu bunko.

[1911] Tennet, Benno. *A World Federation of States*: *Some Suggestions.* Johannesburg, South Africa: Central News Agency, 1943. 94 pp.

[1912] Thomas, Harold T. *Federal Union*: *Victory and Lasting Peace.* Auckland, New Zealand: Brookdale, 1943. 21 pp.

[1913] Torre Espinosa, Adolfo. *Un mundo nuevo, estados unidas del mundo.* Mérida, Mexico: 1945. 85 pp.

[1914] Trinker, Frederick W. *The Anatomy of World Order*: *Or a Glimpse at a Multifold World Organization.* Mexico: Talleres de B. Costa-Amic, 1946. 132 pp.

[1914]a Tyson, J. *World Peace and World Government*: *From Vision to Reality.* Oxford: Ronald, 1986. 106 pp.
"In this book we shall examine the reasons why world government is essential, the arguments commonly given against world government, and the compelling Bahá'í responses. . . . The creation of a world government is, in itself, only a small part of the process of establishing peacefulness between the diverse elements of mankind. This larger process requires the spiritual upliftment of humanity and the recognition of the oneness of mankind. It may well take several generations and will eventually lead to the establishment of what Bahá'u'lláh called 'the Most Great Peace.'"

[1915] Unwin, Colin. *Blasted Fools?* *A Plea and a Plan for World Federation*: *The Unism Plan to Feed and Federate the World.* Perth: By the author, 1947. 96 pp.

[1916] Vaz, Delfim. *Primeiro programa da nova ordem mundial.* Laurenço Marques, Moçambique: Notícias, 1950. 57 pp.

[1917] Vergara Robles, Enrique. *Panamérica en la órbita universal.* Santiago de Chile: Imprenta universitaria, 1945. 157 pp.

[1918] Virion, Pierre. *El govierno mundial y la contra-Iglesia.* Buenos Aires: Editorial Cruz y Fierro, 1965. 262 pp.

[1919] "World Unity and World Citizenship." *Values* (Kaggalipura), 1 (June, 1956), whole issue.

[1920] Yasugi, Issho. *A View of the New World*: *A World State.* Tokyo: 1963. 91 pp.

[1921] Yoshihara, Shōhachirō. *Sekai seifu no kiso riron.* [Fundamental Theories of World Government.] Tokyo: 1962.
Quotes Reves, Meyer, Clark and Sohn.

13

Universal Federation—
Soviet Union, Russia

There is no known popular or citizens' movement for world federation
in the Soviet Union or the Soviet bloc analogous to that in the West. Russian authors consistently confuse the world federalist movement with the
allegedly imperialistic foreign policy of the United States, as if federalists were well received in Washington and lavishly supported by Wall Street
capitalists. In the West, this view is similar to the extreme Right position that world federalists are in alliance with international communism.
In fact, they are independent of both.

Nevertheless, the very violence of the Russian attacks is evidence of
some popularity of the idea, or at least of the Communist Party's perception of its potential power. "Homeless cosmopolitanism" was a special term
of opprobium coined for all notions of international friendship, universal
culture, and world government when the Soviet Union began an ideological
campaign to prepare the Soviet peoples for possible war with the West in
1947. The Russian philosopher B. M. Kedrov was forced to publicly recant
ideas of "cosmopolitanism" (which in his case apparently did not include
world government) in 1949. Many sources, including an unsigned editorial in
Voprosy filosofii, of which Kedrov was editor-in-chief, make it very clear
that the key concept of "cosmopolitanism" was world government.

Apart from the corruptive effects of perceived threats of war, which
lead to the transformation of both communism and capitalism into war ideologies, and even to lumping world federalism into one or the other, the
Soviet Union's fundamental view is that, at the present stage of history, a
world federal union would put her economic and social progress at the mercy
of Western majorities "on whose benevolent attitude toward the Soviet Union
the Soviet people cannot count," as Andrei Gromyko remarked at the time of
his rejection of the Baruch plan (1947). Soviet authors consistently dwell
on the themes of covert imperialism, lack of world community, and the
strength of nationalism. They held on to their veto for the same reason the
United States now does -- as a defense when in a minority.

Nevertheless, nationalism is splitting communism, and communist ideology was originally internationalist, as Elliot Goodman makes clear. The
attitude could change again, especially if a proposal of world federation,
fair to all, were forthcoming. A formal proposal from the U.S. has never
been made. The nearest approach to it came from Albert Einstein; the reply
by Sergei Vavilov and three Soviet scientists was perhaps the fairest Soviet consideration to date of a proposal to establish a limited world feder-

ation to inaugurate a common rule of law over both the United States and the Soviet Union.   The article by the French federalist Jean Diedisheim in the Communist journal *Peace* was also remarkably fair.

The Clark-Sohn plan received reviews by O. Bogdanov and G. I. Tunkin, but the attitude was still that federalism was in the service of American imperialism.

Recently there has been some development of the idea of "convergence," by which Soviet and American societies are becoming more mixed, partly socialist and partly capitalist.   No Soviet political proposals for a federal union have yet come to light, however.

Writings by Andrei Sakharov speak to our time.

"I'm here to stay, too"
   —copyright 1947 by Herblock in The Washington Post on March 13, 1947
Used by permission of HERBLOCK CARTOONS.

[1930] "Against the Bourgeois Ideology of Cosmopolitanism." *Voprosy filoso-fii*, November 2, 1948, *Current Digest of the Soviet Press*, I:1 (1949), pp. 3-11.
Editorial. Fullest source for final Russian thinking on "cosmopoli-tanism." "World government" was the epitome of the "ideological banner" of American imperialism.

[1931] Aspaturian, Vernon V. "The Theory and Practice of Soviet Federalism." *Journal of Politics*, 12 (1950), pp. 20-51.

[1932] Balicki, Jan.   *Dyskryminacja rasowa w świetle prawa międzynarodowego*. [Racial Discrimination in the Light of International Law.] Warzawa: Ossolineum, 1972. 294 pp.

[1933] Barsegov, Yuri, and Khairov, Rustem.   "A Study of the Problems of Peace." *Journal of Peace Research* (Oslo), 10 (1973), pp. 71-80.
By members of the Institute of World Economic and International Re-lations and the Institute of Control Problems, Moscow, respective-ly."Quite naturally, the existence of opposite social systems rules out any possibility for the creation of a 'world government' or of any world-scale organization of a supranational character. . . . [The U.N.O. at the present stage of history] is the only possible form of an international organization of a universal nature. . . . The untenability of the philosophical-historical concepts stems from the fact that they view the spiritual culture of society in isolation from the socio-economic system. . . . The Soviet policy of peace is based on principles of equality and respect for nation-al sovereignty."

[1934] Berdyayev, Nicolay A. "The Crisis of Man in the Modern World." *Inter-national Affairs*, 24 (January, 1948), pp. 100-06.
By the exiled Russian theologian.   "It is only religious belief which will be able to resist the forces which seek to dominate the world."

[1935] Bogdanov, O. "A Soviet View of Disarmament." International Institute for Peace, Vienna. *World Federalist*, January, 1965, pp. 14-16.
Proposals of Clark and Sohn, since they imply interference in the domestic affairs of the Soviet Union, are condemned.   "World law" would be an instrument of Western imperialism, since the West would have a majority in any world assembly or court. By Russian profes-sor of legal science.   "The creation of any type of 'world state' or of a 'world law' under present conditions would be utopian and incompatible with the course of social development in our times."

[1936] --------; Kaliadin, A.N.; and Vorontsov, G.A.   "Prevention of Nuclear War: Soviet Scientists' Viewpoints." United Nations: UNITAR, 1983. E.83.XV.RR/31. 91 pp.
Soviet perspective on political and strategic issues. Cf. Epstein in section 4.

[1937] Borgese, G.A.   "Russland contra Weltregierung." *Die neue Rundschau*, 10 (Frühjahr, 1948), pp. 157-73.
World federation including the U.S.S.R. is our only hope.

[1938] Borisov, S.   "Protiv proektov peresmotra Ustava OON." [Against Pro-jects for the Review of the U.N. Charter.] *Sovetskoe gosudarstvo i pravo* (Moskva), 6 (1955), pp. 92-98.

1939 Breuer, B. Armand. *Testverallam vilagallum*.   Budapest: Vajna es Bo-
      kor, 1947. 39 pp.

1940 Brucan, Silviu. *The Dissolution of Power*: *A Sociology of Internation-
      al Relations and Politics*. New York: Knopf, 1971. 388 pp.
      By a Rumanian scholar.   "The U.N.   must be given the authority to
      plan, to make decisions, and to enforce them -- or it will disap-
      pear altogether."

1941 Burlatsky, Tyodor. *World Peace*: *A Possibility or a Dream?* Moscow:
      Novesti, 1982. 148 pp.
      Includes sections on detente and U.S.-U.S.S.R. relations.

1942 Carr, E. H. *The Soviet Impact on the Western World*.   New York: Fer-
      tig, 1947. 113 pp.

1943 Clemens, Walter C., Jr. "Ideology in Soviet Disarmament Policy." *Jour-
      nal of Conflict Resolution*, 8 (March, 1964), pp. 7-22.
      Distrust of capitalism has produced contempt for Western-style
      "arms control" (as distinguished from their reduction or elimina-
      tion), rejection of "security first" positions (instead of pragma-
      tic steps forward even when all political differences are not re-
      solved), and preference for rapid and maximum solutions (in place
      of security and inspection first, then disarmament).

1944 Coffey, J. I. "The Soviet View of a Disarmed World." *Journal of Con-
      flict Resolution*, 8 (March, 1964), pp. 1-6.
      U.S. concept tends to "world government . . . the end of the pre-
      sent world order in which states are responsible ultimately only to
      themselves." Soviet concept sees world of "sovereign and theoreti-
      cally equal states," in which peaceful settlement of disputes would
      be accomplished by "mutual concessions and seeking mutually accep-
      table settlements."

1945 Dean, Vera Micheles. *The United States and Russia*.   Cambridge: Har-
      vard University Press, 1947. 321 pp.
      "What marks Russia today is not so much that it is either uncommon-
      ly nationalistic or uncommonly propagandist in its foreign policy,
      but that it is telescoping developments which in Western countries
      were spread over centuries. As a result, its impact on the West has
      all the force of a delayed explosive."

1946 Diedisheim, Jean. "World Government." *Peace*:   *A World Review*, Feb-
      ruary, 1951, pp. 6-10.
      One of few instances when world government was viewed fairly in a
      Communist journal.

1947 Fedotov, G. "Russia and Freedom." *Review of Politics*, 8 (January,
      1946), pp. 12-36.
      Hanna Arendt called this article a "masterpiece."

1948 Frantsev, Yu. "Contemporary Idealism in the Service of Imperialism."
      Pravda, March 7, 1949. *Current Digest of the Soviet Press*, I:9
      (1949), pp. 16-18.
      More on "homeless cosmopolitanism."

1949 Golovin, I. N. *I. V. Kurchatov*: *A Socialist-Realist Biography of the*

Soviet Nuclear Scientist. Translated by William H. Doughterty. Bloomington, Ind.: Selbstverlag Press, 1968. 99 pp.
History of Russian atomic bomb project. It started in May, 1942, in Kazan. Crash program began after "atomic blackmail" began, in August, 1945. First sustained chain-reaction a few days before the critical vote on the Baruch Plan at the end of 1946. First Russian test, August 29, 1949.

1950 Goodman, Elliot Raymond. *The Soviet Design for a World State.* New York: Columbia University Press, 1960. 512 pp.
U.S.S.R. has two problems with world government: there is no world community on whose good will the Soviet Union can rely (national sovereignty protects internal life), and nationalism has been particularly strong since defeat of Nazi Germany. Yet nationalism in the satellites is splitting Communism, and Bolshevik ideology was internationalist. Attitude could change again.

1951 --------. "The Soviet Union and World Government." *Journal of Politics*, 15 (May, 1953), pp. 231-53.
Excellent survey, especially for the period after the *Current Digest of the Soviet Press* became available (1949).

1952 Goure, Leon, et al. *Convergence of Communism and Capitalism: The Soviet View.* Miami: University of Miami, Center for Advanced International Studies, Monographs in International Affairs, 1973. 168 pp.

1953 Gromyko, Andrei. "Nations' Interests Coincide -- Warning on Changing the Charter." *Vital Speeches*, 12 (February 15, 1946), pp. 260-62.
Address of Soviet delegate to first General Assembly, London, January 18, 1946.

1954 Grzybowski, Kazimierz. *Soviet Public International Law: Doctrines and Diplomatic Practice.* Leyden: Sijthoff, 1970. 544 pp.

1955 Halpern, Frieda F. "The World Government Plan." *Sunday Worker*, March 19, 1950.
Sponsors of Atlantic Union Committee, United World Federalists, and Citizens Committee for United Nations Reform prove that capitalists and militarists, not workers, are behind world government movement. Object is "putting Russia in her place . . . all under the slogan of the need for peace."

1956 Holloway, David. *The Soviet Union and the Arms Race.* New Haven: Yale University Press, 1983. 211 pp.

1957 Hughes, Thomas. "Marxism and Federalism." *Yale Political Journal*, 1 (February, 1947), pp. 5-11; (October, 1947), pp. 18-24.
Shows that Marxist theory does not necessarily contradict federalist theory.

1958 Israelyan, V. "Against Utilitarianism and Charter Review." In Rubinstein, Alvin Z., *The Foreign Policy of the Soviet Union* (New York: Random House, 1960), pp. 329-34.
Soviet rejection of Sohn's Commission to Study the Organization of Peace proposals of 1969. "The shortcomings and ineffectiveness of the [U.N.] organization, especially in questions of maintaining peace, do not stem from any so-called imperfections of its Charter,

but from the fact that the imperialist powers grossly violate the
high aims and principles expressed in it."

[1959] Kapitza, Peter. "Global Problems, International Solutions." *Bulletin
of the Atomic Scientists*, 37 (January, 1981), pp. 40-43.
An outstanding Soviet scientist calls for international solutions
to technological, economic, ecological, social, and political problems.

[1960] Kedrov, B.M. "To the Editors." *Kultura i zhizn*, March 22, 1949. *Current Digest of the Soviet Press*, I:13 (1949), pp. 12-13.
Public retraction of "cosmopolitanism" by Russian professor and editor-in-chief of *Voprosy filosofii*. Chief offense seems to have
been his denial that questions of priority in science (even if Russian) have importance

[1961] Kennan, George. "The Sources of Soviet Conduct." *Foreign Affairs*, 25
(July, 1947), pp. 566-82.

[1962] Kim, Samuel S. *The Maoist Image of World Order*. Princeton: Occasional Paper No. 5, World Order Studies Program, Center of International Studies, Woodrow Wilson School of Public and International Affairs, 1977. 57 pp.
Cf. Goodman.

[1963] Klark, Grenvil', i Son, Lui B. *Vredenie ko vtoromu (ispravlennomu)
izdaniiu mezhdunarodnyi mir putem mirovogo prava*. [Introduction to
Second (Revised) Edition of World Peace through World Law.] Kem-
bridzh, Mass.: Izd-vo Garvard-skogo universiteta, 1960. 71 pp.
This is the Russian translation of *World Peace through World Law*
that Adlai Stevenson delivered to Nikita Khruschev during the negotiations of the McCloy-Zorin agreement on the principles for general and complete disarmament.

[1964] *K peregovoram mezhdu pravitel'stvom SSSR i pravitel'stvom SShA po
atomnoi probleme*. [Concerning the U.S.S.R.-U.S.A. negotiations on
atomic energy.] Moskva: Gospolitizdat, 1954. 55 pp.

[1965] Kraminov, D. "Zamysly Dallesa v otnoshenii OON." [Intentions of J.F.
Dulles with Regard to the U.N.] *Pravda*, sentiabria 1, 1953; *Current
Digest of the Soviet Press*, 5 (October 10, 1953), p. 21.

[1966] Krehel, Peter. "More on Cosmopolitanism in the U.S.S.R." *Common Cause*,
2 (June, 1949), pp. 435-36.
Continuation of Sandomirsky.

[1967] Krylov, C. "U.N. Charter Must Be Observed." *Izvestia*, April 27, 1955,
p. 4; *Current Digest of the Soviet Press*, 7 (June 8, 1955), pp. 15-
16.

[1968] Kudriavtsev, V. "Za mezhdunarodnoe sotrudnichestvo." [In Favor of International Cooperation.] *Izvestia*, October 24, 1953.

[1969] Kuz'min, Eduard Leonidovich. *Mirovoe gosudarstvo: illiuzii ili real'-
nost'? Kritika burzhuaznykh kontseptsii suvereniteta*. [World Government: Illusions or Reality? Criticism of bourgeois conceptions
of sovereignty.] Moskva: Meshdunarodaia otnosheniia, 1969. 199 pp.

[1970] Lazerson, Maxim. *Russia and the Western World*: *The Place of the Soviet Union in the Comity of Nations*. New York: Macmillan, 1945. 275
pp.
By former member of Kerensky government.

[1971] Levin, D.B. "The Falsification of the Conception of International Law
by the Bourgeois Pseudo-Science." *Sovetskoe gosudarstvo i pravo*, 4
(1952), pp. 55-63.
Contains suggestions re U.N. Charter, Arts. 2, 11, 24, 25, and 55.

[1972] Mastny, Vojtech. *Russia's Road to the Cold War*: *Diplomacy, Warfare,
and the Politics of Communism, 1941-1945*. New York: Columbia University Press, 1979. 409 pp.
Based on American, British, and accessible Soviet and East European
sources. Stalin would not base Russian security on cooperation with
West. He did not know where to draw the line for his sphere of influence. West's failure was not to actively oppose his expansion
earlier.

[1973] McCagg, William O., Jr. *Stalin Embattled, 1943-1948*. Detroit: Wayne
State University Press, 1978. 423 pp.
Defensive and reactive character of Stalin's actions, 1947-1948.
Cf. Mastny.

[1974] Modrzhinskaĩa, E. D. "Cosmopolitanism." *Great Soviet Encyclopedia*,
3rd ed. (1976), 13:190.
"Proletarian internationalism is opposed to bourgeois cosmopolitanism. Cosmopolitanism calls for the merging of nations . . . by for-
cible assimilation. Marxists, on the other hand, envision the gradual and voluntary drawing together and then merging of nations because of the objective course of social development. . . ."

[1975] Molotov, V.M. Address to the United Nations, October 29, 1946. *Pravda*, November 1, 1946. Quoted in "Statements from the Soviet Union."
Common Cause, 1 (July, 1947), p. 29.
Highest level Soviet pronouncement against world government.
"[Some] seek to establish their world domination by way of political pressure, . . . military preparation and economic expansion,
clothing such a policy as a program for the creation of a United
States of Europe or for the establishment of a single world government."

[1976] Morozov, Gregory I. "Chto skryvaetsĩa za popytkami peresmotra Ustava
OON." [What Is Concealed by Attempts to Review the U.N. Charter.]
Moskovskii propagandist, 11 (1955), pp. 65-71.

[1977] --------. "O novykh planakh revizii Ustava OON." [On New Plans to Reform the U.N. Charter.] *Sovetskoe gosudarstvo i pravo*, 5 (mai,
1959), pp. 116-24.

[1978] --------. *International Organization*: *Some Theoretical Problems*. Moscow: Mysl, 1969. 231 pp.

[1979] Morozov, Platon D. "Soviet Views on Peace-Keeping." Interview with
Richard Hudson, August 27, 1964. *War/Peace Report*, October, 1964.
By deputy permanent representative of the Soviet Union to the U.N.
Soviet views on an international police force to be drawn from
Western, neutral, and socialist countries and used strictly to re-

pel aggression (collective security) under the U.N. Charter as originally conceived.

1980 Mrázek, I.   "O změnách mezinárodních smluv a zvláště jejich revisi."
     Právník (Praha), 46 (1957), pp. 148-65.

1981 Muszkat, Marian.   *Atomnaia energiia i bor'ba za mir*.   Perevod s pol'-
     skogo.   [Nuclear energy and the struggle for peace.]   Moskva: Iz-
     dat. Inostr. Liter., 1951.   358 pp.

1982 Nabliudatel' [pseud.].   "Vragi OON: Vragi mirnogo uregulirovaniia mezh-
     dunarodnykh problem."   [Enemies at the U.N.:   Enemies of the Peace-
     ful Settlement of Disputes.] *Izvestia*, 4 (sentiabria 6,   1953),   p.
     6; *Current Digest of the Soviet Press*, 5 (October 17, 1953), p. 9.

1983 Nogee, Joseph L.   *Soviet Policy towards International Control of Atom-
     ic Energy*.   Notre Dame: Notre Dame University Press, 1961.   306 pp.
     Based on available Soviet sources.   "To the Kremlin, non-Soviet in-
     trusion   into the   Soviet industrial   structure   constituted a   far
     greater   threat to   its long-term   stability and   survival than   an
     atomic arms race."

1984 Nove, Alec.   *The Soviet Economy*:   *An Introduction*.   London: Allen &
     Unwin, 1961.   328 pp.
     Soviet and   Western economies   may soon   "meet in   the middle"   (p.
     303).

1985 Pavlov, Yu.   "Cosmopolitanism: Ideological Weapon of American Reac-
     tion."   *Pravda*, April 7, 1949.   *Current Digest of the Soviet Press*,
     I:14 (1949), p. 25.
     "Cosmopolitanism is   the gospel   of so-called   'world citizenship,'
     the abandonment   of any allegiance   to any nation   whatsoever,   the
     liquidation of the   national traditions and culture   of the peoples
     under the screen of creating a 'world' culture."

1986 Polents, O.   E.   *"Vsemirnoe gosudarstvo"* -- *oruzhie amerikanskikh im-
     perialistov v bor'be za mirovoe gospodstvo*.   ["World government" --
     The weapon of American imperialism in   its struggle for world domi-
     nation.] Moskva: Pravda, 1950.   31 pp.

1987 Ramundo, Bernard A.   *Peaceful Coexistence*:   *International Law in the
     Building of Communism*.   Baltimore: Johns Hopkins University Press,
     1967.   262 pp.

1988 "Reshit' problemy reorganizatsii OON."   [To Solve the   Problem of the
     Reorganization of the U.N.] *Kommunist*, 4 (mart, 1961), pp. 12-15.

1989 Rubinstein, Alvin Z., ed. *The Foreign Policy of the Soviet Union*. New
     York: Random House, 1960; 3rd ed., 1972.   457 pp.

1990 --------. *The Soviets in International Organizations*: *Changing Policy
     toward Developing Countries, 1953-1963*.   Princeton: Princeton Uni-
     versity Press, 1964.   380 pp.

1991 --------, and Ginsburgs, George, eds.   *Soviet and American Policies in
     the United Nations*: *A Twenty-five Year Perspective*.   New York: New
     York University Press, 1971.   211 pp.
     Contains bibliography of Soviet   works on   international organiza-

tion.

[1992] --------. *Soviet Foreign Policy since World War II*: *Imperial and Global*. Cambridge, Mass.: Winthrop, 1981. 295 pp.
Brief work, concentrating on period from 1945 to present. ". . . the Kremlin leadership is wedded to the preservation of its imperial system; it has little interest in interdependence or involvement with the outside world beyond what it sees as necessary for strengthening its own society. Moscow may not be isolationist, but neither is it internationalist in the Western sense of the word."

[1993] Rubinstein, M. "A New Sect of the Atomic Religion." *New Times* (Moscow), December 10, 1947.
Condemnation of article by Joseph and Stewart Alsop in the *Saturday Evening Post* about new intercontinental ballistic missiles developed from the German V-2. In context of Einstein's appeal.

[1994] Sakharov, Andrei Dmitrievich. *Thoughts on Progress, Peaceful Coexistence, and Intellectual Freedom*. New York: Norton, 1968. 158 pp.
Great plea for a new Soviet domestic and foreign policy by a prominent Russian atomic scientist. Predicts world government by the year 2000 through convergence of communism and capitalism.

[1995] --------. *My Country and the World*. New York: Knopf, 1975. 109 pp.

[1996] Sandomirsky, Vera. "Zhdanov's Formula in Operation." *Common Cause*, 1 (May, 1948), pp. 393-94.
Report on new Russian ideological campaign against the West in aftermath of Truman Doctrine and Marshall Plan. Typical notions to be rooted out: "formalism," "servile worship of all things foreign," American "bourgeois culture," and literary themes of war weariness, suffering, and destruction. Sandomirsky followed the Russian press and the English language *Soviet Monitor* before appearance of the *Current Digest of the Soviet Press*.

[1997] --------. "Russian Cosmopolitanism: 1949." *Common Cause*, 2 (April, 1949), pp. 341-46.
Critique of "cosmopolitanism."

[1998] --------. "We Who Loved Thee, O Russia." *Common Cause*, 3 (November, 1949), pp. 199-208.
On universalism in both Russian literature and Bolshevik ideology.

[1999] Sholokhov, Mikhail. Moscow Domestic Broadcast, December 20, 1947. *Pravda*, January 23, 1948. Quoted by Robert S. Bird, *New York Times*, March 1, 1948.
Ideological campaign against former ally, in response to Truman Doctrine, Marshall Plan, and atomic threat. "While, like profligates, they spend billions of dollars in the making of atom bombs and for the preparation of a monstrous war, let our indestructable hatred of them continue."

[2000] Sorokin, Pitirim A. "Mutual Convergence of the United States and the U.S.S.R. to the Mixed Socio-Cultural Type." *International Journal of Comparative Sociology*, 1 (1960), pp. 143-76.
Leading Western source for doctrine of "convergence." "The preceding brief analysis . . . demonstrates indeed that in all these basic fields both countries have been becoming increasingly similar to

each other and converging mutually toward a mixed type, neither
Communist nor Capitalist, neither Totalitarian nor Democratic, neither Materialistic nor Idealistic, neither totally Religious nor
Atheistic-Agnostic, neither purely Individualistic nor Collectivistic. . . ."

2001 Soviet Draft Convention for Immediate, Complete, and General Disarmament, February 15, 1928. League of Nations Documents, V.165.M.50.
League of Nations Publications, 1928.IX.6, pp. 324-37.
Cited by A.   A. Sobolev during the Baruch Plan negotiations as a
Soviet "plan for world government." The Permanent International
Commission of Control was an approach to a world authority, with
representation from national legislative bodies, trade unions, and
other workmen's organizations.   Decisions were to be by majority
vote. But enforcement was by *national* legislation, which distinguishes this plan from a full world government proposal.

2002 Spiro, George. *Workers Democratic World Government versus National
Bureaucratic "Soviet" and Capitalist Regimes.* New York: Red Star
Press, 1951. 1068 pp.

2003 "The Stalin and Wallace Letters." *New York Herald Tribune*, May 18,
1948.
Stalin's apparently favorable response to Henry Wallace's overtures
for negotiations on East-West issues after the Czech coup and before the Berlin blockade.

2004 Strauss, Joshua. "Is 'World Government' the Answer?" *New Masses*, July
16, 1946, pp. 3-5; July 23, 1946, pp. 19-22.
"A world state can conceivable be created out of the imperialist
world in one of two ways. The imperialist way would be the complete
triumph of one imperialist nation (or alliance of nations,   as
Churchill proposes) over the rest of the world in a war, or wars.
The only other way is through the achievement of socialism in all
countries, through the final abolition of capitalism and its state
forms. . . ."

2005 "The Superstate Hoax." *Free Bulgaria* (Sophia), January 15, 1949, pp.
1-2.
Response to Yugoslav proposals for a Danubian federation, and hence
world federation.

2006 Taubman, William. *Stalin's American Policy: From Entente to Detente
to Cold War.* New York: Norton, 1982. 291 pp.
Defensive and reactive character of Stalin's actions, 1947-1948.
Note pp. 128-92.

2007 Tunkin, Gregorii I. *Theory of International Law.* Translated with introduction by William E. Butler. Cambridge: Harvard University
Press, 1974. 497 pp.
Most authoritative Soviet book on international law.   Denies the
Stalinist concept that there is a socialist and a bourgeois international law.   Basis of international law is   "*agreement* between
states." Contains a fair critique of *World Peace through World Law.*

2008 Uralsky, Anatoly. *Security and Co-operation: The Soviet Viewpoint.*
Moscow: Novosti, 1978. 71 pp.
Exposition of the Peace Program of the CPSU.   Sections on disarma-

ment, detente, development, causes of war, and community of aims and interests.

2009 Vavilov, Sergei, et al.   "About Certain Fallacies of Professor Albert Einstein." *New Times* (Moscow), November 26, 1947.   Reprinted in *Bulletin of the Atomic Scientists*, 4 (February, 1948), pp. 34, 37-38.
Response to Einstein's open letter in *United Nations World* of October, 1947.   Only fairly considered response from Russia to Western proposal of world government until perhaps the mid-1970s.

2010 "Why They Attack the Charter." *New Times* (Moscow), 41 (October 10, 1953), pp. 5-10.

2011 Zaslawski, D. "The Utopia of the Universal Gendarme." *Pravda*, July 6, 1948.
Response to W.T. Holliday's article in the *Reader's Digest* of January and February, 1948.   "A world government -- this is a universal gendarme . . . a dirty Utopian sketch of Hitler's 'New Order.'"

2012 Zhdanov, A.A.   Address to Founding Convention of Cominform, Poland, September, 1947.   Quoted by Vera Sandomirsky.
"The idea of 'world government,' which some bourgeois intellectuals of the dreamer and pacifist type have taken up, is being used not only as a means of pressure for the purpose of an ideological disarmament of peoples who defend their independence from the encroachment of American imperialism, but also as a slogan especially directed against the Soviet Union, which indefatigably and consistently defends the principles of genuine equality and of safeguarding the sovereign rights of all peoples, great and small."

2013 Zhukov, Yuri.   "What Is Behind the Plan to Revise the U.N. Charter?" *Pravda*, mai 11, 1948.

Cartoon originally appearing in the *Daily Worker*, March 19, 1950. Used by permission of the *Daily World*, Long View Publishing Co.

14

European Federation

Arnold Toynbee once remarked that "'Pan-Europa' had already become an anachronism without our ever having had an opportunity of creating her." He meant that, by 1948, "Europe," even if united, was already too small and too weak to be a viable independent unit. The concept ignored world realities. Was the British Commonwealth "in" Europe? What about the European empires in Africa and Asia? How could Europe be a "third force" between Russia and America?

World federalists have argued that European federation could follow, but not precede, a world federation, which would provide the military security and economic coordination necessary for all regional federations.

Nevertheless, the dream of European union has generated more efforts and achieved more successes than any other. The modern movement dates from the efforts of the Hungarian count Richard N. Coudenhove-Kalergi, who published *Pan-Europa* in 1923 and prevailed on French Foreign Minister Aristide Briand to issue a formal invitation of union to the states of Europe in 1930. But the idea of national sovereignty was too strong. After the war, the work of that national sovereignty, Coudenhove-Kalergi returned to Europe from exile in New York, bringing careful studies and a draft constitution for a federation of Europe. Winston Churchill then lent his enormous prestige to the cause in a dramatic appeal at The Hague in 1948. Generally, European sentiment was that economic cooperation had to precede political unification, so the Council of Europe that resulted from these efforts (1949) had a pronounced confederal structure, like the U.N.

In the next decade, a new line of European integration under the inspiration of French international banker, Jean Monnet, led to major economic achievements: the European Coal and Steel Community (1952), European Economic Community or Common Market (1957), and Euratom (1958), each of whose Commission and Council of Ministers were merged in 1967. The European Defense Community, regarded as a necessary step to political union, failed (1955). In these years, a protean conflict developed between Monnet, the prophet of a United States of Europe, and Charles de Gaulle, custodian of the grandeur of France. In 1965, in a dispute over the relative power of the European Commission (a "federal" body) and the Council of Ministers (a body representative of sovereign states), President de Gaulle *vetoed* the Commission by withdrawing French delegates for six months. This act of sovereign power set back progress of the Community for years. But the European Parliament was made elective in 1979, and five years later, under the

leadership of Altiero Spinelli, it produced the Draft Treaty Establishing
the European Union -- the most significant supranational federal constitution proposed in years. At time of writing the appointive Council had
still successfully turned aside the initiative of the elective Parliament,
but the trend was clear. The sovereignty of the people was asserting itself over the sovereignty of the state. This can also be seen in the European Court, which has now been granted some jurisdiction in cases involving
individuals vs. states.

Accounts by Hallstein, Mayne, Robertson, and Zurcher are particularly
useful for a general understanding of these complex developments. Leading
theorists of integration or community formation include Carl Friedrich,
Ernst Hass, Charles Pentland, and William Riker.

There is a decided anti-communist animus in European Union but not to
the extent of implying an open challenge for power with the Soviet Union,
as in the project of Atlantic Union.

Monnet's *Memoirs* is a classic for federalists of all stripes. It is
full of ripe political wisdom for the great task of uniting sovereignties.
His method, after he resigned the presidency of the European Coal and Steel
Community, was to form an Action Committee for the United States of Europe,
a committee that consisted of as few as thirty leaders of democratic political parties and trade union federations in the member states of the Community. Over a twenty-year period (1955-1975), they met several times a
year to produce able, well-received political reports on the issues of European union for the guidance of their governments.

From the very beginning, European unionists have claimed that their
union was the key to world union, and not the reverse. This view is evident, for instance, in the writings of Frances Josephy, Christopher Layton,
and John Pinder. The leading umbrella organization in Europe is the Union
des fédéralistes européens, based in Brussels.

Crawford cartoon, in *The Newark News*, December 2, 1951. Used by permission of Media General, Inc.

2023 Aben, H.J.M. *Europa onderweg*: *Ooggetuigen brengen verslag uit*. Amsterdam: Agon Elsevier, 1967. 200 pp.

2024 Action Committee for the United States of Europe. *Statements and Declarations, 1955-1967*. London: Royal Institute of International Affairs, European Series No. 9, Chatham House, 1969. 122 pp.

2025 Ad hoc Assembly Instructed to Work Out a Draft Treaty Setting Up a European Political Community. *Debates and Official Report*. Strasbourg: European Community, 1953. 578 pp.

2026 --------. *Draft Treaty Embodying the Statute of the European Community*. Paris: Secretariat of the Constitutional Committee, 1953. 178 pp.

2026a Albertini, Mario. *Lo stato nazionale*. Napoli: Guida Editori, 1958; 2nd ed., 1980. 152 pp.

2026b --------. *Il risorgimento e l'unità europea*. Napoli: Guida Editori, 1979. 83 pp.

2027 Albonetti, Achille. *Preistoria degli Stati Uniti d'Europa*. Intro. di Roberto Ducei. Milano: Giuffre, 1960. 336 pp.
       Also in French and German.

2028 --------. *Europeismo e atlantismo*. Firenze: Vallecchi, 1963. 100 pp.

2029 Alder, Claudius. *Koordination und Integration als Rechtsprinzipien ein Beitrag zum Problem der derogatorischen Kraft des europäischen Gemeinschaftsrechts gegenuber einzelstaatlichem Recht*. Bruges: De Tempel, 1969. 344 pp.

2030 Alting von Geusau, Frans A.M. *Beyond the European Community*. Leyden: Sijthoff, 1969. 247 pp.

2031 Ambrosini, Gaspare. *Autonomia regionale e federalismo*: *Austria, Spagna, Germania, U.R.S.S.* Roma: Edizioni italiane, 1944. 230 pp.

2032 American Committee on United Europe. *The Union of Europe*: *Declarations of European Statesmen*. New York: By the Committee in cooperation with the European Movement, 1950. 75 pp.

2033 --------. *Études sur le fédéralisme*. Bruxelles: European Movement, 1952-1953. 7 vols.
       Harvard studies of the government of a European federation. Precedents sought in Australia, Canada, West Germany, Switzerland, and the United States. Louis B. Sohn wrote study on foreign affairs. Also in English.

2034 André, Charles. *L'Europe à la croisée des chemins*. Lyon: Fédérop, 1979. 317 pp.

2035 Araujo, Braz José de. *Le Plan Fouchet et l'union politique européenne*. Nancy: Centre européen universitaire de Nancy, 1967. 56 pp.

2036 Arbuthnott, Hugh, and Edwards, Geoffrey, eds. *A Common Man's Guide to the Common Market*: *The European Community*. London: Federal Trust for Education and Research, Macmillan, 1979. 213 pp.

2037 Armand, Louis, et Drancourt, Michel. *Le Pari européen*. Paris: Fayard, 1968. 315 pp.

2038 --------. *The European Challenge*. Trans. by Patrick Evans. New York: Atheneum, 1970. 256 pp.

2039 Armitage, Paul. *The Common Market*. London: MacDonald Educational Fund, 1978. 63 pp.

2040 Aron, Robert, et Marc, Alexandre. *Principes du fédéralisme*. Paris: Le Portulan, 1948. 147 pp.

2041 Aronco, Gianfranco d'. *Federazione europea e autonomie regionali*. Urdine: "Il Nuovo Friuli," 1953. 14 pp.

2042 Associazione italiana Fulbright. *Stati Uniti d'America e integrazione europea*. Firenze: L.S. Olschki, Atti del convegno nazionale, 5, 1964. 132 pp.

2043 *Der Aufbau Europas*: *Plane und Dokumente, 1945-1980*. Hrsg. von Jurgen Schwartz. Bonn: Osang, 1980. 698 pp.

2044 Avenol, Joseph. *L'Europe silencieuse*. Neuchâtel: La Baconnière, 1944. 91 pp.
Politics, 1918-1945.

2045 Bailey, Sydney D. *United Europe*: *A Short History of the Idea*.   London: National News Letter, 1948. 76 pp.

2046 Bakke, Elliv. *Tre slags borgerskap*: *Alternativet til Romatraktaten*. Lillehammer, Oslo: Mesna-trykks forlag, 1967. 41 pp.

2047 Ball, Mary M. *NATO and the European Union Movement*. London: Stevens, 1959. 486 pp.

2048 Baltus, René. *De la vieille à la nouvelle Europe*.   Préf. de Robert Schuman. Paris: Le Centurion, 1953. 141 pp.

2049 Barrat, Robert. "A Neutral Europe." *Commonweal*, June 16, 1950, pp. 245-46.

2050 Baumann, Carol E., comp. *Western Europe*: *What Path to Integration?* Boston: Heath, 1967. 156 pp.
Includes leading statements by Winston Churchill, George Marshall, Ernest Bevin, Jean Monnet, Charles de Gaulle, Karl Deutsch, Ernst Haas, Robert Aron, Zbignew Brezenski, et al.   Communist views discussed.

2051 Beales, A.C.F., et al. *Der Kampf um den Frieden*: *Ein neuer Weltkrieg oder eine neue Ordnung?* Koblenz: Historische-Politischer Verlag, 1948. 178 pp.
Führende Politiker und Wissenschaftler aus allen Ländern und aus allen Lagern fordern als Ausweg aus der Krisis der Gegenwart ein föderiertes Europa in einer föderierten Welt.

2052 Bellezza, Giuliano. *La Comunità economica europea*.   Roma: Riuniti,

1980. 150 pp.

2053 Beloff, Max.　*Europe and the Europeans*:　*An International Discussion.*
Introduction by Denis de Rougemont. London: Chatto & Windus, 1957.
288 pp.
Report requested by Council of Europe at critical period.

2054 --------.　*The United States and the Unity of Europe.*　Washington:
Brookings, 1963. 124 pp.

2055 Berthaud, Claude.　*Le Marché commun.*　Paris:　Masson, 2e ed., 1981.
290 pp.

2056 Bertolino, Alberto.　*Cooperazione internazionale e sviluppo economico.*
Firenze:　La Nuova Italia, Il pensiero economico, Nuova serie, 6,
1961. 198 pp.

2057 Beugel, Ernst Hans van der.　*From Marshall Aid to Atlantic Partnership: European Integration as a Concern of American Foreign Policy.*
Foreword by Henry Kissinger. Amsterdam: Elsevier, 1966. 480 pp.

2058 Bieber, Roland, und Nickel, Dietmar, red.　*Das Europa der zweiten Generation: Gedachtnissschrift fur Christoph Sasse.* Baden-Baden: Nomos
Verlagsgesellschaft, 1981.

2058a --------; Jacque, Jean-Paul; and Weiler, Joseph H.H.　*An Ever Closer
Union.* Brussels: European Commission, 1985. 345 pp.
Detailed study, sponsored by the European University Institute
(Florence), of the European Parliament's Draft Treaty on European
Union.

2059 Bikkal, Dénes.　*Los Estados Unidos de Europa*:　*Precursores y programa.*
Madrid:　By the author, 1955. 158 pp.

2060 Bingham, Alfred M.　*The United States of Europe.*　New York:　Duell,
Sloan & Pearce, 1940. 336 pp.

2061 Blacksell, Mark.　*Post-war Europe*:　*A Political Geography.*　London:
Hutchinson, 2nd ed., 1981. 220 pp.

2062 Blanchard, Louis.　"L'union pan-americaine et les projects de fédération européenne." *Esprit, revue internationale* (Paris), 8 (1940),
pp. 25-36.

2063 Bliesener, Erich.　*Europäische integration als Thema der Karikature.*
Heidelberg: Impula Verlag, 1962. 96 pp.

2064 Bloes, Robert.　*Le "Plan Fouchet" et le problème de l'Europe politique.*
Bruges:　Collège d'Europe, Dijver, 1970. 542 pp.

2065 Bodenheimer, Susanne J.　*Political Union*:　*A Microcosm of European Politics, 1960-1966.*　Preface by Daniel Lerner. Leyden:　Sijthoff,
1967. 229 pp.

2066 Bombach, Gottfried, et al.　*Sciences humaines et intégration européenne.*　Préf. de Robert Schuman. Leyde: Sythoff, 1960. 423 pp.

2067 Bonnefous, Edouard.　*L'idée européenne et sa réalisation.*　Paris: Édi-

tions du grand siècle, 1950.   357 pp.
History of European Movement.

2068 --------. *L'Europe en face de son destin*.   Paris: Éditions du grand
siècle, 1952.   386 pp.

2069 Bonvicini, G., e Sassoon, J., et al.   *Governare l'economia europea*:
Divergenze e processi integrativi.   Torino: Fondazione Giovanni
Agnelle, 1978.   329 pp.

2070 Bozeman, Ada B. *The Future of Law in a Multicultural World*.   Princeton: Princeton University Press, 1971.   229 pp.
Conflict resolution by mediation by peers in African societies is
compared to adjudication by officials in Europe.

2071 Brandstätter, Leopold.   *Der Ausweg, Europas letzte Chance und die Zukunft der Menschheit*. Linz: Spirale-Verlag, 1968.   155 pp.

2072 Brecht, Arnold.   "European Federation -- The Democratic Alternative."
Harvard Law Review, 55 (February, 1942), pp. 561-94.
Hegemony of any one state in Europe to be checked not by partition
or discrimination, but by legislative balances, general disarmament, federal supremacy, continental economic and financial programs, non-national education, and regional organizations.

2073 Briand, Aristide. "Memorandum on the Organization of a Regime of European Federal Union Addressed to Twenty-six Governments of Europe
. . . May 17, 1930." *International Conciliation*, Special Bulletin
(June, 1930), pp. 323-53.
Formal proposal by French Foreign Minister.   Coudenhove-Kalergi's
greatest achievement. For replies, see *International Conciliation*,
265 (December, 1930), pp. 651-769.

2074 Brogan, Denis W.   *The Idea of European Union*.   Leeds: University of
Leeds Press, 1949.   15 pp.

2075 Brugmans, Hendrik. *Fundamentals of European Federalism*.   Foreword by
Lord Layton, translation by F. L. Josephy. London: European Union
of Federalists, 1947.   11 pp.
Precursor to Churchill's European Movement.   Brugmans became first
rector of the College of Europe.

2076 --------, et al. *Federazione europea*. Firenze: La nuova Italia, 1948.
322 pp.
Includes essays by Luigi Einaudi and Altiero Spinelli.

2077 --------. *La cité européenne*: *Programme fédéraliste*. Paris: Le Portulan, 1950.   99 pp.

2078 --------. *Pour un gouvernement européen*. Paris: La Fédération, 1952.
30 pp.

2079 --------. *Auf dem Weg zur Europa-Regierung*. Paris: Verlag der Euro-
paischen Jugendkampagne, 1952.   38 pp.

2080 --------. *Schets van een Europese samenleving*.   Rotterdam: Donker,
1952. 135 pp.

2081 --------. *Skizze eines europäischen Zusammenlebens.* Frankfurt-am-Main: Verlag der Frankfurter Hefte, 1953. 229 pp.

2082 --------. *Towards a European Government.* Paris: European Movement, International Youth Secretariat, 1953. 29 pp.

2083 --------. *Europa west èn oost.* Den Haag: Europese Beweging, 1956. 26 pp.

2084 --------. *Les origines de la civilisation européenne.* Liege: G. Thone, 1958. 264 pp.

2085 --------. *Panorama del pensiero federalista.* Milano: Edizione di Comunità, 1960. 214 pp.

2086 --------. *L'Europe prend le large.* Préface de Salvador de Madariaga. Liege: G. Thone, 1961. 367 pp.

2087 --------. *Europa en het vaderland: Een culturele benadering.* Den Haag: Europese Beweging, 1962. 34 pp.

2088 --------, et Duclos, Pierre. *Le fédéralisme contemporain: Critères, institutions, perspectives.* Leyde: Sythoff, 1963. 191 pp.

2089 --------, et al. *L'Europe de demain et ses responsables. Leaders for the Europe of Tomorrow.* Bruges: Collège de l'Europe, De Tempel, 1967. 366 pp.

2090 --------. *La pensée politique du fédéralisme.* Avant-propos de Robert Aron. Leyde: Sythoff, 1969. 144 pp.

2091 --------. *L'Europe des nations.* Paris: Librarie générale de droit et de jurisprudence, 1970. 478 pp.

2092 --------. *Levend in Europa: Ontmoetingen en herinneringen.* Alphen a/d Riin: Sijthoff, 1980. 224 pp.

2093 --------. *Volti d'Europa: I momenti-chiave della storia europea.* Brescia: La Scuola, 1981. 223 pp.

2094 Brunner, Karl, et al. *Die Integration des europäischen Westens.* Zürich: Polygraphischer, 1954. 157 pp.
Essays on European union by Karl Brunner, Ludwig Erhard, Robert Schuman, Alcide de Gasperi, and others.

2094a Burgess, Michael. "Federal Ideas in the European Community: Altiero Spinelli and European Union, 1981-1984." *Government and Opposition,* 19 (Summer, 1984), pp. 339-47.

2095 Burrows, Bernard; Denton, Geoffrey; and Edwards, Geoffrey, eds. *Federal Solutions to European Issues.* London: Macmillan, Federal Trust for Education and Research, 1977. 225 pp.
Scholarly articles on political needs and institutions of the European Economic Community, its economic and social policies, Europe and the world, and the value of federalism. Includes John Pinder, "A Federal Community in an Ungoverned World Economy."

2096 Campagnolo, Umberto. *Republica federale europea: unificazione giuri-*

dica dell'Europa. Milano: L'Europa unita, 1945. 130 pp.

2097 ————. *Der europäische Bundesstaat*: *die juristische Einigung Europas.* Übersetzung von Walter Eckstein. Bern: Francke, 1947. 84 pp.

2098 Camps, Miriam. *What Kind of Europe? The Community since de Gaulle's Veto.* London: Royal Institute of International Affairs, Oxford University Press, 1965. 140 pp.

2099 ————. *European Unification in the Sixties*: *From Veto to the Crisis.* New York: Council on Foreign Relations, McGraw-Hill, 1966. 273 pp.

2100 Canfora, Fabrizio. *Federalismo europeo e internazionalismo da Mazzini ad oggi.* Firenze: Parenti, 1954. 100 pp.

2101 Carandini, Nicolo. *Europa*: *problema del mondo.* Roma: Soc. ABETE, 1949. 27 pp.

2102 ————. *Verso l'Europa unita.* Roma: Soc. ABETE, 1949. 29 pp. Work of Movimento federalista europeo.

2103 Cardis, Francois. *Federalisme et intégration européenne.* Préf. de Georges Rigassi. Lausanne: Centre des recherches européennes, École des H.E.C., Université de Lausanne, 1964. 269 pp.

2104 Caron, Giuseppe. *Scritti e discorsi sull'unione europea.* Roma: Litostam, 1958. 167 pp.

2105 Carter, William H. *Speaking European*: *The Anglo-Continental Cleavage.* London: Allen & Unwin, 1966. 233 pp.

2106 Cartou, Louis. *Communautés européennes.* Paris: Dalloz, 6e ed., 1979. 668 pp.

2107 Cassimatis, Gregoire. *Les bases essentielles de l'union de l'Europe*: *synthèse politique, synthèse économique et sociale, synthèse culturelle.* Athènes: Éditions du "Présent," 1949. 23 pp.

2108 Castanos, Stelios. *Les tendances juridiques de l'intégration européenne.* Paris: Librairie du Recueil Sirey, 1957. 53 pp.

2109 Castarede, Jean. *De l'Europe de la raison à celle du coeur.* Paris: Nathan, 1979. 393 pp.

2110 Catholic Church, Roman. *His Holiness Pope Pius XII on Europe, 1948-1957.* Strasbourg: Catholic Information Office on European Problems, 1958. 15 pp.

2111 Catlin, George E.G. *The Unity of Europe.* London: Temple, 1944. 31 pp.

2112 ————. *The Stronger Community.* New York: Hawthorn, 1966. 217 pp.

2113 Centre d'action pour la fédération européenne. *L'Europe de demain.* Neuchâtel: La Baconnière, 1945. 220 pp.

[2114] Chiti-Batelli, Andrea. *Il Parlamento europea*: *Struttura, procedura, codice parlamentare*. Padova: Cedam, 1982. 412 pp.

[2115] Churchill, Winston S. *A United Europe*: *One Way to Stop a New War*. London: 1946. 7 pp.

[2116] --------. *The Sinews of Peace*. Ed. by Randolph S. Churchill. London: Cassell, 1948. 256 pp.
Speeches, 1945-1946, including those at Metz and Zurich bravely calling for Franco-German rapproachment and a European union.

[2117] --------. *Europe Unite*. Ed. by Randolph S. Churchill. London: Cassell, 1950. 506 pp.
Speeches, 1947-1948, including that at The Hague and three others on United Europe. Initiative by Churchill when out of office that led to creation of the (confederal) Council of Europe. "Unless some effective World Super-Government can be set up and brought quickly into action, the prospects for peace and human progress are dark and doubtful."

[2118] --------. *In the Balance*. Ed. by Randolph S. Churchill. Boston: Houghton Mifflin, 1952. 456 pp.
Speeches, 1949-1950.

[2119] Clavel, Jean-Claude, et Collet, Pierre. *L'Europe au fil de jours*: *Les jeunes années de la construction européenne, 1948-1978*. Paris: La Documentation française, 1979. 404 pp.

[2120] Cleveland, Harold Van B. *The Atlantic Idea and Its European Rivals*. New York: Council on Foreign Relations, McGraw-Hill, 1966. 186 pp.

[2121] Coffey, Peter. *Economic Policies of the Common Market*. London: Macmillan, 1979. 212 pp.

[2122] Collier, David S., and Glaser, Kurt, eds. *Western Integration and the Future of Eastern Europe*. Chicago: Foundation for Foreign Affairs, Regnery, 1964. 207 pp.

[2123] -------- and --------, eds. *Western Policy and Eastern Europe*. Chicago: Foundation for Foreign Affairs, 1966. 245 pp.

[2123]a Coombes, David. *Politics and Bureaucracy in the European Community*: *A Portrait of the Commission of the E.E.C.* London: Allen & Unwin, 1970. 343 pp.

[2124] Corbett, John P. *Europe and the Social Order*. Leyden: Sijthoff, 1959. 188 pp.

[2125] Cornelis, Petrus A. *Europeans about Europe*: *What European Students Know and Expect of the Unification of Europe*; *A Study in Social Psychology*. Amsterdam: Swets & Zeitlinger, 1970. 174 pp.

[2126] Coudenhove-Kalergi, Richard N. *Pan-Europa*. Wien: Pan Europa Verlag, 1923; 2n ed., 1928; 3rd, 1966. 167 pp.
Book which launched the movement for European federation.

[2127] --------. *Europe Must Unite*. London: Secker & Warburg, 1940. 160 pp.

2128 --------. "America and Europe." *Common Sense*, October, 1941, pp. 296-300.
While in exile during the war, Coudenhove-Kalergi abandoned his earlier notion of a European confederation under Franco-German leadership for a bipolar Europe of two full federations. Analogy for world split into Soviet and American blocs.

2129 --------. *Crusade for Pan-Europe*. New York: Putnam, 1943. 318 pp.
A Streitian, anti-Russian figure who labored for years to unite Europe. Churchill upstaged him, but actually both were disappointed that no European federation was achieved immediately after the war.

2130 --------. *Memorandum on the European Question and America*. New York: By the author, 1945. 18 pp.

2131 --------. *J'ai choisi l'Europe*. Avant-propos de Winston Churchill. Paris: Plon, 1952. 356 pp.

2132 --------. *Die europäische Mission der Frau*. Zürich: Thomas Verlag, 1953. 43 pp.

2133 --------. *Mutterland Europa*. Zürich: Thomas Verlag, 1953. 29 pp.

2134 --------. *An Idea Conquers the World*. Introduction by Winston Churchill. London: Hutchinson, 1953. 310 pp.

2135 --------. *Eine Idee erobert Europa: meine Lebenserinnerungen*. Wien: Desch, 1958; 2nd ed., 1966. 392 pp.

2136 --------. *Weltmacht Europa*. Stuttgart: Seewald Verlag, 1971. 195 pp.

2137 Council of Europe. Directorate of Information. *La culture européenne et le Conseil de l'Europe*. Strasbourg: Conseil de l'Europe, 1955. 79 pp.

2138 Crawford, Oliver. *Done This Day: The European Idea in Action*. London: Hart-Davis, 1970. 399 pp.
On Council of Europe.

2139 Criddle, Byron. *Socialists and European Integration: A Study of the French Socialist Party*. London: Routledge & Paul, 1969. 116 pp.

2140 Davies, David, baron. *A Federated Europe*. London: Gollancz, 1940. 141 pp.

2141 Dean, Vera Micheles. *Can Europe Unite?* New York: Foreign Policy Association, Headline Series No. 80, 1950. 62 pp.
Includes John Kenneth Galbraith, "America and Western Europe."

2142 Debre, Michel. *Projet de pacte pour une union d'états européens*. Paris: Nagel, 1950. 59 pp.

2143 Dehousse, Fernand. *L'Europe et le monde: recueil d'études, de rapports et de discours, 1945-1960*. Paris: Librairie générale de droit et de jurisprudence, 1960. 618 pp.

2144 Dell'Omodarme, Marcello. *Europa: Mito e realta del processo d'integrazione*. Milano: Marzorati, 1981. 381 pp.

2145 Derfler, Michael. *Europa -- ja oder nein?* Wien: Zeit & Zukunft Verlag, 1947. 196 pp.

2146 Deutsche Gesellschaft fur Auswärtige Politik, ed. *Prognosen für Europa: die siebziger Jahre twischen Ost und West*. Opladen: C.W. Leske, 1968. 140 pp.

2147 Dichter, Ernest. *Europas unsichtbare Mauern, die Rolle nationaler Vorurteile und ihre Überwindung: eine Motivuntersuchung zur europäischen Einigung für die Europa-Union Deutschland*. Düsseldorf: Europa Union Verlag, 1962. 54 pp.

2148 Døcker, Henrik. *De europaeiske enhedsbestraebelser*. København: Borgen, 1967. 296 pp.

2149 Domenedò, Francesco M. *Introduzione all'Europa*. Roma: Società editrice libraria italiana, 1949. 100 pp.

2150 Doublet, M. *Les problèmes sociaux démographiques posés par la réalisation de l'unité de l'Europe*. Nancy: Centre européen universitaire, 1952. 79 pp.

2151 Drancourt, Michel. *Les clés du pouvoir*. Avec une conclusion de Louis Armand. Paris: Fayard, 1964. 238 pp.

2152 Dutoit, Bernard. *La neutralité suisse à l'heure européenne*. Paris: Université de Paris, Institut des hautes études internationales, Bibliotheque de droit international, 24, 1962. 138 pp.

2153 Economidès, Constantin P. *Le pouvoir de décision des organisations internationales européennes*. Leyde: Sythoff, 1964. 167 pp.

2154 Einaudi, Luigi. *I problemi economici della Federazione europea*. Milano: "La Fiaccola," 1945. 112 pp.

2155 --------. *La guerra e l'unità europea*. Milano: Edizioni di Comunità, 1948. 154 pp.
By the President of Italy.

2156 Elgozy, Georges. *L'Europe des européens*. Paris: Flammarion, 1961. 332 pp.

2157 Erler, Georg H.J. *Die Krise der europäischen Gemeinschaften: Europäischer Bundesstaat oder Europa der Väterlander?* Göttingen: Vandenhoeck & Ruprecht, 1966. 30 pp.

2158 *Europa: Chronik, Probleme, Ziele, Partner, Parteien, Gemeinschaften, Organe, Politik, Finanzen, Wahrung, Landwirtschaft, Handel, Dritte Welt*. Bonn: Presse- und Informationsamt der Bundesregierung, 1980. 112 pp.

2159 *Europa -- Gemeenschap in wording*. Den Haag: Nijhoff, 1978. 207 pp.

2160 Europäische Aktionsgemeinschaft. *Taschenbuch für die Freunde Europas: ein Europa-Wegweisen*. Bad Godesberg, 1961. 237 pp.

[2161] *Europe*: *Guide européen.* Paris: Société générale européenne, 1980.

[2162] European Movement. *Europe Unites*: *The Hague Congress and After.* Foreword by Winston Churchill. London: Hollis & Carter, 1949.
Story of the campaign for European unity, including a full report on the Congress of Europe, held at The Hague, May, 1948.

[2163] --------, International Council. *European Movement and the Council of Europe.* Forewords by Winston Churchill and Paul-Henri Spaak. London: Hutchinson, n.d., c. 1949.

[2164] European Parliament.   *Draft Treaty Establishing the European Union.* [Spinelli Plan.] Directorate-General for Information and Public Relations, Publications and Briefings Division, P.O. Box 1601, L-2920 Luxembourg, February, 1984. 46 pp.
A federal constitution for Europe, developing and extending the institutions of the European Community.   "Where this Treaty confers exclusive competence on the Union, the institutions of the Union shall have sole power to act; national authorities may legislate only to the extent laid down by the law of the Union" (Art. 12). Draft adopted by Parliament on 14 February 1984 by vote of 237 for, 31 against, 43 abstentions.

[2164a] Everling, Ulrich; Kloten, Norbert; et al. *Zwischenbilanz Europa.* Baden-Baden: Nomos Verlagsgesellschaft, 1979. 175 pp.

[2165] Falck, Enrico. *Saggi politici e sociali.* Milano: Ambrosianeum, 1955. 415 pp.

[2166] Ferrari Aggradi, Mario.   *Europa*: *tappe e prospettive di unificazione.* Roma: Editrice Studium, 1958. 356 pp.

[2167] Firsoff, V.A. *The Unity of Europe*: *Realities and Aspirations.* London: Drummand, 1947. 305 pp.

[2168] Fischer, Helmut. *Der Weg nach Europa*: *übernationale Gemeinschaften und der Europarat.* München: Heyne, 1953. 96 pp.

[2169] Florinski, Mikhail Timofeyevich. *Integrated Europe?* New York: Macmillan, 1955. 182 pp.

[2170] Der Föderalist. *Die Bildung Europas.* Heidelberg: Centre international de formation européenne, Moos, 1962. 48 pp.

[2171] Foighel, Isi. *EF*: *Funktion og regler.* København: Berlingske Forlag, 1972. 301 pp.

[2172] Fontaine, François, et al. *Quelle Europe?* Paris: Centre catholique des intellectuels français, Recherches et debats 22, Fayard, 1958. 249 pp.

[2173] Fontaine, Pascal. *Une course sans retour*: *Fondation Jean Monnet pour l'Europe.* Lausanne: Centre de recherches européennes, 1981. 149 pp.

[2174] Forschungsinstitut der Deutschen Gesellleschaft für Auswartige Politik, Frankfurt am Main. *Europa*: *Dokumente zur Frage der europäischen*

Einigung. München: ITS Dokumente und Berichte, 17, Oldenbourg, 1962. 2 vols.

2174a Forsyth, Murray. *Unions of States: The Theory and Practice of Confederation.* New York: Leicester University Press, Holmes & Meier, 1981. 236 pp.

2175 Fouère, Yann. *L'Europe aux cent drapeaux: essai pour servir à la construction de l'Europe.* Préf. de Alexandre Marc. Paris: Presses d'Europe, 1968. 209 pp.

2176 Freytag, Werner. *Politik für Jedermann: deutsche Probleme, politische Systeme und Europa.* Nachwort von E. Meyer. Göttingen: Musterschmidt Verlag, 1968. 264 pp.

2177 Friedrich, Carl J. *Europe: An Emergent Nation?* New York: Harper & Row, 1969. 269 pp.

2178 Frisch, Alfred. *L'Europe et son unité: sur la voie du progrès.* Paris: Les Cahiers africains, 9, "Création de presse," 1962. 80 pp.

2179 Frydenberg, Per, et al. *Integrasjon og sikkerhet: Klipp fra debatten om Europas aktuelle problemer.* Oslo: Norsk utenrikspolitisk institutt, 1966. 150 pp.

2180 Garelli, Francois. *Pour une monnaie européenne.* Paris: Éditions du Seuil, 1969. 159 pp.

2181 Gerbet, Pierre. "L'intégration européenne: problèmes et institutions, état des travaux." *Revue française de sciences politiques* (Paris), 11 (septembre, 1961), pp. 691-719.

2182 Germany, Federal Republic. *Europa: Dokumente zur Frage der europäischen Einigung.* Bonn: Verlag Bonner Universitäts-Buchdruckerei, 1953. 393 pp.

2183 Giancola, Luigi. *Europeismo e civiltà cristiana.* Roma: Coliana de studi sociali, 5, Belardetti, 1953. 131 pp.

2184 Giannini, Amedeo. *Unione europea.* Mazara: Inchieste d'attualità, 2, Società editrice siciliana, 1948. 48 pp.

2185 Gilson, Etienne. "Neutrality for France?" *Bulletin of the Atomic Scientists,* 6 (July, 1950), pp. 203-05.

2186 Gimenez Caballero, Ernesto. *La Europa de Estrasburgo: vision española del problema europeo.* Madrid: Instituto de estudios politicos, 1950. 154 pp.

2187 Gladwyn Jebb, H.M., baron. *The European Idea.* London: Weidenfeld & Nicolson, 1966. 159 pp.

2188 Goormaghtigh, John. *European Integration.* New York: Carneige Endowment for International Peace, 1953. 109 pp.

2189 Gori, Umberto. *Organizzazione internazionale e Comunità europee; problemi dell'insegnamento universitario.* Preface di Ricardo Monaco. Padova: CEDAM, Pubblicazioni della Società italiana per l'organizzazione internazionale, 1965. 43 pp.

2190 Gorny, Léon. Les politiques européennes face aux États-Unis. Préf. de
     Lord Warwick. Paris: Éditions Émile-Paul, 1967. 313 pp.

2191 Gouzy, Jean Pierre. Les pionniers de l'Europe communautaire. Lausanne:
     Centre de recherches européennes, 1968. 171 pp.

2192 Great Britain. Central Office of Information. Western Cooperation in
     Brief. London: H.M. Stationery Office, 1958; 2nd ed., 1960. 39 pp.

2193 Groeben, Hans von der.   Die europäische Wirtschaftsgemeinschaft als
     Motor der gesellschaftlichen und politischen Integration. Tübingen:
     Walter Eucken Institut, Vortrage und Aufsätze, 25, Mohr, 1970.   30
     pp.

2194 Gross, Feliks. Crossroads of Two Continents: A Democratic Federation
     of East-Central Europe. New York: Columbia University Press, 1945.
     162 pp.
     An alternative vision for Eastern Europe. Includes documents.

2195 Grosser, Dieter, und Neuss, Beate.   Europa zwischen Politik und Wirt-
     schaft. Hildesheim: Olms, 1981.   270 pp.

2196 Guérard, Albert. Europe Free and United.   London: Oxford University
     Press, 1945. 206 pp.
     Exploration of the historical possibility of uniting Europe, with
     respect to the problems of England, the Soviet Union, and Germany.
     By Stanford University professor of literature who became a member
     of the Committee to Frame a World Constitution.

2197 Haas, Ernst B.   "Regionalism, Functionalism, and Universal Organiza-
     tion." World Politics, 8 (January, 1956), pp. 238-63.
     Process of political integration or community formation at work.

2198 --------. The Uniting of Europe: Political, Social, and Economic For-
     ces, 1950-1957. Stanford: Stanford University Press, 1958.   552
     pp.
     Common Market federalism.

2199 --------. "International Integration: The European and the Universal
     Process." International Organization, 15 (Summer, 1961), pp. 336-
     93.
     European and world unification as process of community formation.

2200 --------.   "The Obsolescence of Regional Integration Theory." Paper,
     Institute of International Studies,   University of California,
     Berkeley, 1976.
     New decision-making styles and technological change have made inte-
     gration theory obsolescent. European union to follow world union?

2201 Haesele, Kurt W. Europas letzter Weg: Montan-Union und EWG.   Frank-
     furt am Main: Knapp, 1958. 352 pp.

2202 Haines, C. Grove, ed. European Integration. Introduction by Paul Van
     Zeeland. Baltimore: Johns Hopkins University Press, 1957. 310 pp.
     Papers at conference of Bologna in 1956 to "relaunch" Europe. Con-
     tains Altiero Spinelli, "The Growth of the European Movement since

World War II."

2203 Hallstein, Walter. *Economic Integration as a Factor of Political In-tegration*. Brussels: Publishing Services of the European Communities, 1961. 18 pp.

2204 --------. *United Europe*: *Challenge and Opportunity*. Cambridge: Harvard University Press, 1962. 109 pp.
The analogy for the world is Europe, not the United States in 1787.

2205 --------, und Schlochauer, Hans-Jurgen, eds. *Zur Integration Europas*: *Festschrift für Carl Friedrich Ophüls*. Karlsruhe: Müller, 1965. 258 pp.

2206 --------. *Wege nach Europa*: *Walter Hallstein und die junge Generation*. Einleitung und biographische Skizze von Theo M. Loch. Hangelar bei Bonn: Pontes-Verlag, 1967. 199 pp.

2207 --------. *Europa 1980*. Einleitung und biographische Skizze von Theo M. Loch. Bonn: Eicholz-Verlag, 1968. 215 pp.
Collection of author's addresses, lectures, and speeches.

2208 --------. *Europe in the Making*. Introduction by George Ball. New York: Norton, 1972. 343 pp.
By former West German Secretary of State for Foreign Affairs. Authoritative political analysis of European Economic Community -- neither a federation nor a confederation.

2209 --------. *Die Europäische Gemeinschaft*. 5. überarbeitete und erwieterte Auflage. Dusseldorf: Econ Verlag, 1979. 499 pp.

2210 --------. *Europäische Reden*. Hrsg. von Thomas Oppermann unter Mitarbeit von Joachim Kohler. Stuttgart: DVA, 1979. 707 pp.

2211 Hammar, Conrad H. *Toward a Simpler World*: *The Community Idea*. New York: Vantage, 1978. 337 pp.

2212 Harbrecht, Wolfgang. *Die Europäische Gemeinschaft*. Stuttgart: Fischer, 1978. 228 pp.

2213 Harrison, George, and Jordan, Peter. *Central Union*. London: By the authors, 1943. 48 pp.

2214 Harrison, Reginald J. *Europe in Question*: *Theories of Regional International Integration*. London: Allen & Unwin, 1974. 256 pp.
Good survey of European federalist movement.

2215 Haug, Hans. *Neutralität und Völkergemeinschaft*. Zürich: Polygraphischer Verlag, 1962. 191 pp.

2216 Hawtrey, Ralph G. *Western European Union*: *Implications for the United Kingdom*. London: Royal Institute of International Affairs, 1949. 126 pp.

2217 Hay, Peter. *Federalism and Supranational Organizations*: *Patterns for New Legal Structures*. Urbana: University of Illinois Press, 1968. 335 pp.

[2218] Healey, Denis. *Western Europe*: *The Challenge of Unity*.   Toronto: Canadian Association for Adult Education,   Behind the Headlines, 9,
1950. 24 pp.

[2219] Heiser, Hans Joachim.   *British Policy with Regard to the Unification
Efforts on the European Continent*. Leyden: European Aspects, Series C, Politics 3, Sijthoff, 1959. 121 pp.

[2220] Held, Ronald, en Schretlen, Joke.   *De bazen van Europa*. Utrecht: Spectrum, 1979. 109 pp.

[2221] Herriot, Edouard. *The United States of Europe*. New York: Viking, 1930.
330 pp.
By the French Premier and President.

[2222] Hersch, Jeanne, et al. *L'Europe au défi*. Paris: Plon, 1959. 240 pp.

[2223] Herter, Christian A. *Toward an Atlantic Community*. New York: Council
on Foreign Relations, Harper & Row, 1963. 107 pp.

[2224] Hill, Walter. *Grand-Bretagne et Occident européen*.   Intro. de François Charles-Roux. Paris: Comité d'action économique et douanière,
SPID, 1946. 33 pp.

[2224a] Hoffmann, Stanley.   "Reflections of the Nation State in Western Europe Today." *Journal of Common Market Studies*, 21 (September-Decem-
ber, 1982), pp. 21-37.

[2225] Hogan, Willard N. *Representative Government and European Integration*.
Lincoln: University of Nebraska Press, 1967. 246 pp.
Cf. his *Encyclopedia Britannica* article on world federalism.

[2226] Holzer, Werner. *Europa*: *woher--wohin*? *Die Deutschen und die Franzo-
sen*. Frankfurt am Main: Vom Gestern zum Morgen, 17/18, Ner-Tamid-
Verlag, 1963. 79 pp.

[2227] Home, Alexander Frederick Douglas-Home, earl.   *Britain's Attitude towards a United Europe*. Heule, Belgium: Uitgeverij voor Gemeente-
administratie, 1967. 18 pp.
Lecture at International Centre of European Studies and Research.

[2228] Hurd, Volney D. *The Council of Europe*: *Design for a United States of
Europe*. New York: Manhattan, 1958. 56 pp.

[2229] Istituto per le relazioni tra l'Italia e i paesi dell'Africa, America
latina, e Medio Oriente.   *Europa, 1978*: *I risultati, le scadenze,
il dibattito in Italia*. Roma: Istituto, 1978. 218 pp.

[2229a] Jansen, Max, and DeVree, Johan K. *The Ordeal of Unity*: *The Politics
of European Integration, 1945-1985*. Bilthoven: Prime Press, 1985.
406 pp.
Comprehensive, penetrating, and theoretically interesting work by
two Dutch scholars.

[2230] Jennings, W. Ivor. *A Federation for Western Europe*.   New York: Macmillan, 1940. 196 pp.
Influential on formation of Union Européenne des Fédéralistes.

2231 Jeune Europe. *La révolution nationale-européenne*: *pour une société communautaire dans une Europe unitaire*. Bruxelles: Jeune Europe, 1962. 32 pp.

2232 Jezerník, Vladimir. *Západoslovanská federální unie a Svaz středoevropských států*. London, Edinburgh: Nákladem Západoslovanského ruchu, 1942. 79 pp.

2233 Joad, C.E.M. "World vs. Regional Federation." *New Statesman and Nation*, 36 (November 27, 1948), pp. 459-60.
Antagonism between world and European federalists.

2234 Josephy, Frances L. *Europe: The Key to Peace*. London: Federal Union, 1944. 16 pp.

2235 Jüttner, Alfred. *Die europäische Einigung*: *Entwicklung und Stand*. München: Olzog, 1968. 160 pp.

2236 Kasten, Hans. *Die europäische Wirtschaftsintegration*: *Grundlagen*. München: Fink, 1978. 130 pp.

2237 Kautter, Eberhard. *Paneuropa als Problem der Wirtschafts- und Socialgestaltung*. München: Pflaum, 1950. 48 pp.

2238 Keith, A. Berriedale. "The Practicability of Working a Federation." *New Commonwealth Quarterly*, 6 (1940), pp. 3-24.

2239 Kindt-Kiefer, Johann Jakob. *Eidgenossenschaft im neuen Europa*. Bern: Haupt, 1941. 125 pp.
Confederation to consolidate Hitler's new order.

2240 Kirkby, Alan G. *The Key Problem of the Peace*: *A United States of Europe*. Toronto: Ryerson, 1943. 45 pp.

2241 Klepacki, Zbigniew M. *Zachodnieuropejskie zgromadzenia międzyparlamentarne studium porównawcze*. Warszawa: Książka i Wiedza, 1967. 300 pp.

2242 Klompé, Marga. *Europa bouwt*. Den Haag: Diebon, 1954. 51 pp.

2243 Knapton, E.O. "A German View of European Federation." *New Commonwealth Quarterly*, 7 (1941), pp. 25-35.

2244 Knorr, Klaus Eugen. *Union of Western Europe*: *A Third Center of Power?* New Haven: Yale Institute of International Studies, 1948. 118 pp.

2245 Kölner Schriften zum Europarecht. *Publications de droit européen*. Köln: Institut für das Recht der Europäischen Gemeinschaften, Universität Köln, Heymann, 1965-

2246 Kraus, Herbert. *Über kulturelle Zusammenarbeit der Völker*. (UNESCO-EUROPAPLAN.) Göttingen: Fleischer, 1948.

2247 --------. *Probleme des europäischen Zusammenschlusses*. Würzburg: Holzner Verlag, 1956. 74 pp.

2248 Kuby, Heinz. *Provokation Europa*: *die Bedingungen seines politischen Überlebens*. Köln: Kiepenheuer & Witsch, 1965. 391 pp.

2249 Kurtz, Waldemar. *Briefe für den Frieden*. Stuttgart: Im Selbstverlag, 1954. 64 pp.

2250 Labour Party. *Feet on the Ground*: *A Study of Western Union*. London: Labour Party, 1948. 22 pp.

2251 La Malfa, Ugo. *Contro l'Europa di de Gaulle*: *scritti e discorsi a cura di Adolfo Battaglia*. Milano: Cultura e realità, universale contemporanes, 64, Edizioni di Comunità, 1964. 201 pp.

2252 Lambert, Henri. *Européens sans Europe*. Paris: Rivière, 1960. 131 pp.

2253 Lambert, John. *Britain in a Federal Europe*. London: Chatto & Windus, 1968. 208 pp.

2254 Lasok, Dominik, et Panayotis, Soldatos. *Les Communautés européennes en fonctionnement*. Bruxelles: Bruylant, 1981. 604 pp.

2255 Lau, Alfred, ed. *Forward to Europe*, *Auf nach Europa*, *En route pour l'Europe*. Bielefeld: Univers, 1979. 148 pp.

2256 Lawson, R. C. "European Union or Atlantic Union?" *Current History*, 19 (December, 1950), pp. 328-33.

2257 Layton, Walter T., baron. *United Europe*: *The Way to Its Achievement*. London: News Chronicle, 1948. 31 pp.

2258 Lecerf, Jean. *Histoire de l'unité européenne*. Préf. de Jean Monnet. Paris: Gallimard, 1965. 382 pp.

2259 Lehmann-Rüssbuldt, Otto. *Europa den Europäern*. Mit einer wirtschaftlichen Ergänzung von Alexander Hirsch. Hamburg: Oetinger, 1948. 184 pp.

2260 Leone, Ugo. *Le origini diplomatiche del Consiglio d'Europa*. Milano: Giuffrè, 1966. 355 pp.

2261 "Les mouvements fédéralistes." *La Tribune des Nations*, 14 (nouvelle serie) (15 août 1947), pp. 1-2.
Survey of world and European federalist movement in Europe.

2262 Levi, Lucio. *Federalismo e integrazione europeo*. Palermo: Palumbo, 1978. 148 pp.

2263 --------. *Verso gli Stati Uniti d'Europa*: *Analisi dell'integrazione europea*. Napoli: Guida, 1979. 285 pp.

2264 Lindberg, Leon L. *The Political Dynamics of European Integration*. Stanford: Stanford University Press, 1963. 367 pp.

2264a --------, and Scheingold, Stuart A. *Europe's Would-Be Polity*: *Patterns of Change in the European Community*. Englewood Cliffs, N.J.: Prentice-Hall, 1970. 314 pp.
Study of the European Community as a political system in terms of functions and institutions (structures, rules, norms). Public demands and national leadership are decisive in the process of inte-

gration.

2265 Linden, Fred van der. *Les territoires d'outre-mer et la communauté européenne*. Bruxelles: Institut royal colonial, Sections des sciences morales et politiques, Memoires, 31, 1953. 52 pp.

2266 Lindsay, Kenneth. *European Assemblies: The Experimental Period, 1949-1959*. London: Stevens, 1960. 267 pp.

2267 Linthorst Homan, Johannes. *Europese integratie: de spanning tussen economische en politieke factoren*. s'Gravenhage: M. Nijhoff, 1955. 256 pp.

2268 Lipgens, Walter, ed. *Europa-Föderationsplane der Widerstandsbewegungen, 1940-1945: eine Dokumentation gesammelt*. München: Oldenbourg, 1968. 547 pp.

2268a --------. *A History of European Integration, 1945-1947: The Formation of the European Unity Movement*. Oxford: Clarendon, 1982. Vol. I.
A major work, the first of several volumes.

2268b --------. *Documents on the History of European Integration*. Berlin: De Gruyter, 1985. 2 vols.

2269 Liska, George. *Europe Ascendant: The International Politics of Unification*. Baltimore: Johns Hopkins University Press, 1964. 182 pp.
"Unity in Western Europe . . . has become a global event even before it has been consummated as a regional reality."

2270 Ljubisavljevic, Bora. *Les problèmes de la ponderation dans les institutions européennes*. Préf. de Paul Reuter. Leyde: European Aspects, Series C, Politics 1, Sythoff, 1959. 199 pp.

2271 Loch, Theo M. *Walter Hallstein: ein Portrait*. Freudenstadt: Eurobuch Verlag Lutzeyer, 1969. 72 pp.

2272 Lochen, Einar. *Europabevegelsen og Europarådet*. Bergen: Institutt for videnskap og åndsfrihet, Tidens ekko, småskrifter om storpolitikk, 3, Grieg, 1950. 31 pp.

2272a Lodge, Julliet, ed. *Institutions and Policies of the European Community*. London: Frances Pinter, 1983.
Symposium of articles particularly on external policy.

2272b --------, ed. *European Union: The European Community in Search of a Future*. London: Macmillan, St. Martin's Press, 1986.
Symposium on the European Parliament's Draft Treaty Establishing the European Union.

2273 Longo, Domenico. *Verso un'unione europea e mondiale*. Roma: Minerva, 1959.

2274 Lucas Verdú, P. "Notas sobre federalismo y funcionalismo europeos." In *Estudios de derecho internacional: homenaje al Profesor Camilo Barcia Trelles* (Zaragosa: Universidad de Santiago de Compostela, 1958), pp. 195-203.

[2275] Lukas, John A. *Decline and Rise of Europe*: *A Study in Recent History with Particular Emphasis on the Development of a European Consciousness*. Garden City, N.Y.: Doubleday, 1965. 295 pp.

[2276] Lund, Erik; Pihl, Mogens; og Slok, Johannes. *De europaeiske idéers historie*. København: Gyldendal, 1980. 396 pp.

[2277] Lundstedt, Anders V. *Europas demokratier*: *förenen eder!* Stockholm: Natur och kultur, 1948. 96 pp.

[2278] Lyons, Francis S.L. *Internationalism in Europe, 1815–1914*. Leyden: Sijthoff, 1963. 413 pp.

[2279] Maas Geesteranus, Henry. *The Organisation of Peace*: *Ideas of an Old Dutchman*. The Hague: Boucher, 1947. 62 pp.

[2280] McCallum, Ronald B. *Public Opinion and the Last Peace*. London: Oxford University Press, 1944. 214 pp.

[2281] MacKay, R. W. G. *Federal Europe*: *The Case for European Federation, together with a Draft Constitution for a United States of Europe*. Foreword by Norman Angell. London: M. Joseph, 1940. 323 pp. After the war, MacKay was prominent in Usborne's Parliamentary group; then in 1948 he joined Churchill's European Movement.

[2282] ––––––––. *Peace Aims and the New Order*. New York: Dodd, 1941.   306 pp. Revised and popular American edition of *Federal Europe*.

[2283] ––––––––. *Britain in Wonderland*. London: Gollancz, 1948. 222 pp.

[2284] ––––––––. *You Can't Turn the Clock Back*. Chicago: Ziff-Davis, 1948. 367 pp.

[2285] ––––––––. *European Unity*: *The Strasbourg Plan for a European Political Authority with Limited Functions but Real Powers*. Foreword by Paul-Henri Spaak. Oxford: Basil Blackwell, 1951. 34 pp. Proposal to transform the Council into a European government.

[2286] ––––––––. *Towards a United States of Europe*: *An Analysis of Britain's Role in European Union*. Preface by Paul-Henri Spaak. London: Hutchinson, 1961. Argument for British participation in Common Market.

[2287] Madariaga, Salvador de. *Europe, a Unit of Human Culture*. Brussels: European Movement, 1952. 32 pp.

[2288] Maddox, William P. *European Plans for World Order*. Philadelphia: American Academy of Political and Social Science, 1940. 44 pp.

[2289] Maier, Hedwig. *Deutscher und europäischer Föderalismus*. Stuttgart: Riederer, 1948. 175 pp.

[2290] Maignial, Charles. *L'Europe commencée*: *les structures, les options*. Tournai: Casterman, 1964. 202 pp.

[2291] Mander, John. *Great Britain or Little England?* Boston: Houghton-Mifflin, 1964. 205 pp.

.

[2292] Maritain, Jacques. "Europe and the Federal Idea." *Commonweal*, 31 (April 19, 1940), pp. 544-47; 32 (April 26, 1940), pp. 8-12.

[2293] --------. *De la justice politique: notes sur la présente guerre*. Paris: Librairie Plon, 1940. 114 pp.

[2293]a Marquand, David. *Parliament for Europe*. London: Cape, 1979. 147 pp.

[2294] Marlin, Jan Frederic. *Das Konzil der abendländischen Elite: der Weg zur europäischen Einheit*. Zürich: Thomas-Verlag, 1955. 180 pp.

[2295] Massip, Roger. *Voici l'Europe*. Paris: Fayard, 1958. 190 pp.

[2296] --------. *De Gaulle et l'Europe*. Paris: Flammarion, 1963. 203 pp.

[2297] Maury, René. *L'intégration européenne*. Paris: Sirey, 1958. 338 pp.

[2298] Mayne, Richard. *The Community of Europe*. London: Gollancz, 1962. 192 pp.

[2299] --------. *The Institutions of the European Community*. London: Royal Institute of International Affairs, European Series 8, Chatham House, 1968. 82 pp.

[2300] --------. *The Recovery of Europe, 1945-1973*. New York: Harper & Row, 1970, 1973. 458 pp.

[2301] Mayrzedt, Hans, and Binswanger, Hans Christoph, eds. *Die Neutralen in der europäischen Integration: Kontroversen, Konfrontationen, Alternativen*. Wien: Braümuller, 1970. 496 pp.

[2302] Melanges, Fernand Dehousse. *Ouvrage publie sous les auspices de l'Institut d'études juridiques européennes Fernand Dehousse de l'Université de Liege*. Introduction générale de Pierre-Henri Teitgen. Paris: Nathan, 1979. 2 vols.

[2303] Mérei, Gyula. *Die Idee der europäischen Integration in der westdeutschen bürgerlichen Geschichtsachreibung*. Budapest: Akademiai Kiadó, 1966. 206 pp.

[2304] Meyer, Werner. *Die Wiederaufbau Europas: Raum, Geschichte und Kultur in der Gestaltung eines europäischen Bunder*. Zürich: 1946. 47 pp.

[2305] Middleton, Drew. *The Atlantic Community: A Study in Unity and Diversity*. New York: McKay, 1965. 303 pp.

[2305]a Milward, Alan S. *The Reconstruction of Western Europe, 1945-1951*. London: Methuen, 1984. 527 pp.
Major work of new generation of historians. Based on recently opened archives. Critical of some of Lipgen's conclusions.

[2306] Moersch, Karl. *Europa für Anganger: Falten zur Volljahrigkeit*. Frankfurt am Main: Societäts-Verlag, 1979. 231 pp.

[2307] Mollet, Guy. *L'Europe unie. Pourquoi? Comment?* Arras: Societé d'éditions du Pas-de-Calais, 1953. 44 pp.

2308 --------. *The New Drive for European Union*. New York: American Committee on United Europe, 1955. 11 pp.

2309 Monnet, Jean. *Les États-Unis d'Europe ont commencé*: *la Communauté europénne du charbon et d'acier*. Paris: Laffont, 1955. 171 pp. Discours et allocutions, 1952-1954.

2310 --------. *La Communauté européenne et la Grande-Bretagne*. Lausanne: Centre des recherches européennes, École HEC, Université de Lausanne, 1958. 15 pp.

2311 --------. *Memoires*. Paris: Fayard, 1976. 642 pp.

2312 --------. *Memoirs*. Trans. by Richard Mayne. Forword by Roy Jenkins. London: Collins: 1978. 544 pp.

2313 --------. *Memoirs*. Trans. by Richard Mayne. Intro. by George Ball. Garden City, N.Y.: Doubleday, 1978. 544 pp.
"Have I said clearly enough that the Community we have created is not an end in itself? It is a process of change, continuing that same process which in an earlier period of history produced our national forms of life. Like our provinces in the past, our nations today must learn to live together under common rules and institutions freely arrived at. The sovereign vations of the past can no longer solve the problems of the present: they cannot ensure their own progress of control their future. And the Community itself is only a stage on the way to the organized world of tomorrow."

2314 --------. *Cittadino d'Europa*: *75 anni di storia mondiale*. Milano: Rusconi, 1978. 402 pp.

2315 --------. *Erinnerungen eines Europaers*. Vorwort von Helmut Schmidt. Munchen: Hauser, 1978. 671 pp.

2316 Monte, Hilda. *The Unity of Europe*. Intro. by H.N. Brailsford. London: Gollancz, 1943. 196 pp.

2317 Mosley, Oswald. *Europe: Faith and Plan*; *A Way Out from the Coming Crises and an Introduction to Thinking as a European*. Essex: Washburn, 1958. 147 pp.

2318 --------. *La Nation Europe*. Trad. par Georges Portal. Paris: Nouvelles éditions Tatines, 1962. 156 pp.

2319 Mouskheli, Michel, et Stefani, Gaston. *L'Europe face au fédéralisme*. Strasbourg: Le Roux, 1949. 180 pp.

2320 --------. *Confédération ou fédération européenne?* Avant-propos de Henri Frenay. Paris: Campagne européenne de la jeunesse et Union européenne des fédéralistes, 1952. 43 pp.

2321 Naets, Guido. *Europa-abc*. Woord vooraf door Leo Tindemans. Leuver: Davidsfonds, 1979. 209 pp.

2322 *New Model for Europe?* London: National Peace Council, Peace Aims Pamphlet No. 32, 1945. 24 pp.
Discussion of proposal for an association of Western European coun-

tries. Reprinted from the *Economist*.

[2323] Nielsen, Rolf. *Veien til europeisk enhet*. Oslo: Elingaard, 1967.
187 pp.

[2324] Nikuradse, Alexander. *Vom Traum zur Tat*: *Sätze zur Europa-Idee*. Wiesbaden: Klemm, 1951. 87 pp.

[2325] Noël, Émile.   *La fusion des institutions et la fusion des Communautés européennes*. Nancy: Centre européen universitaire, Collection des conferences européens 1, Carnot, 1966. 51 pp.

[2326] --------. *Het raderwerk van Europa*: *Hoe de instellingen van de Europese Gemeenschap functioneren*. Voorwoord van Leo Tindemans. Brussels: Labor, 1979. 145 pp.

[2327] --------. *So funktioniert Europa*. Mit einem Vorwort von Willy Brandt. Baden-Baden: Nomos, 1978. 104 pp.

[2328] --------.   *Les rouages de l'Europe*: *Comment fonctionnent les institutions de la Communauté européenne*.   Paris: Nathan, 2e ed., 1979. 138 pp.

[2329] --------.   *The European Community*: *How It Works*.   Luxembourg: European Commission, 1979. 97 pp.

[2330] Northrop, F.S.C.   *European Union and United States Foreign Policy*: A *Study in Sociological Jurisprudence*.   New York: Macmillan, 1954. 230 pp.

[2331] Nothomb, Pierre. *L'Europe naturelle*. Préf. de Pierre Wigny.   Paris: Éditions universitaires, 1960. 198 pp.

[2332] Nouvelles équipes internationales. *L'État chrétien dans l'Europe unie*. Paris: Éditions A. Pedone, 1951. 87 pp.

[2333] Nowak, Zdzisław.   *Koncepeja integracji Europy zachodniej na tle procesów rozwoju ekonomicznego*. Poznań: Instytut zachodni, Prace, nr. 37, 1965. 297 pp.

[2334] Nutting, Anthony. *Europe Will Not Wait*: *A Warning and a Way Out*. New York: Praeger, 1960. 122 pp.

[2334a] Nye, Joseph S., ed. *International Regionalism*. Boston: Little, Brown, 1968. 432 pp.
Contains Stanley Hoffmann, "Obstinate or Obsolete? The Fate of the Nation State and the Case of Western Europe."

[2334b] --------.   *Peace in Parts*: *Integration and Conflict in Regional Organization*. Boston: Little, Brown, 1971. 210 pp.

[2335] Olivi, Bino.   *Il tentativo Europa*: *Storia politica della Comunità europea*. Milano: Etas Libri, 1979. 309 pp.

[2336] Orda, Hans. *Zur Wirtschaft und Einheit Europas*. Bonn: Athenäum-Verlag, 1959. 95 pp.

[2337] Otto, Archduke of Austria.   *Soziale Ordnung von Morgen*: *Gesellschaft und Staat im Atomzeitalter.* Wien: Herold, 1957. 172 pp.

[2338] Padover, Saul K., and Leonard, L. Larry. *Europe's Quest for Unity.* New York: Foreign Policy Association, Headline Books 97, 1953. 63 pp.

[2339] Palmer, M.; Lambert, J.; et al. *European Unity: A Survey of the European Organisations.* London: Allen & Unwin, 1959; 2nd ed., 1968. 519 pp.

[2340] Pan-European Conference, New York, 1943. *Draft Constitution of the United States of Europe.* Intro. by Richard Coudenhove-Kalergi. New York: New York University, Seminar for European Federation, 1944. 23 pp.

[2341] Parry, David Hughes. *Ewrop yn un.* Aberystwyth: Pamffledi Harlech, Rhif 12, 1940. 29 pp.

[2342] Patijn, S., ed. *Landmarks in European Unity. Jalons dans l'Europe unie.* Intro. par Henrik Brugmans. Leyden: European Aspects, Series E, Law 10, Sijthoff, 1970. 223 pp.

[2343] Pedini, Mario. *Rapporto sull'Europa: Scritti e discorsi, 1959-1979.* Milano: Mursia, 1979. 227 pp.

[2344] Pentland, Charles. *International Theory and European Integration.* London: Faber & Faber, 1973. 283 pp.

[2345] Petrescu-Comnen, Nicolas M. *Anarchie, dictature ou organisation internationale?* Genève: Perret-Gentil, 1946. 204 pp.

[2346] Pettee, George Sawyer. *Union for Europe.* Chicago: Human Events Pamphlet 20, 1947. 28 pp.

[2347] Petwaidie, Walter. *Europa: Traum oder Drohung.* Köln: Verlag Wissenschaft und Politik, 1963. 126 pp.

[2348] Pflimlin, Pierre, et Legrand-Lane, Raymond. *L'Europe communautaire.* Paris: Plon, 1966. 300 pp.

[2349] Philip, Andre. *L'unité européenne: l'heure de la décision.* Paris: Éditions du Mouvement socialiste pour les États-Unis d'Europe, 1950. 23 pp.

[2350] Philip, Oliver. *Le problème de l'union européenne.* Préf. de Denis de Rougemont. Neuchâtel: La Baconnière, 1950. 381 pp.

[2351] Picard, Roger. *L'unité européenne par l'intercitoyenneté.* Paris: SPID, 1948. 117 pp.

[2352] Picot, Albert. *La neutralité suisse et intégration européenne.* Genève: Parti national democratique de Genève [liberal], 1957. 22 pp.

[2353] Pinder, John, and Pryce, Roy. *Europe after de Gaulle.* Hammondsworth: Penguin, 1969. 191 pp.
Issues that cross national boundaries and hence must be regulated by a supranational authority include modern industrial production, monetary stability, communications, and multinational corporations.

2353a --------. "European Community and the Nation State: A Case for Neo-
Federalism." *International Affairs* (London), 62 (Winter, 1985-86),
pp. 41-54.
By president of the Union of European Federalists. "The tendency
to identify federalism with a great leap to a federation with unitary and coercive power inhibits practical thought about the prospects for taking further steps in a federal direction. . . . Such
thought would be helped by a systematic study of the specific steps
that could be taken, and of the conditions that favor or impede
them."

2354 Pinto, Roger. *Les organisations européennes.* Paris: Payot, 1963. 443
pp.

2355 Platz, Hans Joachim. *Europa Weg und Aufgabe: ein Handbuch für die politische Bildung.* Bad Godesberg: Europäische Aktionsgemeinschaft,
1962. 304 pp.

2356 --------. *Das grosse Europa-Handbuch.* Köln: Europa-Union-Verlag,
1965. 228 pp.

2357 Plessia, R. *L'Europe unie: problèmes et perspectives économiques.*
Préf. de René Courtin. Paris: A. Pedone, 1949. 150 pp.

2358 Pohl, Hermann P.A. *Das europäische Manifest.* Berlin: Drei Enkel Verlag, 1967. 23 pp.

2359 Politis, Jacques. *L'avenir de l'Europe.* Neuchâtel: La Baconnière,
1946. 147 pp.

2360 Pordea, G. *Aspects et problèmes de l'intégration européenne.* Paris:
Bellenand, 1951. 187 pp.

2361 --------. *Fédéralisme et minorités en Europe orientale.* Paris: Pedone, 1952. 173 pp.

2362 Prat Ballester, Jorge. *La lucha por Europa.* Con un prólogo de E.A.
Pascual. Barcelona: Colección patrocinada por el Instituto de estudios europeos 1, L. Miracle, 1952. 303 pp.

2363 Pryce, Roy. *The Political Future of the European Community.* London:
Federal Trust, Marshbank, 1962. 107 pp.

2363a --------, ed. *The Dynamics of European Union.* London: Croon Helm,
forthcoming.
Study by the Trans-European Policy Studies Association of succes-
sive attempts at closer union since 1945, including the 1985 Single
European Act.

2364 Quaroni, Pietro. *L'Europa al bivio.* Milano: Ferro edizioni, 1965.
187 pp.

2365 Racine, Raymond, ed. *Demain l'Europe sans frontières.* Paris: Centre
européen de la culture, Plon, 1958. 231 pp.

2366 Raestad, Arnold C. *Europe and the Atlantic World.* Oslo: I kommisjon
hos Aschelroug, 1958. 114 pp.

2367 Rappard, William E. *La Suisse et l'organisation de l'Europe.* Neuchâtel: La Baconnière, 1950. 81 pp.

2368 Redlhammer, H.H. *Handelt: Völker Europas!* Frankfurt: Ammelburg, 1958. 64 pp.

2369 Reuter, Paul. *Organisations européennes.* Paris: Presses universitaires de France, 1965. 452 pp.

2370 Reynaud, Paul. *Unite or Perish: A Dynamic Program for a United Europe.* New York: Simon & Schuster, 1951. 214 pp.
By the former French Prime Minister to whom Churchill made his proposal of a Franco-British union in 1940.

2371 Ridley, Francis A., and Edwards, Bob. *The United Socialist States of Europe.* London: National Labour Press, 1943. 111 pp.

2372 Riker, William H. *The Theory of Political Coalitions.* New Haven: Yale University Press, 1962. 300 pp.
Extreme view of the political factors underlying the establishment of actual federations. The main motives, Riker argued, were not to guarantee freedom or the independence of the units, nor to respond to social processes that had created some common interest, but to defend those uniting against some external military or diplomatic threat, or to prepare for aggression themselves. Cf. Friedrich, Deutsch, and Wheare.

2374 Ritsch, Frederick F., Jr. *The French Left and the European Idea, 1947-1949.* New York: Pageant, 1966. 277 pp.

2375 Ritzel, Heinrich G. *Europa und Deutschland, Deutschland und Europa.* Offenbach am Main: Bollwerk-Verlag, 1947. 37 pp.

2376 Robertson, Arthur H. *European Institutions: Co-operation, Integration, Unification.* London: Stevens, 1959; 2nd ed., 1966; 3rd, 1973. 372 pp.
Authoritative single-volume account of the European organizations: Council, OECD, NATO, the Communities, and prospects.

2377 Röling, Bernard V.A., ed. *Europese toenadering: een bundel opstellen betreffende de Europese integratie.* Haarlem: Volkuniversiteits bibliothek, Recks 2, no. 63, Bohn, 1959. 295 pp.

2378 Röpke, W. "La communauté économique européenne." Banque nationale de Belgique, *Bulletin d'information et de documentation,* 27 (novembre, 1952), pp. 337-57.

2379 Röpke, Wilhelm. *Die Schweiz und die Integration des Westens.* Zürich: Schweizer Spiegel, 1965. 65 pp.

2380 Rougemont, Denis de. "L'attitude fédéraliste." *La Nef* (Paris), 4 (octobre, 1947), pp. 49-60.

2381 --------, et al. *Dix ans d'efforts pour unir l'Europe, 1945-1955.* Paris: Bureau de liason franco-allemand, 1955. 127 pp.

2382 --------. *The Meaning of Europe.* Trans. by Alan Braley. London: Sidgwick & Jackson, 1963. 126 pp.

[2383] --------. *L'Europe en jeu*: *trois discours suivis de documents de la Haye*. Neuchâtel: Evolution du monde et des idees, La Baconnière, 1948-1970. 2 vols.

[2384] --------. *Lettre ouvert aux Européens*. Paris: Éditions Albin Michel, 1970. 213 pp.
Integral federalism.

[2385] --------; Schwamm, Henri; Calinescu, Matei; et al. *Vers la rélance de debat européen*: *Le déclin de l'Europe, mythe et histoire*. Genève: Centre européen de la Culture, Institut universitaire d'études européennes de Genève, 1978. 120 pp.

[2386] Ruini, Meuccio. *Dal nazionale al sovranazionale*. Milano: Giuffrè, 1961. 654 pp.

[2387] Salmon, Guy. *La France fédérale dans l'Europe fédérée*. Besançon: Jacques et Demontrond, 1957. 90 pp.

[2388] Saran, Mary. *The Future Europe*: *Peace or Power Politics?* London: Supplement to Socialist Vanguard Commentary, 1942. 27 pp.

[2389] Sartre, Jean Paul. "European Declaration of Independence." *Commentary*, July, 1950, pp. 596-98.

[2390] Scelle, M. *Le fédéralisme européen et ses difficultes politiques*. Nancy: Centre européen universitaire, Departement des sciences politiques, fasc. no. 4, 1952. 57 pp.

[2391] Schmid, Karl. *Europa zwischen Ideologie und Verwirklichung*: *Psychologische Aspekte der Integration*. Zürich: Artemis-Verlag, 1966. 192 pp.

[2392] Schmitt, Hans A. *European Union*: *From Hitler to de Gaulle*. New York: Van Nostrand Reinhold, 1969. 159 pp.

[2393] Schmitt, Walter E. *Zwischenrufe von der Seine*: *die Entwicklung der Europa-Politik und das deutsch-französische Verhaltnis*. Stuttgart: Kohlhammer, 1958. 207 pp.

[2394] Schneider, Heini. *Europäische "Völksdemokratie"*: *Kritik eines politischen Trugbildes*. Bonn: Junge europäische Föderalisten, 1958. 43 pp.

[2395] Schoendube, Claus. *Europa Taschenbuch*. 7. neubearbeitete Auflage. Bonn: Europa Union Verlag, 1980. 477 pp.

[2396] Schuman, Robert. *Pour l'Europe*. Paris: Nagel, 1963. 209 pp.
By the French Prime Minister who was responsible for the Schuman Plan to create the Coal and Steel Community (1950).

[2397] Secrétan, Jacques. *Nations unies ou fédéralisme?* Paris: Recueil Sirey, 1958. 86 pp.
Military alliances and the Coal and Steel Community are the nearest approaches so far to world federation.

[2398] Sennholz, Hans F.   *How Can Europe Survive?*   New York: Van Nostrand, 1955. 336 pp.

[2399] Serafini, Umberto. *La via communitaria del socialismo.* Roma: "I Dialoghi," 1, 1956. 50 pp.

[2400] Sforza, Carlo, conte. *O Federazione europea, o nuove guerre.* Firenze: "La nuova Italia," 1948. 117 pp.
By the Italian Foreign Minister.

[2401] Shibley, George H. *The Coming United States of Europe and the World State to End the Mad Race in Armament Building, Attain Justice, World Peace and Prosperity Unprecedented.* Denver, Colo.: By the author, 1939. 64 pp.

[2402] Sidjanski, D. *Erfolge und Krisen der Integration.* Köln: Europa Union Verlag, 1969. 136 pp.

[2403] Siegler, Heinrich von, ed. *Europäische politische Einigung, 1949-1968*: *Dokumentatation von Vorschlagen und Stellungnshmen.* Bonn: Verlag für Zeitarchive, 1968. 435 pp.

[2404] Silberman, David. *A United Europe -- Or Else!* New York: Smith, 1946. 116 pp.
One world or none.

[2405] Silj, Alessandro. *Europe's Political Puzzle: A Study of the Fouchet Negotiations and the 1963 Veto.* Cambridge: Harvard University, Center for International Affairs, No. 17, 1967. 178 pp.

[2406] Socialist Vanguard Group. *Europe and World Peace.* London: By the group, 1944. 7 pp.

[2407] Socini, Roberto. *Rapports et conflits entre organisations européennes.* Leyde: Sythoff, 1960. 168 pp.

[2408] Sorensen, Max.   "The Council of Europe: A New Experiment in International Organisation." *Yearbook of World Affairs* (London), 6 (1952), pp. 75-97.

[2409] Soucek, Theodor. *Wir rufen Europa: Vereinigung des Abendlandes auf sozial-organischer Grundlage.* Wels: Verlag Welsermühl, 1956. 320 pp.

[2410] Sozialdemokratische Partei Deutschlands. *Die Europapolitik der Sozialdemokratie.* Bonn: SPD, 1953. 51 pp.

[2411] Spaak, Paul Henri Charles.   "L'Europa unita." *La Communità Internazionale* (Padova), 6 (1951), pp. 3-15.

[2412] Spinelli, Altiero. *Dagli stati sovrani agli Stati Uniti d'Europa.* Pref. di Aldo Garosci. Firenze: Nuova Italia, 1950. 347 pp.

[2413] --------. *Manifest der europäischen Föderalisten.* Frankfurt am Main: Europäische Verlaganstalt, 1958. 69 pp.

[2414] --------. *Political Report, Congress of Europe, 1953.* Brussels: European Movement, Action Committee for the Supranational Community,

1953. 31 pp.

2415 --------. *Manifesto dei Federalisti europei*. Parma: Collana clandestina 21, Guanda, 1957. 108 pp.

2416 --------. *L'Europa non cade dal cielo*. Bologna: Il Mulino, 1960. 357 pp.

2417 --------. *The Eurocrats: Conflict and Crisis in the European Community*. Trans. by C. Grave Haines. Baltimore: Johns Hopkins Press, 1966. 229 pp.

2417a --------. "L'Europa verso l'unità." *Politica internazionale*, (June, 1978).

2418 --------. *La mia battaglia per un'Europa diversa*. Manduria: Laciata, 1979. 193 pp.

2418a --------. *Towards European Union*. Florence: European University Institute, 1983. 28 pp.
Sixth Jean Monnet lecture.

2419 Spinelli, C. *Unità europea e piano di ricostruzione: Memorandum del Labour party*. Napoli: 1st. poligraphico editoriale meridonale, 1948. 94 pp.

2420 Starzewski, Jan. *International Importance of Central-Eastern Europe*. London: Free Course of Central-Eastern European Studies, 1954. 32 pp.
Includes T. Komarnicki, "Political Unions of the Nations of Central Eastern Europe in the Past."

2421 Steinbüchel, Theodor. *Europa als Verbundenheit im Geist*. Tübingen: Universität Reden, No. 36, 1946. 26 pp.

2422 Sternberg, Fritz. "Can Europe Be United?" *Nation*, June 17, 1950, pp. 586-98.

2423 Stewart, Michael, et al. *One Europe -- Is It Possible?* London: British Broadcasting Corp, 1966. 40 pp.

2424 Stranner, Henri. *Neutralité suisse et solidarité européenne*. Lausanne: Payor, 1960. 295 pp.

2425 Strauss, Walter. *Fragen der Rechtsangleichung im Rahmen der europäischen Gemeinschaften*. Frankfurt am Main: Schriften des Instituts für Ausländisches und Internationales Wirtschaftsrecht, Bd. 9, V. Klostermann, 1959. 39 pp.

2426 Suha, A. *Economic Problems of Eastern Europe and Federalism*. Cambridge: Galloway & Porter, 1942. 46 pp.

2427 Svahnström, Bertil. *Europa mellan öst och väst*. Stockholm: Kooperativa förbundets bokförlag, 1948. 167 pp.

2428 Taber, George M. *John F. Kennedy and a Uniting Europe: The Politics of Partnership*. Bruges: College of Europe, European Issues 2, 1969. 188 pp.

[2429] Tagliamonte, Francesco. *Europa, oggi*. Bologna: Cappelli, 1966.   134 pp.

[2430] Teitgen, Pierre-Henri. *Origines, objectifs et nature des Communautés européennes*. Paris: DEPP, 1979. 111 pp.

[2431] Thiel, Rudolf. *Die dritte Weltmacht*: *Bundesstaat Europa in 4 Wochen*. Darmstadt: By the author, 1953. 40 pp.

[2432] Tigerschiöld, Brita. *Europarädet och Europarörelsen*. Stockholm: Världspolitikens dagsfrägor, nr. 9, 1949. 32 pp.

[2433] Tillich, Paul J.O. *War Aims*: *A Discussion of the Most Important Problem Facing the Democratic World Today*. New York: The Protestant, 1942. 22 pp.

[2434] Tošević, Dimitri J. *The World Crisis in Maps*: *Its Background and Course*. Toronto: Ryerson, 1949. 36 pp.

[2435] Trempont, Jacques. *L'unification de l'Europe, conditions et limites*. Préf. de Paul Van Zeeland. Amiens: Éditions Scientifiques et Litteraires, 1955. 418 pp.
Theory of European union before Common Market.

[2435]a Tsoukalis, Loukas. *The Politics and Economics of European Monetary Integration*. London: Allen & Unwin, 1977. 192 pp.

[2436] Uhlig, Karl-Heinz. *EG*: *Gemeinschaft von Rivalen*. Berlin: Verlag Die Wirtschaft, 1980. 247 pp.

[2437] Union Européenne des Fédéralistes.   "L'integration économique et sociale de l'Europe." Paris: UEF, 1950.
The Union Européenne des Fédéralistes was a companion organization to the World Movement for World Federal Government.

[2438] --------.   "European Federation Now." Loos: Danel, 1951.

[2439] --------.   *Économie de la Fédération Européenne*. Paris: ICO, Movimento federalista europeo, 10, Ivrea, 1952. 119 pp.

[2440] *Uniting Europe*: *Ireland Cooperates*. Dublin: Browne & Nolan, 1950. 36 pp.

[2441] Universidad Internacional Menéndez Pelayo, Santander, Espagna. *Europa en el mundo actual*. Madrid: Delagación nacional de organizaciones, Seminario central de estudios europeos, 1962-1963. 2 vols.

[2442] Valk, W. de. *La signification de l'intégration européenne pour le developpement du droit international moderne*. Leyde: Sythoff, 1962. 142 pp.

[2443] Vansittart, Robert G.V., baron. *Events and Shadows*: *A Policy for the Remnants of a Century*. London: Hutchinson, 1947. 196 pp.

[2444] Vassenhove, Léon van. *L'Europe helvétique*: *étude sur les possibilités d'adapter à l'Europe les institutions de la Confédération Suisse*. Neuchâtel: La Baconnière, 1943. 226 pp.

[2445] Vecchio, Giorgio del. *L'ideale cosmopolitico e il problema dell'unificazione europea*. Milan: Giuffrè, 1957.

[2446] Visine, Francois. *Dictionnaire Visine*: *Dictionnaire de l'Européen*.
Luxembourg: Fondation du mérite européen, 1980. 333 pp.

[2447] Wales, Peter. *Europe Is My Country*: *The Story of West European Cooperation since 1945*. London: Methuen, 1963. 117 pp.

[2447]a Wallace, Helen; Wallace, William; and Webb, Carole, eds. *Policy Making in the European Community*. Chichester: Wiley, 2nd ed., 1983.
451 pp.
Examines theory and practice of decision making in the Communities.
A major scholarly analysis.

[2448] Wandyez, Piotr S. *Zjednoczona Europa*: *teoria i praktyka*. London: Po-
lonia, 1965. 308 pp.

[2449] Wanke, Otto. *Das Europäische Parlament*. Wien: Verlag des Öster-
reichischen Gewerkschaftsbundes, 1965. 76 pp.

[2450] Watson, George. *The British Constitution and Europe*. Leyden: European Aspects, Series C, Politics No. 2, Sijthoff, 1959. 79 pp.

[2451] Wehe, Walter. *Das werden Europas*: *Zeittafel der europäischen Eini-
gungsbestrebungen, 1946-1955*. Frankfurt am Main: Agenor, 1955. 278
pp.

[2452] --------. *Zeittafel für Zusammenschluss Europas*. Bonn: Bundeszentrale
für Heimatdienst, Schriftenreihe, Heft 55, 1963. 78 pp.

[2453] Weil, Gordon Lee. *A Foreign Policy for Europe? The External Relations
of the European Community*. Forward by Jean Rey.   Bruges: College
of Europe, 1970. 324 pp.

[2454] Weinfeld, Abraham C. *Towards a United States of Europe*: *Proposals for
a Basic Structure*. Washington: American Council on Public Affairs,
1942. 52 pp.

[2455] Wilcox, Francis O. *The Atlantic Community*: *Progress and Prospects*.
Boston: World Peace Foundation, International Organization 17,
1963. 308 pp.

[2456] Willis, Frank Roy.   *France, Germany, and the New Europe, 1945-1963*.
Stanford: Stanford University Press, 1965. 397 pp.

[2457] Windelen, Heinrich.   *Für Deutschland und Europa*: *Reden und Aufsätze*.
Bonn: Edition Atlantic Forum, 1969. 72 pp.

[2458] Włodarski, Piotr. *Nowy ład a zasada narodowości*.   Rzym, Nakł: Kiubu
federalnego środkowo-europejskiego, 1946. 48 pp.

[2459] Zeeland, Paul Van. *La Belgique et l'Occident européen*. Bruxelles: Le
Maurais, 1946. 43 pp.

[2460] Zellentin, Gerda. *Formen der Willensbildung in den europäischen Organisationen*. Frankfurt am Main: Kölner Schriften zur politischen

Wissenschaft., Bd. 5, Athenäum, 1965. 131 pp.

2461 Zurcher, Arnold J. *The Struggle to Unite Europe*: *1940-1958*. Washington Square: New York University Press, 1958. 254 pp.
"An historical account of the development of the contemporary European Movement from its origin in the Pan-European Union to the drafting of the treaties for Euratom and the European Common Market."

David Low cartoon, in *The New York Times*, December 2, 1951. Reprinted by permission of the London Express News and Feature Services and Mrs. Rachael Whear.

15

World Order

Grenville Clark left at his death (1967) three quarters of a million dollars to the World Law Fund. The Fund grew into the Institute for World Order, recently renamed the World Policy Institute. As the possibility of an international agreement to establish the rule of law seemed ever more "unrealistic" with every passing year of the Cold War, the Institute has turned its attention to the preconditions for a legal world order, and to alternative forms of conflict management without the centralization of power implicit in a world federation. A large literature has been produced, including legal studies, policy analyses, future perspectives, and college teaching materials. Two scholarly journals maintain vigorous and world-wide discussion: *Alternatives* and *World Policy*.

Almost all works with any connection to world federalism whatsoever published since 1975 have been works on world order. The term "world order" has emerged as distinct from "world government" as world government is from a league of sovereign states. The central idea seems to be Richard Falk's concept of "central governance," in which existing international institutions and transnational popular peace movements will restrain national governments from recourse to war. The goal is not a centralized world legal order but a decentralized, less bureaucratic, less coercive international system in which peace is maintained by popular opposition to war.

The world order school has effectively challenged the simplistic "federate or perish" attitude of early world federalists. More realistic assumptions are now in vogue. Great resourcefulness has been shown in analyzing the current international system and in discovering existing popular resources. The school defied the tradition of "value-free" social and political analysis, which seemed to have brought the United States to the War in Vietnam, and it upheld such values for a preferred world order as peace, justice, wealth, nature, and democracy, or in the school's terms, peace, social justice, economic well-being, ecological balance, and political participation. Justice particularly has drawn much study, with a series of readers on a just world order. So has the *transition* to any more effective international organization, with the school's identification with the "struggle of the oppressed."

In an effort to break the ideal American perspective that has dominated world federalism from the beginning, a major project was begun to support scholars from every major region of the earth in formulating their desires for a preferred world. The result was the six volumes of the World

Order Models Project, under the general editorship of Saul Mendlovitz. Falk, Kothari, Mazrui, Lagos and Godoy, and Galtung wrote studies. A comparable work was sought from the Soviet Union, but it was not produced.

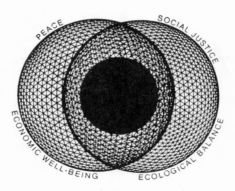

Logo of World Order Models Project. Used by permission of the World Order Models Project.

2471 Ajami, Fouad. *Human Rights and World Order Politics*. New York: In-
       stitute for World Order, 1978. 33 pp.

2471a --------. "World Order: The Question of Ideology." *Alternatives*, 6
       (1980), pp. 473-85.

2472 Baldwin, Ian, Jr. "Thinking about a New World Order for the Decade
       1990." *War/Peace Report*, January, 1970, pp. 3-8.
       Preliminary report on World Order Models Project. Values differ in
       the seven regions (including U.S.S.R.) of the project.   Corrective
       to world federalism, which has tended to be a Western or even Amer-
       ican ideology.

2473 Beres, Louis René. "Examining the Logic of World Federal Government."
       Publius, 4 (Summer, 1974), pp. 75-87.
       Most federalists neglect the realities of power.   Their writing is
       generally superficial and "enthusiastic." "As a result, large num-
       bers of people have been diverted from a variety of potentially
       more productive courses to international order."

2474 --------, and Targ, Harry R. *Reordering the Planet*: *Constructing Al-
       ternative world Futures*. Boston: Allyn & Bacon, 1974. 264 pp.

2474a --------, and --------.   "Perspectives on World Order: A Review."
       Alternatives, 2 (1976), pp. 177-98.

2575 --------. *People, States, and World Order*.   Itasca, Ill.: Peacock,
       1981. 237 pp.
       Two paths to replacement of *realpolitik* by world order: institu-
       tional change (international law and world federal government) and
       behavioral change (people and states). Chapter on "World Federal
       Government" does not reflect work of Grenville Clark or Chicago
       Committee.

2476 Bhagwati, Jadish N., ed. *Economics and World Order*: *From the 1970s
       to the 1990s*. New York: Free Press, World Law Fund, 1972. 365 pp.
       Includes capitalist, socialist, and Third World perspectives.

2477 Brucan, Silviu.   "The Establishment of a World Authority: A Working
       Hypothesis." *Alternatives*, 8 (Fall, 1982), pp. 209-23.

2478 Bull, Hedley. *The Anarchical Society*: *A Study of World Order in World
       Politics*. New York: Oxford University Press, 1977. 335 pp.
       Dismisses world government by contract and by conquest, then re-
       signs himself to the "age of the disintegration of empires." Pro-
       claims the need for "new concepts and normative principles" in in-
       ternational relations. Blinded by "realism."

2479 --------.   "Order and Justice in International Society." *Political
       Studies*, 19 (1971), pp. 269-83.

2480 Claude, Inis L. *Swords into Plowshares*: *The Problems and Progress of
       International Organization*. New York: Random House, 1956; 3rd ed.,
       1964. 458 pp.

2481 --------. *Power and International Relations*. New York: Random House,
       1962. 310 pp.
       Misunderstands proposal of world government -- claims that world

government promises to be perfectly free from even civil wars, or
that it would rule by a monopoly of armed force. Institutions of
world government, according to Claude, could not accommodate "political adjustment," as institutions of national governments do.
Clark's World Equity Tribunal and World Conciliation Board are designed to meet just this need.

2482 Falk, Richard A. *Legal Order in a Violent World*. Princeton: Princeton University Press, 1968. 610 pp.
Basic for transition from world government thought to that of world
order.

2482a --------. "Can International Law Contribute to World Order?" *American Journal of International Law*, 66 (September, 1972), pp. 268-78.

2483 --------. *This Endangered Planet*: *Prospects and Proposals for Human
Survival*. New York: Random House, 1971. 495 pp.

2484 --------. *A Global Approach to National Policy*. Cambridge: Harvard
University Press, 1975. 320 pp.

2485 --------. *A Study of Future Worlds*. New York: Free Press, 1975. 506
pp.
American perspective for World Order Models Project. His own "preferred world" (pp. 224-76) seems virtually identical with the Chicago constitution, yet Falk everywhere avoids the clear language of
world government.

2486 --------. "Contending Approaches to World Order." *Journal of International Affairs*, 31 (Fall-Winter, 1977), pp. 171-98.
"World order" carefully defined and distinguished from world government and traditional nationalism. Other articles in this issue
by Karl Deutsch, Robert C. Johansen, Ervin Laszlo, Wassily Leon-
tief, Saul Mendlovitz, and Jan Tinbergen.

2487 --------. "The World Order Models Project and Its Critics: A Reply."
International Organization, 31 (Spring, 1978), pp. 531-45.
World order is link to traditionalists (power), modernists (interdependence), and utopians (world government). Defense of populist
politics and efforts to control self-destructive tendencies of our
time.

2488 --------. *Human Rights and State Sovereignty*. New York: Holmes &
Meier, 1982. 215 pp.
Argues that regional and global institutions and popular citizens'
movements can challenge state governments in the pursuit of human
goals.

2489 --------. *The International Quest*. New York: Holmes & Meier, 1982.
349 pp.
Outlines a new world order in which states are destructured and non-
territorial central guidance is provided by organizational mechanisms already in existence

2490 --------. *Normative Initiatives and Demilitarization*: *A Third System
Approach*. New York: Institute for World Order, 1982. 18 pp.

2490a --------, and Kim, Samuel S. *An Approach to World Order Studies and*

the World System. New York: Institute for World Order, WOMP Working
Paper No. 22, 1982. 33 pp.
Guide to concept and discipline of world order: assumptions, framework of inquiry, history, and bibliography. "World order studies
has two ambitions: to establish an enduring academic presence and
to provide a basis for a movement for social change that encompas-
ses issues of global scale. Only time will tell whether its reading
of contemporary history as disaster-prone and as favorable to the
struggles of oppressed peoples is correct, and whether if correct,
these struggles can be carried to completion without provoking catastrophe. As it is, the world order approach provides an alternative to both Machiavellianism and Marxism for student concerned
about the shape of things to come in international life.

[2491] --------.   *The End of World Order.*   New York: Holmes & Meier, 1983.
358 pp.
Criticizes the durability and adequacy of the sovereign state system and proposes alternative "world order" systems of politics for
global transformation. A farewell to the field?

[2492] --------; Mendlovitz, Saul H.; and Kim, Samuel S., eds. *Toward a Just*
World Order. Boulder, Colo.: Westview Press, 1982. 652 pp.
College text on the present international system, its problems and
strategies for realizing World Order Models Project values. Vol. I
of three.

[2493] --------; --------; and Kratochwil, Friedrich, eds. *International Law*:
A Contemporary Perspective. Boulder, Colo.: Westview, 1984.   702
pp.
Vol. II in Studies on a Just World Order Series.

[2494] --------; --------; and Kim, Samuel S., eds. *The United Nations and a*
Just World Order. Boulder, Colo.: Westview, 1984.
Vol. III.

[2495] Farer, Tom J. "The Greening of the Globe: A Preliminary Appraisal of
the World Order Models Project." *International Organization*, 31
(Winter, 1977), pp. 129-47.
Critique of WOMP. Reply by Falk in next issue.

[2496] Frank, Andre Gunder. "The World Crisis: Theory and Ideology." *Alter-*
natives, 6 (Spring, 1981), pp. 497-523.

[2497] Galtung, Johan. *A World Central Authority.* Oslo: International Peace
Research Insitute, December, 1972. 14 pp.
The coming world state cannot simply be the Western model writ
large. It must have representative institutions not only for nations but also for minorities, international non-governmental organizations, and transnational associations. Powers must include
positive developmental ones as well as punitive ones.

[2498] --------.   *The True Worlds*: *A Transnational Perspective.*   New York:
Free Press, 1980. 544 pp.
Last of World Order Models Project studies. Synthesizes the region-
al perspectives.

[2499] --------.   *The North-South Debate*: *Technology, Basic Human Needs, and*
the New International Economic Order. New York: Institute for World

Order, 1980. 50 pp.

2500 --------. *There Are Alternatives*! *Four Roads to Peace and Security.*
Chester Springs, Pa.: Dufour, 1984. 221 pp.

2501 Geusau, Frans A. M. Alting von. *European Perspectives on World Order.*
Leyden: Sijthoff, 1975. 341 pp.

2501a Henrikson, Alan K., ed. *Negotiating World Order*: *The Artisanship and
Architecture of Global Diplomacy.* Wilmington, Del.: Scholarly Resources, 1986. 265 pp.
Basic for the transition. "The field of international relations has
long been divided between two traditional modes of thinking.   One
is that of the 'world order' builder -- the international architect
-- who envisions global structures and grand designs, and every-
thing fitting into them.   From this intellectual perspective, the
meaning of international relations consists, at a basic level, in
the logical symmetry and symbolic unity of their patterns.   Such
structures may be conservative and historical, as in the balance-
of-power concept, or progressive and utopian, as in the idea of
world government.   The other traditional style of internationalist
thought is that of the 'negotiator' -- the diplomatic artisan. From
the point of view of the professional diplomat or other regular par-
ticipant in international affairs, often the most important value
to be preserved is the actual process, the give and take, of diplomacy itself.   The blueprint may be of less significance to him than
the task of building. . . .   The challenge facing us is somehow to
combine globalist architecture with diplomatic artisanship. 'There
is no substitute,' as Stanley Hoffmann has written, 'for universal
bargaining, issue by issue, deal by deal.' A 'double revolution' is
called for, in the scope of diplomacy and in the diplomatic process
itself.   Negotiating world order, the diplomacy of consensus, is
such a universal process."

2502 Hoffmann, Stanley. *Duties beyond Borders*: *On the Limits and Possibilities of Ethical International Politics.* Syracuse, N.Y.: Syracuse University Press, 1981. 252 pp.
Concern to reconcile realistic approach to international politics
with demands of morality. Cf. Beitz.

2503 Johansen, Robert C. *Toward a Dependable Peace*: *A Proposal for an Appropriate Security System.* New York: Institute for World Order,
1978; 1983. 58 pp.
Compressed argument for a strategy to move from the insecurity of
present military policies to a security system provided by an array
of national and international institutions. Calls for a world social movement.

2504 --------. *The National Interest and the Human Interest*: *An Analysis
of U.S. Foreign Policy.* Princeton: Princeton University Press,
1980. 517 pp.
Analyzes American foreign policy from perspective of WOMP values:
peace, human rights, economic justice, and environment.   Considers
alternative policy.

2505 --------. *Toward an Alternative Security System*: *Moving beyond the
Balance of Power in the Search for World Security.* New York: World
Policy Institute, 1983. 52 pp.

[2506] Kaldor, Mary. *Beyond the Blocs*: *Defending Europe the Political Way*.
New York: World Policy Institute, 1983. 20 pp.

[2507] Kim, Samuel S. *The Maoist Image of World Order*. Princeton: Occasional Paper No. 5, World Order Studies Program, Center of International Studies, Woodrow Wilson School of Public and International Affairs, 1977. 51 pp.

[2507]a --------. *China, the United Nations, and World Order*. Princeton:
Princeton University Press, 1979.

[2507]b --------. "The World Order Models Project and Its Strange Critics."
Journal of Political and Military Sociology, 9 (Spring, 1981), pp.
109-15.

[2508] --------. *The Quest for a Just World Order*. Boulder, Colo.: Westview, 1984. 440 pp.

[2509] Kohler, Gernot. *Global Apartheid*. New York: Institute for World Order, 1979. 14 pp.

[2510] Kothari, Rajni. *Footsteps into the Future*: *Diagnosis of the Present
World and a Design for an Alternative*. New York: Free Press, 1974.
173 pp.
Indian perspective for WOMP.

[2511] -------- . *Toward a Just World*. New York: Institute for World Order,
1980. 42 pp.

[2512] Lagos, Gustavo, and Goday, Horatio H. *Revolution of Being*: *A Latin
American View of the Future*. New York: Free Press, 1977. 226 pp.
Latin American perspective for WOMP.

[2513] Mazrui, Ali A. *A World Federation of Cultures*: *An African Perspective*. New York: Free Press, 1976. 528 pp.
African view for WOMP.

[2514] Mendlovitz, Saul H, ed. *Legal and Political Problems of World Order*.
New York: The Fund for Education Concerning World Peace through
World Law, 1962. 858 pp.
Seminar guide, supporting materials, critical articles, and biblio-
graphies for *World Peace through World Law*.

[2515] --------, and Falk, Richard A., eds. *The Strategy of World Order*. New
York: World Law Fund, 1966. 4 vols.
Valuable collection of articles on the development of international
law. Transition to world order studies.

[2516] --------, ed. *On the Creation of a Just World Order*: *Preferred Worlds
for the 1990s*. New York: Free Press, 1975. 302 pp.
Lead volume for World Order Models Project. "It is my considered
judgment that there is no longer a question of whether or not there
will be world government by the year 2000. As I see it, the questions we should be addressing ourselves are: how it will come into
being -- by cataclysm, drift, more or less rational design -- and
whether it will be totalitarian, benignly elitist, or participatory
(the probabilities being in that order)."

[2516]a --------. "The Program of the Institute for World Order." *Journal of International Affairs*, 31 (1977), pp. 259-65.

[2516]b --------. "A Perspective on the Cutting Edge of World Order Inquiry: The Past, Present, and Future of WOMP." *International Interactions*, 8 (1981), pp. 151-60.

[2517] --------. *The Struggle for a Just World Order*: An Agenda of Inquiry and Praxis for the 1980s. New York: Institute for World Order, 1982. 23 pp.

[2518] --------, and Wallach, Ira D. "A Perspective on the Cutting Edge of World Order Inquiry: The Past, Present, and Future of WOMP." *International Interactions*, 8 (1981), pp. 151-60.
     Rajni Kothari understands "world order" as oppression of the Third World. WOMP researchers have been aware of this danger. They have produced a series of shared-values models, with transition strategies grounded in present reality. Their contribution on the "cutting edge" of scholarly discussion has five elements: (1) introduction of a struggle theory of history (Lenin, Wilson, Third World); (2) focus on demilitarization; (3) focus on global culture and civilization; (4) abandonment of state perspectives; (5) analysis of the relationship between global and local perspectives.

[2518]a Michalak, S.J. "Richard Falk's Future World: A Critique of WOMP--USA." *Review of Politics*, 42 (January, 1980), pp. 3-17.

[2519] Mische, Gerald, and Mische, Patricia. *Toward a Human World Order*: Beyond the National Security Straitjacket. New York: Paulist Press, 1977. 399 pp.
     "Two types of world order must be distinguished. The first is the order that presently exists on the planet, an order of dependent relationships between allegedly independent sovereignties that are dominated by raw economic, monetary and military power rather than by law. . . . The second type envisions an order of relationships determined by law and based on universal social justice for all persons; an order whose operative principles embrace the centrality and sovereignty of the human person."

[2520] Nathan, James A., and Oliver, James K. *United States Foreign Policy and World Order*. Boston: Little, Brown, 1976, 2nd ed., 1981. 467 pp.
     Viewpoint not of international anarchy but of international interdependence -- a "global systems perspective." Good on economic interdependence. Traditiona world politics began to shift to interdependent politics about the mid-1960s. "We are at a historic watershed, a time not unlike the early cold war years from 1945 to 1955."

[2520]a Oakes, G., and Stunkel, K.R. "In Search of WOMP." *Journal of Political and Military Sociology*, 9 (Spring, 1981), pp. 83-99.

[2520]b Sakamoto, Y. "The Rationale and the World Order Models Project." *American Journal of International Law*, 66 (September, 1972), pp. 245-52.

[2521] Sharp, Gene. *Making the Abolition of War a Realistic Goal*. New York:

Institute for World Order, 1981. 15 pp.

2521a Steiner, M. "Conceptions of the Individual in the World Order Models
      Project (WOMP) Literature." *International Interactions*, 6 (1979),
      pp. 27-41.

2522 Swazo, Norman K. "World Government and Global Anarchy: A Theological
      Projection of the Future." *Alternatives*, 7 (Winter, 1981-82), pp.
      291-316.

2523 Targ, Harry R. "Contending Paradigms in International Relations: State
      Centrism, Global Hegemony, and Global Conflict." Purdue University:
      Mimeographed, 1977. 36 pp.
      Clark and Sohn classed with "global hegemonists." Targ prefered the
      "global conflict" (Marxist) model.

2524 --------. "Reflections of the Rejection of World Order Studies." Pur-
      due University: Mimeographed, 1977. 13 pp.

2524a --------.   "World Order and Future Studies Reconsidered." *Alterna-
      tives*, 5 (1979), pp. 371-83.

2525 Waskow, Arthur I.   "New Roads to a World without War." *Yale Review*,
      54 (October, 1964), p. 85.
      Various substitutes for world law in a disarmed world where sover-
      eign states continue to pursue their selfish national interests are
      considered: economic competition, political pressure, sanctions,
      subversion, blackmail, espionage, propaganda.   All unilateral mea-
      sures short of military operations.

2526 Weston, Burns, ed. *Toward Nuclear Disarmament and Global Security*: *A
      Search for Alternatives*. Boulder, Colo.: Westview Press, 1984.   746
      pp.
      "Balanced, fair, and comprehensive" essays on confronting the nuc-
      lear crisis, understanding the arms race, combating the crime of
      silence, rethinking security, deterrence, "the enemy," breaking the
      momentum towards nuclear war, and pursuing global security alterna-
      tives.

2527 Wien, Barbara, ed. *Peace and World Order Studies*: *A Curriculum Guide*.
      New York: World Policy Institute, 4th ed., 1985. 742 pp.
      Comprehensive guide to foundations, programs, syllabi, and biblio-
      graphies on world order.

2528a Wilkinson, D. "World Order Models Project: First Fruits." *Political
      Science Quarterly*, 91 (Summer, 1976), pp. 329-35.

2528 Wiesner, Jerome B., and York, Herbert F.   "National Security and the
      Nuclear Test Ban." *Scientific American*, 211 (October, 1964), pp.
      27-35.
      U.S. national security based on nuclear deterrence has decreased
      every year since World War II.

2529a Yalem, R.J.   "Conflicting Approaches to World Order." *Alternatives*,
      5 (1979), pp. 384-93.

2529 Wright, Quincy. *The Study of International Relations*. New York: Ap-
      pleton Century Crofts, 1955. 642 pp.

Fundamental thinking in transition to world order school.

John W. Collins cartoon, in Arthur C. Millspaugh, *Peace Plans* (Brookings Institution, 1942). Used by permission of the Brookings Institution.

16

Diplomacy of the Cold War

Since the Vietnam War in the 1960s, a serious and sometimes acrimonious controversy has been going on among American historians about the origins of the Cold War. Very generally, the "liberal" or "traditionalist" account, in which Russia was held to blame, gave way to "revisionist" accounts, in which the United States was primarily blamed. This was followed by a "post-revisionist" or synthetic school of interpretation, in which the blame is apportioned more or less equally. Neither Russia nor America aimed to "conquer the world."

Since the Cold War was what developed when world federation was rejected as national policy about 1947, important and representative works of Cold War historiography are listed here for context. Few, if any, of the authors of these histories had the fate of world federalism in mind, but they do show why the Soviet Union and the West soon after World War II found themselves on the verge of war. Readers interested in world federalism will want to be informed about this context.

When the history of the world federalist movement is written, it will necessarily fall into the post-revisionist category, for the central view of world federalists is that anarchy is the cause of wars. The Cold War was caused, they claimed, not by "that gang in the Kremlin," nor by the "Wall Street capitalists," but by the weakness of the United Nations.

Traditionalist works are represented here by selected writings of Feis, Kennan, Lukacs, and Schlesinger. Also included are memoirs by the main characters of the drama: Acheson, Byrnes, Forrestal, and Truman.

Revisionist writings include those by Alperowitz, Bernstein, Fleming, Freeland, Gardner, Kolko, LeFeber, Lieberman, Myrdal, Sherwin, Spanier, and Williams.

There is a large literature on the international control of atomic energy, which is generally revisionist or post-revisionist: Alperowitz, Baratta, Bernstein, Borowsky, Gerber, Gormly, Herken, Hewlett, and Sherwin.

Post-revisionist writings include: Gaddis, Gimbel, Ireland, Paterson, Ulam, and Yergin. Thomas G. Paterson's On Every Front: The Making of the Cold War might be the place to begin.

Surveys of the controversy are found in Gaddis, Leffler, Richardson,

Tucker, and Walker.

Accounts of the Nuremberg trials, with their great implications for the world rule of law, are listed here because the trials were rooted, not in any internationalist or federalist movement, but in the practice of diplomacy. That diplomacy itself should acknowledge crimes against the peace, crimes against humanity, and war crimes, and should acknowledge some standard of universal justice, is evidence again of the new reality of interdependence in the mid-twentieth century.

One of the most interesting developments of the reinterpretation of the Cold War from a world federalist perspective is the complete rehabilitation of the reputation of Henry Wallace. He is now regarded as a courageous politician, who might have piloted the nation toward a less disastrous course over the last forty years. This view can be seen in works by Blum, Markowitz, Walker, and especially Richard Walton.

Albert Einstein observed, at the start of the Cold War, that there were three fundamental alternatives for national policy: empire, preventive war, and world government. The diplomatic history of the last forty years is largely an account of trends toward the first -- or the second.

Stan McGovern cartoon, in the *New York Post*, September 27, 1948. Reprinted by permission of the *New York Post*. Copyright News Group Publications, Inc.

2538 Acheson, Dean. *Present at the Creation*: *My Years in the State Department*. New York: Norton, 1969. 798 pp.
Memoirs, 1941-1953.

2539 Alperovitz, Gar. *Atomic Diplomacy*: *Hiroshima and Potsdam*. New York: Vintage, 1965. 317 pp.
"It is now evident that, far from following his predecessor's policy of cooperation, shortly after taking office Truman launched a powerful foreign policy initiative aimed at reducing or eliminating Soviet influence from Europe." Atomic bomb, as Truman said, "put us in a position to dictate our own terms at the end of the war." Explains why there was no American world federalist foreign policy at the end of World War II.

2540 --------. *Cold War Essays*. Garden City, N.Y.: Anchor, 1970. 150 pp.
Repeated U.S. interventions before, during, and after the Cold War were "products of our deeply expansionist institutions and traditions." The future task of Americans will be the "negative and essentially conservative work of halting the interventionist course of American policy" and the "positive work of attempting to change our basic attitudes and institutional arrangements" that have led to so much national disaster.

2541 Bailey, Thomas A. *A Diplomatic History of the American People*. New York: Crofts, 1940; many subsequent editions. 973 pp.
Standard history of U.S. diplomacy, emphasizing domestic, rather than elite, influence on foreign policy. United World Federalists could make no progress because of "Soviet obstruction."

2542 Baratta, Joseph Preston. "Was the Baruch Plan a Proposal of World Government?" *International History Review*, 7 (November, 1985), pp. 592-621.
The Baruch Plan was the nearest approach to a world government proposal by the United States; a full proposal could have been more "fair" to the Russians, who in the circumstance of 1946 probably still would have rejected it, but at least they would not have been alarmed by the deceptiveness of the plan actually offered; and the story of the failure to make the plan a complete world government proposal casts a sidelight on the origins of the Cold War, and offers some guidance for a way out of the present nuclear arms race.

2543 Barton, John H. *The Politics of Peace*: *An Evaluation of Arms Control*. Stanford: Stanford University Press, 1981. 257 pp.

2544 Bernstein, Barton J. "American Foreign Policy and the Origins of the Cold War." In Bernstein, Barton J., ed. *Politics and Policies of the Truman Administration*. Chicago: Quadrangle, 1970.
". . . American leaders sought to reshape much of the world according to American needs and standards, and thereby contributed significantly to the origins of the Cold War. . . . The fear of communism, often mixed with a misunderstanding of Munich and the sense that compromise may be appeasement, has led policy-makers generally to be intransigent in their response to communism. They have allowed their fears to distort their perceptions and their ideology to blur reality. . . . It is this defective world view, so visible in the early Cold War, that has led some to lament that the American self-conception has lost its utopian vision."

[2545] --------. "The Quest for Security: American Foreign Policy and International Control of Atomic Energy, 1942-1946." *Journal of American
History*, 60 (March, 1974), pp. 1003-44.
"Neither the United States nor the Soviet Union was prepared in
1945 or 1946 to take the risks that the other power required for
agreement."

[2546] Blum, John Morton, ed. *The Price of Vision*: *The Diary of Henry A.
Wallace*. Boston: Houghton Mifflin, 1973. 707 pp.
"The irony of history should have restored Wallace's reputation,
but in the early 1970s he was still remembered more for his occasional fallibility than for his extraordinary foresight. Three decades earlier he had imagined a splendid century which still had
yet convincingly to begin. He would have welcomed a century of the
common man, as he welcomed the New Deal, whenever it began. . . ."

[2547] Borowski, Harry R. *A Hollow Threat*: *Strategic Air Power before Korea*.
Westport, Conn.: Greenwood, 1982. 242 pp.
Actual weakness of the atomic threat at beginning of Cold War.

[2548] Bosch, William J. *Judgment on Nuremberg*: *American Attitudes toward
the Major German War-Crime Trials*. Chapel Hill, N.C.: University
of North Carolina Press, 1970. 272 pp.

[2549] Burns, Richard Dean, ed. *Guide to American Foreign Relations since
1700*. Santa Barbara, Calif.: 1982. 1213 pp.
Major guide for research.

[2550] Byrnes, James F. *Speaking Frankly*. New York: Harper & Bros., 1947.
324 pp.
Basic on foreign policy of 1946.

[2551] --------. *All in One Lifetime*. New York: Harper, 1958. 432 pp.
Completes memoirs.

[2552] Caute, David. *The Great Fear*: *The Anti-Communist Purge under Truman
and Eisenhower*. New York: Simon & Schuster, 1978. 697 pp.
Large scale narrative of McCarthyism. World federalists are passed
over in silence -- they had already purged themselves.

[2553] Clifford, J. Garry. "President Truman and Peter the Great's Will."
Diplomatic History, 4 (1980), pp. 371-85.
Reviews Grenville Clark's letters to Stimson, Taft, and others in
1948 re Truman's credulity toward this fake will that purportedly
showed Russia's plans (1725) for domination of the world. Incident
demonstrates Truman's "simplistic and hostile" attitude toward Soviet Union in early Cold War.

[2554] DeConde, Alexander, ed. *The Encyclopedia of American Foreign Policy*:
Studies of the Principal Movements and Ideas. New York: Scrib-
ner's, 1978. 3 vols.
Authoritative essays on internationalism, international law, pacifism, and peace movements, in addition to many others on concepts
such as American attitudes toward war, the Cold War, containment,
nuclear weapons, power politics, realism and idealism.

[2555] Deutscher, Issac. *Stalin*: *A Political Biography*. New York: Oxford
University Press, 1949; 2nd ed., 1967. 661 pp.

Even-handed account of the Russian dictator.

[2556] Divine, Robert A.   *Second Chance*: *The Triumph of Internationalism in America during World War II*. New York: Atheneum, 1967. 371 pp.
Standard history of U.S. part in creation of United Nations.

[2557] Douglas, Roy. *From War to Cold War, 1942-1948*.   New York: St. Martins, 1981. 224 pp.
Closely argued diplomatic history by British scholar. Main "lesson" is that both Marxists and defenders of capitalism mistook the other for the enemy: Europe, though ripe for revolution according to Marxist theory, did not fall into the Communist basket after World War II, and the Third World, where real poverty has created conditions favorable to communism, has only been prevented from falling because of Western capitalist alliance with a small, repressive land owning class. Common enemy is the land system.

[2558] Feis, Herbert. *The Atomic Bomb and the End of World War II*.   Princeton: Princeton University Press, 1966. 223 pp.
Traditional account for use of atomic bomb. Cf. Alperovitz.

[2559] Fleming, Denna F.   *The Cold War and Its Origins*.   Garden City, N.Y.: Doubleday, 1961. 2 vols.
Early revisionism, by historian who was consultant to Bernard Baruch at time of formulation of U.S. plan for international control of atomic energy.

[2560] Freeland, Richard M. *The Truman Doctrine and the Origins of McCarthyism*: *Foreign Policy*, *Domestic Politics*, *and Internal Security*, *1946-1948*. New York: Knopf, 1972.
Shows that McCarthyism was fully in place by early 1948, "as the result of a deliberate and highly organized effort by the Truman administration in 1947-48 to mobilize support for the program of economic assistance to Europe. . . ." The Soviet "threat" was manufactured as an ideological weapon to complete the defeat of isolationism in America.

[2561] Gaddis,   John L.   *The United States and the Origins of the Cold War*. New York: Columbia University Press, 1972. 396 pp.
Multi-causal explanation for coming of Cold War. Much responsibility remains with the U.S. Truman *led* public opinion in support of his "get tough with Russia" policy. Stalin's ambitions were limited to security, but he failed to make that clear. Hence Americans, having just defeated one dictator with suspected ambitions to conquer the world, could hardly help regarding another with similar feelings of apprehension and anger.

[2562] ‑‑‑‑‑‑‑‑. *Strategies of Containment*: *A Critical Appraisal of Postwar American National Security Policy*.   New York: Oxford University Press, 1982. 432 pp.
Attempt at new synthesis of the meaning of the Cold War in aftermath of revisionism.   Gaddis finds it in the changing *strategy* of containment: Kennan's original concept and Truman's implementation, NSC-68 during the Korean War, the later Eisenhower-Dulles policy, Kennedy and Johnson's "flexible response" strategy, and Nixon and Kissenger's "detente." The strategy is conceived by Americans as *defensive*. Offensive implications are passed over as unintentional.

[2563] --------.   "The Emerging Post-Revisionist Synthesis on the Origins of
the Cold War." *Diplomatic History*, 7 (Summer, 1983), pp. 171-90.
Guide to recent scholarly literature. Cf. Walker and Leffler.

[2564] Gardner, Lloyd C.   *Architects of Illusion*: *Men and Ideas in American
Foreign Policy, 1941-1949*. Chicago: Quadrangle, 1970. 365 pp.
"This book is premised on the assumption that the United States was
more responsible [than the Russians] for the *way* in which the Cold
War developed . . . to 1949."

[2565] --------; Schlesinger, Arthur M.; and Morgenthau, Hans J.   *The Origins
of the Cold War*. Waltham, Mass.: Ginn, 1970. 112 pp.
Traditionalist-realist-revisionist debate.

[2566] George, Alexander, and Smoke, Richard.   *Deterrence in American Foreign
Policy*: *Theory and Practice*. New York: Columbia University Press,
1974. 666 pp.
Concentrates not on strategic deterrence to prevent nuclear war,
but on deterrence of limited conflicts,   like those of Berlin in
1948 or Hungary in 1956.   In effect, a review of peace through
strength. Finds need for "positive incentives" in policy, which can
best be provided by "classical diplomacy at its best."

[2567] Gerber, Larry G.   "The Baruch Plan and the Origins of the Cold War."
Diplomatic History, 6 (Winter, 1982), pp. 69-95.

[2568] Gimbel, John F.   *The American Occupation of Germany*: *Politics and the
Military, 1945-1949*.   Stanford: Stanford University Press, 1968.
335 pp.
Re implied threat of revival of Germany against Russia -- key element in coming of Cold War in Russian view. No aggressive *intent*.
"Besides wanting to denazify, demilitarize, decartelize, democra-
tize, and reorient Germans and Germany, Americans were also interested in seeing to their own continued security, bringing about the
economic rehabilitation of Germany and Europe, and guaranteeing the
continuance of free enterprise. They wanted to frustrate socialism,
to forestall Communism, to spare American taxpayers' money, to
counteract French plans to dismember Germany, and to contain the
Soviet Union in Central Europe." Cf. Herz.

[2569] Gormly, James L.   "The Washington Declaration and the 'Poor Relation':
Anglo-American Atomic Diplomacy, 1945-1946." *Diplomatic History*, 8
(Spring, 1984), pp. 125-43.
Diplomatic account of Truman-Attlee-King Declaration and Moscow
Declaration of 1945, ushering in negotiations on the international
control of atomic energy. U.S. "simply wanted to retain her exist-
ing monopoly." Failure to establish international control was "hu-
manity's greatest and final failure."

[2570] Graebner, Norman A.   *America as a World Power*:   *A Realist Appraisal
from Wilson to Reagan*. Scholarly Resources, 1984.

[2571] Green, Philip. *Deadly Logic*: *The Theory of Nuclear Deterrence*.   Co-
lumbus: Ohio State University Press, 1966. 361 pp.
Contains bibliographical essay on pre-1966 critiques of deterrence
theory.

²⁵⁷² Hazard, Leland. *Empire Revisited*. Homewood, Ill.: R.D. Irwin, 1965.
     138 pp.
     Contributions by Bernard Brodie et al.

²⁵⁷³ Henrikson, Alan K. "The Map as an 'Idea': The Role of Cartographic
     Imagery during the Second World War." *American Cartographer*, 2
     (1975), pp. 19-53.
     During the war, the "airman's view" of the earth, typified by the
     North Pole-centered azimuthal map projection, supplanted the old
     "seaman's and landsman's view," given by the Mercator projection.
     The new maps changed people's common sense of the world. Russia
     and America were actually quite close, across the Arctic. The world
     was one, but the new political rivals were uncomfortably close.

²⁵⁷⁴ Herken, Gregg. *The Winning Weapon*: *The Atomic Bomb in the Cold War*,
     1945-1950. New York: Knopf, 1980. 425 pp.
     Bomb was used *both* to defeat Japan and to exert diplomatic pressure
     on Russia. American monopoly a hollow threat (12 A-bombs by 1947).
     U.S. policy led not to security and prestige, but to arms race,
     tensions, and loss of civil liberties.

²⁵⁷⁵ Herz, John H. "The Fiasco of Denazification in Germany." *Political
     Science Quarterly*, 63 (December, 1948), pp. 569-94.
     Of 12,750,000 Germans registered in accordance with the denazifica-
     tion regulations, 836,000 were tried, 16,750 were classified as of-
     fenders, and 840 as major offenders. In the end, 7,776 were sen-
     tenced to labor camps, most for less than five years, 18,543 were
     made ineligible to hold office, and 107,246 were restricted in
     their employment. A U.S. report of December, 1947, found that 46%
     of the upper middle civil service were former Nazis, 40% of the
     higher civil service, and 30% of owners and partners in private in-
     dustry.

²⁵⁷⁶ Hewlett, Richard G., and Anderson, Oscar E., Jr. *A History of the
     United States Atomic Energy Commission*. University Park, Pa.: Penn-
     sylvania State University Press, 1962. 2 vols. Vol. I: *The New
     World*, *1939-1946*. 766 pp.
     Official history, including Baruch Plan.

²⁵⁷⁷ Holloway, David. *The Soviet Union and the Arms Race*. New Haven:
     Yale University Press, 1983. 211 pp.

²⁵⁷⁸ Ireland, Timothy P. *Creating an Entangling Alliance*: *The Origins of
     the North Atlantic Treaty Organization*. Westport, Conn.: Green-
     wood, 1981. 245 pp.
     In the "revolutionary" international situation following first use
     of atomic weapons and the end of the war, the United States would
     not go so far as to join a limited world government, but it would
     join an entangling alliance with Western Europe. This in itself,
     after the tradition of Washington and Monroe, was a "revolution" in
     American foreign policy. "In essence, in order to reconstitute a
     balance of power against the Soviet Union, the United States had to
     become part of a more intricate balance designed both to contain
     the Soviet threat and permanently to end the threat of German domi-
     nation of western Europe by integrating the western portion of that
     divided country into a large Atlantic framework."

²⁵⁷⁹ Jackson, Robert H. *The Nuremberg Case*. New York: Knopf, 1947. 268

pp.

2580 --------. "Nuremberg and International Law." *American Thought* (New York), (1947), pp. 213-22.

2581 Johnson, Andrew Nissen. *Enforceable World Peace*: *Thoughts of a Diplomat*. Minneapolis: Burgess, 1973. 156 pp.

2582 Kennan, George F. *American Diplomacy, 1900-1950*. Chicago: University of Chicago Press, 1951. 127 pp.
A prime example of the "legalistic-moralistic approach to international problems" that Kennan condemned was the belief in "World Law and World Government." He misunderstood world government as a bulwark of the status quo, like the United Nations, while actually it is conceived as an agency for peaceful change. By the architect of the containment policy.

2583 --------. *Memoirs, 1925-1950*. Boston: Little, Brown, 1967. 583 pp.

2583a Keohane, Robert O. *After Hegemony*: *Cooperation and Discord in the World Political Economy*. Princeton: Princeton University Press, 1984. 320 pp.
On international regime formation.

2584 Kolko, Gabriel. *The Politics of War*: *The World and United States Foreign Policy, 1943-1945*. New York: Random House, 1968. 685 pp.
Broadly conceived history of World War II with following twenty-five years of social revolution in mind. U.S. had only fleeting interest in U.N. and world government because leaders and people heedlessly assumed that American national interest was identical with the world interest. "In considering the postwar world political order, and especially the United Nations as a forum for the resolution of future problems, the United States had to shape its position to adjust for its Western Hemispheric policies and needs, its desire for military security via bases, and its rapidly growing spheres of interest elsewhere."

2585 --------, and Kolko, Joyce. *The Limits of Power*: *The World and United States Foreign Policy, 1945-1954*. New York: Harper & Row, 1972. 820 pp.
Bid for world economic empire after the war precluded leadership for world government. "Surrounded by this vast upheaval [in war-torn and colonized areas] the United States found itself immeasurably enriched and, without rival, the strongest nation on the globe. It emerged from the war self-conscious of its new strength and confident of its ability to direct world reconstruction along lines compatible with its goals. . . . Essentially, the United States' aim was to restructure the world so that American business could trade, operate, and profit without restrictions everywhere." A classic of new left historiography.

2586 LeFeber, Walter. *America, Russia, and the Cold War, 1945-1971*. New York: Wiley, 1972. 339 pp.
Domestic policy influences foreign policy. For the coming of the Cold War, this meant that American leaders were much influenced by considerations of American economic advantage. The "open door" struck against the "iron curtain."

[2587] Leffler, Melvyn.   "The American Conception of National Security and
      the Beginnings of the Cold War." *American Historical Review*,   89
      (April, 1984), pp. 346-81.
      Fundamental on traditionalist-revisionist historiography.

[2588] Leigh, Michael. *Mobilizing Consent*: *Public Opinion and American For-
      eign Policy, 1937-1947*. Westport, Conn.: Greenwood, 1976. 187 pp.

[2589] Levin, N. Gordon, Jr.   *Woodrow Wilson and World Politics*: *America's
      Response to War and Revolution*. New York: Oxford University Press,
      1968. 340 pp.
      Standard work on preceding phase of international organization.
      "This ultimate Wilsonian goal may be defined as the attainment of a
      peaceful liberal capitalist world order under international law,
      safe from both traditional imperialism and revolutionary socialism,
      within whose stable liberal confines a missionary America could
      find moral and economic pre-eminence."

[2590] Lieberman, Joseph I. *The Scorpion and the Tarantula*: *The Struggle to
      Control Atomic Weapons, 1945-1949*. Boston: Houghton Mifflin, 1970.
      460 pp.
      "This is the story of a disastrous failure of statecraft. . . . In
      the guilt and responsibility for this epic failure, the United
      States shares equally with the Soviet Union."

[2591] Lukacs, John.   *A History of the Cold War*. Garden City, N.Y.: Double-
      day, 1961. 288 pp.
      Stalin rushed into vacuum, while the American people,   to their
      credit, did not use their greater power to exploit the distress of
      a ruined world to build an empire. Traditionalist.

[2592] Lundestad, Geir.   *America, Scandinavia, and the Cold War, 1945-1949*.
      New York: Columbia University Press, 1980. 434 pp.
      A regional study with wide implications.

[2593] McCagg, William O., Jr. *Stalin Embattled, 1943-1948*.   Detroit: 1978.
      423 pp.
      Defensive and reactive character of Stalin's policy, 1947-1948.

[2594] Markowitz, Norman D. *The Rise and Fall of the People's Century*: *Henry
      A. Wallace and American Liberalism, 1941-1948*. New York: Free
      Press, 1973. 369 pp.
      The "world New Deal" was world federalism in all but name. Progres-
      sive capitalism like Wallace's, Markowitz thinks, is unattainable;
      a "democratic socialist America" is the true goal.

[2595] Mastny, Vojtech.   *Russia's Road to the Cold War*: *Diplomacy, Warfare,
      and the Politics of Communism, 1941-1945*. New York: Columbia Uni-
      versity Press, 1979. 409 pp.
      Based on American, British, and accessible Soviet and East European
      sources. Stalin would not base Russian security on cooperation with
      West. He did not know where to draw the line for his sphere of in-
      fluence.   West's failure was not to actively oppose his expansion
      earlier. Cf. McCagg.

[2596] May, Ernest R. "An American Tradition in Foreign Policy: The Role of
      Public Opinion." In William Nelson, ed., *Theory and Practice in
      American Politics* (Chicago: University of Chicago Press, 1964), pp.

101-22.

[2597] Millis, Walter, ed.   *The Forrestal Diaries*.   New York: Viking, 1951.
581 pp.

[2598] Morgenthau, Hans.   *In Defense of the National Interest*:   *A Critical Examination of American Foreign Policy*.   New York: Knopf,   1951.
283 pp.
The "utopianism" he criticizes is the notion that U.S. foreign policy is animated by universal moral principles,   instead of   by a sense of selfish advantage or national interest, like that of other countries.   The United   Nations could never mean the   end of power politics.

[2599] Myrdal, Alva.   *The Game of Disarmament*: *How the United States and Russia Run the Arms Race*.   New York: Pantheon, 1976.   397 pp.
"Disarmament is a common world interest,   not least for the peoples in the lands of the superpowers and their all too silent military and political allies.   My proposals for independent action are directed, at a deeper level,   not against but for their true national interests.   They are, however, directed against their present policies, which are headed for disaster.   These policies are irrational from the national as well as the international point of view.   And they are deeply immoral."

[2600] Nogee, Joseph L.   *Soviet Policy towards International Control of Atomic Energy*.   Notre Dame: Notre Dame University Press, 1961.   306 pp.
Based on available Soviet sources.   "To the Kremlin, non-Soviet intrusion   into the   Soviet industrial   structure   constituted a   far greater   threat to   its long-term   stability and   survival than   an atomic arms race."

[2600]a Nye, Joseph S., Jr., and Keohane, Robert O.   *Transnational Relations and World Politics*.   Cambridge: Harvard University Press,   1972.
428 pp.

[2600]b -------- and --------.   *Power and Interdependence*:   *World Politics in Transition*.   Boston: Little, Brown, 1977.

[2601] Osgood,   Robert Endicott.   *Ideals and Self-Interest in America's Foreign Relations*:   *The Great Transformation of the Twentieth Century*.
Chicago: University of Chicago Press, 1953; 2nd ed.,   1964.   491 pp.
A standard work for the tension between realism and idealism in the American experience.   Cf. Britain's E. H. Carr.

[2602] Paterson, Thomas G, ed.   *Cold War Critics*:   *Alternatives to American Foreign Policy in the Truman Years*.   Chicago: Quadrangle Books, 1971.   313 pp.
Critics included Grenville Clark, Leo Szilard, Albert Einstein, A. J. Muste, and Vito Marcantonio.

[2603] --------.   *Soviet-American Confrontation*:   *Postwar Reconstruction and the Origins of the Cold War*.   Baltimore: Johns Hopkins University Press, 1973.   287 pp.
Account of American concept of "peace and prosperity" following the war.   "Because the United States was maneuvering from an uncommonly powerful [economic] position and on a global scale,   its foreign

policy often was haughty, expansionist, and uncompromising. Washington attempted to exploit Europe's weaknesses for its advantage and must share a substantial responsibility for the division of the world into competing blocs.   This is not to ignore or excuse the Soviet grip on eastern Europe, but . . . Soviet policy was flexible in the immediate postwar years."

2604 --------. *On Every Front*: *The Making of the Cold War*. New York: Norton, 1979. 210 pp.
Brief synthesis on origins of Cold War. Causes found in anarchical international system, disparate national interests, and peculiar diplomatic conduct or tactics of American and Russian leaders. Both Russia and America to blame. Best short history.

2605 Range, Willard. *Franklin D. Roosevelt's World Order*.   Athens, Ga.: University of Georgia Press, 1959. 219 pp.
Roosevelt had no vision of world federation and the rule of world law.

2606 Richardson, J. L.   "Cold War Revisionism: A Critique." *World Politics*, 24 (1972), pp. 579-612.
Revisionists have been too selective in finding evidence that U.S. is to blame.   "What we have, then, is not so much Cold War history as Cold War polemic. . . . 'Containment' was not the purely defensive, reactive policy depicted by its supporters and critics alike. The universalist, idealist strand in American foreign policy had hegemonial overtones."

2607 Rosenberg, David A.   "American Atomic Strategy and the Hydrogen Bomb Decision." *Journal of American History*, 66 (1979), pp. 62-87.

2608 --------. "The Origins of Overkill: Nuclear Weapons and American Strategy, 1945-1960." *International Security*, 7 (1983), pp. 3-71.
On small size of American atomic arsenal.

2609 Rubinstein, Alvin Z. *Soviet Foreign Policy since World War II*: *Imperial and Global*. Cambridge: Winthrop, 1981. 295 pp.
Brief work, concentrating on period from 1945 to present. ". . . the Kremlin leadership is wedded to the preservation of its imperial system; it has little interest in interdependence or involvement with the outside world beyond what it sees as necessary for strengthening its own society. Moscow may not be isolationist, but neither is it internationalist in the Western sense of the word."

2610 Schlesinger, Arthur M.   "Origins of the Cold War." *Foreign Affairs*, 46 (October, 1967), pp. 22-52.
Traditional account at height of revisionist controversy.

2611 Shafer, Boyd C. *Nationalism*: *Myth and Reality*. New York: Harcourt, Brace, 1955. 319 pp.

2612 --------.   "Nationalism: Its Nature and Interpreters." Washington: American Historical Association, Pamphlet 701, 1959, 1976. 33 pp.
". . . If there is to be at any future time a truly international authority or world state above the nation, that international or world government will have to evolve somewhat as national governments did."

2613 --------. *Faces of Nationalism*: *New Realities and Old Myths*. New York: 1972. 535 pp.
Leading study of nationalism.

2614 --------. "Webs of Common Interests: Nationalism, Internationalism, and Peace." *Historian*, 36 (1974), pp. 403-33.

2615 Sherwin, Martin J. *A World Destroyed*: *The Atomic Bomb and the Grand Alliance*. New York: Knopf, 1975. 315 pp.
Parallels Hewlett. "To comprehend the relationship between atomic energy and diplomatic policies that developed during the war, the bomb must be seen as both scientists and policymakers saw it before Hiroshima: as a possible means of controlling the postwar course of world affairs."

2616 Sorokin, Pitirim A. "Mutual Convergence of the United States and the U.S.S.R. to the Mixed Socio-Cultural Type." *International Journal of Comparative Sociology*, 1 (1960), pp. 143-76.
Leading Western source for doctrine of "convergence." "The preceding brief analysis . . . demonstrates indeed that in all these basic fields both countries have been becoming increasingly similar to each other and converging mutually toward a mixed type, neither Communist nor Capitalist, neither Totalitarian nor Democratic, neither Materialistic nor Idealistic, neither totally Religious nor Atheistic-Agnostic, neither purely Individualistic nor Collectivistic. . . ."

2617 Spanier, John W., and Nogee, Joseph L. *The Politics of Disarmament*: *A Study in Soviet-American Gamesmanship*. New York: Praeger, 1962. 226 pp.
Baruch Plan considered. Preferred approach between "utopian" and "realist" schools.

2618 --------. *World Politics in an Age of Revolution*. New York: Praeger, 1967. 434 pp.
World government not even theoretical answer until a "global consensus" exists.

2619 Stimson, Henry L., with Bundy, McGeorge. *On Active Service in Peace and War*. New York: Harper & Bros., 1947. 698 pp.
Memoirs. Some discussion of Grenville Clark's association.

2620 Taubman, William. *Stalin's American Policy*: *From Entente to Detente to Cold War*. New York: Norton, 1982. 291 pp.
Account of Stalin's foreign policy by American observer who made ingenius use of available Russian sources. Cf. Mastny and Rubinstein. Cold War was product of deep-seated national forces and misperceptions on both sides.

2621 Taylor, Telford. "Nuremberg Trials: War Crimes and International Law." *International Conciliation*, 450 (April, 1949), pp. 241-371.

2622 Theoharis, Athan. *Seeds of Repression*: *Harry S. Truman and the Origins of McCarthyism*. Chicago: Quadrangle, 1971. 238 pp.

2623 Thornton, Archibald P. *Imperialism in the Twentieth Century*. Minneapolis: University of Minnesota Press, 1977. 363 pp.
A thoughtful study of imperialism through its modern forms of Sov-

iet and American expansionism. Alternative to voluntary establishment of world federation.

[2624] Truman, Harry S. *Memoirs*: *Year of Decisions* and *Years of Trial and
Hope*. Garden City, N.Y.: Doubleday, 1955. 2 vols.

[2625] Tucker, Robert W. *The Radical Left and American Foreign Policy*. Baltimore: Johns Hopkins University Press, 1971. 156 pp.
Critique of New Left historiography. "More than the explanatory
power of radical criticism, it is the moral fervor and idealism of
this criticism that must account for its influence. . . . The radical does not foreswear the belief in America's providential mission.   Indeed, he changes the content of that mission and sees its
fulfillment in the future. A condemnation of the past and the present is accordingly joined to a promise of a future in which a sin-
ful nation may yet redeem itself and, by so doing, serve as an example to the world."

[2626] Tugwell, Rexford Guy. *Off Course*: *From Truman to Nixon*. New York:
Praeger, 1971. 326 pp.
Popular revisionism by a former New Dealer and member of the Chi-
cago Committee

[2627] Ulam, Adam. *The Rivals*: *America and Russia since World War II*. New
York: Viking, 1971. 405 pp.
Brilliant essay -- corrective of many illusions -- aiming to teach
Americans respect for diplomacy and power politics, like that held
maturely in Europe.

[2628] --------. *Stalin*: *The Man and His Era*. New York: Viking, 1973.   760
pp.
Large canvas of Stalin and Russian history.   Less analytical and
more negative than Deutscher. Stalin's goal in Eastern Europe was,
as he said, the establishment of friendly governments, not necessarily Communist ones.

[2629] Walker, J. Samuel. *Henry A. Wallace and American Foreign Policy*.
Westport, Conn.: Greenwood, 1976. 224 pp.
Clear and brief.   Contrasts fundamental views, like Wallace's and
Truman's on aid to Greece and Turkey, but does not decide between
them.

[2630] --------.   "Historians and Cold War Origins: The New Consensus." In
Haines, Gerald K., and Walker, J. Samuel, eds. *American Foreign
Relations*: *A Historiographical Review* (*Westport*, Conn.:   Greenwood, 1981).
A cool and balanced account.   Fair guide to the literature.   New
consensus has emerged that America and Russia shared responsibility
for the Cold War.   Such a conflict between the two great powers to
survive the war was probably inevitable. U.S. policies were provo-
cative and hence contributed to the bitterness of the inevitable
conflict.   The pattern was one of challenge and response, action
and reaction, by the two powers, rather than one side simply res-
ponding honorably to the aggressive expansion of the other.   Neither aimed to "conquer the world."

[2631] Walton, Richard J. *Henry Wallace, Harry Truman, and the Cold War*.
New York: Viking, 1976. 388 pp.

Most sympathetic and readable of the recent works restoring Wallace's reputation. Wallace is regarded as a courageous politician in FDR's tradition who might have saved the United States from its disastrous course after 1947. Cause of Cold War and Vietnam War was not expansionist capitalism but popular hubris in American greatness after World War II. "This hubris took the shape of globalism, a new imperialism, a Pax Americana."

2632 Wechsler, Herbert. *Principles, Politics, and Fundamental Law: Selected Essays*. Cambridge: Harvard University Press, 1961. 171 pp.
Includes "The Issues of the Nuremberg Trial," "Towards Neutral Principles of Constitutional Law," "The Political Safeguards of Federalism."

2633 Widenor, William C. "American Planning for the United Nations: Have We Been Asking the Right Questions?" *Diplomatic History*, 6 (Summer, 1982), pp. 245-65.
Since the U.N. has proved quite inadequate to keep the peace, the right questions include: Why did American policy makers and Congressional leaders make such exaggerated claims for it in 1945? Did they not understand the requirements of a workable international security organization, or did they use inflated rhetoric to mask a continuation of national policy? Author hints that world government was necessary, then shows how U.N. was sold to the American people as an instrument "to force the rest of the world to measure up to American standards."

2634 Williams, William Appleton. *The Tragedy of American Diplomacy*. New York: World, 1959; revised ed. 1962. 309 pp.
The work which inspired the revisionist school. American overseas economic expansion was at root of Cold War.

2635 ————. *Empire as a Way of Life: An Essay on the Causes and Character of America's Present Predicament, Along with a Few Thoughts about an Alternative*. New York: Oxford University Press, 1980. 226 pp.

2636 Woetzel, Robert K. *The Nuremberg Trials in International Law*. New York: Praeger, 1960; 2nd ed., 1962. 287 pp.

2637 Yergin, Daniel. *Shattered Peace: The Origins of the Cold War and the National Security State*. Boston: Houghton Mifflin, 1977. 526 pp.
Riga and Yalta axioms competed in minds of American policy elite at start of Cold War. "At the heart of the first set was an image of the Soviet Union as a world revolutionary state, denying the possibilities of coexistence, committed to unrelenting ideological warfare, powered by a messianic drive for world mastery. The second set downplayed the role of ideology and the foreign policy consequences of authoritarian domestic practices, and instead saw the Soviet Union behaving like a traditional Great Power within the international system rather than trying to overthrow it."

17

Peace Movement

The movement for world federation was, of course, a peace movement. It needs to be understood in the context of peace movements as much as in that of diplomacy.

Grenville Clark once said, "I believe in advancing religious liberalism because I believe that God is at the foundation of life, and the truest possible understanding of God is the best road to peace and progress on earth." He then explained why he worked for world law:

"What I would emphasize, however, is that if this affirmance is to be more than a pious generality it must be implemented by severe thought as to the practical political solutions that are required if world order is not to remain a mere dream. . . .

"The churches of all sects continually and properly call for a 'moral revolution' as the solution for the cruelties and injustices that afflict mankind. They stress the necessity for radical change in the heart of man. Who will deny the truth of this? -- And yet I venture that it is not the whole truth.

"For thousands of years man has needed a moral revolution. Perhaps he will for thousands more. The basic task is no doubt to work for this year by year and century by century, but it is also true that if we are to make some tangible progress towards world unity we cannot wait until the golden rule prevails among all men or even the majority.

"We must do what we can in our own time and in our present state of morals and intelligence."

Here is found as fair a statement as was ever made about the difference between world federalism and pacifism. It is a difference mainly of timing, like that between minimalism and maximalism, world community and world government, European federation and world federation. Federalists seek to establish the rule of world law as a more practicable next step to peace. If peace could be made and maintained by government on the world level, as it is on the national, then the precondition would exist for the truly religious work of regenerating the heart of man.

Law is only one step away from violence -- that is why so much of the literature on world peace through world law is a discussion of war -- but

it is a necessary step.   World federalism is merely a doctrine for the organization of power, including military and police power, in the interests
of the people. It needs to be rooted in moral principle and universal religious teaching if the world statesmanship it contemplates is to produce a
good world government.

    The   leaders of the peace movements have been wrestling with such
issues since long before the League of Nations failed.   Works listed here
are standards in the field.   Here are general histories by Beales,   Curti,
DeBenedetti,   and Lange, and more specialized histories of American movements since the late 19th century by Chatfield,   Patterson, and Wittner.
Internationalism in the United States is covered by Kuehl and Divine.   A
few collections of documents edited by Cook, Dougall, Kuehl, and Lynd are
listed.

Bill Mauldin cartoon, in the *Chicago Sun-Times*, 1962. By permission of
Bill Mauldin and Wil-Jo Associates, Inc.

[2647] Beales, Arthur C. F. *The History of Peace*: *A Short Account of the Or-ganised Movements for International Peace*. London: Dial, 1931; New York: Garland, 1971. 355 pp.
European and American peace activism. Standard. Augmented for U.S. by Curti.

[2648] Berman, Edward H. *The Ideology of Philanthropy*: *The Influence of the Carnegie, Ford, and Rockefeller Foundations on American Foreign Policy*. New York: State University of New York Press, 1983.   227 pp.

[2649] Brock, Peter. *Pacifism in the United States from Colonial Times to the First World War*. Princeton: Princeton University Press, 1968. 1005 pp.

[2650] --------. *Twentieth Century Pacifism*.   New York: Van Nostrand Rein-hold, 1970. 274 pp.

[2651] --------. *Pacifism in Europe to the First World War*.   Princeton: Princeton University Press, 1972. 556 pp.

[2652] Brown, Lester. *World without Borders*. New York: Random House, 1972. 395 pp.
National borders are obsolete.

[2653] Carnegie Endowment for International Peace. *Perspectives on Peace, 1910-1960*. New York: Praeger, 1960. 202 pp.
Fundamental essays by James Shotwell, H. Nicolson, Salvador de Madariaga ("Blueprint for a World Commonwealth"), Dag Hammarskjold ("Towards a Constitutional Order"), Paul-Henri Spaak, Jean Monnet, Lester Pearson, and Norman Angell.

[2655] Chatfield, Charles. *For Peace and Justice*: *Pacifism in America, 1914-1941*. Knoxville: University of Tennessee, 1971. 447 pp.
Complements Patterson. Interwar pacifists did not see in time that their support for neutrality would work to the advantage of nation-alists, so they lost initiative to Socialists, isolationists, and internationalists.

[2656] --------, ed. *Peace Movements in America*. New York: Schocken, 1973. 191 pp.
Chapter on United World Federalists by Jon A. Yoder. Another on "Internationalism as a Current in the Peace Movement: A Symposium."

[2657] Cook, Blanche Wiesen; Chatfield, Charles; and Cooper, Sandi, eds. *The Garland Library of War and Peace*: *A Collection of 360 Titles Bound in 328 Volumes*. Introduction by Merle Curti.   New York: Garland, 1971. 136 pp.
"The reappearance of the books and phamphlets in this series testi-fies to a growing concern, both academic and public, over the causes of war and the necessity for peace."

[2658] Curti, Merle. *Peace or War*: *The American Struggle, 1636-1936*.   New York: Norton, 1936; New York: Garland, 1972. 374 pp.
Standard for U.S. Updated by DeBenedetti.

[2659] DeBenedetti, Charles L. "The American Peace Movement and the National Security State, 1941-1971." *World Affairs*, 141 (Fall, 1978), pp.

118-29.

2660 --------. *The Peace Reform in American History*. Bloomington: Indiana
      University Press, 1980. 245 pp.
      Incorporates recent scholarship. Updates Curti.

2661 --------. "Peace History, in the American Manner." Paper Delivered
      to the Conference on Peace Research in History, Washington, August
      4, 1983.
      Bibliographical essay on historical field: pacifism, non-violence,
      anti-militarism, draft resistance, conscientious objection, anti-
      preparedness, anti-intervention, internationalism, and the modern
      peace movement.

2662 Divine, Robert A.   *Second Chance*: *The Triumph of Internationalism in
      America during World War II*. New York: Atheneum, 1967. 371 pp.
      Standard history of U.S. part in creation of United Nations.

2663 --------.   *Blowing on the Wind*:   *The Nuclear Test Ban Debate, 1954-
      1960*. New York: Oxford University Press, 1978. 393 pp.
      Relevance of peace activists in case of test-ban controversy.

2664 Dougall, Lucy, comp.   *War and Peace in Literature*: *Prose, Drama, and
      Poetry which Illuminate the Problem of War*. Chicago: World without
      War Publications, 1982. 171 pp.

2665 Ekirch, Arthur. *The Civilian and the Military*. New York: Oxford Uni-
      versity Press, 1956. 340 pp.
      Standard on anti-militarism.

2666 Josephson, Harold. *James T. Shotwell and the Rise of Internationalism
      in America*. London: Associated University Presses, 1975.   330 pp.
      Shotwell, director of the Carnegie Endowment for International
      Peace, was the leading protagonist of internationalism and collec-
      tive security in the U.S. Historian turned activist.   Idealist --
      believed that man, through exercise of reason, could remake his
      world.   "Shotwell never achieved more than secondary importance as
      molder of public opinion or as a State Department advisor."

2667 Kuehl, Warren F. *Hamilton Holt*: *Journalist, Internationalist, Educa-
      tor*. Gainsville: University of Florida Press, 1960.   303 pp.
      Life of leading spirit of the League to Enforce Peace of 1915-1920,
      which had parallels to world government movement of 1940s.

2668 --------.   *Seeking World Order*:   *The United States and International
      Organization to 1920*. Nashville: Vanderbilt University Press, 1969.
      385 pp.
      Standard history of American contributions to founding of the
      League of Nations. Completes Bartlett. By 1920, American interna-
      tionalists had accepted six essential principles: universal member-
      ship, peaceful settlement of disputes, enforcement under legal
      safeguards, democratic organization, continuous functioning, and
      gradual evolution.

2669 --------.   "The Principle of Responsibility for Peace and National Se-
      curity." *Peace and Change*, 3 (1975).

2670 --------, ed. *The Library of World Peace Studies*.   New York: Clear-

water, 1982. 1252 fiche.
Reproduction of journals and other research materials in fields of
peace, pacifism, internationalism, and international law.

[2671] Lange, Christian. *Histoire de la doctrine pacifique et son influence
sur le développement du droit international, recueil de cours.*
Paris: 1926; New York: Garland, reprint ed., 1973. 249 pp.
According to Boyd Shafer, "the best and most complete single study
of the history of internationalism."

[2672] --------, and Shou, August. *Histoire de l'internationalisme.* Oslo:
1919-1963. 3 vols.

[2673] Lentz, Theodore. *Toward a Science of Peace: Turning Point in Human
Destiny.* Foreword by Julien Huxley. London: Halcyon, 1955. 194
pp.

[2674] Lynd, Staughton, ed. *Nonviolence in America: A Documentary History.*
Indianapolis: Bobbs-Merrill, 1966. 535 pp.
Statements by American practitioners of non-violent social change.

[2675] MacArthur, Kathleen W. *What Can Unite the World?* New York: Church
Peace Union, 1950. 53 pp.

[2676] Muste, A.J. *Not by Might.* New York: Harper & Bros., 1947. 227 pp.
Pacifist policy convincingly argued.

[2677] Nuttall, Geoffrey. *Christian Pacifism in History.* London: Blackwell
& Mott, 1958.
Religious underpinnings of pacifism.

[2678] Patterson, David S. "Andrew Carnegie's Quest for World Peace." *Proceedings of the American Philosophical Society,* 114 (October 20,
1970), pp. 371-83.
Ideals, which included world government, of the founder of the Carnegie Endowment for International Peace.

[2679] --------. *Toward a Warless World: The Travail of the American Peace
Movement, 1887-1914.* Bloomington: Indiana University Press, 1976.
339 pp.
Complements Chatfield. Movement was elitist, coldly intellectual,
and overly optimistic. Defeated by national and imperial rivalries
and by messianic interventionism in World War I. Though divided
over arbitration treaties and world court, movement had tended to
progress from non-institutional pacifism to institutional internationalism.

[2680] Stockholm International Peace Research Institute. *Yearbooks on World
Armaments and Disarmament,* 1968-   .
Invaluable data on present war system.

[2681] Swaab, Maurice. *The Solution: A New Pattern for World Self-Government.* New York: Carlton, 1963. 183 pp.

[2682] Wittner, Lawrence S. *Rebels against War: The American Peace Movement,
1941-1960.* New York: Columbia University Press, 1969; revised and
expanded ed., 1984. 364 pp.
Places world government movement into context of peace movement.

[2683] Zeitzer, Glen.   "A Place for All: Recent Trends in American Peace
            Writing." *American Studies International*, 19 (Spring-Summer, 1981),
            pp. 49-57.
            Critical survey of recent peace scholarship.

Derso and Kelen cartoon, originally appearing in their *United Nations
Sketchbook* (Funk & Wagnalls, 1950).

18

International Education

"Human history," H.G. Wells wrote in a famous passage, "becomes more and more a race between education and catastrophe." The catastrophe of world war and other man-made disasters like world economic depression, ecological collapse, or overpopulation has been clearly foreseen since Wells' time, and many educators, scholars, novelists, humanists, and people of good will have labored patiently against the nationalist traditions that seem to be tending toward some such calamity. But the kind of international education necessary to avoid it has been profoundly disputed.

Some have called for the founding of a world university that would openly aim at the creation of international loyalties in the next generation of business and political leaders. Others, who were only too aware of how school systems are deeply rooted in national polities, advocated the immediate establishment of federal world government in order to create the necessary political basis for a truly universal education. Still others argued that state universities or private universities with international curricula were the only practical alternatives. Many have adhered to the classical tradition of liberal education, which in its best forms has never been *national*.

Michael Zweig has argued that there are six broad objectives that international education must meet: a broader sense of national interest in the body politic of every country, a new sense of international responsibility, improved intellectual cooperation, practice of new techniques of conflict resolution, experience of diverse world cultures, and intellectual and moral preparation for the creation of lawful institutions of world order.

Zweig continues that such an education must take place in a new world university, since the alternative forms of international education achieved to date are inadequate. International exchanges of students and faculty benefit too few people for too short a time. Centers for the study of international relations and programs for area studies at existing national universities tend to be dominated by the foreign policies of their national governments. The UNESCO series of seminars, conferences, projects, and publications are limited by the mere recommendatory powers of UNESCO. International academic associations, while they assist scholars in communicating with one another, have little educational impact on students. Lastly, the international exchanges of books and journals in the humanities, social sciences, and especially natural sciences make an impressive contribution to world understanding, but no one could doubt, from a glance at the daily news, that they have made a negligible impact so far on the culture of war.

International education is not simply higher education as practiced in the separate nations of the world.   Fundamentally, it is an education of intellectual confrontation with and of resolution of the ideological differences -- and now of powerful vested economic interests -- that are at the root of the immense conflicts of the twentieth century.   International education is a reassertion of the power of reason over the drift of world politics. It may be defined simply as education for world citizenship.

The history of international education may be divided into three periods: the heroic, the idealistic, and the realistic.

The heroic period was inaugurated by Paul Otlet, a Belgian educator, who, in the first flush of enthusiasm for the League of Nations, presented the League in 1919 with a detailed proposal for the establishment and funding of an international university near Brussels. His efforts led to creation of an international information office in 1924, but the larger project fell on deaf ears.   League officials did not feel strong or independent enough to support a major innovation in international education. The League could give advice and exert moral suasion, but it could not challenge the nation state by attempting to create a world university, whose probable failure, caused in part by the refusal of national universities to recognize its degrees, would be a proof of the League's own impotence.

So the catastrophe that Wells foresaw, the Second World War, came, in large part because of the failure of international education.   During and immediately after the war, however, a new trend -- called "idealistic" by its enemies -- developed among some leading American educators and emigré European teachers.   The group centered around Robert M. Hutchins and G.A. Borgese at the University of Chicago came to the conclusion that, if the League had proved too weak to prevent war, and incidentally too weak to give effective support to international education, then the solution had to be to replace a confederation of states like the League with a true federation of states and peoples.   Moral suasion had to give way to the rule of law.   "World government is necessary; therefore, it is possible," became their motto.   Hutchins, Borgese, Mortimer Adler, Richard McKeon, Robert Redfield, Rexford Tugwell, Stringfellow Barr and other distinguished academics drafted a model world constitution, entered the politics of the day, became leaders in the World Movement for World Federal Government, acquired a million dollars for the Foundation for World Goverment, and tried to direct public sentiment toward a world constitutional convention in 1950. They had some influence on the French educator, Alexandre Marc, who tried to establish a world university at Royaumont, near Paris.   In following years, Marc succeeded in founding the Centre international de formation europeenne in Nice, which in turn has established the College universitaire d'etudes federalistes in Aosta, Italy.

But the popular federalist movement was not able to maintain headway against the new national policies of containment (in the West) and of strategic defense (in the East).   With the coming of the Korean War and McCarthyism, the dream of some sort of rule of law, bringing even the great powers into ordered freedom, faded away.   Educators, many of whom were inspired by the ideal of world federalism, saw the necessity of more realistic courses.   War could not be abolished at a stroke of the constitutional framer's pen. So friends of peace looked to more modest intermediate steps. UNESCO has drawn many contributions, many new centers for the study of international relations have been established at national universities, and cooperative research centers like CERN (1954) and the U.N. University (1973) have been set up.   A large literature, reflected in this bibliography, has been written.   In Europe, as vehicles for the "idea" of Europe (European Economic Community and European Union), the College of Europe was founded at Bruges (1949), as were other educational institutions such as the Centre international in Nice.   In the United States, a great spurt of interest in international education came with President Lyndon Johnson's International Education Act of 1966, which authorized $131 million for the purpose.   "Ideas, not armaments," Johnson said, "will shape our lasting prospects for peace.   The conduct of our foreign policy will advance no faster than the curriculum in our classrooms."

But, with the coming of the Vietnam War, Congress never appropriated the money.   By the mid-1970s, when it was evident that the act was a dead letter, American international educators seemed to be without a symbol, without financial support, and without enlightened national leadership. Politics has retained its priority over education, which remains overwhelmingly national.

Nevertheless, the struggle continues, especially in other parts of the world.   In 1978, President Rodrigo Carazo of Costa Rica, a nation which abolished its army in 1948 and has been a model of democracy in Latin America, proposed to create a University for Peace.   It is now in operation, with plans to develop into a true teaching university.   Seven fields of study are provided: peace, education, human rights, communications, scientific and technological transfers, natural resources, and conflict resolution.   If one case can prove a rule, one might venture to predict that the next phase of international education will be led by Third World countries, like Costa Rica or perhaps Julius Nyerere's Tanzania.   The United Nations, like the League, has been rendered impotent by the national governments that created it; no enlightened national leadership is calling for a policy of ultimately establishing federal world government; and East and West are locked into the frightful dead end of nuclear deterrence.   The heroes are dispirited, the idealists are silenced, and the realists have run out of ideas.

[2688] Alger, Chadwick. "'Foreign' Policies of U.S. Publics." *International Studies Quarterly*, 21 (June, 1977), pp. 277-318.

[2689] --------. *"People* in the Future Global Order," *Alternatives*, 4 (April 1978).

[2690] American Council on Education. *Education for Global Interdependence: A Report with Recommendations to the Government-Academic Interface Committee.* Washington: ACE, International Education Project, 1975.

[2691] Anderson, Lee F. *Schooling and Citizenship in a Global Age: An Exploration of the Meaning and Significance of Global Education.* Bloomington, Ind.: Mid-America Program for Global Perspectives in Education, Social Studies Development Center, Indiana University, 1979. 486 pp.
By professor of political science and education at Northwestern. Suitable for high school and college teachers. Chapter on "Development of a Global Political System" never once uses the words world federation, but it provides a useful historical survey and concludes with the "international system of planet Earth." Extensive bibliography.

[2692] --------. "An Evaluation of the Structure and Objectives of International Education." *Social Education*, 33 (November, 1969).

[2693] Arndt, Christian O., and Everett, S., eds. *Education for a World Society: Promising Practices Today.* New York: Harper, 1951. 273 pp.
The editors contribute a fair analysis of the basic assumptions of international education and of the means to a free world order. Science, for instance, has made world order inevitable, but the political question is whether it will be based on armaments or cooperation. They also provide a more political essay, written during the Korean War, favoring an education based on "democratic" values.

[2693]a Bailey, Stephen K. "International Education: An Agenda for Interdependence." *International Educational and Cultural Exchange*, 11 (Fall, 1975).

[2694] Barr, Stringfellow. "Education: For Nationals or Human Beings." *Common Cause* (Chicago), 1 (September, 1947), p. 83.
"To flourish, liberal education must be universal. It is either education for all men, or it is hypocrisy. . . . Only a reign of law between nations will permit any government to concern itself seriously with the liberal education of its citizens."

[2695] Becker, James M. *Education for a Global Society.* Bloomington, Ind.: Phi Delta Kappa Educational Foundation, 1973. 42 pp.
"No nation today has sufficient power to guarantee protection of its citizens or to assure its own prosperity in isolation. To gain control over our future, sovereignty must be pooled with that of other nations in various international organizations or international agreements."

[2696] Bidwell, Percy Wells. *Undergraduate Education in World Affairs.* New York: King's Crown, 1962. 215 pp.

[2697] Botkin, James W.; Elmandjra, Mahdi; and Malitza, Mircea. *No Limits to Learning: Bridging the Human Gap; A Report to the Club of Rome.* New

York: Oxford University Press, 1979.   159 pp.

2698 Boulding, Kenneth.   "Education for the Spaceship Earth." *Social Education*, 32 (November 1968), pp. 648-52.
Special issue on international education for the 21st century. Includes articles by Chadwick Alger, Robert C. North, and Robert A. Harper. By 1968, Boulding had rejected world government as contrary to the "folk culture" of national sovereignty; talk of world federation aroused irrational fears. Yet his own solution is actually federalist, properly understood, for he calls for "solutions to the problem of war . . . short of world government and not inconsistent with the preservation of local and national cultures and organizations."

2699 Boyer, William H. "Education for Survival." *Phi Delta Kappan*, 52 (January 1971), pp. 258-62.
Sharp criticism of the schools for the "perpetuation of ignorance." Theodore Roszak is quoted on their "entrenched social irrelevance," and Boyer develops the theme of their "criminal delinquency." Schools must come to grips with such survival problems as cataclysmic war, uncontrolled population expansion, resource depletion, and pollution. "A society without control over change is a society with its future out of control."

2700 --------. "Universities and Social Priorities." *Prioritas*, (February 1978), pp. 13-17.
Criticizes American universities for irresponsiveness to social needs. Proposes a responsible ethical core of teaching that would make the university a "leadership institution."

2701 Boyle, Edward. *Education for International Understanding*. London: David Davies Memorial Institute of International Studies, 1965. 16 pp.
By former British Minister of Education and UNESCO official. Four reasons why educators should pay closer attention to their country's place in the world: (1) students must be placed in jobs in a world economy; (2) culture, particularly of science, is international; (3) young people travel widely, feel genuine moral involvement in other countries, and want to help those less fortunate than themselves; (4) immigration forces us to understand and teach foreign peoples more sincerely. History and geography have greatest role in inducing a world attitude.

2701a Buchanan, Scott. "Imago Mundi." Commencement Speech, St. John's College, June, 1952. In Harris Wofford, ed., *Embers of the World* (Santa Barbara, Calif.: Center for the Study of Democratic Institutions, 1970), pp. 205-23.
Buchanan's brilliant reflections on the political struggle for world government in the context of liberal education. "Some of you . . . will, I take it, become citizens of the world. . . . This may mean that you see the need for a world government or a universal church, as Toynbee suggests, but it more probably will mean that you will want to see that the laws that you live under are made truly universal and the God you serve less like an idol."

2702 Buergenthal, Thomas, and Torney, J.B. *International Human Rights and International Education*. Washington: U.S. National Commission for UNESCO, 1976. 211 pp.

2703 Carr, William George. *Only by Understanding*: *Education and International Organization*. New York: Foreign Policy Association, Headline Series 52, 1945. 96 pp.

2704 Clarke, Fred. "Education and World Order." *International Affairs*, 21
(July, 1945), pp. 376-85.
Education for world order must be conceived within national con-
texts.   Problems of education in forming community in South Africa
and Quebec are taken as analogous to those of world community. Main
emphasis should be on community formation, even national community
as a first step.   Then teaching should be about people, not states
and sovereignty. People who plunge into "internationalism" tend to
be unconscious national imperialists.   Time is needed to undo old
habits of mind.

2705 Coombs, Philip Hall. *The Fourth Dimension of Foreign Policy*: *Educational and Cultural Affairs*. New York: Council on Foreign Relations, Harper, 1964. 158 pp.

2706 --------. *The World Education Crisis*: *A Systems Analysis*. New York:
Oxford University Press, 1968. 241 pp.

2707 --------. *Future Critical World Issues in Education*:   *A Provisional
Report of Findings*. Essex, Conn.: International Council for Educational Development, 1981. 79 pp.

2708 Costa Rica, Council of the University for Peace. *University for Peace*.
Ciudad Colon: By the council, n.d., c. 1984.
"Peace is the primary and irrevocable obligation of a nation and
the fundamental objective of the United Nations; it is the reason
for its existence. . . .   Many nations and international organizations have attempted to attain peace through disarmament. This effort must be continued; yet facts show that man should not be too
optimistic as long as the human mind has not been imbued with the
notion of peace from an early age.   It is necessary to break the
vicious circle of struggling for peace without a educational foundation." The university, founded in 1981, is conceived as a teaching institution of higher education, ultimately with about 2,000
students and an international faculty.   Areas of study include:
education for peace, human rights, communications, economic development, non-violence, conflict resolution, scientific cooperation,
cultural studies, and disarmament.

2709 Deutsch, Steven E.   *International Education and Exchange*: *A Sociological Analysis*. Cleveland: Case Western Reserve University Press,
1970. 207 pp.

2710 Dunn, Frederick S. *War and the Minds of Men*. New York: Harper, Council on Foreign Relations, 1950. 115 pp.

2711 Education and World Affairs. *International Education Act of 1966*. New
York: EWA, 1966. 65 pp.
Collection of the most important House and Senate documents relating to the act.   President Johnson signed the bill in Thailand in
late 1966, but the $131 million provided was never appropriated.
The program for international education, like so many social programs of the Johnson administration, was sacrificed to the Vietnam

War.

2712 Gardiner, Robert. *A World of Peoples*. London: Longmans, 1966. 93 pp.
Color solidarity crosses national boundaries. "We live in one world and share a common fate."

2713 Goodwin, G.L., ed. *University Teaching of International Relations*. Oxford: Blackwell, 1951. 126 pp.
Report on the conference by that title in Windsor, England, 1950.

2714 Guéard, Albert. "A Federal Language for a World Commonwealth." *Free World*, 5 (February, 1943), pp. 173-76.
Language differences seem to concentrate and embitter the pride and jealousy of men. We need, therefore, a language that stands for brotherhood and that can be used in world institutions.

2715 Guéron, Geneviève; Cohen, R.; and Meyer, J. *Education sans frontieres: ecole europeenne, ecoles internationales*. Paris: Presses Universitaires de France, L'educateur 13, 1967. 187 pp.

2716 Haavelsrud, Magnus, ed. *Education for Peace: Reflection and Action*. Guildford, Surrey, England: IPC Science and Technical Press, 1976. 407 pp.
Proceedings of first conference of the World Council for Curriculum and Instruction, University of Keele, September, 1974. Includes Johan Galtung, "Peace Education: Problems and Conflicts." Education for peace is a fraction of that for war. Education is already politicized; educators must resist.

2717 Harbison, Frederick. *Human Resources as the Wealth of Nations*. New York: Oxford University Press, 1973. 173 pp.

2717a Harper, Robert. "Geography's Role in General Education." *Journal of Geography*, 65 (April, 1966).

2718 Hartnett, Robert C. *Education for International Understanding*. New York: America Press, 1950. 46 pp.

2719 Henderson, James L. *Education for World Understanding*. London: Pergamon, 1968. 160 pp.
A workable system of world order is urgent, and education can help to create and maintain such a system. A humanistic program is proposed.

2720 Hoopes, David S. *Global Guide to International Education*. Yarmouth, Me.: Intercultural Press, 1985. 704 pp.
Sourcebook of information on international educational opportunities, organizations, and publications in the United States.

2721 Hutchins, Robert M. *The Atom Bomb and Education*. London: National Peace Council, 1947. 15 pp.
"Civilisation can be saved only by a moral, intellectual, and spiritual revolution to match the scientific, technological, and economic revolution in which we are now living." Argument for developing world community, as the necessary condition for a world state, by means of a restored liberal education, with appropriate changes in adult, vocational, teacher, and graduate education. "The princi-

ple of order is the intellect.   If we do not know what is good or
what is the right order of goods, the failure is an intellectual
failure."

2722 --------. *The Future of International Education.* New York: U.N. Institute for Training and Research, 1970.
Address given on May 7, 1970, in honor of 25th anniversary of the
U.N. All educational systems are now instruments of national power.
Yet liberal, universal eduction would be useful even for national
systems. That Americans regard education as an economic investment
is an illusion -- American universities are dedicated to preparation for jobs, and they fail at that.   True education aims not at
manpower but at manhood.   Nations would be wise to think of education as an instrument, not to power, prosperity, and prestige, but
to the full humanity of their populations. Educators should prepare
students for national *and* world communities. Ultimately, the world
republic of learning will become the world political republic.

2723 "International Education for the Twenty-first Century." *Social Education,* 32 (November, 1968), whole issue.

2724 Kerr, Clark.   "Education for Global Perspectives." *Annals,* American
Academy for Political and Social Science, 442 (March, 1979), pp.
109-16.
American education must graduate from isolationism to global citizenship. Three kinds of education are recommended: (1) systems approaches; (2) knowledge of other nations and cultures; (3) cross-
cultural awareness. U.S. funding cutbacks jeopardize such programs.
Hope is in the tradition of universal education.

2725 King, David C. *International Education for Spaceship Earth.* Washington: Foreign Policy Association, 1971. 184 pp.
Summation of more elaborate report for U.S.   Office of Education.
Allays fear that studying the world system must somehow lead to an
oversimplified, idealistic, one-world picture.   "Teachers do not
have to fear that they must start teaching about the breakdown of
the nation state system and the immanence of some form of world
government."

2726 Laves, Walter, and Thomson, Charles. *UNESCO: Purpose, Progress, Prospects.* Bloomington: Indiana University Press, 1957.

2727 Lawson, Terence, ed. *Education for International Understanding.* Hamburg: UNESCO Institute for Education, 1969. 92 pp.
Report on twelve seminars, 1955-1966, organized by UNESCO on subject of international understanding. Cautious thinking by educators
from East and West who had no grand vision of a World Republic.
Grounded in "reality."

2728 Leach, Robert J. *International Schools and Their Role in the Field of
International Education.* Oxford: Pergamon, 1969. 272 pp.
"Quite obviously, the communism-noncommunism international tension
postponed world federalism to an indefinitely distant future, despite growing interdependence in such areas as the Common Market.
There was still the slower, surer field of building a sense of international community among young people of all nationalities."

2728a Leestma, Robert. "Global Education." *American Education.* Washington: U.S. Dept. of Health, Education, and Welfare, Office of Education, June, 1978, pp. 6-13.

[2729] Lewis, Sulwyn. *Towards International Cooperation*. Oxford: Pergamon, 1966. 327 pp.
There are eight basic components of nationalism: (1) self-determination, (2) the super-human nature of the state, (3) the virtue of struggling with other states, (4) the need for diversity, (5) a national language, (6) racial identity, (7) religious identity, (8) educational identity. International education must supply substitutes for all these.

[2730a] Lipset, Seymour Martin. *Student Politics*. New York: Basic Books, 1969. 403 pp.
Analysis of role of students in politics and higher education, with emphasis on situation in developing countries. First in series on students worldwide by the Comparative University Project of the Center for International Affairs at Harvard.

[2730] Maddox, John B. *The Doomsday Syndrome*: *An Attack on Pessimism*. New York: McGraw-Hill, 1972. 293 pp.

[2731] Malinowski, Halina W., and Zorn, V. *The United Nations International School*: *Its History and Development*. New York: U.N. International School, 1973. 184 pp.

[2732] Marc, Alexandre. "Mission of an International University." *International Social Science Bulletin of UNESCO*, 4 (Spring 1952), pp. 225-29.
"The aim of higher education is to create human beings worthy of the name, regardless of all utilitarian considerations. . . . And the tradition of a full thousand years goes to prove that it is impossible to force such human beings, without maiming them, into the spiritual straightjacket of rigorous historical and geographical separatism. . . . An irresistible tendency towards union is visible in every sphere -- economic, scientific, cultural, social, and even political. To regard this as a merely spiritual attitude, dismissing it with a smile as 'idealistic,' would be to misinterpret it. For it is not a spiritual attitude, but a historical urge to which spirit and hard fact are both lending their impetus. . . . Diversity and unity, indissolubly linked, form the hallmark and the patent of nobility of our human condition."

[2732a] Marker, Gerald W. "Global Education: An Urgent Claim on the Social Studies Curriculum." *Social Education*, 41 (January, 1977).

[2733] Marshall, Robert A. *Can Man Transcend His Culture? The Next Challenge in Education for Global Understanding*. Washington: American Association of State Colleges and Universities, 1973. 106 pp.
Report on seminar on internationalization of curricula held at Lake Chapala, Mexico, February 19-27, 1972. Goal: "integrating education into effort to awaken a new mentality of *rapprochement* among peoples."

[2734] Meiklejohn, Alexander. *Education between Two Worlds*. New York: Harper, 1943. 303 pp.
The two worlds are not those of communism and capitalism, but the old world in which the Church had accepted the responsibility for

educating all men and the modern world in which the Church has lost
that authority and no one short of the State can pick it up.   But
the contemporary state is woefully disqualified for one reason: it
is not universal.   Stringfellow Barr called this a "wise" book,
which was in favor of a world state.   By the president of Amherest
College who was closely connected to Barr and Robert M. Hutchins.

2735 Melvin, Kenneth H.   *Education in World Affairs*: *A Realistic Approach
to International Education*.   Lexington, Mass.:   Heath, 1970.   198
pp.
Powerful argument for *Weltpolitik* (between *Realpolitik* and *Ideal-
politik*).   Clear continuation of spirit of world federalist movement.

2736 Meutter, Léon de.   *La conscience mondiale et la paix*.   Illustrations
par Jan Delandtsheer.   Bruxelles: Vanderlinden, 3eme ed.,   1947.
159 pp.
Etude approfondie.   Education mondiale a l'usage de tous les peuples, de tous les educateurs, de tous les pays de l'univers.

2737 Mitchell, Morris R. *World Education*: *Revolutionary Concept*. New York:
Pageant, 1967.   315 pp.
Revolutionary concepts now at work: world government, racial equality,   universal suffrage,   social   planning,   regional development,
consumer co-ops, socialism, intentional communities, world education. Impassioned argument for progressive education. Cf. Zweig.

2738 Mudd, Stuart, ed. *Conflict Resolution and World Education*. Blooming-
ton: Indiana University Press, 1967. 294 pp.
Contains Harold Taylor, "Existing International Institutions which
Approximate or Might Become World Universities."

2739 Muller, Robert. *The Need for Global Education*. Dundas, Ontario: Peace
Research Institute -- Dundas, 1984. 8 pp.

2739a Newland, Kathleen.   *The UNU in the Mid-Eighties*.   Tokyo: United Nations University, 1984.   63 pp.
Short, independent account of the UNU's program of research, training, and communication, written by a senior researcher at the World-
watch Institute.

2740 Otlet, Paul.   *Address to the World Federation of Educational Associations*.   Proceedings of the First Biennial Conference.   Edinburgh:
1925.

2741 Pei, Mario.   *One Language for the World*.   New York: Devin-Adair, 1958.
291 pp.

2742 --------. "Ending the Language Traffic Jam." *Saturday Review*, September 9, 1961, pp. 14-16, 51.

2743 Preston, Ralph C. *Teaching World Understanding*. New York: Prentice-
Hall, 1955. 207 pp.

2743a Reischauer, Edwin O.   *Toward the 21st Century*: *Education for a Changing World*. New York: Knopf, 1973. 195 pp.

2744 Reisner, Edward H.   *Nationalism and Education since 1789*.   New York:

Macmillan, 1923. 575 pp.

[2745] Riggs, Fred W., ed. *International Studies: Present Status and Future Prospects*. Philadelphia: American Academy of Political and Social Science, Monograph 12, 1971. 271 pp.

[2746] Sanders, Irwin T. *Professional Education for World Responsibility*. New York: Education and World Affairs, Occasional Report No. 7, 1968. 32 pp.
Speech at Berkeley, May, 1968, summarizing full report: *The Professional School and World Affairs* (Albuquerque: University of New Mexico Press, 1968).

[2747] --------, and Ward, Jennifer C. *Bridges to Understanding: International Programs of American Colleges and Universities*. New York: Carnegie Foundation for the Advancement of Teaching, 1970. 285 pp.
Post-mortem on failure of Congress to fund International Education Act of 1966.   Survey of surviving schools and programs.   National perspective.

[2748] Scanlon, David G., ed. *International Education: A Documentary History*. New York: Columbia University, Teachers College, Bureau of Publications, 1960. 196 pp.
Includes such classics as the letters between Gilbert Murray and Rabindranath Tagore.

[2749] --------, and Shields, James J., eds. *Problems and Prospects in International Education*. New York: Columbia University, Teachers College Press, 1968. 399 pp.
Articles at peak of international education movement, just after President Johnson's message of 1966.

[2750] Sinauer, Ernst M. *The Role of Communication in International Training and Education: Overcoming Barriers to Understanding with the Developing Countries*. New York: Praeger, 1967. 155 pp.

[2751] Taylor, Harold. "The Idea of a World College." *Saturday Review*, November 14, 1964, pp. 29-32, 63-64.
Taylor was a former president of Sarah Lawrence College and director of a pilot project for a world college, held on Long Island in 1963.

[2752] --------, ed. *Conference on World Education*. Washington: American Association of Colleges for Teacher Education, 1967. 57 pp.
Report of conference at peak of interest in international education, December, 1966. Harris Wofford, who attended, later attempted to create a world university at SUNY, Old Westbury.

[2752]a --------. *The World as Teacher*. Garden City, N.Y.: Doubleday, 1969. 322 pp.
Masterful argument for international education, in principle and practice, by a leading American educator.   Special focus on educating teachers for a "world society." The place to begin.

[2752]b --------.   "Strangers in the World Community." *World Magazine*, July 17, 1973, pp. 30-31.
Comment on lack of relations between American students and the international student community, with suggestions for remedy.

[2752]c --------. *A University for the World: The United Nations Plan*. Bloomington, Ind.: Phi Delta Kappa Educational Foundation, Fastback No. 51, 1975. 50 pp.
Brilliant survey of the student movement of the 1960s and '70s, with critical suggestions for the development of the U.N. University. "What is at stake in the development of the United Nations University is nothing less than the development of a planetary ethic and a radical transformation in the way the world looks at its own problems. The university can, if the circumstances are right, become the world's most trusted source of information, enlightenment, and ideas for global action."

[2752]d Thant, U. "Can Scholars Succeed Where Diplomats Have Failed?" *World Magazine*, August 1, 1972, pp. 32-34, and August 29, 1972, pp. 38-39.
Description of origins of the U.N. University, its rationale, and projections of future research programs.

[2752]e Ulich, Robert, ed. *Education and the Idea of Mankind. New York: Harcourt, Brace* & World, 1964. 279 pp.

[2753] United Nations Educational, Scientific, and Cultural Organization. *Catalogue of UNESCO Publications*. Paris: UNESCO, 1983. 117 pp.
U.S. distributor of UNESCO publications is: UNIPUB, 205 E. 42nd St., New York, NY 10017.

[2754] --------. *Comparability of Degrees and Diplomas in International Law: A Study of the Structural and Functional Aspects*. By Rene Jean Dupuy and Gregory Tunkin. Paris: UNESCO, 1973. 75 pp.

[2755] --------. *Education for International Understanding*. UNESCO Institute for International Studies in Education, 18 (1969). 92 pp.

[2756] --------. *Education Today for the World of Tomorrow*. By Charles Hummel. Paris: UNESCO, 1977. 200 pp.

[2757] --------. *Educational Goals*. Paris: UNESCO, 1981. 231 pp.

[2758] --------. *Experimental Period of the International Baccalaureate: Objectives and Results*. By Gerard Renaud. Paris: UNESCO, 1974. 69 pp.

[2759] --------. *Higher Education and the New International Order*. Ed. by Bikas C. Sanyal. Paris: UNESCO, 1982. 242 pp.
Analysis of educational and social implications of U.N. resolution on the New International Economic Order and of each nation's contribution to it by its system of higher education.

[2760] --------. *International Conference on Education: Recommendations, 1934-1977*. Paris: UNESCO, 1979. 430 pp.

[2761] --------. *The International Dimensions of Human Rights*. Ed. by Karel Vasak and Philip Alston. Paris: UNESCO, 1982. 755 pp.
Intended for teaching human rights in faculties of law and political science. Structured around standard setting and enforcement, with respect to principal legal systems of the world.

2762 --------. *International Directory of Higher Education Research Insti-tutions*, vol. 33. Prepared by the European Center for Higher Educa-tion (CEPES). Paris: UNESCO, 1981. 139 pp.

2763 --------. *Learning To Be: The World of Education Today and Tomorrow*. By Edgar Faure et al. Paris: UNESCO, 1972; 7th printing, 1982. 313 pp.

2764 --------. *Many Voices, One World: Communication and Society, Today and Tomorrow*. Paris; UNESCO, 1980; 2nd printing, 1983. 312 pp. Text of Final Report of the International Commission for the Study of Common Problems, under the presidency of Sean MacBride. Prob-lems discussed: government controls, censorship, concentration of media ownership, cultural dominance, freedom and responsibility of press, commercialization of mass media, protection of journalists, power of trans-national corporations, technological revolution, and right to communicate.

2765 --------. *Peace on Earth: A Peace Anthology*. Paris: UNESCO, 1980. 227 pp. Selection of famous and lesser-known writings from different cul-tures on possible paths to peace.

2766 --------. *The Process of Educational Innovation: An International Perspective*. By Raymond S. Adams with David Chen. Paris: UNESCO, 1981. 284 pp. Examines internal process of planned innovation and reform in edu-cational systems in seven countries.

2767 --------. *Some Suggestions on Teaching about Human Rights*. Paris: UNESCO, 1968; 3rd printing, 1978. 155 pp.

2768 --------. *Study Abroad: International Scholarships, International Courses*, vol. 24, 1983-1986. Paris: UNESCO, 1983. 1104 pp. Popular reference book of some 2600 international study programs in all academic and professional fields (mostly at undergraduate lev-el) in 115 countries.

2769 --------. *Teaching for International Understanding of Peace and Human Rights*. Paris: UNESCO, forthcoming.

2770 --------. *Thinking Ahead: UNESCO and the Challenges of Today and To-morrow*. Paris: UNESCO, 1977. 363 pp.

2771 --------. *World Guide to Higher Education: A Comparative Survey of Systems, Degrees, and Qualifications*. Paris: UNESCO, 2nd ed., 1982. 236 pp. Includes for each country a general description of its system of higher education, a glossary of its degrees and qualifications, and a table showing the periods of study required.

2772 United Nations, General Assembly. *Report of the Council of the United Nations University (January-December, 1985)*. 57 pp. A/41/31, 1986, GAOR, 41st sess., 31st sup. Full report on UNU programme: peace and security; global economy; hunger and poverty; social development; science and technology.

2773 *United Nations University: A Summary*. Tokyo: UNU, 1985. 25 pp.

Basic pamphlet on profile, program, reports, fellowships and training, dissemination of materials, institutional developments, budget, collaboration, and personnel.

2774 *The United Nations University Today*:   *Introduction and Basic Facts*.
Tokyo: UNU Information Services, 1985. 42 pp.
The UNU, established in 1973, is not a teaching university but an
"international community of scholars, engaged in research, postgraduate training and dissemination of knowledge in furtherence of
the purposes and principles of the Charter of the United Nations."
It supports and publishes studies in five areas: peace and security, global economy, poverty, social development, and science and
technology.

2776 United States Congress, House. Committee on Education and Labor, Task
Force on International Education. *International Education*: *Past*,
Present, *Problems*, *and Prospects*. Selected Readings to Supplement
HR-14643. 89th Cong., 2nd sess. October, 1966. House Doc. 527.
565 pp.
Essential testimony re President Johnson's message of February 2,
1966, on an International Education Act. It was never funded.

2777 Wilson, Howard E. *Universities and World Affairs*. New York: Carnegie
Endowment for International Peace, 1951. 88 pp.

2778 Zweig, Michael. Foreword and edition by Harold Taylor. *The Idea of a
World University*. Carbondale, Ill.: Southern Illinois University
Press, 1967. 204 pp.
Argument for the establishment of a world university in order to
achieve the goals of international education. Zweig counts about
1,000 such proposals in the twentieth century.

19

Films, Plays, and Videos

Early federalism:

[2784] *The Beginning or the End*. Written and directed by Pare Lorentz. Never completed, 1948.
A dispute between the Chicago Committee and United World Federalists over the cost ($35,000) and the political line (minimalism or maximalism) led to cancellation of what could have been a superior film on world government.

[2785] *Grass Roots*. Written and directed by Edward Levitt and John Chadwick, narrated by Peter Charlton. A New Age release, Los Angeles, 1948. 16mm, 11 min.
First motion picture on world government.

[2786] *How to Conquer War*. By Sydna White. Federalist Films, New York, 1948. 16mm, 40 min (forum), 15 or 25 min (classroom).
Showed development of government through family, tribe, city-state, and nation. Seen in 42 states and 17 foreign countries.

[2787] *The Myth That Threatens the World* [national sovereignty]. By the Writers' Board for World Government; produced and directed by Oscar Hammerstein II. 1949-1952.
Theatrical sketches and succession of speeches leading logically and dramatically to an understanding of the necessity for world government to keep the peace. First performed with members of the cast from *South Pacific*, and such speakers as Norman Cousins, Alan Cranston, Walter Cronkite, Clifton Fadiman, Cord Meyer, and Rex Stout at the Coronet Theater in New York, December 4, 1949. Later played in San Francisco, Chicago, Minneapolis, Baltimore, Philadelphia, Boston, Detroit, and again in New York.

[2788] *Rip Van Winkle Renascent*. Produced by Mr. Hill of the Todd School in Woodstock, Illinois, c. 1948. Color.
A satire on the apathy of the Common Man through the ages, and on his final awakening, under atomic thunder, to his responsibilities to establish a necessary world government.

Contemporary federalism:

[2789] *Freedom of the Seize*: *A Gentle Satire on the Third United Nations Conference on the Law of the Sea.*   Written, produced, and directed by John Logue. New York, 1977.
A five-act play on the Law of the Sea Conference, presented at the United Nations and other places.

[2790] *The Equipment of Peace.*   Written by David Graybeal,   produced by Jo Bales Gallagher of United Methodist Communications.   15 minute slide show with sound track.   1985.   Available from Office of Interpretation, Presbyterian Church (U.S.A.),   341 Ponce de Leon Avenue NE, Atlanta, GA   30365.

[2790]a *Make the U.N. Work*:   *The Case for the Binding Triad.*   Produced by Richard Hudson, November, 1985. VHS video, 27 min. Available from the Center for War/Peace Studies,   218 East 18th Street,   New York, NY 10003.
Superior video on changing the voting process in the U.N. General Assembly. Hudson faces the tough questions like Would it work? and Is it politically acceptable?

[2790]b *The United Nations*: *Are Forty Years Enough?* New York Public Television, WNET-Channel 13, in cooperation with Rutgers University, March 23, 1986. VHS video, 57 min. Available from Center for U.N. Reform Education, 139 East McClellan Avenue, Livingston, NJ   07039.
Tape of panel discussion on Channel 13's Symposium series.   Participants: Charles Lichenstein, former Asst. U.S. Ambassador to the U.N.; Brian Urquhart, former Under-Secretary-General at the U.N.; Steven Lewis, Canadian Ambassador to the U.N.; Midge Dector, Committee for a Free World; Myron Kronish, CURE; Saul Mendlovitz, Professor of International Law, Rutgers; Erskine Childers, Third World Economics; Theodore Childs, delegate to San Francisco conference, 1945; Theodore Achilles, Vice-Chairman,   Atlantic Council of the United States.

[2791] *World Federalism*:   *A Realistic Peace Strategy.*   Written by and starring John Logue.   Public Interest Video Network, Washington, 1985. VHS, 45 min. Available from World Federalist Association, 418 Seventh Street SE, Washington, DC 20003.
Basic argument for world federalism against a background of famous Washington sites, using quotations from Presidents Washington, Jefferson, and Lincoln.   Also included is footage from President Kennedy and WFA president Norman Cousins.

Early films on atomic energy and the horrors of atomic war:

[2792] *Atomic Power*. March of Time, 1946.
Nuclear physics and Mahatten Project.

[2793] *How to Live with the Atom*. 1946.

[2794] *One World or None*. Narrated by Raymond Swing.   Atomic Scientists of Chicago, 1946.
Crucial scientific and political nature of problem.

[2795] *Operation Crossroads*. U.S. Navy, 1946.
   Bikini tests.

[2796] *Tale of Two Cities*. U.S. Army, 1946.
   Hiroshima and Nagasaki.

[2797] *Way of Peace*. Narrated by Lew Ayres. Religious Film Association,
   1947.
   Christian implications.

[2798] *Atomic Energy*. Encyclopedia Britannica, 1947.
   Pure science -- no political implications.

[2799] *Boundary Lines*. 1948.

[2800] *Where Will You Hide*? Council on Atomic Implications, 1948.
   No one will escape nuclear war.

Contemporary films on nuclear war:

[2801] *Atomic Cafe*. 1982. Archives Project, P.O. Box 438, Canal Street Sta-
   tion, New York, NY 10013.
   Schocking, at times hilarious, history of the atomic bomb told entirely through clips from Army, Atomic Energy Commission, and other
   documentary films of Cold War vintage.

[2802] *The Arms Race and Us*. 1981. Color videotape (3/4 inch), 30 min. Riv-
   erside Church, 490 Riverside Drive, New York, NY 10027.
   Highlights of 1981 conference at the Riverside Church, featuring
   Rev. William Sloan Coffin, Richard Hatcher, Dr. Helen Caldicott,
   Richard Barnet, and others.

[2803] *Between Men*. 1979. 57 min. United Documentary Films, P.O. Box 315,
   Franklin Lakes, NJ 07417.
   Award-winning examination of masculinity in the military.

[2804] *The Bomb*. 1981. 60 min. Concord Films Council, 201 Flexstowe Road,
   Ipswich, Suffolk IP3-9BJ, England.
   Moving look at the nuclear war issue from British perspective.

[2805] *Dark Circle*. 1981. Independent Documentary Group, 394 Elizabeth Street,
   San Francisco, CA 94114.
   Footage of an arms bazaar interwoven with personal stories of radi-
   ation victims, Hiroshima survivors, and people working to end the
   dangers posed by the Rocky Flats nuclear arsenal.

[2806] *The Day after Trinity*. 1981. 90 minutes. Pyramid Films, P.O. Box
   1048, Santa Monica, CA 90406.
   Story of the father of the A-bomb, J. Robert Oppenheimer -- what it
   was like to work on the bomb, and how it felt to live with the decision to use it on Hiroshima and Nagasaki.

[2807] *The Defense of the United States*. CBS, 1981. CBS News, 624 West 57th
   Street, New York, NY 10019.

Five part series on effects of nuclear weapons, European forces,
conventional warfare, military-industrial complex, and Russian ca-
pability.

²⁸⁰⁸ *Eight Minutes to Midnight*. 1981.   60 minutes.   Direct Cinema, Ltd.,
P.O. Box 315, Franklin Lakes, NJ 07417.
Helen Caldicott's warning on the drift toward nuclear war.

²⁸⁰⁹ *The Fatal Competition*. 1976. 60 minutes. Films, Inc., 733 Green Bay
Road, Wilmette, IL 60091.
Perceptive examination of the economic roots of the Cold War by
John Kenneth Galbraith.

²⁸¹⁰ *The Last Epidemic*: *The Medical Consequences of Nuclear Weapons and Nuclear War*.   Council for a Liveable World, 1981.   36 minutes.
Resource Center for Nonviolence, P.O.   Box 3024, Santa Cruz, CA
95063.
Highlights of a conference of Physicians for Social Responsibility.

²⁸¹¹ *Nuclear Nightmares*. 1980. 90 minutes.   Corinth Films, 410 East 62nd
Street, New York, NY 10021.
Penetrating investigation of nuclear weaponry, the military doctrines of East and West, and the frightening probability of nuclear
war. Narrated by Peter Ustinov.

²⁸¹² *The Red Army*.   1981.   60 minutes.   King Features Entertainment, 235
East 45th Street, New York, NY 10017.
Best film dispelling the myth of Soviet military superiority.   It
contrasts the Reagan administration's charges with the hard realities of obsolete and dangerous equipment, inadequate training, al-
coholism, drug abuse, and racial violence.

²⁸¹³ *The SALT Syndrome*. 1976. 30 minutes. American Security Council, Co-
alition for Peace through Strength, Boston, VA 22713.
Disparages SALT and advocates U.S.   nuclear superiority over the
Soviet Union.

²⁸¹⁴ *Survival or Suicide*. 1978. 24 minutes.   American Committee on East-
West Accord, 227 Massachusetts Avenue NE, Washington, DC 20002.
Simulates military war game players in action as they create a
scenario for World War III.   Film reviews risks inherent in continued arms race, and points toward SALT and areas of U.S.-Soviet
cooperation.

²⁸¹⁵ *Thinking Twice*.   1982.   60 minutes.   Public Interest Video Network,
1736 Columbia Road NW, Washington, DC 20009.
Follows a typical American family through their changes in outlook
as they are exposed to the nuclear war issue through a series of
personal encounters, films, and forums.   A second part focuses on
people who are doing something to change policies which could lead
to nuclear war.

²⁸¹⁶ *War Without Winners*.   Center for Defense Information, 1979.   38 minutes. Films, Inc., 733 Green Bay Road, Wilmette, IL 60091.
Filmed in the U.S. and the U.S.S.R. "A fresh and delightful appeal
to reason," says the *Bulletin of Atomic Scientists*.

²⁸¹⁷ *Who's In Charge Here?* 1981. 15 minutes.   Institute for World Order,

777 United Nations Plaza, New York, NY 10017.
Looks at the impact of military spending on the U.S. economy --
jobs, taxes, inflation -- from the personal viewpoints of a group
of employees of a military production plant.

Contemporary United Nations films on political affairs and on the U.N.'s history, organization, and structure:

[2818] *The Big If*. Animated film by Czech artist Bretislav Pojar. No narration; titles in Arabic, English, French, and Spanish. United Nations, 1982. 9 minutes, color.
What would happen *if* we turned our tanks into tractors, our uni-
forms into dresses and shoes? On the economic consequences of the
arms race.

[2819] *B O O O M*. Animated film by Bretislav Pojar. No narration; sound effects and music. United Nations, 1979. 11 minutes, color.
Humorous look at history of aggression and the theory that might
makes right. Projects into the future various scenarios for planetary self-destruction, planned and accidental. Asks, Is this *the
end*?

[2820] *The Court*. United Nations, 1981. 16 minutes, color.
The International Court of Justice is the U.N.'s principal judicial
body. This film examines its role in the development of international law and illustrates some of the issues brought to the Court
over the years, from fishing and mineral rights in the North Sea to
nuclear testing in the Pacific. Available in English, French, and
Spanish.

[2821] *Design for a Better World*. Produced in cooperation with the U.N. Post-
al Administration. United Nations, 1979. 20 minutes, color.
U.N. activities in such areas as child care, peacekeeping, agriculture, health, and civil aviation are illustrated by scenes from the
making of U.N. stamps. For layman and philatelist alike. Available
in English, French, and Spanish.

[2822] *In the Minds of Men*. United Nations, 1982. 30 minutes, color.
Produced in response to a resolution of the General Assembly to
make a film to create a "genuine aversion to all wars in the future." The horrors of war from antiquity to modern times are power-
fully presented through rarely viewed historical footage, graphic
art, drawings by Hiroshima atom bomb victims, and children. Original music and sound effects; minimal narration.

[2823] *The Law of the Sea*. United Nations, 1973. 27 minutes, color.
A graphic look at maritime law as the third session of the Law of
the Sea began its work. Examines such questions as, Who has fishing rights, or mineral rights, and where? Is there truly "freedom
of the seas?" Is there hope for the U.N.'s "common heritage" approach? Available in English and Spanish.

[2824] *The League of Nations, Part I: The First Experiment*. United Nations,
1970. 29 minutes, color.
Review of the history of the League of Nations from the Treaty of

Versailles to the Great Depression to the rise of fascism and Naz-
ism. Available in English and French.

2825 *The League of Nations, Part II: Decline and Fall.* United Nations,
1970. 27 minutes, color.
Historic failure of the League in the face of resurgent nationalism. Review of the onset of agression in Manchuria and Ethiopia,
Hitler's expansion into Austria and Czechoslovakia, and the final
slide into World War II. Available in English and French.

2826 *1945: Year of Decision.* United Nations, 1969. 28 minutes, black and
white.
No year in world history was so packed with decisive events: Yalta,
Victory over Germany, Potsdam, San Francisco, Hiroshima, Victory
over Japan, the Founding of the United Nations.

2827 *Nuclear Countdown.* United Nations, 1978. 28 minutes, color.
The nuclear arms race, with its inherent threat of ultimate disaster, is the greatest peril the world faces today. Lasting peace
cannot be based on nuclear weapons, but on disarmament and international cooperation. This film traces the history of the arms race
and of efforts to establish international control. Scenes of nuclear testing by lesser powers emphasizes the danger.

2828 *Overture.* United Nations, 1958. 9 minutes, black and white.
Beethoven's *Egmont Overture* is performed by the Vienna Philharmonic
Orchestra amid scenes of war and attempts at recovery, of suffering
caused by famine and disease, of hunger, homelessness, ignorance,
and poverty. The work of devoted men and women of the U.N. to address these problems is shown, ending with a view of the inscrip-
tion from Isaiah at headquarters: "They shall beat their spears
into plowshares, and their spears into pruning hooks. Nation shall
not lift up sword against nation, neither shall they learn war any
more."

2829 *The Security Council.* United Nations, 1981. 18 minutes, color.
Describes the role, functions, and composition of the Security Coun
cil within the U.N. structure. A meeting and its effects are followed to illustrate the difficulties and responsibilities of the
Council. Past responses to crises in Palestine, Korea, Congo, and
Zimbabwe are also reviewed. Available in Arabic, English, French,
and Spanish.

2830 *This Is the United Nations.* United Nations, 1976. 15 minutes, color.
Explains background, organs, and specialized agencies of the U.N.
system. Available in Arabic, English, French, and Spanish.

2831 *UNIDO.* United Nations, 1982. 20 minutes, color.
Tells the story of the U.N. Industrial Development Organization,
whose primary purpose is to help developing nations with their industrial growth.

2832 *Workshop for Peace.* United Nations, 1973. 23 minutes, color.
The viewer is taken on a tour of headquarters in New York: the General Assembly, Security Council, Economic and Social Council, and
the Secretariat. Available in English and French.

Current guides to related films:

[2833] Dowling, John, ed. *War-Peace Film Guide*. Chicago: World without War
Publications, revised ed. 1980.

[2834] Public Interest Video Network. Seminars, consultation, production, and
distribution of public interest programming. 1736 Columbia Road NW,
Washington, DC   20009.   202-797-8997.

[2835] United Nations. *Film and Video Catalogue, 1983*. Radio and Visual Services Division, Department of Public Information, United Nations,
New York, NY 10017.

Rube Goldberg cartoon, in *California Monthly*, June 1948. Pulitizer prize
winner. Reprinted with special permission of King Features Syndicate,
Inc.

20

Journals

Journals listed with a preceding asterisk (*) are still being published. For addresses, see list of current organizations in last section.

2845 *Across Frontiers.* London: People's World Convention [Crusade for World Government], fl. 1949. Gerry Kraus, ed.

2846* *Across Frontiers.* Lakewood, Colo.: World Constitution and Parliament Association, 1968– . Philip Isely, ed.

2847* *Aizen World.* Madras: Universal Love and Brotherhood Association, current.

2848* *The Atlantic Community Quarterly.* Washington: Atlantic Council of the United States, 1963– . Francis O. Wilcox and John D. Hickerson, eds.

2849* *Atlantic Papers.* Boulogne-sur-Seine: Atlantic Institute, 1965. Occasional papers.

2850* *Alternatives: A Journal of World Policy.* New Delhi: Institute for World Order [now World Policy Institute], 1975– . Rajni Kothari and Saul Mendlovitz, eds.

2851 *Atlantic Union News.* Washington: Atlantic Union Committee, 1949-1960. Owen J. Roberts, president.

2852* *Bulletin of the Atomic Scientists.* Chicago: Atomic Scientists of Chicago, 1945– . Eugene Rabinowitch and H. H. Goldsmith, eds.

2853 *Bulletin of the Commission to Study the Organization of Peace.* New York: Commission to Study the Organization of Peace, 1941-1944. Clark Eichelberger, director.

2854* *Bulletin of the European Communities.* Luxembourg: Office des publications officielles des Communautés européennes, 1958– .

2855 *Le Bulletin Fédéraliste.* Paris: La Fédération, 1948-1952. M. Feuillade, ed.

²⁸⁵⁶ *Le Bulletin Fédéraliste.* Luxembourg: Jeunesses fédéralistes luxembourgeoises, fl. 1949. Jean Jaans, secretaire.

²⁸⁵⁷ *Bulletin d'information.* Paris: World Movement for World Federal Government, 1949-1951. Henri Koch, ed. Also issued as *Informaciones* (Spanish edition) and *Newsletter* (English).

²⁸⁵⁸ *Canadian World Federalist.* Ottawa: World Federalists of Canada, 1955-1968. Continued by *World Federalist* (Ottawa).

²⁸⁵⁹ *CCUNR Bulletin.* New York: Citizens Committee for United Nations Reform, 1946-1951. Ely Culbertson, chairman; Lucinda Hazen, ed.

²⁸⁶⁰ *Changing World.* New York: League of Nations Association and American Association for the United Nations, 1940-1949. Clark Eichelberger, director.

²⁸⁶¹ *Le Citoyen du monde.* Bruxelles: Le Citoyen du monde, fl. 1949. J.M. Brugat, ed.

²⁸⁶² *Common Cause: A Journal of One World.* Chicago: Committee to Frame a World Constitution, 1947-1951. G.A. Borgese, director; Gertrude S. Hooker, editor.

²⁸⁶³ *La Comunità internazionale.* Roma: Società italiana per l'organizzazione internazionale, 1946-1955.

²⁸⁶⁴ *Continents.* Paris: L'Association universitaire pour un gouvernement fédéral européen et pour un gouvernement fédéral mondial, 1947-   . Jacques Almeras, directeur.

²⁸⁶⁵ *Le Document fédéraliste.* Paris: Comité pour une fédération européenne et mondiale, 1946-1951. H. Vausrot, E. Zmirou, eds.

²⁸⁶⁶ *Een Verden.* København: Een Verden, 1946-1950. Knud Nielsen, chairman; Svend-Age Hestoft, ed. Suceeded by *Verden Og Vi*, c. 1950.

²⁸⁶⁷* *Én Verden.* Oslo: Én Verden, 1948-   . Leif Caspersen, ed.

²⁸⁶⁷a* *Europa.* Bern: Europa-Union Schweiz. Christina Gafner, ed.

²⁸⁶⁷b* *Europa Eén Federaal.* Wilrijk/Antwerpen: BVSE und Union des Fédéralistes Européens. Erwin Dirks, ed.

²⁸⁶⁷c* *Europa in Beweging.* Den Haag: Europese Beweging. Marion van Emden, ed.

²⁸⁶⁷d* *Europäische Zeitung.* Bonn: Europa-Union Deutschland. Walter Böhm, ed.

²⁸⁶⁷e* *Europa-Stimme.* Feldbach: Europäische Föderalistische Bewegung und BEJ. Reinhart Zweifler, ed.

²⁸⁶⁸* *Evolution.* Milano: Evoluzione italiana, c. 1978-   . Bruno Micheli, ed.

²⁸⁶⁸a* *Facts.* London: European Movement. Ernest Wistrich, ed.

[2868]b* *Fédéchoses*. Lyon: Jeunesses des fédéralistes européens. Jean-Luc Prevel, ed.

[2869] *Federal Union News*; after 1944, *Federal News*. London: Federal Union, 1939-1955. Jack Grove, ed. Continued by *World Affairs*.

[2870] *Federal Union World*. Washington: Inter-Democracy Federal Unionists, 1939-1945. Clarence Streit, ed.

[2871] *Federal World*. Tokyo: Institute for International Studies on Federal World Community, 1956-1958?. Morikatsu Inagaki, ed. Continued by *Rempō sekai koku*.

[2872] *The Federalist*. New York: United World Federalists, 1951-1956. Richard Strause, ed. Continued by *World Federalist* (Washington).

[2873]* *The Federalist*: *A Political Review*. Pavia: EDIF, 1959-   . Mario Albertini, ed.

[2874]* *The Federalist*. Florence: Euro-Atlantic Review for a Federalist Democracy, 1980-   . Antonluigi Aiazzi, ed.

[2874]a* *Il Federalista*. Pavia: Movimento Federalista Europeo. Elio Cannillo, ed.

[2875]* *Federalist Caucus*. Portland, Oregon: annual. Betsy Dana, ed.

[2876] *La Fédération*: *Revue de l'ordre vivant*. Paris: La Fédération, 1945-1956. Max Richard, rédacteur en chef.

[2877]* *The Federator*. Washington: Association to Unite the Democracies, 1983-   . Ira Straus, ed.

[2878] *Freden*. Stockholm: Svenska Freds och Skiljedomsföreningen, 1928-   . Holger Eriksson, ed. Continued by *Pax*.

[2879] *Freedom and Union*. Washington: Federal Union, 1946-1986. Clarence Streit, ed. Continued by *The Federator*.

[2880] *FYI*: *For Your Information*. New York: United World Federalists, 1950-1951. Richard Strause, ed. Continued by *The Federalist* (New York).

[2881]* *Global Report*. New York: Center for War/Peace Studies, 1979-   . Richard Hudson, ed.

[2882] *Hitotsu No Sekai* [One World]. Tokyo: Institute for Permanent Peace, 1947-1949. Mitsuo Tokoro, ed.

[2883] *Humanity*. Glasgow: United World, 1947-1951. Alex Smith, ed.

[2884] *Informations Fédéralistes*: *UEF*. Paris: Union Européenne des Fédéralistes, 1953-   . Gabriel Badarau, secrétaire-général.

[2884]a* *Integration*. Bonn: Institut für Europäische Politik. Heinrich Schneider und Woldgang Wessels, eds.

[2885]* *The Interdependent*. New York: United Nations Association--U.S.A., 1974-   . Frederic Eckhard, ed.

2886 *International Conciliation.* New York: Carnegie Endowment for International Peace, 1907-1972. Nicholas Murray Butler, dir.

2887* *International Education Journal.* Scarsdale: Association for Research on International Education, 1984-   . Juan Cobarrubias, ed.

2888* *International Organization.*   Boston: World Peace Foundation, 1947-   .   . Leland M. Goodrich, chairman of ed. board.

2889 *Italia-Europa-Universo.*   Milano: c. 1970-1977.   Bruno Micheli, ed. Continued by Europe-Universe, European Evolution, World Evolution, and Evolution.

2889a* *J.E.F.-info.* Bruxelles: Jeunesses des fédéralistes européens. Eva Finzi, ed.

2890* *Journal of World Peace.* Morris: University of Minnesota, 1985-   . William O. Peterfi, ed.

2891 *Message de Paix.* Naumur, Belgique: Pro Pace, fl. 1949. J. Toussaint, ed.

2892 *Monde uni.*   Paris: Union fédéraliste mondiale et l'union des mouvements européens et mondiaux pour un monde sans guerre, 1954-1963. Guy Marchand, directeur-gerant.

2893 *News from World Citizens.* Oberlin, Ohio: World Citizenship Movement, 1940-1948. M. Thomas Tchou, dir.

2894 *Newsletter.* Paris: World Student Federalists, 1948-1953. Norman Hart, Svend-Age Hestoft, eds. Continued by *Young World Federalist.*

2894a* *Nieuw Europa.* Den Haag: Europese Beweging. Marion van Emden, ed.

2895 *Nouvelles équipes internationales.* Paris: Les Cahiers des NEI, 1949-1952. Robert Bichet, secrétaire-général.

2896* *Occasional Papers.*   Amsterdam: Institute for Global Policy Studies, 1984-   . Finn Laursen, ed.

2897 *One World.* London: National Peace Council, 1946-1958. Gerald Bailey, ed.

2898 *One World*: *A Forum of Federalist Opinion.* Chicago: CURE, Conference upon Research and Education, 1953-1970. Everett Lee Millard, ed.

2899 *Pacifismo.* Cordoba: Asociación Pacifista Argentina, fl. 1949. S. Savary, ed.

2900 *Parlement.* St. Martin, Belgique: Organisation Parlement, 1948-1956. Gevaert, ed.

2901 *Peace*: *A World Review.* Paris: World Peace Council [Communist], 1949-1951. Claude Morgan, ed.

2902* *Peace Research Abstracts Journal.*   Dundas, Ontario: Canadian Peace Research Institute, now Peace Research Institute--Dundas, 1964-   .

Hanna and Alan Newcombe, eds.

2903* *Peace Research Reviews*. Dundas, Ont.: Canadian Peace Research Institute, now Peace Research Institute--Dundas, 1967-   . Hanna and Alan Newcombe, eds.

2904 "Peuple du Monde," two-page center insert every other Sunday in *Combat*. Paris: Citoyens du Monde, December, 1948 - July, 1949. Robert Sarrazac, ed.

2905 *The Planet*. Chicago: World Republic, 1946-1949.   Jack Whitehouse, chairman.

2906 *La Praktiko*. The Hague: Universala Ligo [Esperanto], fl. 1949.

2907 *Rempō sekai koku*. [Federal World Community.] Tokyo: Learned Society for World Federation, 1958-1972? Morikatsu Inagaki, ed.

2908 *La Republique federale: socialiste, syndicaliste, europeene*.   Paris: Cercles socialistes et federalistes, 1948-1951.

2909 *Revue de Presse*. Paris: Union Européenne des Fédéralistes, 1952-1953.

2910 *Student Federalist*. Scarsdale, New York, and Washington: Student Federalists, 1942-1951. Harris Wofford, ed.

2911* *Transnational Perspectives*. Geneva: 1974-   . René V. L. Wadlow, ed.

2912* *The XXth Century and Peace*. [XX-i Vek i Mir.] Moscow: Soviet Peace Committee, 1967-   .

2913 *U.E.F.: Union Européenne des Fédéralistes, Bulletin*. Paris: UEF, 1949-1953. Albert Lohest, secrétaire-général. Continued by *Informations Fédéralistes*.

2914a* *UN Kaj Ni*. Rotterdam: Universala Esperanto-Asocio, 1975-   .

2914 *L'Unità Europea*, later *Europa Federalista*. Torino: Movimento Federalista Europeo, 1945-1955.

2914a* *L'Unità Europea*.   Milano: Movimento Federalista Europeo.   Massimo Malcovati, ed.

2915 *United Nations News*. New York: Woodrow Wilson Foundation, 1946-1949.

2916 *ULMWG News*. London: University of London Movement for World Government, fl. 1949. J. H. Clark, ed.

2916a* *University for Peace Newsletter*. Cuidad Colon, Costa Rica: University for Peace, 1984-   . Elizabeth Escalante, coordinator.

2817 *United Nations World*. New York: 1947-1953. Louis Dolivet, ed.

2917a* *UNU Work in Progress*. Tokyo: United Nations University, 1976-   . John M. Fenton, ed.

2918* *Världen och Vi*. Stockholm: 1953-   . Gunnar Ekegard, ed.

[2919] *Världsfederations--Nytt*. Stockholm: Swedish Movement for World Federation [SAV]. 1949-1953. S. Leander, ed. Continued by *Världen och Vi*.

[2920] *Voice of the World Citizen*. London: Crusade for World Government, 1953-1954? B.E. Cain, ed.

[2920]a *War/Peace Report*. New York: Center for War/Peace Studies, 1961-1976. Richard Hudson, ed.

[2921] *Washington Bulletin*. Washington: Americans United for World Organization, 1945-1946.

[2922] *Die Welt von Morgen*. Köln: Liga für Weltregierung, 1949-1951. Julius Stocky, ed.

[2923] *Der Weltstaat*. Frankfurt: Weltstaat-Liga, 1947-1950. Joe Heydecker, ed.

[2924] *Wereld Parlement*. Ghent, Belgique: Wereld Parlement, fl. 1949.

[2925] *Windham County* (Connecticut) *Observer*. 1946-1955. George Holt weekly column.

[2925]a* Wir Europaër. Linz: Europäische Föderalistische Bewegung und BEJ Oberösterreich. Alexander F. Barasits-Altempergen, ed.

[2926] *World Affairs*. London: Federal Union, 1956-1962.

[2927] *World Citizen*. London: Service-Nation, then World Citizen Movement, 1941-1949.

[2928] *World Citizen*. Cincinati: American Federation of World Citizens, fl. 1954. Mary Weik ed.

[2929]* *World Federalist*. Washington: World Federalists Association, 1975- . . Lawrence Abbott, ed.

[2930] *World Federalist*. Amsterdam: World Movement for World Federal Government, 1951-1956; The Hague: World Association of World Federalists, 1956-1968. Peter Holland, ed.

[2931] *World Federalist*. Ottawa: World Association of World Federalists, 1968-1973. Andrew Clarke, ed. Continued by *Transnational Perspectives*.

[2932]* *World Federalist News*. Amsterdam: World Association of World Federalists, 1980- . Henk van der Most, ed.

[2933]* *World Federalist Newsletter*. London: Association of World Federalists, 1977- . John Roberts, ed.

[2934] *World Federation*. New Delhi: 1929-1941, 1946-1962. Mahendra Pratap, ed.

[2935]* *World Federation--Now*. Chicago: Campaign for World Government, 1938- . . William Bross Lloyd and Georgia Lloyd, eds.

[2936] *World Frontiers*. Philadelphia: Interim Committee of American Federal-
     ist Youth, 1951-1954. John Logue, ed.

[2937] *World Government News*. New York: [Independent] 1943-1952. Tom Gries-
     semer and Stewart Ogilvy, eds.

[2937]a* *World Order*. New York: Bahá'í Community, 1935-1949; Wilmette, Ill.:
     National Spiritual Assembly of the Bahá'ís of the United States,
     1965-   . Firuz Kazemzadeh, ed. in chief.

[2938]* *World Peace News*. New York: American Movement for World Government,
     1970-   . Tom Liggett, ed.

[2939]* *World Perspectives*. San Francisco: Academy of World Studies, 1979-
     .   . Keith Beggs, ed.

[2940]* *World Policy Journal*. New York: World Policy Institute, 1983-   .
     Robert C. Johansen, ed.

[2941] *World Union--Goodwill*. Pondicherry 2, India: Sri Aurobindo, 1962-
     1965?.

[2942] *Young World Federalist*. Amsterdam: World Movement for World Federal
     Government, 1951-1956. W. McLean Maclean and Virginia Lastayo Ri-
     orden, eds. Continued by *World Federalist* (Amsterdam).

21

Archives

2952 Americans United for World Organization (later Americans United for World Government).
No known archives but some records in United World Federalists Papers, Eichelberger Papers, and Hoover Institution on War, Revolution, and Peace. Americans United were a major component of United World Federalists on formation in 1947.

2953 Atomic Scientists Papers. Regenstein Library, University of Chicago:
Association of Cambridge Scientists;
Association of Los Alamos Scientists;
Association of Oak Ridge Engineers and Scientists;
Association of Pasadena Scientists;
Association of Scientists for Atomic Education;
Atomic Scientists of Chicago (and *Bulletin*);
Emergency Committee of the Atomic Scientists;
Federation of Atomic Scientists;
Federation of American Scientists;
Washington Association of Scientists.
Papers of atomic scientists as they organized politically, after Hiroshima, for the international control of atomic energy.

2954 Baruch, Bernard, Papers. Mudd Library, Princeton University.
Background of the United States plan for the international control of atomic energy in the United Nations Atomic Energy Commission, 1946.

2955 Blaine, Anita McCormick, Papers. State Historical Society of Wisconsin.
Foundation for World Government records, correspondence with Stringfellow Barr, Henry Wallace, and others in world government movement and Progressive Party; World Citizenship Association records.

2956 Blake, Mildred Riorden, Reminiscences. Oral History Research Office, Butler Library, Columbia University.
Reminiscences of formation of World Federalists after split with Streit in 1941. World Federalists became the second major component of United World Federalists in 1947.

2957 Carnegie Endowment for International Peace Archives. Butler Library,

Columbia University.
Extensive holdings on private groups favoring international organization, notably the Commission to Study the Organization of Peace.

[2958] Clark, Grenville, Papers. Baker Library, Dartmouth College.
Papers of the New York lawyer, associate of Elihu Root, Sr., and
Henry L.   Stimson, who became the "elder statesman" of the world
government movement after 1944. Clark was the leading proponent of
minimal or limited world government.

[2959] Committee to Frame a World Constitution Papers.   Regenstein Library,
University of Chicago.
Records of the Committee under Robert M. Hutchins and G. A. Borgese
that issued the "Preliminary Draft of a World Constitution," a maximalist document. "Peace and justice stand or fall together."

[2960] Cousins, Norman, Papers. Brooklyn College Library, Brooklyn, New York.
Papers re the *Saturday Review of Literature*, Americans United, and
United World Federalists.

[2961] Culbertson, Ely, Papers.   Yale University Library, New Haven, Conn.;
Syracuse University Library, Syracuse, New York.
Papers of the famous bridge expert, who devoted the last years of
his life to world federalism.

[2962] Eichelberger, Clark, Papers. New York Public Library.
Papers of Eichelberger's directorship of the League of Nations Association, Commission to Study the Organization of Peace, and American Association for the United Nations.

[2963] Finletter, Thomas K., Papers.   State Historical Society of Wisconsin,
Madison.
Papers of brains of Americans United for World Government, occa-
sional antagonist of Grenville Clark, and Secretary of the Air
Force in Truman's administration.

[2964] Holt, Hamilton, Papers.   Mills Library, Rollins College, Winter Park,
Florida.
Papers of the founder of the League to Enforce Peace, who in 1946
organized the Rollins College conference on world government.   Records of the Institute for World Government, which came out of the
conference, are also here.

[2965] Hudson, Manley O., Papers.   Harvard Law Library (Langdell Building).
Harvard University.
Personal and professional papers of law professor, judge, interna-
tional mediator, and legal scholar whom the public reguarded as
"Mr. World Court."

[2966] Hutchins, Robert M., Papers. Regenstein Library, University of Chicago.
Correspondence with prominent citizens and leaders of the movement.

[2967] Mowrer, Edgar Ansel, Papers. Library of Congress, Washington, D.C.
Papers of journalist who worked particularly with Grenville Clark
at the United Nations.

[2967]a Ogilvy, Stewart, Papers. Tulane University, New Orleans.

Papers of a coeditor (with Tom Griessemer) of *World Government News* and an independent observer of the whole movement from earliest days.

2968 Schwimmer-Lloyd Collection. New York Public Library.
Extensive collection on the Ford Peace Ship, pacifism, and world government organizations. Mme Rosika Schwimmer was the radical forebear of the peoples' convention approach to world government.

2969 Shotwell, James T., Papers. Carnegie Endowment Archive, Butler Library, Columbia University.
Papers of the distinguished defender of the League of Nations and leading proponent of the "realist" concept of international organization.

2970 Sohn, Louis B., Papers. Harvard Law Library (Langdell Building), Harvard University.
MSS, writings, correspondence (with Grenville Clark, e.g.) of law professor, international organizer, and legal scholar.

2971 Stimson, Henry L., Papers. Yale University Library. Microfilm, 1973.
For Stimson's "unguarded" views on world government to succeed the U.N., see letter to George Wharton Pepper, October 27, 1947 (118).

2972 United World Federalists Archive. Lilly Library, Indiana University.
Organizational files, including much correspondence, of the mainstream mass membership world government organization in the United States. Additional material on all branches of the movement.

2973 Warburg, James P., Papers. John F. Kennedy Library, Boston, Mass.
Papers of prominent New York banker and critic of U.S. foreign policy.

2974 World Citizens Association Papers. Regenstein Library, University of Chicago.
Files of an organization which during the war supported the Commission to Study the Organization of Peace. Some additional records in Blaine Papers.

2975 World Knowledge Bank. Academy of World Studies, 2820 Van Ness Avenue, San Francisco, Calif. 94109.
80,000-item research file on world historical, political, economic, and social issues. Collected by Bennet Skewes-Cox, who took a broad view of the trends, since the advent of nuclear weapons, toward federal world government. An invaluable repository of primary sources for world history.

2976 World Movement for World Federal Government Papers. Regenstein Library, University of Chicago.
Records especially valuable for European branches of the movement.

2977 World Republic Papers. Regenstein Library, University of Chicago.
Papers of radical veteran and student group, which for a time threatened to rival United World Federalists with a grassroots popular movement for world government.

2978 Wright, Quincy, Papers. Regenstein Library, University of Chicago.
Papers of distinguished professor of international law and leading

political theorist,   whose thought   provides a   connective between
United Nations and world government supporters.

European Collections

See those of Guy Marchand (Paris), Hendrik Brugmans (Bruges),   Patrick Armstrong (London),   the   Federal Union archives at   Sussex University (Brigh-
ton), the Union des fédéralistes européens archives (in formation, Torino),
and the Bahá'í World Center (Haifa).

22

Dissertations and Manuscripts

[2988] Abou-Ali, Sayed Anwar. "Le contrôle de l'utilisation pacifique des matières fissiles fournies par l'Agence internationale de l'energie atomique." Thèse, Université de Paris, Faculté de Droit et des Sciences Économiques, 1969. 436 pp.

[2989] Babcock, Robert S. "Limitations to International Federalism." Ph.D. Dissertation, Northwestern University, April, 1949. 371 pp.

[2990] Bantell, John Frank. "Perpetual Peace through World Law: The United World Federalists and the Movement for Limited World Government, 1945-1951." Ph.D. Dissertation, University of Connecticut, 1979. 371 pp.

[2991] Baratta, Joseph Preston. "Bygone 'One World': The Origin and Opportunity of the World Government Movement, 1937-1947." Ph.D. Dissertation, Boston University, 1982. 515 pp.

[2992] Baskin, Myron A. "American Planning for World Organization, 1941-1945." Ph.D. Dissertation, Clark University, 1950. 179 pp.

[2993] Benkert, Gerald Francis. "The Thomistic Conception of An International Society." Ph.D. Dissertation, Catholic University of America, 1942.

[2994] Beres, Louis Rene. "The Management of World Power: A Theoretical Analysis. Ph.D. Dissertation, Princeton University, 1971. 242 pp.

[2995] Bernhard, John Torben. "United Nations Reform: An Analysis." Ph.D. Dissertation, University of California at Los Angeles, 1950. 251 pp.

[2996] Birmingham, Francis R. "The Atlantic Union Committee, 1949-1961: The Plan, the Program, the Organization." M.A. Thesis, Georgetown University, June, 1967.

[2997] Bodager, Bill Warren. "An Inquiry into the History, Background, and Progress of the Atlantic Union Committee." M.A. Thesis, University of Omaha, June, 1959.

[2998] Bourne, Frank. "The Public Opinion Poll as Opinion Evidence in World

Government, 1946-1954." M.A. Thesis, Columbia University, 1955.

[2999] Bresler, Robert Joel. "American Policy toward International Control of Atomic Energy, 1945-1946." Ph.D. Dissertation, Princeton University, 1964. 169 pp.

[3000] Burroway, Jessie J. "Christian Witness Concerning World Order: The Federal Council of Churches and Postwar Planning, 1941-1947." Ph.D. Dissertation, University of Wisconsin, 1954.

[3001] Dworkis, Martin Bernard. "An Analytical Survey of Concepts and Plans of World Government." Ph.D. Dissertation, New York University, 1952. 334 pp.

[3002] Engle, Harold Edward. "A Critical Study of the Functionalist Approach to International Organization." Ph.D. Dissertation, Columbia University, 1957. 565 pp.

[3003] Farr, Thomas S. "Some Considerations on Western European Federation." Ph.D. Dissertation, University of Chicago, 1953. 621 pp.

[3004] Gasteyger, Curt Walter. "Die politische Homogenität als Factor der Föderation." Dissertation, Universität Zürich, 1954. 151 pp.

[3005] Goodman, Elliot Raymond. "The Soviet Design for a World State." Ph.D. Dissertation, Columbia University, 1957. 686 pp.

[3006] Griessemer, Tom. "Force and Peace." Unpublished MS on the problems of world government, n.d., ante 1966. By the founder and editor of *World Government News*. In Stewart Ogilvy Papers.

[3007] Hilmi, A. "Die Unvollkommenheit der Satzung der Vereinten Nationen." Dissertation, Rheinische Friedrich Wilhelms Universität, Reichs- und Staatswissenschaftliche Facultät, 1952. 74 pp.

[3008] Israel, Thomas Andrew. "Significance of Social Contract Theory for International Organization." Ph.D. Dissertation, University of Illinois, 1959. 158 pp.

[3009] Keck, Daniel Newton. "Designs for the Post-War World: Anglo-American Diplomacy, 1941-1945." Ph.D. Dissertation, University of Connecticut, 1967. 291 pp.

[3010] Lent, Ernest S. "Fact and Fancy on World Federalism: The United World Federalists' Approach to World Government." M.A. Thesis, Columbia University, February, 1952.

[3011] Mangone, Gerard J. "The Idea and Practice of World Government." Ph.D. Dissertation, Harvard University, 1949.

[3012] Osgood, Robert E. "Realism and Idealism in American Foreign Relations: An Interpretation of the Evolution of the American Attitude toward World Politics in the Twentieth Century." Ph.D. Dissertation, Harvard University, 1952. 247 pp.

[3013] Panzella, Emmett E. "The Atlantic Union Committee: A Study of a Pressure Group in Foreign Policy." Ph.D. Dissertation, Kent State University, 1969. 328 pp.

3014 Perrard, Roger.   "Essai sur les doctrines fédéralistes de langue ang-
      lais et de langue française." Thèse, Université de Grenoble, Fa-
      culté de Droit, 1950. 471 pp.

3015 Price, John W.   "British Attitudes toward European Unity as Reflected
      by the Participation of the United Kingdom in the Council of Eur-
      ope." Ph.D. Dissertation, University of Michigan, 1957. 275 pp.

3016 Rienthal, Umberto. "World Republic." M.A. Thesis, Northwestern Univer-
      sity, 1954. 132 pp.

3017 Riorden, Shane E.   "'Now It Is Proposed . . .' A History of the Move-
      ment in the United States for World Government from Its Beginning
      to the Present." S.B. Thesis, Harvard University, April, 1948. 186
      pp.

3018 Ritsch, Frederick F., Jr.   "The French Political Parties of the Left
      and European Integration, 1947-1949." Ph.D. Dissertation, Univer-
      sity of Virginia, 1962. 297 pp.

3019 Rohn, Peter H. "European Integration: A Comparison of Institutions."
      Ph.D. Dissertation, University of Washington, 1958. 292 pp.

3020 Romm, Avrom N.   "Contemporary American World Government Proposals."
      M.A. Thesis, Georgetown University, December, 1947.

3021 Shallchy, Mandob al-. "Les travaux des Nations Unies en vue de la ré-
      vision de la Charte; application des Articles 108 et 109 de la
      Charte." Thèse, Université de Neuchâtel, Faculté de Droit et des
      Sciences Économiques, 1966. 164 pp.

3022 Skewes-Cox, Bennet. "The United Nations Charter and World Federalism."
      M.A. Thesis, Georgetown University, December, 1947. 181 pp.

3023 Tiffany, Victor Scott. "Quantum Rationality and the Inexhaustible Pro-
      cess of Peace: An Essay Exploring the Extant Structure of Peace
      and the Possibility for Synergistic Institutional Transformation."
      M.A. Thesis, Graduate School of the State University of New York at
      Binghamton, 1984. 355 pp.

3024 Vega, Angelina de la. "Le problème international du contrôle de l'en-
      ergie atomique." Thèse, Université de Paris, Faculté de Droit,
      1951. 232 pp.

3025 Wadlow, René V. L.   "Beyond Nuclear Deterrents: The Assumptions of
      World Government." M.A. Thesis, University of Chicago, March, 1958.

3026 Wagar, Walter W. "The Open Conspirator: H.G. Wells as a Prophet of
      World Order." Ph.D. Dissertation, Yale University, 1959.

3027 Weber, Robert J.   "Proposals Involving World Federation Supported by
      U.S. Non-governmental Political-Action Organizations since World
      War II." Ph.D. Dissertation, School of International Service, Amer-
      ican University, 1969. 342 pp.

3028 Whitmer, Edith. "Expressions of Ideas on the Problem of Peace by Scho-
      lars in Higher Learning in the United States, 1915-1950." Ed.D.

Dissertation, University of Missouri-Columbia, 1954.   547 pp.

3029 Winterhager, Eva Marie.   "Die Revision von Grundungsvertragen interna-
      tionaler und supernationaler Organisationen." Dissertation, J. W.
      Goethe Universität, Reichtswissenschaftliche Facultät, 1963. 87 pp.

3030 Wofford, Harris, Jr.   "A Cold War Odyssey: The Story of the Foundation
      for World Government; An Adventure of Ideas by a Million Dollar
      Foundation Whose Donor Wanted a Gay and Timeless Affair." Unpub-
      lished MS, n.d., c. 1956.   926 pp. In possession of author, Phila-
      delphia, Pa.

23

Bibliographies

[3040] Albrektsen, Beatrice, and Valla, Gerd-Liv. "Documentation on a World Authority." 1974. 63 pp. Dundas, Ont.: World Federal Authority Committee.

[3041] Atherton, Alexine L. *International Organizations*: *A Guide to Information Sources*. Detroit: Gale Research Co., 1976. 350 pp.

[3042] Atomic Scientists. Leikind, Morris C., comp. "A Bibliography of Atomic Energy." March 1, 1946 - February 1, 1947. 19 pp. *Bulletin of the Atomic Scientists*, 3 (April-May, 1947), pp. 127-35.

[3043] Atomic Scientists. "Bibliography on Bacterial Warfare." 1947. 1 p. *Bulletin of the Atomic Scientists*, 3 (December, 1947), p. 364.

[3044] *Bibliographie fédéraliste*, No. 1. Paris: Union fédéraliste inter-universitaire, 1950; 2nd ed., 1952. 40 pp.
Les précurseurs, Ouvrages généraux, Fédération européenne, Gouvernement fédéral mondial, et Fédéralisme interne.

[3045] --------, No. 2. Paris: 1950. 40 pp.
Additional articles and volumes, 1945-1950. Includes section on Action federaliste.

[3046] --------, No. 3. Paris: 1951. 40 pp.
British works.

[3047] --------, No. 4. Paris: 1953. 40 pp.
Swiss and German works.

[3048] Bouche, Monique, ed. *L'Europe? Dossier de documentation*. Paris: Ministère de l'education, Centre national de documentation pedagogique, 1978. 135 pp.

[3049] Boulding, Elise, et al., eds. *Bibliography on World Conflict and Peace*. Boulder, Colo.: Westview, 1979. 168 pp.

[3050] Burns, Richard Dean, ed. *Guide to American Foreign Relations since 1700*. Santa Barbara, Calif.: 1983. 1311 pp.
Major guide for research.

3051 Carroll, Bernice A.; Fink, Clinton F.; and Mohraz, Jane E. *Peace and*
      War: A Guide to Bibliographies. Santa Barbara, Calif.: ABC Clio,
      1983. 580 pp.
      Chapter 20, "World Order, World Society, World Government," lists
      many bibliographies, especially for the pre-World War II period.

3052 Center for the Study of Democratic Institutions. "World Community" in
      "Index," *The Center Magazine*, January-February, 1978, p. 55.

3053 Commission of the European Communities. *Bulletin of the European Com-*
      munities (monthly).

3054 --------. *Documentation Bulletin* (weekly).

3055 --------. Centres de documentation européenne, Bibliotheques déposi-
      taires, Centres de reference sur les Communautés européennes:
      Liste d'adresses. European Documentation Centres, Depositary Lib-
      raries, European Reference Centres: *Addresses.* Bruxelles: Com-
      mission des Communautés européennes, Information universitaire,
      1984. 133 pp.

3056 --------. *The European Community as a Publisher, 1984-85.* Luxembourg:
      Office des publications officielles des Communautés européennes,
      9th ed., 1985. 78 pp.
      Abridged version of Community's annual multilingual catalogue of
      publications. Lists main official publications and common publi-
      cations for general information. Available at press offices of the
      Commission.

3057 --------. *Postgraduate Degrees in European Integration.* Brussels:
      Commission of the European Communities, University Information,
      1985. 79 pp.
      List of post-graduate "European" courses available within member
      countries of the Community.

3058 --------. *Publications of the European Communities: Catalogue 1983.*
      Luxembourg: Office des publications officielles des Communautés
      européennes, 1984. 87 pp.
      Source bibliography for press pamphlet above.

3059 --------. Centre for European Studies, University of Louvain. *Re-*
      cherches universitaires sur l'intégration européenne. University
      Research on European Integration. No. 13, 1985. [No. 1, 1972?]
      Luxembourg: Office des publications officielles des Communautés
      européennes, 1985. 457 pp.
      Register of doctorate theses and other university studies relating
      to European integration completed since 1980 as well as studies in
      progress during the academic year 1983-84. Studies are listed in
      their original languages.

3060 Commission to Study the Organization of Peace. Aufricht, Hans, comp.
      "General Bibliography on International Organization and Post-War
      Reconstruction." *Bulletin*, 2 (May-June, 1942). 28 pp.
      Contains 3 pp. on federations.

3061 --------, --------. "II. Bibliography on Post-War Reconstruction."
      Ibid., 3 (January-February, 1943), pp. 20-24.

3062 --------. "Bibliographical Notes on Federation." Ibid., 2 (August-September, 1942), pp. 19-20.

3063 Committee to Frame a World Constitution. Hooker, Gertrude S., comp. "A Selected World Government Bibliography." *Common Cause*, 1 (September, 1947), pp. 115-18.

3064 --------. Ishida, Gladys, comp. "World Government Bibliography." *Common Cause*, 2 (September, 1948), pp. 72-77.

3065 --------. Ishida, Gladys, comp. "World Government Bibliography." *Common Cause*, 3 (November, 1949), pp. 212-19.

3066 --------. Harrod, Elizabeth B., comp. "An Analytic Bibliography of World Constitutional Drafts, Part I." *Common Cause*, 3 (January, 1950), pp. 325-31.

3067 --------. Harrod, Elizabeth B., comp. "An Analytic Bibliography of World Constitutional Drafts, Part II." *Common Cause*, 3 (February, 1950), pp. 384-88.

3068 --------. Eck, Hannelore Z., comp. "World Government Bibliography." *Common Cause*, 4 (April, 1951), pp. 460-67.

3069 --------. "Index of Committee Documents." *Common Cause*, 1 (March, 1948), pp. 355-58.
Proceedings and position papers now available on microfilm from the Regenstein Library, University of Chicago.

3070 Conference on the North Atlantic Community (Bruges, 1957). *Atlantic Community: An Introductory Bibliography*. Leyden: Sijthoff, 1962. 2 vols.

3071 Conover, Helen F., comp. *World Government: A List of Selected References*. Library of Congress, General Reference and Bibliography Division, September 16, 1947. 11 pp.

3072 Cook, Blanche Wiesen, ed. *Bibliography of Peace Research in History*. Santa Barbara, Calif.: ABC-Clio, 1969. 72 pp.

3073 Dworkis, Martin B. *World Government and Related Problems: A Selected Bibliography*. Mimeographed, March 1, 1949. 80 pp. United World Federalists Papers, Box 67, Lilly Library, Indiana University.

3074 European Parliament. *Bibliography, 1981-1982*. [Other editions?] Strasbourg: European Parliament, Directorate-General for Research and Documentation, mimeographed, 1983. 43 pp.

3075 Federal Union. Brennan, Ann Marie, comp. *Comprehensive Bibliography on Federalism and Atlantic Area Studies*. N. d., post 1973. 32 pp. Federal Union, Box 75920, Washington, DC 20013.

3076 Federation of American Scientists. *Articles on Atomic Energy in Current Magazines*. June - October, 1946. 6 pp. Federation of American Scientists Papers, Box 5.1, Regenstein Library, University of Chicago.
Typical atomic scientists articles at crucial introduction of Baruch Plan.

[3077] Haas, Michael, comp. *International Organization: An Interdisciplinary Bibliography.* Stanford: Hoover Institution Press, 1971. 944 pp.

[3078] Hannigan, Jane A., comp. *Publications of the Carnegie Endowment for International Peace, 1910-1967, Including International Conciliation, 1924-1967.* New York: CEIP, 1971. 229 pp.

[3079] Josephson, Harold, ed. *Biographical Dictionary of Modern Peace Leaders.* Westport, Conn.: Greenwood, 1985. 864 pp.
Complements Kuehl.

[3080] Kuehl, Warren F. *Internationalism.* Los Angeles: Center for the Study of Armament and Disarmament, California State University, 1973. 42 pp.

[3081] --------. *Biographical Dictionary of Internationalists.* Westport, Conn.: Greenwood, 1983. 934 pp.
Biographical sketches of about 650 internationalists from most countries, plus chronology and tabulations of the internationalists by country, career, and type.

[3081]a Lodge, Julliet. *The European Community: Bibliographical Excursions.* London: Frances Pinter, 1983.
Useful series of bibliographical guides to theories about the EC and its institutions and policies.

[3082] Luna, Antonio de, comp. "Bibliografia acerca de la federatión europea." *Revista de estudios políticos,* 31 (1950), pp. 285-99.

[3083] Newcombe, Hanna. "Alternative Approaches to World Government." *Peace Research Reviews,* 5, 3 (February, 1974). 94 pp.

[3084] --------, comp. *World Unification Plans and Analyses.* Dundas, Ontario: Peace Research Institute--Dundas, 1980. 259 pp. *Supplement* (1984). 128 pp.
With abstracts.

[3085] Paklons, L. L., comp. *Bibliographie européenne.* Bruges: De Tempel, 1964.
History and the basic organizations.

[3086] Peace Palace Library, The Hague. *Systematic Catalog.* New York: Clearwater, 1982.
Contains:
Periodicals Reference Guide,
        Chronological Section, 70,000 cards, 435 fiche;
        Author Index, 75,000 cards, 291 fiche;
Universal Bibliographic Catalog,
        Chronological Section, 170,000 cards, 413 fiche;
        Author Index, 180,000 cards, 677 fiche.

[3087] Pickus, Robert, and Woito, Robert, eds. *To End War: An Introduction to the Ideas, Books, Organizations, Work That Can Help.* Berkeley, Calif.: World without War Council, 1970. 261 pp.

[3088] Rubinstein, Alvin Z., and Ginsburgs, George, eds. *Soviet and American*

Policies in the United Nations: *A Twenty-five Year Perspective*. New York: New York University Press, 1971. 211 pp.
Contains bibliography of Soviet works on international organization.

[3089] Spencer, Richard E., and Awe, Ruth, comps. *International Education Exchange*: *A Bibliography*. New York: Institute of International Education, 1970. 156 pp.
Comprehensive bibliography on exchanges of students, teachers, and specialists between nations. Additional sections on curriculum (primarily languages), cross-cultural studies, and general works (foreign policy, development, critiques). No annotations or page headings. Little on education for internationalism.

[3089]a UNESCO. *World Directory of Peace Research Institutions*. Paris: UNESCO, 5th ed., 1984. 230 pp.

[3090] United Nations, Atomic Energy Commission. *Index to Documents of the Atomic Energy Commission*, . . . *General Assembly, and Security Council on the Subject of the International Control of Atomic Energy and the Prohibition of Atomic Weapons, 1946-1951*. New York: AEC, 1952. 72 pp. AEC/C.1/81/Rev.1.

[3091] United Nations, Dag Hammarskjold Library. *Bibliographical Series on U.N. Charter Amendment*. ST/LIB/SER.B/3 (1955.I.7), Part III, 2, Revision.

[3092] United Nations, General Assembly. *Ad Hoc* Committee on the Restructuring of the Economic and Social Sectors of the United Nations System. *Bibliography*. 30 January 1976. 20 pp. A/AC.179/3.
Contains references to U.N. documents on the Economic and Social Council, regional cooperative structures, coordination and planning, operations, organs, specialized agencies, and general strengthening of the organization.

[3093] --------. --------. *Bibliography*. 30 January 1976. 19 pp. A/AC.-179/3/Add.1.
List of General Assembly resolutions relevant to restructuring the U.N. Not an addendum so much as a rearrangement of material in A/AC.179/3.

[3094] United States, Library of Congress, Legislative Reference Service, Foreign Affairs Division. *Strengthening Free World Security*: *NATO and Atlantic Cooperation, the United Nations and World Government*; *A Collection of Excerpts and Bibliographies*. Washington: Government Printing Office, Senate Doc. No. 124, 1960. 91 pp.

[3095] United World Federalists. *Literature List*. January, February, April, 1948. 8 pp. UWF Papers, Lilly Library, Indiana University.

[3096] --------. *Study Program*. March, 1948. 14 pp. UWF Papers, Box 60, ibid.
UWF Literature on League of Nations, United Nations, world government, and international control of atomic energy.

[3096]a *UNU Publications*: *June, 1985*. Tokyo: United Nations University, 1985. 121 pp.
Lists periodicals and publications on natural resources; energy;

food and nutrition; economics, culture, and politics; international
law; UNU network publications; general information; audio-visual
materials; UNU depository libraries; and distributors.

3097 Walch, J. Weston. *Complete Handbook on World Government*.   Portland,
Me.: Walch, 1947.
Guide to 1947–48 college debate topic.   Contains valuable chrono-
logically arranged references, pro and con, and bibliography.

3098 Wien, Barbara, ed. *Peace and World Order Studies*: *A Curriculum Guide*.
New York: World Policy Institute, 4th ed., 1985. 742 pp.
Comprehensive guide to foundations, programs, syllabi, and biblio-
graphies on world order.

3099 Williams, Stillman P. *Toward a Genuine World Security System*: *An An-
notated Bibliography for Layman and Scholar*.   Washington: United
World Federalists, 1964. 64 pp.
Particularly strong on arms control and disarmament in early 1960s.

3100 Windegger, F.R. von. *List of Phamphlets Prepared by the Plaza Bank of
St. Louis, 1942–1947*.   3 pp. Emergency Committee of the Atomic Scientists Papers, Box 1.7, Regenstein Library, University of Chicago.
Speeches, broadcasts, and brief articles on world government by
prominent persons.

3101 World Law Fund. *Catalogue of Instructional Materials*. New York: Institute for International Order, n.d., c. 1967. 19 pp.

3102 World Law Institute. *International Law . . . and Constitutional Government. . . .*   1949. 10 pp.

3103 Wynner, Edith, comp. *A Selected Bibliography on World Government*. New
York: American Movement for World Government, mimeographed, 1985.
10 pp.

3104 Yalem, Ronald J. "The Study of International Organization, 1920-1965."
Background, 10 (May, 1966), pp. 1-56.

24

Current Organizations

3114

Academy of World Studies
    2820 Van Ness Avenue
    San Francisco, CA 94109
      Mr. Bennet Skewes-Cox, President
      415-441-1404

3115

Aizen World   Alternative addresses:
    218 Ramakrishna Math Road Kameoka   415 Galle Road
    Madras 4   Kyoto-fu   Colombo 3
    India   Japan   Sri Lanka

3116

All India Association of World Federalists (WAWF National Organization)
    6A Telegraph Lane
    New Delhi 110 001
    India
      Mr. T.N. Chopra, President

3117

American Movement for World Government
    One World Trade Center, Suite 7967
    New York, NY 10048
      Mr. William H. D. Cox, Jr., President
      212-321-1747

3118

Arms Control and Foreign Policy Caucus
    (formerly Members of Congress for Peace through Law)
    U.S. House of Representatives
    House Annex II, Room 501
    Washington, DC 20515
      Ms. Edith B. Wilhie, Executive Director
      202-226-3440

3119

Association of World Federalists (WAWF National Organization)
    43, Wallingford Avenue
    London W10 6PZ
    United Kingdom
      Mr. Bruce Ritchie, Executive Director

3120

Association to Unite the Democracies (formerly Federal Union)
    P.O. Box 75920
    Washington, DC   20013
      Mr. Clarence Streit, President
      Mr. Ira Straus, Executive Director
      Dr. Julius Strickler, Director, Center for the Study of Federalism
        202-544-5150

3120a

Bahá'í World Center   Bahá'í Community of the United States
    Haifa   415 Linden Avenue
    Israel   Wilmette, IL   60091
                                 312-869-9039

3121

Campaign for U.N. Reform
    418 Seventh Street, SE
    Washington, DC   20003
      Mr. Franklin C. Stark, President
      Mr. Walter Hoffman, Executive Director
        202-546-3950

3122

Campaign for World Government
    331 Park Avenue, Room 304
    Glencoe, IL   60022
      Miss Georgia Lloyd, Executive Secretary
        312-835-3685

3123

Carnegie Endowment for International Peace
    11 Dupont Circle, NW
    Washington, DC   20036
      Mr. Thomas L. Hughes, President
        202-797-6400

3124

Center for U.N. Reform Education (CURE)
    139 East McClellan Avenue
    Livingston, NJ   07039
      Mr. Myron Kronish, Executive Director
      Ms. Michele Freidus, Executive Secretary
      Ms. Judith Tritschler, Director of Development
        201-992-8350

3125

Center for War/Peace Studies
    218 East 18th Street
    New York, NY   10002
      Mr. Richard Hudson, Executive Director
        212-475-1077

3126

Centre international de formation européenne
    4 blvd. Carabacel
    06000 Nice
    France
      Prof. Ferdinand Kinsky, Secrétaire-Général
        Collège universitaire d'études fédéralistes
        Aoste, Italie

3127

Club humaniste
    15, rue Victor Duruy
    75015 Paris
    France
      M. Guy Marchand, Secrétaire-Général
      33-1-531-2999

3128

Commission of the European Communities
    Directorate-General for Information
    Division IX-C-1
    Rue de la Loi, 200
    B-1049 Bruxelles
    Belgique
      32-2-235-1111

3129

Common Heritage Institute (formerly World Order Research Institute)
    Villanova University
    Villanova, PA 19085
      Prof. John Logue, Director
      Ms. Colleen D. Sullivan, Associate Director
      215-645-7300

3130

Communidad mundial
    Avenue de la Hacienda, 124
    Atizapan
    Mexico
      Sra. M. de Lourdes Escargega, Director

3130a

Congrès des peuples
    15, rue Victor Duruy
    75015 Paris
    France
      M. Guy Marchand, Secrétaire-Général
      33-1-531-2999

3131

Consortium on Peace Research, Education, and Development (COPRED)
    911 West High Street, Room 100
    University of Illinois at Urbana-Champaign
    Urbana, IL 61801
      Mr. Clinton F. Link, Executive Director
      217-333-2069

3132

COPRED Midwest Office
    Center for Peaceful Change, Stopher Hall
    Kent State University
    Kent, OH 44202

3133

Crusade to Abolish War and Armaments by World Law
    174 Majestic Avenue
    San Francisco, CA 94112
      Ms. Mia Lord, Director
      415-587-0600

3134

Delegation of the Commission of the European Communities
    1 Dag Hammarskjold Plaza
    245 East 47th Street
    New York, NY 10017
      Ms. Elizabeth Grant, Public Information Officer
      212-371-3804

3136

Emergency World Council
    Frederik Hendriklaan, 26
    The Hague
    The Netherlands
      Dr. J.H.C. Creyghton, Director

3137

Én Verden (WAWF National Organization)
    Riddervoldsgatan 10
    0258 Oslo 2
    Norway

3138

European Community Information Service
    2100 M Street, Suite 707, NW
    Washington, DC 20037
      Sir Roy Denman, Head of Delegation
      Mr. Denis Corboy, Executive Officer
      202-862-9500

3139

Evolution (formerly Europa-Universe)
    Via Marco Agrate, 19A
    20139 Milano
    Italia
      Sig. Bruno Micheli, Editor

3140

Federal Trust for Education and Research (continuing Federal Union)
    Europe House
    1A Whitehall Place
    London SW1A 2HA
    England
      Dr. Roy Pryce, Director

3141

The Federalist
    Via Silvio Pellico, 1
    Firenze
    Italia
      Sig. Antonluigi Aiazzi, Editor

3142

The Federalist
    EDIF
    Via Porta Pertusi, 6
    27100 Pavia
    Italia
      Sig. Mario Albertini, Editor

3143

The Federalist Caucus
    Box 19482
    Portland, OR   97219
      Mr. Neal Potter, President
      Ms. Betsy Dana, Secretary-Treasurer
      503-292-4586

3144

Les Fédéralistes mondiaux (WAWF National Organization)
    c/o M. Gerard Bourgeois
    26, rue du 4 Septembre
    75002 Paris
    France

3145

Federation of American Scientists
    307 Massachusetts Avenue, NE
    Washington, DC   20002
      Dr. Jeremy J. Stone, Director
      202-546-3300

3146

FN-Forbundet (WAWF National Organization)
    Kronprinsengade 9
    1114 København K
    Denmark

3147

Global Education Associates
    552 Park Avenue
    East Orange, NJ   07017
      Mr. Gerald F. Mische, President
      Ms. Harriet Zullo, U.N. Representative
      Dr. Charles Guettel, Representative concerning U.N. Mediation
        and Conciliation Service
      201-675-1409

3148

Grenville Clark Institute
    95 North Main Street
    Concord, NH   03301
      Mr. Robert H. Reno, Director

3149

Institut d'études mundialistes
    15, rue Victor Duruy
    75015 Paris
    France
      M. Guy Marchand, Secrétaire-Général
      33-1-531-2999

3150

Institute for Global Policy Studies
    Leliegracht 21
    1016 GR Amsterdam
    The Netherlands
      Prof. Finn Laursen, General Director
      31-20-227502

3151

Iranian Association of WAWF (WAWF National Organization)
    12 Azimi Street Gulhak
    Teheran
    Iran
      Mr. Ebrahim Khadje Nouri, Director

3152

Japan Council of Local Authorities for Realization of World
    Federalism (WAWF National Organization)
    Kocho-koho-ka, Chiji-shitau, Okayama-ken
    Okayama
    Japan

3153

Japan Women's Council of World Federation Societies (WAWF National
    Organization)
    6 Izumikawa-cho, Shimogamo
    Sakyo-ku, Kyoto 606
    Japan
      Mrs. Sumi Yukawa, Director

3154

Mondcivitan Republic (Servant Nation)
    1038A Finchley Road
    London NW11 7ES
    England
      Dr. Hugh Schonfield, Ambassador General

3155

National Peace Council
    29 Great James Street
    London WC1N 3ES
    England
      44-1-242-3228

3156

Nepalese National Organization for WAWF
    P.O. Box 1558
    Kimdol, Swoyambhu
    Kathmandu
    Nepal

3157

Office des publications officielles des Communautés européennes
    Rue du Commerce, 5
    L-2985 Luxembourg
        352-49-0081
        352-49-0191

3158

One World
    4030 Irving Park Road
    Chicago, IL 60641
      Mr. Everett Lee Millard, Director
        312-777-4030

3159

Pakistan Association of World Federalists (WAWF National Organization)
    113-A Singhi Muslim Society
    Shahrah-E-Faisal
    P.O. Box 7482
    Karachi 0302
    Pakistan
      Mr. Ahmed E.H. Jaffer

3160

Parliamentarians Global Action (formerly Parliamentarians for World Order)
    220 East 42nd Street, Suite 3301
    New York, NY 10017
      Mr. Nicholas Dunlop, Secretary General
      Ms. Regina Montecone, Executive Director
        212-687-7755

3161

Parliamentary Group for World Government
    House of Commons
    London SW1A 0AA
    England
      Mr. Patrick Armstrong, Honorable Secretary

3162

Peace Research Institute--Dundas
    25 Dundana Avenue
    Dundas, Ontario L9H 4E5
    Canada
      Drs. Hanna and Alan Newcombe, Directors
        416-628-2356

3163

People's Assembly for the United Nations
    51 East 90th Street
    New York, NY 10028
      Dr. Jeffrey Segall, Founder
      Dr. Harry Lerner, Convenor
        212-549-6520

3165

Planetary Citizens
    Box 2722
    San Anselmo, CA 94960
        Mr. Donald Keys, President
        415-325-2939

3166

Political World Union (Emergency World Council)
    Frederik Hendriklaan 26
    The Hague
    The Netherlands
        Mr. J.M.I.F. Keijser, Secretary General

3167

Registre international des citoyens du monde
    66 boulevard Vincent Auriol
    75013 Paris
    France
        M. Roger Wellhoff, Secrétaire-Général

3168

Soviet Peace Committee
    36, Prospekt Mira
    129010 Moscow
    U.S.S.R.
        Mr. Yuri Zhukov, President
        280-3382
        411426 MIRSU

3169

Soviet Peace Fund
    10, Kropotkin St.
    119034 Moscow
    U.S.S.R.
        Mr. Anatoli Karpov, Chairman of the Board

3170

Stanley Foundation
    420 East Third Street
    Muscatine, IA 52761
        Mr. J. Maxwell Stanley, Director
        319-264-1500

3171

Sveriges Världsfederalister (WAWF National Organization)
    P.O. Box 224
    S-10122 Stockholm
    Sweden

3172

The XXth Century and Peace
    Sovetskii Komitet Zashchity Mira
    Kropotkinskaya 10
    Moskva
    U.S.S.R.

3173

Transnational Perspectives
    Casa Postal 161
    1211 Geneva 16
    Switzerland
        Mr. René Wadlow, Editor

3174

Umano Foundation and Orchestra
    62-24 Grand Avenue
    Maspeth, NY 11378
        Thom and Lorry Gambino, Co-founders
        718-894-7683

3174a

Union des fédéralistes européens (UEF)
    (formerly Union européenne des fédéralistes)
    Rue de Toulouse, 49
    1040 Bruxelles
    Belgium
        Dr. Caterina Chizzola, Secrétaire-Général
        02-230-0416

3175

United Nations Association (UNA-USA)
    300 East 42nd Street
    New York, NY 10017
        Mr. Edward C. Luck, President
        212-697-3232

3176

United Nations Association (Canada)
    63 Sparks, Suite 808
    Ottawa, Ontario K1P 5A6
    Canada
        613-232-5751

3176a

United Nations University
    Information Services
    Toho Seimei Building
    15-1, Shibuya 2-chome
    Shibuya-ku, Tokyo 150
    Japan
        81-3-499-2811

3177

United World Federalists of Japan (WAWF National Organization)
    Sekai Rempō Kense tsu Domei
    Dai-chi Fuji-Kawa Blvd., 3F
    23, 4-chome, Yotsuya
    Shinjuku-ku, Tokyo-to
    Japan

³¹⁷⁷a
University for Peace
    P.O. Box 199
    Eseazu
    Costa Rica
        Pres. Rodrigo Carazo, President of the Council
        Mr. Robert Muller, Chancellor
        506-49-10-72

³¹⁷⁸

Vereingung der Weltföderalisten in der Schweiz (WAWF National
    Organization)
    Postfach 210
    CH-3000 Bern 31
    Switzerland

³¹⁷⁹

Weltföderalisten Deutschlands (WAWF National Organization)
    Kaiserstrasse 59
    2300 Kiel-Gaarden
    Federal Republic of Germany

³¹⁸⁰

Wereld Federalisten Beweging Nederland (WAWF National Organization)
    Vondelstraat 15
    2251 KG Voorschoten
    The Netherlands

³¹⁸¹

World Association for the School as an Instrument of Peace (EIP)
    27, rue des Eaux-Vivres
    CH-1207 Geneva
    Switzerland

³¹⁸²

World Association of World Federalists (WAWF)
Mouvement Universel pour une Fédération Mondiale
    (formerly World Movement for World Federal Government)
    Leliegracht 21
    1016 GR Amsterdam
    The Netherlands
        Dr. Hermod Lannung, President
        Ms. Ria Mullaart, Administrative Officer and Head of Secretariat
        31-20-227502

³¹⁸³

WAWF Asian Center
    Konko-kyo Church of Izuo
    21-8 Nishi 3-chome, San-gen-ya
    Taisho-ku, Osaka 551
    Japan
        Rev. Toshio Miyake, Senior Minister
        81-6-551-003435

3184

WAWF Belgium Section (WAWF National Organization)
      50, Corniche Verte
      Bruxelles 15
      Belgium
         M. M. von Mach, Secrétaire-Générale

3185

WAWF Geneva Office
      Casa Postal 161
      1211 Geneva 16
      Switzerland
         Mr. René Wadlow, U.N. Representative

3186

WAWF Hong Kong Branch (WAWF National Organization)
      P.O. Box 74504
      Kowloon
         Mr. Sung Tit Hop, Chairman

3187

WAWF North American Office
      410 South Michigan Avenue, Room 468
      Chicago, IL 60605
         Rev. G. G. Grant, S.J., Vice-President
         312-427-5409

3188

WAWF United Nations Office
      777 U.N. Plaza
      New York, NY 10017
         Dr. Joseph P. Baratta, U.N. Representative
         Prof. John J. Logue, Alternate
         212-599-1320

3189

World Citizens Assembly
      World Affairs Center, Suite 506
      312 Sutter Street
      San Francisco, CA 94108
         Dr. Lucile Green, President
         Mr. Douglas Mattern, Secretary General
         415-421-0836

3190

World Citizen's Party
      Friedrikstrasse, 26
      Wolfach Brd. 7620
      Federal Republic of Germany
         Herr Emil Peter, Coordinator

3191

World Conference on Religion and Peace
      777 U.N. Plaza
      New York, NY 10017
      Rev. Kenryo T. Tsuji, President
      Prof. John Borreli, Secretary-General, U.S. Committee
         212-687-2163

3192

World Constitution and Parliament Association
     1480 Hoyt Street, Suite 31
     Lakewood, CO 80215
       Mr. Philip Isely, Secretary General
         303-233-3548

3193

World Council for Mundialization
Conseil Mondial pour la Mondialisation
     Hiroshima
     Japan

3194

World Federal Authority Committee
     25 Dundana Avenue
     Dundas, Ontario L9H 4E5
     Canada
       Dr. Hanna Newcombe, President
       Ms. Sally Curry, Director of Literature Service
         416-628-2356

3195

World Federalist Association (WAWF National Organization)
     (formerly United World Federalists and World Federalists, U.S.A.)
     418 7th Street, SE
     Washington, DC 20003
       Prof. Norman Cousins, President
       Mr. Walter Hoffman, Executive Director
         202-546-3950

3196

World Federalists of Australia (WAWF National Organization)
     Trinity Peace Research Institute
     72 St. George's Terrace
     Perth, W.A. 6000
     Australia
       Dr. Keith D. Suter, Director

3197

World Federalists of Bangladesh (WAWF National Organization)
     P.O. Box 2095
     Dacca 2
     Bangladesh

3198

World Federalists of Canada (WAWF National Organization)
     46 Elgin Street, Suite 32
     Ottawa, Ontario K1P 5K6
     Canada
       Mr. Dieter Heinrich, President
       Mr. Fergus Watt, Executive Director
         613-232-0647

3199

World Federalists of Greece (WAWF National Organization)
    c/o Dr. D. Poulantzas
    P.O. Box 14082
    Ampelokipi
    11510 Athens
    Greece

3200

World Federalists Association of India (WAWF National Organization)
    World Federalists Chamber
    Apeejay House, 1st Floor
    15 Park Street
    Calcutta 700 016
    India
        Mr. M.K. Banerji, Secretary General

3200a

World Federalists of New Zealand
    7 Bolton Street
    Blockhouse Bay
    Auckland 7
    New Zealand
        Mr. W.M. Harper, Director

3200b

World Federalists of Sri Lanka
    28 Hodder Street
    Brighton East
    Victoria 3187
    Australia
        Mr. Kenneth Hanibelsz, Director

3201

World Federalist Youth / New International Order Youth
    Leliegracht 21
    1016 GR Amsterdam
    The Netherlands
        Mr. Paol Hvilsted, Chairman
        Mr. Jan Pakulski, Coordinator
        Ms. Inge van de Kamp, Coordinator
        31-20-261993

3202

World Federation of United Nations Associations
    United Nations, DC1-1177
    One United Nations Plaza
    New York, NY 10017
        Mrs. Annabelle Wiener, U.N. Representative
        212-754-6033

3203

World Government Organizations Coordinating Council (WGOCC)
    774 Colusa Avenue
    El Cerrito, CA 94530
        Dr. Lucile Green, Facilitator
        Mr. John Eubank, Facilitator
        415-525-5057

3204

World Peace Foundation
    22 Batterymarch Street
    Boston, MA 02109
      Mr. Richard J. Bloomfield, Director
        617-482-3875

3205

World Peace News
    777 United Nations Plaza
    New York, NY 10017
      Mr. Thomas Liggett, Editor

3206

World Peace through Law Center
    1000 Connecticut Avenue, Suite 800, NW
    Washington, DC 20036
      Mr. Charles S. Rhyne, President
        202-466-5428

3207

World Policy Institute
    777 U.N. Plaza
    New York, NY 10017
      Mr. Archibald L. Gillies, President
      Dr. Robert C. Johansen, Editor in Chief
        212-490-0010

3208

World Service Authority
    Continental Building, Suite 1101
    1012 14th Street, NW
    Washington, DC 20005
      Mr. Garry Davis, Coordinator
        202-638-2662

3209

World Union International
    Sri Aurobindo Ashram
    Pondicherry 605002
    India
      Sri A.B. Patel, Secretary General

3210

World Without War Council
    1730 Martin Luther King, Jr., Way
    Berkeley, CA 94709
      Mr. Robert Pickus, President
        415-845-1992

Author Index

Wittner, Lawrence S. 2682
Włodarski, Piotr. 2458
Woetzel, Robert K. 641-643, 2636
Wofford, Harris. 15, 90, 644, 1104-1106, 2910, 3030
Woito, Robert. 1349, 3087
Women's International League for Peace and Freedom. 1107
Wood, Alex. 763
Wood, Hugh McKinnon. 1560
Woodrow Wilson Foundation. 2915
Woodward, E.L. 764, 892, 1561
Wooley, Wesley T., Jr. 1350
Wooton, Barbara. 1562, 1563
World Association for the School as an Instrument of Peace. 3181
World Association of World Federalists (WAWF). 1791, 1792, 1794, 2931, 2932, 3182, 3183, 3185, 3187, 3188
World Citizen Movement. 2927
World Citizens Assembly. 3189
World Citizens Association. 112, 210, 211, 2974
World Citizenship Movement. 2893
World Citizens Party. 3190
World Conference on Religion and Peace. 3191
World Constitution and Parliament Association. 2846, 3192
World Council for the People's World Convention. 1793
World Federal Authority Committee. 3194
World Federalist Association(U.S.A.) 2929, 3195
World Federalists of Australia. 3196
World Federalists of Bangladesh. 3197
World Federalists of Canada. 1351, 2858, 3198
World Federalists of Greece. 3199
World Federalists of India. 3200
World Federalist Youth / New International Order Youth. 3201
World Federation of United Nations Associations. 3202
World Government Association. 212
World Government Organizations Coordinating Council. 3203
World Law Fund. 3101

World Law Institute. 3102
World Movement for World Federal Government. 645, 646, 1794-1796, 2857, 2930, 2942, 2976
World Parliament Association. 647
World Peace Council. 2901
World Peace Foundation. 1214, 2888, 3204
World Peace through Law Center. 3206
World Policy Institute. 2850, 2940, 3207
World Republic. 2905, 2977
World Service Authority. 1183, 3208
World Student Federalists. 2894
World Union International. 3209
World Without War Council. 3210
Wright, Quincy. 213, 648-651, 765, 1068, 1109, 1352-1354, 2528, 2978
Wynner, Edith. 214, 652, 1110, 1111, 1355, 1356, 3103
Yakemtchouk, R.O. 653, 654
Yalem, Ronald J. 2529a, 3104
Yasugi, Issho. 1920
Yepes, J.M. 655
Yergin, Daniel. 2637
Yoder, Jon A. 2656
Yokota, Kisaburo. 656
Yoshihara, Shohachiro. 1921
Yost, Charles W. 1357
Young, George. 1564
Younger, Kenneth. 657
Yudell, Esther. 1205
Yukawa, Sumi. 3153
Zacklin, Ralph. 658
Zaslawski, D. 2011
Zeitzer, Glen. 2683
Zellentin, Gerda. 2460
Zenkl, Petr. 1797
Zhdanov, A.A. 2012
Zhukov, Yuri. 659, 2013, 3168
Ziccardi, P. 1798
Ziff, William B. 1112, 1113
Zimmerman, Carle C. 1358
Zmirou, E. 2865
Zoll, Allen A. 1114
Zoller, Elisabeth. 660, 661
Zorn, V. 2731
Zucher, Arnold J. 2461
Zullo, Harriet. 3147
Zweig, Michael. 2778

Nation Index

Subject Index

1137, 1505, 1792
World government, criticized. Front
for anti-communist U.S. foreign
policy. 1930, 1935, 1948, 1955,
1966, 1974, 1975, 1985, 1986,
2004, 2011, 2012
It is an independent policy
proposal. 881, 914
World government, criticized. Legalistic-moralistic fallacy for the
conduct of foreign policy. 2582
It is the preferred alternative
to "realistic" use of force;
idealism is legitimate in foreign
policy. 2, 3, 4, 903, 1037,
1097, 1173, 1271, 1417, 1419,
1714, 2502, 2521, 2554, 2601,
2606, 2666, 2732, 2735, 3012
World government, criticized. Loyalty to humanity is too weak. 849,
930, 1005, 1060, 1530
Human brotherhood is the spirit
of our age. 12, 13, 849, 926,
936, 988, 1037, 1060, 1224, 1243,
1340, 1394, 1473, 1530, 1537,
1746, 1865, 1914a, 2694, 2701a,
2721, 2722, 2732
World government, criticized. Luna-
tic fringe. 799, 821, 935, 1061,
1423
World government, criticized. Nations are too diverse for union;
world is not ready to submit to
law. 118, 127, 128, 1253, 1291,
1518
The world is ready. 6, 12, 13,
461, 824, 836, 899, 923, 962,
1037, 1109, 1151, 1161, 1197,
1269, 1282, 1285, 1286, 1424,
1513, 1537, 1540, 1549-1554,
1646, 1713, 1826, 1896, 1897,
1914a, 1950, 1994, 1995, 1998,
2269, 2313, 2652, 2695, 2712,
2735
World government, criticized. Political and social conditions are
not met; no consensus exists,
especially between communism and
capitalism. 255a, 1068, 1095,
1241, 1244, 1417, 1510, 1518,
1933, 1935, 1969, 1974, 1985,
1997, 2002, 2004, 2009
Forces of convergence are rapidly
building a world community. 7,
11, 12, 13, 186, 349, 461, 808,
822, 849, 866, 900, 905, 930,
960, 963, 964, 997, 999, 1000,
1040, 1109, 1144, 1146, 1148,

1151, 1156, 1157, 1161, 1184,
1187, 1190, 1244, 1258, 1260,
1269, 1282, 1283, 1297, 1339,
1345, 1353, 1443, 1463, 1469,
1472, 1499, 1513, 1516, 1537,
1540, 1549, 1551-1554, 1592,
1609, 1620, 1621, 1642, 1646,
1662, 1696, 1699, 1700, 1730,
1740, 1781, 1782, 1787, 1798,
1849, 1852, 1890, 1896, 1897,
1904, 1907, 1914a, 1933, 1950,
1952, 1970, 1985, 1994, 2000,
2007, 2107, 2313, 2518, 2693,
2704, 2721, 2728, 2732, 2863,
2975, 3004, 3051, 3052
World government, criticized. Russia
or America is opposed. 127, 128,
868, 891, 918, 966, 1039, 1095,
1114, 1144, 1245, 1261, 1372,
1523, 1974, 1975, 1985, 1986,
2011, 2012
Both have universalist roots and
should lead. America: 6, 9,
121, 208, 325, 738, 807, 923,
986, 987, 1050, 1062, 1063, 1190,
1249, 1255, 1372, 1375-1377,
1539, 2625; Russia: 1240, 1538,
1937, 1944, 1950, 1957, 1994,
1998, 2001, 2009
World government, criticized. Tyrannical; not even theoretically
right. 1127, 1291, 1491, 1492,
1510, 2481, 2523
Checks and balances can preserve
liberties. 3, 4, 5, 126, 841,
1066, 1163, 1171, 1447, 1628-1636
World government, criticized. Unrealistic -- theoretically right,
but impractical now. 168, 425,
572, 692, 775, 869, 871, 951,
974, 979, 980, 995, 996, 1014,
1021, 1031, 1039, 1051, 1068,
1140, 1157, 1179, 1228, 1346,
1354, 1471, 1515, 1523, 1577,
1594, 1726, 2009, 2473, 2478,
2725, 2989
Time has come for courageous
action. 3, 4, 7, 8, 10, 186,
826, 852, 857, 877, 878, 879,
889, 914-916, 971-976, 1027-1029,
1035, 1037, 1069, 1097, 1098,
1104, 1111, 1136, 1137, 1161,
1167, 1172, 1173, 1176, 1197,
1248, 1271, 1285, 1286, 1298,
1356, 1372, 1473, 1524, 1542,
1543, 1713, 1814, 2735
World government, criticized. U.S.
federal analogy is misapplied.

About the Compiler

JOSEPH PRESTON BARATTA, Ph.D., is U.N. Representative for the World Association of World Federalists. His work has appeared in the *International History Review*, the *Statesman's Year Book and International Who's Who*, and the *Institute for Global Policy Studies Occasional Paper No. 3*.